Mosaic Chart
DIRECTORY FOR
Knitting + Crochet

A DAVID AND CHARLES BOOK

David and Charles is an imprint of David and Charles, Ltd
Suite A, Tourism House, Pynes Hill, Exeter, EX2 5WS

Conceived, edited, and designed by Quarto Publishing, an imprint of The Quarto Group, 1 Triptych Place, London, SE1 9SH

First published in the UK and USA in 2024

A catalog record for this book is available from the British Library.

ISBN-13: 9781446313862 paperback
ISBN-13: 9781446313886 EPUB

This book has been printed on paper from approved suppliers and made from pulp from sustainable sources.

Printed in China by 1010 Printing International Ltd

10 9 8 7 6 5 4 3 2

Editor: Charlene Fernandes
Copy editor: Lindsay Kaubi
Pattern checkers: Sharon Carter and Linda Brown
Art director: Martina Calvio
Designer: Bess Daly
Photography: Phil Wilkins
Publisher: Lorraine Dickey

David and Charles publishes high-quality books on a wide range of subjects. For more information visit www.davidandcharles.com.

Share your makes with us on social media using #dandcbooks and follow us on Facebook and Instagram by searching for @dandcbooks.

Layout of the digital edition of this book may vary depending on reader hardware and display settings.

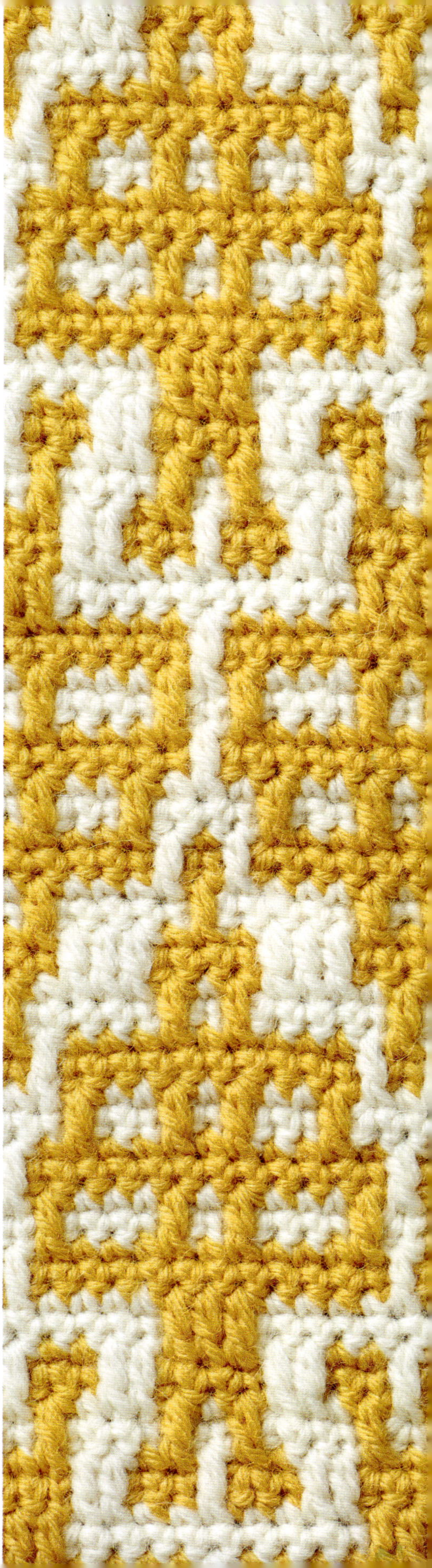

Mosaic Chart DIRECTORY FOR Knitting + Crochet

75 Geometric Designs

Anna Nikipirowicz

DAVID & CHARLES
— PUBLISHING —

www.davidandcharles.com

Contents

Meet Anna

I have been knitting and crocheting for quite a long time now. My love for it was first ignited by my wonderful late mum, Lucy. There is a magic about these two crafts that keeps me excited and constantly wanting more. Despite the years of exploring and practicing, there is still so much to learn, the possibilities are infinite!

One of the many techniques I am fascinated by is mosaic knitting and crochet. It first started with mosaic knitting and the stunning patterns it produces. For this I have Barbara Walker to thank, a knitting expert who coined the term "mosaic knitting" and designed a plethora of extraordinary mosaic patterns. Her books have been both well-used and well-loved on my personal knitting journey.

My exploration of mosaic crochet came later. In this book I concentrate on inset mosaic crochet, which was my first love, overlay mosaic crochet is a far more recent discovery for me. I adore both techniques but inset is the method that I find is more suited to a broader range of projects; however, I will provide you with full instructions on how to convert charts and work the patterns in overlay crochet and Tunisian crochet.

For this book, I have both collected some well-loved patterns and created some, with the hope that they will become much-loved by you, too. The book is divided into five chapters: Geometric, Aztec, General, Nature, and Seasonal. I have tried to include as much variety in each chapter as possible. The Aztec section is full of patterns that I refer to as "stackers," meaning that the patterns are designed to be stacked together to create a beautiful overall design. However, this does not apply only to the Aztec section, each design in this book can also be mixed and matched with another. This is the most wonderful aspect of knitting and crochet, the true freedom of creativity, allowing endless possibilities.

This book has been an idea in my head for a very long time. I'm very thankful that my publisher saw the potential in my vision. It's such a delight to bring this book to you. My hope is that you will find inspiration within its pages and enjoy exploring the potential of mosaic knitting and crochet as much as I do.

Introduction

What is mosaic knitting and crochet?
Mosaic knitting and crochet are colorwork techniques where you use two colors independently. The method is very simple: two contrasting yarn colors are used, one color for every two rows. Unlike other colorwork techniques, such as Fair Isle or stranded, where two or more colors are used per row, the mosaic technique allows the maker to create intricate patterns without having to carry multiple strands of yarn per row.

Mosaic crochet is very similar to mosaic knitting; it follows the same chart, you work with one color at a time, and both techniques give you the opportunity to create beautiful colorwork patterns without changing yarn in one row or round. In mosaic crochet you can simply connect rows or rounds by chaining and skipping a stitch and then "filling" the skipped stitch with a treble two rows or rounds later with the alternate-colored yarn. In mosaic knitting, you simply knit RS rows and purl WS rows, slipping stitches to skip the contrast color.

THE SKILL LEVEL IS INDICATED HERE FOR BOTH KNITTERS AND CROCHETERS.

THE KNITTED PATTERN IS GIVEN FIRST AND CAN BE READ ALONGSIDE THE CHART.

IN EVERY CHART, THE WHITE SQUARE IS YARN A, AND THE BLACK SQUARE (THE CONTRAST COLOR) IS YARN B. I HAVE USED CREAM AS YARN A THROUGHOUT THE BOOK.

Leaves

This sweet leaf design would look amazing if it multicolored yarn as Yarn B and solid yarn as Y

Knit Instructions
Multiple of 20 sts + 3
On RS rows, slip the sts purlwise with yarn in the back.
Cast on using A, k one row and p one row.
Row 1 (RS): Using B, k1, * [sl1, k1] 10 times; rep from * to last 2 sts, sl1, k1.
Row 2 and all WS rows: P the knitted sts and sl the slipped sts purlwise with yarn in the front.
Row 3: Using A, k1, * k5, sl1, k9, sl1, k4; rep from * to last 2 sts, k2.
Row 5: Using B, k1, * sl2, k7, sl2, k1, sl2, k3, sl2, k1; rep from * to last 2 sts, sl1, k1.
Row 7: Using A, k1, * k2, sl1, k5, sl1, k5, sl1, k1, sl1, k3; rep from * to last 2 sts, k2.
Row 9: Using B, k1, * sl1, k2, [sl1, k1] 3 times, k1, sl1, k1, sl1, k2, sl1, k2, sl1, k1; rep from * to last 2 sts, sl1, k1.
Row 11: Using A, k1, * k1, sl1, k7, [sl1, k3] twice, sl1, k2; rep from * to last 2 sts, k2.
Row 13: Using B, k1, * sl1, k1, [sl1, k1] 4 times, sl2, k2, sl1, k1, sl1, k2, sl1; rep from * to last 2 sts, sl1, k1.
Row 15: Using A, k1, * k1, sl1, k7, sl1, k2, sl1, k5, sl1, k1; rep from * to last 2 sts, k2.
Row 17: Using B, k1, * sl1, k2, [sl1, k1] 3 times, k1, sl1, k2, [sl1, k1] 3 times, k1; rep from * to last 2 sts, sl1, k1.
Row 19: Using A, k1, * k2, sl1, k5, sl1, k2, sl1, k7, sl1; rep from * to last 2 sts, k2.
Row 21: Using B, k1, * sl2, k2, [sl1, k1] twice, k1, sl2, k1, [sl1, k1] 4 times; rep

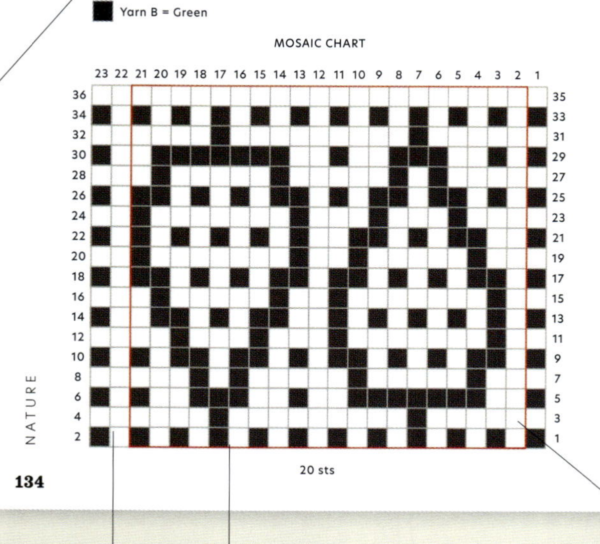

THE MOSAIC TECHNIQUE ALLOWS THE SAME CHART TO BE USED BY KNITTERS AND CROCHETERS.

THE RED BOX INDICATES THE REPEAT IN THE PATTERN.

BOTH THE KNITTED AND CROCHETED SWATCHES ARE SHOWN IN DETAIL SO YOU CAN SEE WHAT THE FINISHED SWATCH SHOULD LOOK LIKE.

:h

1, k1.
* [k3, sl1] 3 times,
ast 2 sts, k2.
* sl1, k1, [sl1, k2]
l1, k1] 3 times, k1;
s, sl1, k1.
k4, sl1, k1, sl1, [k5,
* to last 2 sts, k2.
sl1, k1, sl2, k3, sl2, k1,
last 2 sts, sl1, k1.
k5, sl1, k9, sl1, k4;
s, k2.
* [sl1, k1] 10 times;
s, sl1, k1.
l sts.

KNIT

CROCHET

ons

peat in written
m chart on Rows

d number of

ch, 1 sc, * [2 ch,
rep from * to last
:, turn.
ws: 1 ch,
ch-sps, turn.
1 sc, * [1 Mdc,
h, skip st, [1
Mdc, 2 ch, skip st,
from * to last
.
1 sc, * 3 ch, skip
:, 3 ch, skip 2 sts,
sc, 1 Mdc, 1 sc,
ep from * to last
:, turn.
1 sc, * 2 Mdc, 2 ch,
, 2 Mdc, 1 sc, 2 Mdc,
skip st, 2 Mdc, 1 sc;
s, 1 Mdc, 1 sc, turn.
1 sc, * 2 ch, skip

st, 1 sc, 1 Mdc, [2 ch, skip st, 1 sc] twice, 2 ch, skip st, 1 Mdc, 1 sc, [2 ch, skip st, 1 sc] twice, 1 Mdc, 2 ch, skip st, 1 Mdc, 1 sc, 2 ch, skip st, 1 sc; rep from * to last 2 sts, 2 ch, skip st, 1 sc, turn.

Row 11: Using A, 1 ch, 1 sc, * 1 Mdc, 2 ch, skip st, [1 sc, 1 Mdc] 3 times, 1 sc, 2 ch, skip st, 1 Mdc, 1 sc, 1 Mdc, 2 ch, skip st, 1 sc, 1 Mdc, 1 sc, 2 ch, skip st, 1 Mdc, 1 sc; rep from * to last 2 sts, 1 Mdc, 1 sc, turn.

Row 13: Using B, 1 ch, 1 sc, 2 ch, skip st, * 1 Mdc, [2 ch, skip st, 1 sc] 3 times, 2 ch, skip st, 1 Mdc, 3 ch, skip 2 sts, 1 sc, 1 Mdc, 2 ch, skip st, 1 sc, 2 ch, skip st, 1 Mdc, 1 sc, ** 3 ch, skip 2 sts; rep from * to last 3 sts, ending last rep at **, 3 ch, skip 2 sts, 1 sc, turn.

Row 15: Using A, 1 ch, 1 sc, * 1 Mdc, 2 ch, skip st, [1 Mdc, 1 sc] 3 times, 1 Mdc, 2 ch, skip st, 2 Mdc, 2 ch, skip st, 1 sc, 1 Mdc, 1 sc, 1 Mdc, 1 sc, 2 ch, skip st, 1 Mdc; rep from * to last 2 sts, 1 Mdc, 1 sc, turn.

Row 17: Using B, 1 ch, 1 sc, * 2 ch, skip st, 1 Mdc, 1 sc, [2 ch, skip st, 1 sc] 3 times, 1 Mdc, 2 ch, skip st, 1 sc, 1 Mdc, [2 ch, skip st, 1 sc] twice, 2 ch, skip st, 1 Mdc, 1 sc; rep from * to last 2 sts, 2 ch, skip st, 1 sc, turn.

Row 19: Using A, 1 ch, 1 sc, * 1 Mdc, 1 sc, 2 ch, skip st, [1 Mdc, 1 sc] twice, 1 Mdc, 2 ch, skip st, 1 sc, 1 Mdc, 2 ch, skip st, 1 sc, [1 Mdc, 1 sc] 3 times, 2 ch, skip st; rep from * to last 2 sts, 1 Mdc, 1 sc, turn.

Row 21: Using B, 1 ch, 1 sc, * 3 ch, skip 2 sts, 1 Mdc, 1 sc, [2 ch, skip st, 1 sc] twice, 1 Mdc, 3 ch, skip 2 sts, 1 Mdc, [2 ch, skip st, 1 sc] 3 times, 2 ch, skip st, 1 Mdc; rep from * to last 2 sts, 2 ch, skip st, 1 sc, turn.

Row 23: Using A, 1 ch, 1 sc, * 2 Mdc, 1 sc, 2 ch, skip st, 1 Mdc, 1 sc, 1 Mdc, 2 ch, skip st, 1 sc, 2 Mdc, 2 ch, skip st, [1 Mdc, 1 sc] 3 times, 1 Mdc, 2 ch, skip st; rep from * to last 2 sts, 1 Mdc, 1 sc, turn.

Row 25: Using B, 1 ch, 1 sc, * 2 ch, skip st, 1 sc, 2 ch, skip st, 1 Mdc, 1 sc, 2 ch, skip st, 1 sc, 1 Mdc, 2 ch, skip st, 1 sc, 2 ch, skip st, 1 Mdc, 1 sc , [2 ch, skip st, 1 sc] 3 times, 1 Mdc; rep from * to last 2 sts, 2 ch, skip st, 1 sc, turn.

Row 27: Using A, 1 ch, 1 sc, * [1 Mdc, 1 sc] twice, 2 ch, skip st, 1 Mdc, 2 ch, skip st, [1 sc, 1 Mdc] twice, 1 sc, 2 ch, skip st, [1 Mdc, 1 sc] twice, 1 Mdc, 2 ch, skip st, 1 sc; rep from * to last 2 sts, 1 Mdc, 1 sc, turn.

Row 29: Using B, 1 ch, 1 sc, 2 ch, skip st, * 1 sc, 3 ch, skip 2 sts, 1 Mdc, 1 sc, 1 Mdc, 3 ch, skip 2 sts, 1 sc, 3 ch, skip 2 sts, 1 Mdc, 5 sc, 1 Mdc, ** 3 ch, skip 2 sts; rep from * to last 3 sts, ending last rep at **, 3 ch, skip 2 sts, 1 sc, turn.

Row 31: Using A, 1 ch, 1 sc, * 1 Mdc, 1 sc, 2 Mdc, 1 sc, 2 ch, skip st, [1 sc, 2 Mdc] twice, 3 sc, 2 ch, skip st, 3 sc, 1 Mdc; rep from * to last 2 sts, 1 Mdc, 1 sc, turn.

Row 33: Using B, 1 ch, 1 sc, * [2 ch, skip st, 1 sc] twice, 2 ch, skip st, 1 Mdc, [2 ch, skip st, 1 sc] 4 times, 2 ch, skip st, 1 Mdc, [2 ch, skip st, 1 sc] twice; rep from * to last 2 sts, 2 ch, skip st, 1 sc, turn.

Row 35: Using A, 1 ch, 1 sc in every st and Mdc in every sp.

Row 36: As Row 2.

Rep Rows 1 to 36, ending last rep with Row 35.

LEAVES

135

THESE ARE THE EDGE OR "SELVAGE" STITCHES. SEE PAGE 17 TO LEARN HOW TO READ A MOSAIC CHART.

THE CROCHET PATTERN TEXT IS GIVEN SECOND, AND CAN BE READ ALONGSIDE THE CHART.

YOU ONLY NEED TO KNOW THE BASIC STITCHES, BUT IF YOU NEED A REFRESHER COURSE FOR KNITTING OR CROCHET, TURN TO PAGES 166-173.

The Basics

Before you get started, here is some useful information about yarns, needles, hooks, symbols, and abbreviations, as well as a guide to basic mosaic techniques.

Tools and Materials

Few materials and minimal craft skills are needed to complete the designs featured in this book; however, the yarn type used and yarn color will produce results that vary in scale and texture, so it can be very rewarding to experiment.

1. Yarn

Yarn is available in a range of weights, from fingering to super bulky (learn more on pages 14–15). Because yarns may vary from one manufacturer to another—and certainly change from one fiber to another—the yarn types are not indicated for each pattern and no needle or hook sizes are given as it is a personal preference. However, you do need to be aware of the properties of different yarns, because the construction of a yarn will affect its behavior and characteristics, and that will influence the result. The yarn used in this book is West Yorkshire Spinners The Croft DK (100% Shetland Islands Wool, 246yd/225m, 3½oz/100g). The color codes of the specific yarn used in each chapter are supplied on page 176.

2. Knitting Needles

Match your choice of needle to the yarn you are using. Yarn ball bands indicate a recommended needle size, and this is a good place to start, but you can try different sizes to achieve the desired effect. Pairs of knitting needles are made in a variety of lengths. Most are aluminum, although larger needles tend to be made of plastic to reduce their weight. Bamboo or wooden needles are also available in many sizes. For all of the designs in this book, I have used a pair of US 6 (4mm) circular needles.

3. Crochet Hooks

Crochet hooks are available in a wide range of sizes and materials. Most hooks are made from aluminum or plastic. Small-size steel hooks are made for working with very fine yarns. Handmade wooden, bamboo, and horn hooks are also available. The design of the hook affects the ease of working considerably. Look for a hook that has a comfortable grip. Hook sizes are measured differently in Europe and the United States, and some brands of hook are labeled with more than one type of sizing. See page 14 for a chart showing equivalent hook sizes in the different size systems. Choosing a hook is largely a matter of personal preference, so try some different hooks. I have used size E/4 (3.5mm).

Additional Equipment

4. Tape measure: This is essential for checking gauge and the length or width of a project. Retractable tape measures are most useful as they fit neatly into your project bag.

5. Stitch markers and row counters: Ready-made stitch markers can be used to indicate a repeat or to help count stitches in a chain. Similarly, a row counter may help you to keep track of the number of rows you have worked, but in knitting this is usually easy if you remember to include the stitches on the needle as a row.

6. Scissors: Sharp scissors are a must for any crocheter or knitter. Small, sharp embroidery scissors are best for snipping yarn.

7. Ruler: A ruler can be helpful in checking the gauge or for keeping track of what row you are working on. Simply place it on the chart, above the row you plan to work on.

8. Washi tape: A good way of marking your row so you don't lose track. Place a strip of washi tape above (not below) the row you are working on and move it as you work up. Placing it below will obstruct your view of the previous rows, which you need to see when crocheting, as it will determine if you do a sc or an Mdc.

9. Pencil and pen: You can use a pencil on the chart to mark off your rows. If you plan to scan your chart and print a copy, then a pen is fine to use.

10. Yarn needle(s): Blunt-ended needles are essential for weaving in ends and sewing up projects. Make sure the eye is large enough to thread the yarn through.

2
8
2
6
7
1
4
3
9
10
5

Yarn

With such an amazing variety of yarns on the market, we are truly spoiled for choice. They come in a kaleidoscope of colors and a wide range of weights, and they are all suitable for crochet or knitting.

Yarn weight

Yarn weight refers to the thickness of the yarn; the ball band provides this information. It also gives you a recommendation of the size of knitting needles or crochet hook to use with the specific yarn.

Lace/superfine: Very fine yarns used mostly for delicate openwork.

Sport: Fine yarns used for most types of work, producing a lightweight fabric. This weight in wool with nylon is perfect for making socks.

Light worsted/DK (double knitting): The most commonly used weight of yarn producing medium-weight garments, light worsted/DK is suitable for almost anything.

Worsted/Aran: Both slightly thicker than light worsted/DK, however worsted is lighter than Aran, but both weights can be used for a large number of projects.

Bulky: Works up fast and is used for a range of projects, including blankets, scarves, and garments. It produces a heavy-weight fabric with great stitch definition.

Super bulky: Perfect for supersized cuddly designs, it works up superfast and is perfect for hats, scarves, and cozy garments.

YARN WEIGHTS

Yarn is categorized by the thickness of each strand, known as its weight. This table shows the most common weight categories, with the recommended knitting needle and crochet hook sizes.

CATEGORY	NAMES	KNITTING NEEDLE SIZE RANGE	CROCHET HOOK SIZE RANGE
0 Lace	lace, fingering, 2-ply, 10-count crochet thread	US 000-1 (1.5-2.25mm)	steel size 6-9 (1.6-1.4mm); regular B/1 (2.25mm)
1 Superfine	sock, fingering, baby	US 1-3 (2.25-3.25mm)	B/1-E/4 (2.25-3.5mm)
2 Fine	sport, 4-ply, baby	US 3-5 (3.25-3.75mm)	E/4-G/7 (3.5-4.5mm)
3 Light	light worsted/DK	US 5-7 (3.75-4.5mm)	G/7-I/9 (4.5-5.5mm)
4 Medium	worsted, Aran, Afghan	US 7-9 (4.5-5.5mm)	I/9-K10.5 (5.5-6.5mm)
5 Bulky	bulky, chunky, craft, rug	US 9-11 (5.5-8mm)	K10.5-M/13 (6.5-9mm)
6 Super bulky	super bulky, roving, super chunky	US 11 and larger (8mm and larger)	M/13-P/Q (9-15mm)
7 Jumbo	jumbo, roving	US 19 and larger (15mm and larger)	P/Q (15mm) and larger

Yarn fiber

Yarns are made of many natural fibers such as alpaca and wool, or manmade fibers such as acrylic and nylon, all of which come in a range of thicknesses.

Wool

This very warm fiber is the most popular for crochet and knitting. It comes from the fleece of sheep, and different breeds have different names of wool. Merino wool is one of those types that comes from merino sheep, as is Shetland and Botany. Wool yarns are easy to crochet with and have wonderful bounce.

Cotton

This fiber comes in different grades of softness, with Egyptian cotton being the softest. Cotton is a very kind fiber on the skin and suits a lot of people with skin allergies. Cotton shows off stitch definition beautifully, but it can be heavy and less elastic than wool. However, it does have superb drape.

Mixed yarns

There is a vast array of mixed yarns on the market. They are made by plying different fibers together to produce different textures and weights. They can be natural fibers mixed with synthetic, such as wool and nylon, producing great sock yarn, or all natural, such as mohair and silk or wool and cotton.

Novelty yarns

These yarns are mostly spun from manmade fibers and are made of several plies twisted together. They are perfect for a variety of plain projects that will showcase the yarn.

Manmade fibers

Synthetic fibers are made from crudes and intermediates, including petroleum, coal, limestone, and water. The most common fiber is acrylic, which mimics natural fibers such as wool. Because they are manmade or semi-manmade, they are cheaper and longer, making them more budget-friendly.

Bamboo and soya yarns

These are environmentally friendly yarns. Bamboo is made from the center of the bamboo stalk; it is a soft yarn with very good drape. Soya yarns are made from the soya plant; they are incredibly soft and can often mimic silk yarns.

Abbreviations and Terminology

Listed below are the abbreviations used in the patterns in this book.

KNITTING AND CROCHET ABBREVIATIONS

*	indicates the start of a longer repeat sequence (repeat instructions that follow the asterisk as many times as stated)
[ ]	indicates a short repeat sequence (repeat instruction in brackets as many times as stated)
RS	right side
WS	wrong side
yo	yarn over hook
st(s)	stitch(es)

CROCHET ABBREVIATIONS

BLO	back loop only
ch(s)	chain/chain stitch(es)
ch-sp	chain space
cont	continue
dc	double crochet
FLO	front loop only
FLdc2d	front loop double crochet 2 down, double crochet in FLO of st 2 rows below.
Mdc	mosaic double crochet. Treble worked in skipped st and placed in front of ch in st 2 rows below.
sl st	slip stitch
sc	single crochet
standing sc	Beginning with a slip knot on hook, hold in place, work single crochet into stitch.

KNITTING ABBREVIATIONS

k	knit
p	purl
sl	slip
wyif	with yarn in front
wyib	with yarn in back

TUNISIAN CROCHET ABBREVIATIONS

Tss	Tunisian Simple Stitch
Tdc	Tunisian Double Crochet

AMERICAN/ENGLISH TERMINOLOGY

The patterns in this book use American terminology, which differs somewhat from English terminology. You may find this list of American terms and their English equivalents useful.

AMERICAN	ENGLISH
single crochet **(sc)**	double crochet **(dc)**
double crochet **(dc)**	treble crochet **(tr)**
Tunisian double crochet **(Tdc)**	Tunisian treble crochet **(Ttr)**

How to Read Mosaic Charts

All the patterns in this book are accompanied by mosaic charts. Mosaic charts are a visual representation of the colorwork design. They are compact and easy to read and both mosaic crochet and knitting follow the same chart.

Rules for reading charts

- Read the charts from the bottom to the top.
- Read the charts from right to left on the RS and from left to right on WS:
  - Row 1 and all odd rows (RS)—read from right to left
  - Row 2 and all even rows (WS)—read from left to right
- Each row of the chart represents two actual rows of crochet or knit (worked in one color).
- Each square on the chart represents one stitch.
- The beginning square on each row represents the color of that row.
- The first and last stitch of each row on the chart are the selvage stitches. They are worked in the color used on that row and are always worked in the same way. The selvage stitches are marked in green on the chart adjacent for reference.
- When shaping is involved (for garments), then very often each row of the mosaic chart will be shown on the chart.
- The red box indicates the horizontal pattern repeat.
- Foundation row/rows are not shown on the chart. They will be made in the alternate color to the beginning square of Row 1 and in the same color as the final row/rows.
- If this is your first time following a mosaic chart, I suggest choosing darker yarn for the dark boxes and lighter yarn for light boxes to help you read the chart more easily.

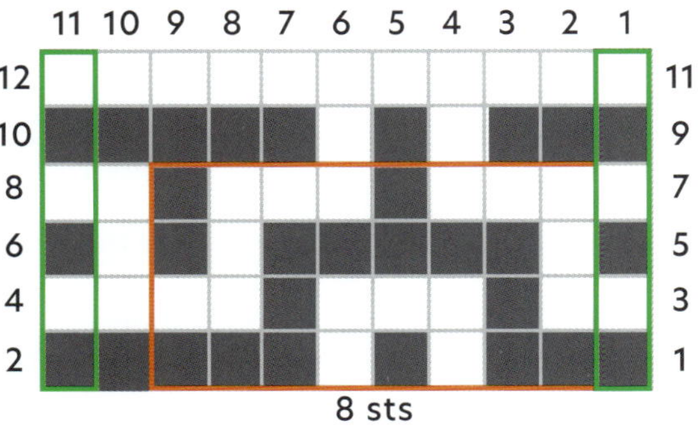

TIP: In this book, all the patterns are worked in stockinette stitch. As stitches are slipped, when you encounter the opposite color they will become elongated, causing the stitches before them to burrow. This will result in stitches that can look uneven. Working on achieving an even gauge is key, however, transferring the designs into garter stitch (knit every row) will also help with this problem. When working on the WS in garter stitch, the slipped stitches must be slipped with yarn in front. Simply move the yarn to the front in between needles, then move it back to knit the next stitch. You can also try working in combination rows: two rows in stockinette stitch and two rows in garter stitch.

Mosaic Knitting

All charts in this book are worked in stockinette stitch, therefore, all RS rows are knit and all WS rows are purled. You can, of course, adapt them for garter stitch, the principle will stay the same, but the WS rows will be knit and not purled.

Using the chart on the previous page, or any chart from the book, start the work by casting on the desired number of stitches in the alternate color to the first row of the chart. Cable cast-on works best here as it gives a nice firm edge (see page 168). Knit one row and purl one row. Now you are ready to start working from chart. The first stitch is 1 x 1 square. Join in a new color simply by starting to knit with that color and catch the tail at the back to secure it. Alternatively, you might find it useful to tie a knot to keep the yarn in place. You will need to undo the knot at the end of the project and weave in the end.

The selvage stitch at each edge is always worked in the color of the stripe you are working. This means that you will never slip the first or last stitch of the pattern. However, they are best worked in garter stitch (knit on both sides). This will create neater edges. You could also add more stitches to the selvage edge, this will help prevent the work from curling if it's worked in stockinette stitch.

1. On knit rows, reading the chart from right to left, knit the selvage stitch using the color indicated, then knit all the stitches on the row that are the same color as the selvage stitch. Slip the opposite-color stitches as if to purl, carrying the yarn in the back of your work (wyib).

2. On purl rows, reading the chart from left to right, purl the stitches that were knit on the preceding row and slip the alternate-color stitches as if to purl with the yarn held in the front (wyif).

3. Work in this way on every row, changing color every two rows. Do not cut the yarn after every color change but carry it with you up the work. For the neatest edge, change the color by placing the yarn you have just worked to the front and pick up the new yarn from the back.

4. Continue as set until your project is complete. End your work with the same color as used for the foundation row. Bind off as usual.

Mosaic Crochet

There are two main types of mosaic crochet: inset and overlay. In this book I concentrate on inset; however, I do give an explanation on how to work and adapt all charts for overlay mosaic crochet later in the book (see page 24). The crochet stitches are a lot larger than knitted ones, this results in crochet mosaic pieces being significantly bigger.

As with mosaic knitting, the selvage stitches are kept the same. In mosaic crochet, work single crochet in the first and last stitch on every row.

Chainless foundation

Mosaic crochet starts with a chainless foundation in the alternate/ contrast color to the first row of the chart. As with mosaic knitting, this foundation row is not shown on the chart. A chainless foundation provides a stretchy, narrow edge which does not pull in and gives you a ready-made row of single crochet, making it a perfect start to mosaic crochet. If you are starting with chain, work one row of single crochet.

1. Start with 2 chains, turn your work on the side, you will see a bump at the back of your chains. Insert your hook into the bump of the second chain from the hook.

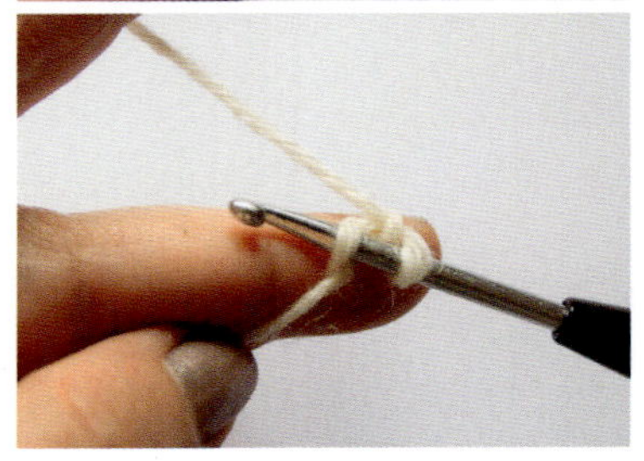

2. Yo and pull through the bump—you now have 2 loops on your hook. Yo again and pull through only 1 loop on the hook.

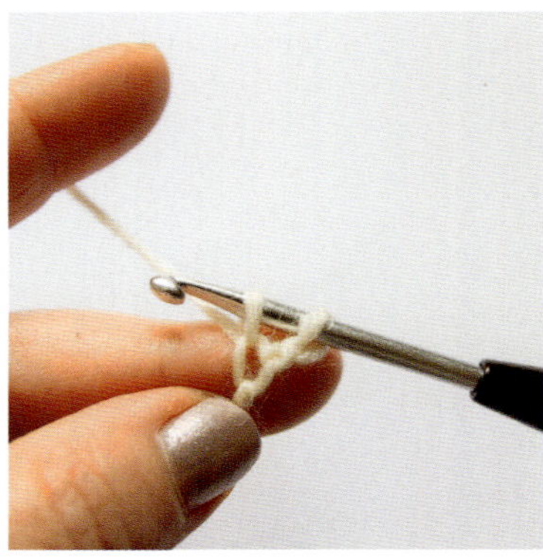

3. You are left with 2 loops on your hook. Yo and pull through both loops. That's the first stitch made. To work the next stitch, turn your work on the side and you will see the front leg of the next stitch to be worked.
Insert the hook into the front and back leg of the stitch (the full V). Yo and pull it through the stitch, so that you have 2 loops on your hook.

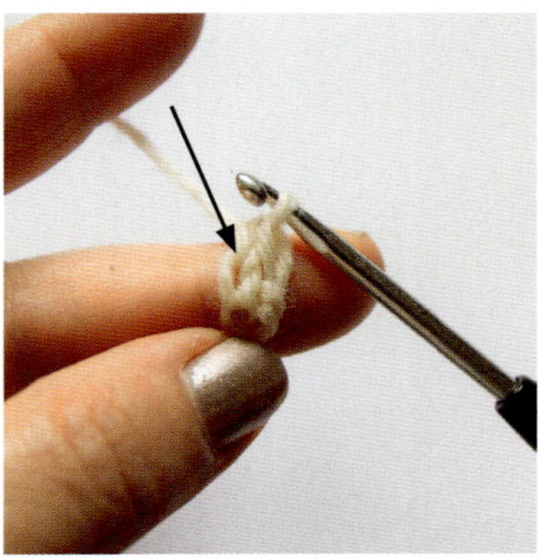

4. Yo and pull through 1 loop, leaving 2 loops on the hook, then yo again, and pull through both loops on the hook. The second stitch is made.

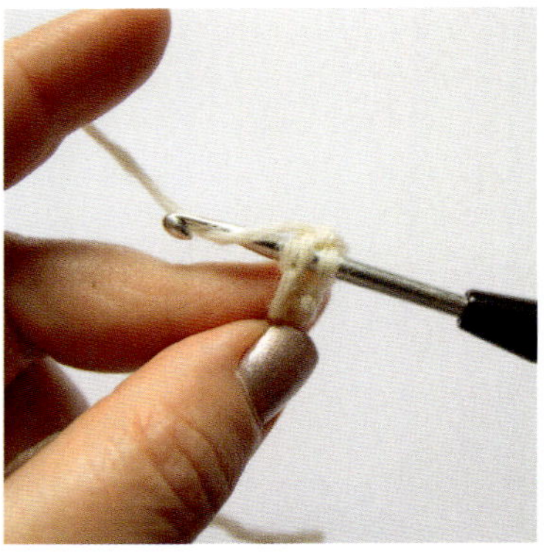

5. Continue repeating steps 4 and 5 until you have the desired number of sc.

Mosaic Crochet: Reading the Rows

Using this chart as an example and starting at the bottom-right of the chart (1 x 1 square), follow the steps below. Always work 1 ch at the beginning of rows, to give the starting stitch the right height. Note that this 1 ch is not counted as a stitch.

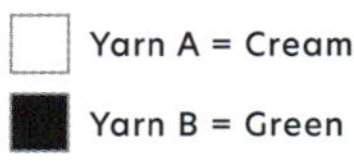

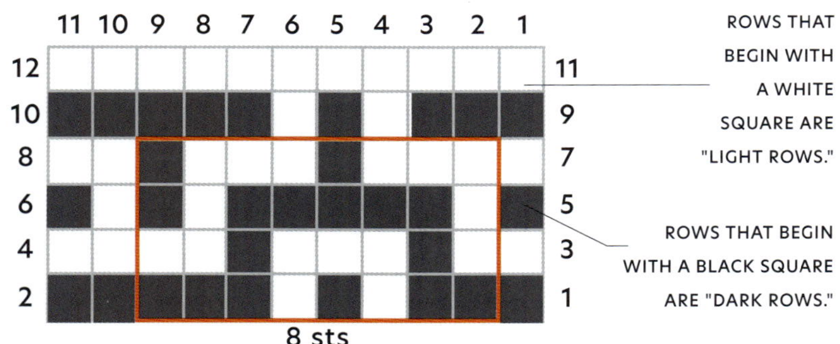

Yarn color
The color of the first square also indicates which color yarn you should use for the entire row.

Starting:

Create your foundation row (see page 20) to your desired length. For this chart, the desired number of chainless single crochet will be a mutiple of 8 stitches plus 3. If you wish to work the foundation row by creating chains, then work single crochet into chains. You will also need to work the WS row by working single crochet in every stitch. This will create a thicker edge. To even this out, when finishing the project, work the last two rows of the chart. It will result in the starting and ending rows being the same thickness.

Dark rows:

Row 1: Whenever you see a dark square, single crochet.
When you see a white square, ch(s) and skip the next st(s).
Note: When chaining (to prevent puckering): 1 sq = 2 ch; 2 sq = 3 ch; 3 sq = 4 ch, and so on.

ROW 1: 2 CH TO SKIP 1 STITCH

ROW 1: SC ON EVERY DARK SQUARE

Row 2: On the next (even) row (still in dark), you do exactly the same: single crochet every dark square and chain (the same number of chains) as on the previous row.

ROW 2

Light rows:

Change color to light yarn. The best way to do this is by working to the last stitch on the previous row, stop when you have 2 loops left of the last stitch, pick up the new yarn and finish off the single crochet as usual with the new yarn.

Always remember to chain 1 at the beginning of every row.

Row 3: On the chart, whenever you see a white square over dark, single crochet.

When you see a white square over a white square (it will actually be over dark chains on your work), drop down two rows by working a mosaic double crochet (Mdc) into the row of the same color as the working yarn and IN FRONT of the chains below (see images below).

Row 4: Then on the next (even) row (still in light), you do exactly the same, but in single crochet and chains. Even in the top of an Mdc you still work single crochet. Work single crochet in every white stitch and chain (the same number of chains) as per previous row.

Dark rows:

Rows 5 and 6: Single crochet on dark squares, ch on light squares and Mdc over dark/dark squares.

Light rows:

Rows 7 and 8: Single crochet on white squares, ch on dark squares and Mdc over white/white squares.
Continue working in this way until your project is finished.

Repeating:

On the last row of repeat, chain spaces will be created, when starting the repeat from Row 1 again those chain spaces need to be filled with Mdc. Simply work Mdc when you come across chain space.

Finishing:

Work RS of last row only in the same color as the chainless foundation, working single crochet and Mdc when required. This will ensure that the foundation and last row are of similar thicknesses and therefore more visually even (in the above example, you finish on Row 11, not 12). If your foundation row was made of chains and two rows of single crochet, work the WS as well to finish off (Row 12).

Special Stitch
Mosaic Double Crochet (Mdc)

MDC STEP 1

Yarn over hook, insert hook in skipped stitch two rows below, making sure that the hook is placed in front of the chains.

MDC STEP 2

Yarn over hook, and pull up a loop (3 loops on hook).

MDC STEP 3

Yarn over hook, pull through 2 loops on hook, twice.

Overlay and Tunisian Mosaic Crochet

The charts in this book can easily be adapted to be used in Tunisian and overlay mosaic crochet.

Overlay Mosaic Crochet

In this technique, you only work with the right side facing you, working each row once only. This requires you to cut and join in new yarn on every row. You start a new row with a standing single crochet. You can hide the ends by enclosing them in an envelope border or you can tie more lengths of yarn to the edges to create fringing. The selvage stitches are always worked in single crochet and indicate the color you will use for the whole row.

In overlay mosaic crochet you do not make chains and skip sts where those chains are created. Instead, you work each st in the back loop only (BLO), and place front loop double crochet 2 down (FLdc2d) when required, working Fldc2d into front loops of stitches from first row below of the same color.

You will notice in the chart below that dark/dark and light/light squares have the letter F. This stands for Fldc2d and is a clear indication of where the front loop double crochet needs to be worked.

The row numbers are now only on the right side, because you will only work on the right side of the work. The chart is read from right to left on every row. You start with a chainless foundation in the alternate color to the first row of the chart, this foundation row is not shown on the chart.

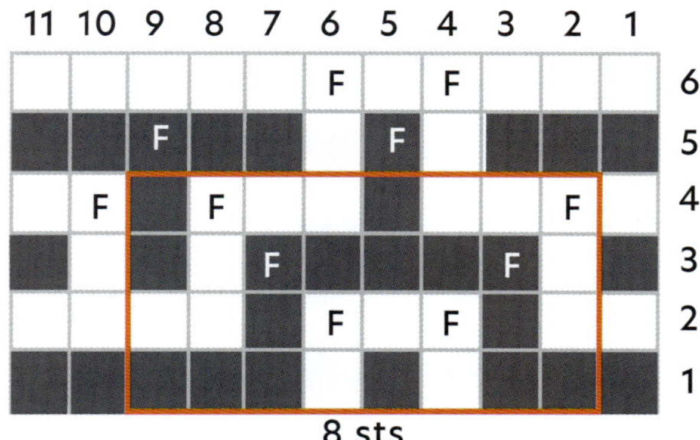

For the next two rows of chart, changing color on each row, start with standing single crochet, 1 single crochet BLO to last stitch, work the last single crochet as normal and not BLO.

From now on

On a light row, when you see:

- Light color square over dark square (L/D)—you will [sc BLO]
- Dark color square over dark square (D/D)—[sc BLO]
- Light color square over light square marked with F (L/L)—[Fldc2d] (front loop only) into corresponding stitch, 2 rows down

On a dark row, when you see:

- D/L—[sc BLO]
- L/L—[sc BLO]
- D/D marked with F—[Fldc2d] (front loop only) into corresponding stitch, 2 rows down

FRONT LOOP DOUBLE CROCHET 2 DOWN (Fldc2d)

Yo, insert hook into the front loop into corresponding stitch 2 rows below. Yo and pull up a loop (3 loops on hook), yo and pull through 2 loops only, yo and pull through remaining 2 loops.

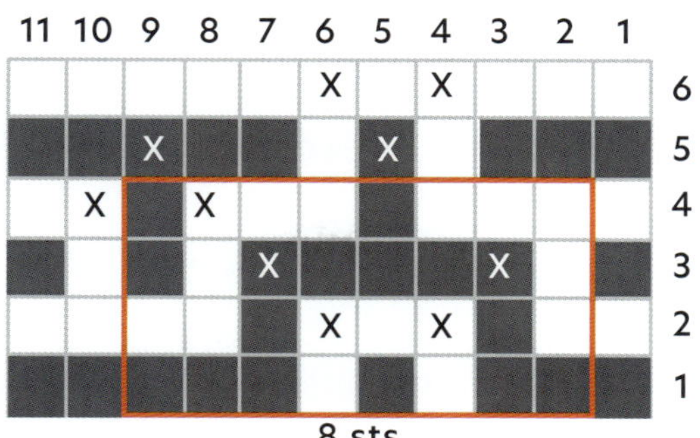

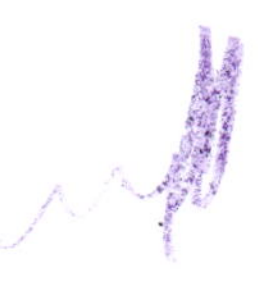

Tunisian Mosaic Crochet

Tunisian mosaic crochet is worked in a very similar way to overlay mosaic crochet.

The chart is adjusted in an almost identical way, with X replacing F. All stitches are worked in Tunisian simple stitch (Tss) and X indicates where Tunisian double crochet (Tdc) needs to be placed.

The selvage stitches are always worked in the same way. With the first stitch being the loop on the hook and the last stitch being worked into two strands of the last stitch of the previous row.

The chart numbers are only written on the right side, showing how to work the forward passes. The return passes are worked in the same way on every row. Start the work with chains and a forward and return pass, this is worked in the alternate color to the first row of the chart. The foundation row is not shown on the chart.

From now on

On a light row, when you see:

- Light color square over dark square (L/D)—you will Tss
- Dark color square over dark square (D/D)—Tss
- Light color square over light square marked with X (L/L)—Tdc into front and back loop of corresponding stitch 2 rows down (row of the same color)

On a dark row, when you see:

- D/L—[Tss]
- L/L—[Tss]
- D/D marked with X—Tdc into front and back loop of corresponding stitch 2 rows down (row of the same color)

TUNISIAN SIMPLE STITCH (Tss)

Insert hook from right to left under front vertical bar of stitch, yo and pull through. Return pass: Yo and pull through 1 loop on hook, *yo and pull through 2 loops; rep from * until 1 loop left on hook.

TUNISIAN DOUBLE CROCHET (Tdc)

Yo, insert hook into the front and back loop of corresponding stitch 2 rows below. Yo and pull up a loop (3 loops on hook), yo and pull through 2 loops only.

Working in The Round

Any chart in this book can be adapted to be worked in the round. You will need to omit the selvage stitches as they will distort the pattern if worked in the round.

When working in the round, the RS will always be facing you, therefore small adjustments are required to individual techniques:

Knit

Because you will be working on the RS only, the even number rows will be worked as the odd number; basically you repeat the RS row twice. It is vital to place a stitch marker to denote the beginning of the round.

Crochet

WS rows will not be worked, only work the RS row once. Place a stitch marker to denote the beginning of the round if you are working in a continuous spiral. Alternatively, slip stitch to first stitch to close round and chain 1 at the beginning of the round. This will result in the designs being shorter and look similar to overlay mosaic crochet.

Geometric

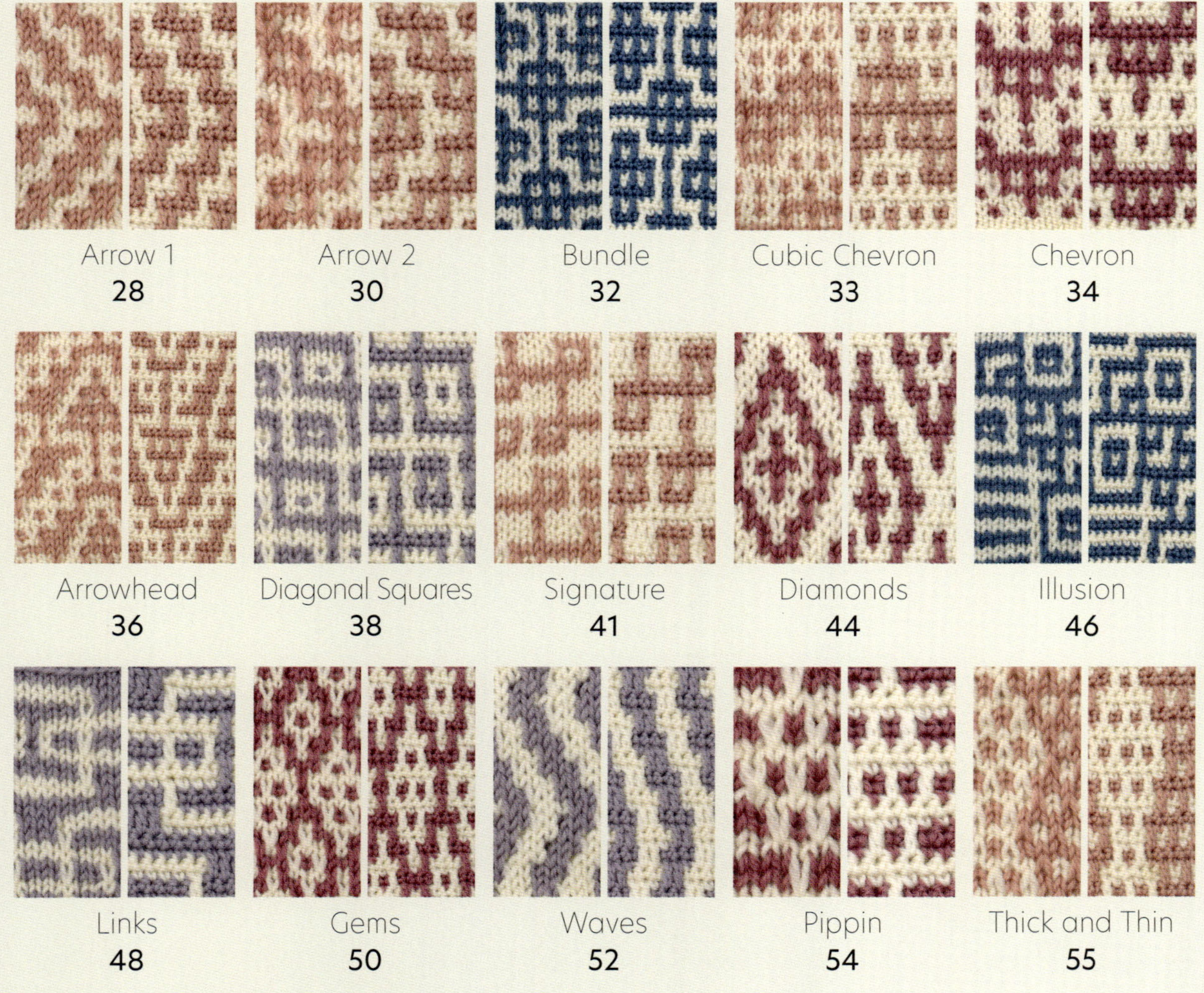

SKILL LEVEL

Arrow 1

This is an ideal pattern for a panel and works best in a horizontal repeat. This pattern produces clean lines and is the easier of the two arrow designs in this chapter.

Knit Instructions

Multiple of 5 sts + 5

On RS rows, slip the sts purlwise with yarn in the back.

Cast on using B, k one row and p one row.

Row 1 (RS): Using A, k1, sl2, * k3, sl2; rep from * to last 2 sts, k2.

Row 2 and all WS rows: P the knitted sts and sl the slipped sts purlwise with yarn in the front.

Row 3: Using B, k3 * sl1, k4; rep from * to last 2 sts, sl1, k1.

Row 5: Using A, k3, * k1, sl2, k2; rep from * to last 2 sts, k2.

Row 7: Using B, k1, sl1, k1, * k3, sl1, k1; rep from * to last 2 sts, k2.

Row 9: Using A, k2, sl1, * sl1, k3, sl1; rep from * to last 2 sts, sl1, k1.

Row 11: Using B, k3, * k1, sl1, k3; rep from * to last 2 sts, k2.

Row 13: Using A, k1, sl1, k1, * k2, sl2, k1; rep from * to last 2 sts, k2.

Row 15: Using B, k2, sl1, * k4, sl1; rep from * to last 2 sts, k2.

Row 17: Using A, k3, * sl2, k3; rep from * to last 2 sts, sl1, k1.

Row 19: As Row 15.

Row 21: As Row 13.

Row 23: As Row 11.

Row 25: As Row 9.

Row 27: As Row 7.

Row 29: As Row 5.

Row 31: As Row 3.

Rep Rows 1 to 32. To finish, work Rows 33 to 36.

Row 33: As Row 1.

Row 35: Using B, k all sts.

Row 36: As Row 2.

Crochet Instructions

Multiple of 5 sts + 5

Pattern note: The repeat in written instructions differs from chart on Rows 9 and 25.

Using B, make desired number of chainless sc.

Row 1 (RS): Using A, 1 ch, 1 sc, 3 ch, skip 2 sts, * 3 sc, 3 ch, skip 2 sts; rep from * to last 2 sts, 2 sc, turn.

Row 2 and all WS rows: 1 ch, 1 sc in sts, ch and skip ch-sps, turn.

Row 3: Using B, 1 ch, 1 sc, 2 Mdc, * 2 ch, skip st, 2 sc, 2 Mdc; rep from * to last 2 sts, 2 ch, skip st, 1 sc, turn.

Row 5: Using A, 1 ch, 3 sc, * 1 Mdc, 3 ch, skip 2 sts, 2 sc; rep from * to last 2 sts, 1 Mdc, 1 sc, turn.

Row 7: Using B, 1 ch, 1 sc, 2 ch, skip st, 1 sc, * 1 sc, 2 Mdc, 2 ch, skip st, 1 sc; rep from * to last 2 sts, 2 sc, turn.

Row 9: Using A, 1 ch, 1 sc, 1 Mdc, 3 ch, skip 2 sts, * 2 sc, 1 Mdc, 3 ch, skip 2 sts; rep from * to last st, 1 sc, turn.

Row 11: Using B, 1 ch, 2 sc, 1 Mdc, * 1 Mdc, 2 ch, skip st, 2 sc, 1 Mdc; rep from * to last 2 sts, 1 Mdc, 1 sc, turn.

Row 13: Using A, 1 ch, 1 sc, 2 ch, skip st, 1 sc, * 1 sc, 1 Mdc, 3 ch, skip 2 sts, 1 sc; rep from * to last 2 sts, 2 sc, turn.

Row 15: Using B, 1 ch, 1 sc, 1 Mdc, 2 ch, skip st, * 2 sc, 2 Mdc, 2 ch, skip st; rep from * to last 2 sts, 2 sc, turn.

MOSAIC CHART

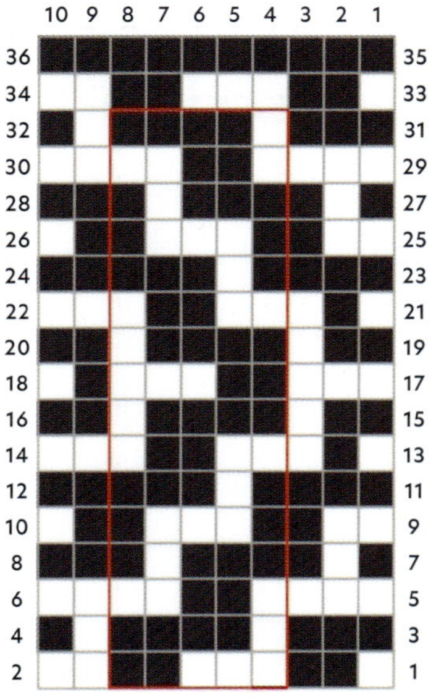

5 sts

Yarn A = Cream

Yarn B = Pale pink

Row 17: Using A, 1 ch, 2 sc, 1 Mdc, * 3 ch, skip 2 sts, 2 sc, 1 Mdc; rep from * to last 2 sts, 2 ch, skip st, 1 sc, turn.
Row 19: Using B, 1 ch, 2 sc, 2 ch, skip st, * 2 Mdc, 2 sc, 2 ch, skip st; rep from * to last 2 sts, 1 Mdc, 1 sc, turn.
Row 21: Using A, 1 ch, 1 sc, 2 ch, skip st, 1 Mdc, * 2 sc, 3 ch, skip 2 sts, 1 Mdc; rep from * to last 2 sts, 2 sc, turn.
Row 23: Using B, 1 ch, 1 sc, 1 Mdc, 1 sc, * 1 sc, 2 ch, skip st, 2 Mdc, 1 sc; rep from * to last 2 sts, 2 sc, turn.
Row 25: Using A, 1 ch, 2 sc, 3 ch, skip 2 sts, * 1 Mdc, 2 sc, 3 ch, skip 2 sts; rep from * to last st, 1 sc, turn.
Row 27: Using B, 1 ch, 1 sc, 2 ch, skip st, 1 Mdc, * 1 Mdc, 2 sc, 2 ch, skip st, 1 Mdc; rep from * to last 2 sts, 1 Mdc, 1 sc, turn.
Row 29: Using A, 1 ch, 1 sc, 1 Mdc, 1 sc * 1 sc, 3 ch, skip 2 sts, 1 Mdc, 1 sc; rep from * to last 2 sts, 2 sc, turn.
Row 31: Using B, 1 ch, 3 sc, * 2 ch, skip st, 2 Mdc, 2 sc; rep from * to last 2 sts, 2 ch, skip st, 1 sc, turn.
Rep Rows 1 to 32, placing 1 Mdc in sps as required on Row 1. To finish, work Rows 33 to 35.
Row 33: Using A, 1 ch, 1 sc, 3 ch, skip 2 sts, * 1 Mdc, 2 sc, 3 ch, skip 2 sts; rep from * to last 2 sts, 1 Mdc, 1 sc, turn.
Row 35: Using B, 1 ch, 1 sc, 2 Mdc, * 3 sc, 2 Mdc; rep from * to last 2 sts, 2 sc, turn.

KNIT

CROCHET

Arrow 2

This arrow design is a little more difficult than Arrow 1 as it requires more concentration. Give this design some space on a larger project.

Knit Instructions

Multiple of 6 sts + 7

On RS rows, slip the sts purlwise with yarn in the back.

Cast on using A, k one row and p one row.

Row 1 (RS): Using B, k4, * sl1, k5; rep from * to last 3 sts, sl1, k2.

Row 2 and all WS rows: P the knitted sts and sl the slipped sts purlwise with yarn in the front.

Row 3: Using A, [k1, sl1] twice * k3, sl1, k1, sl1; rep from * to last 3 sts, k3.

Row 5: Using B, k4, * sl1, k5; rep from * to last 3 sts, sl1, k2.

Row 7: Using A, k1, sl1, k2 * [k1, sl1] twice, k2; rep from * to last 3 sts, k1, sl1, k1.

Row 9: Using B, k2, sl1, k1, * k4, sl1, k1; rep from * to last 3 sts, k3.

Row 11: Using A, k3, sl1, * k1, sl1, k3, sl1; rep from * to last 3 sts, k1, sl1, k1.

Row 13: Using B, k4, * k2, sl1, k3; rep from * to last 3 sts, k3.

Row 15: Using A, [k1, sl1] twice, * k3, sl1, k1, sl1; rep from * to last 3 sts, k3.

Row 17: As Row 13.

Row 19: As Row 11.

Row 21: As Row 9.

Row 23: As Row 7.

Rep Rows 1 to 24. To finish, work Rows 25 to 32.

Row 25: As Row 5.

Row 27: As Row 3.

Row 29: As Row 1.

Row 31: Using A, k all sts.

Row 32: As Row 2.

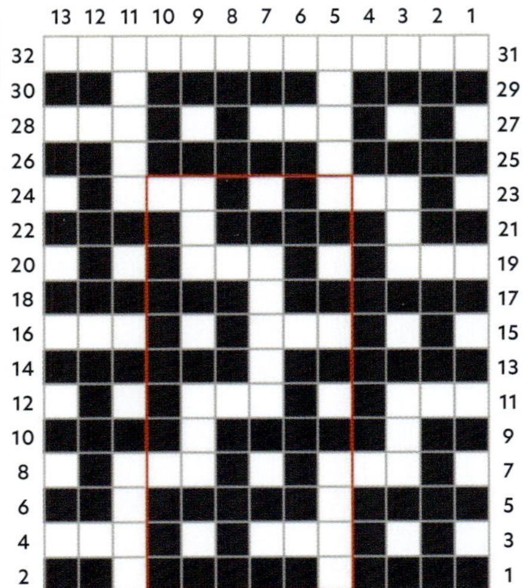

Crochet Instructions

Multiple of 6 sts + 7

Using A, make desired number of chainless sc.

Row 1 (RS): Using B, 1 ch, 4 sc, * 2 ch, skip st, 5 sc; rep from * to last 3 sts, 2 ch, skip st, 2 sc, turn.

Row 2 and all WS rows: 1 ch, 1 sc in sts, ch and skip ch-sps, turn.

Row 3: Using A, 1 ch, [1 sc, 2 ch, skip st] twice, * 1 Mdc, 2 sc, 2 ch, skip st, 1 sc, 2 ch, skip st; rep from * to last 3 sts, 1 Mdc, 2 sc, turn.

Row 5: Using B, 1 ch, [1 sc, 1 Mdc] twice, * 2 ch, skip st, 2 sc, 1 Mdc, 1 sc, 1 Mdc; rep from * to last 3 sts, 2 ch, skip st, 2 sc, turn.

Row 7: Using A, 1 ch, 1 sc, 2 ch, skip st, 2 sc, * 1 Mdc, [2 ch, skip st, 1 sc] twice, 1 sc; rep from * to last 3 sts, 1 Mdc, 2 ch, skip st, 1 sc, turn.

Row 9: Using B, 1 ch, 1 sc, 1 Mdc, 2 ch, skip st, 1 sc, * [1 sc, 1 Mdc] twice, 2 ch, skip st, 1 sc; rep from * to last 3 sts, 1 sc, 1 Mdc, 1 sc, turn.

Row 11: Using A, 1 ch, 2 sc, 1 Mdc, 2 ch, skip st, * 1 sc, 2 ch, skip st, 2 sc, 1 Mdc, 2 ch, skip st; rep from * to last 3 sts, 1 sc, 2 ch, skip st, 1 sc, turn.

Row 13: Using B, 1 ch, 3 sc, 1 Mdc, * 1 sc, 1 Mdc, 2 ch, skip st, 2 sc, 1 Mdc; rep from * to last 3 sts, 1 sc, 1 Mdc, 1 sc, turn.

Row 15: Using A, 1 ch, [1 sc, 2 ch, skip st] twice, * 2 sc, 1 Mdc, 2 ch, skip st, 1 sc, 2 ch, skip st; rep from * to last 3 sts, 3 sc, turn.

Row 17: Using B, 1 ch, [1 sc, 1 Mdc] twice, * 2 sc, 2 ch, skip st, 1 Mdc, 1 sc, 1 Mdc; rep from * to last 3 sts, 3 sc, turn.

Row 19: Using A, 1 ch, 3 sc, 2 ch, skip st, * 1 sc, 2 ch, skip st, 1 Mdc, 2 sc, 2 ch, skip st; rep from * to last 3 sts, 1 sc, 2 ch, skip st, 1 sc, turn.

Row 21: Using B, 1 ch, 2 sc, 2 ch, skip st, 1 Mdc, * 1 sc, 1 Mdc, 2 sc, 2 ch, skip st, 1 Mdc; rep from * to last 3 sts, 1 sc, 1 Mdc, 1 sc, turn.

Row 23: Using A, 1 ch, 1 sc, 2 ch, skip st, 1 Mdc, 1 sc, * 1 sc, 2 ch, skip st, 1 sc, 2 ch, skip st, 1 Mdc, 1 sc; rep from * to last 3 sts, 1 sc, 2 ch, skip st, 1 sc, turn.

Rep Rows 1 to 24, placing 1 Mdc in sps as required on Row 1. To finish, work Rows 25 to 31.

Row 25: Using B, 1 ch, 1 sc, 1 Mdc, 2 sc, * 2 ch, skip st, 1 Mdc, 1 sc, 1 Mdc, 2 sc; rep from * to last 3 sts, 2 ch, skip st, 1 Mdc, 1 sc, turn.

Row 27: Using A, 1 ch, [1 sc, 2 ch, skip st] twice, * 1 Mdc, 2 sc, 2 ch, skip st, 1 sc, 2 ch, skip st; rep from * to last 3 sts, 1 Mdc, 2 sc, turn.

Row 29: Using B, 1 ch, [1 sc, 1 Mdc] twice, * 2 ch, skip st, 2 sc, 1 Mdc, 1 sc, 1 Mdc; rep from * to last 3 sts, 2 ch, skip st, 2 sc, turn.

Row 31: Using A, 1 ch, 4 sc, * 1 Mdc, 5 sc; rep from * to last 3 sts, 1 Mdc, 2 sc, turn.

TIP: For the knit version: As stitches are slipped they will become elongated, causing the stitches before them to burrow. This will result in stitches that can look uneven. Try knitting the design in garter stitch if this is an issue in your work.

KNIT

CROCHET

KNIT

CROCHET

Bundle

A stunning pattern that works equally well as a horizontal or vertical panel or large repeat. When worked over a few rows of repeat, it looks like decorative tiling.

Knit Instructions

Multiple of 10 sts + 3

On RS rows, slip the sts purlwise with yarn in the back.

Cast on using A, k one row and p one row.

Row 1 (RS): Using B, k all sts.

Row 2 and all WS rows: P the knitted sts and sl the slipped sts purlwise with yarn in the front.

Row 3: Using A, k1, * [sl1, k1] twice, k4, sl1, k1; rep from * to last 2 sts, sl1, k1.

Row 5: Using B, k1, * k3, sl1, k3, sl1, k2; rep from * to last 2 sts, k2.

Row 7: Using A, k1, * sl1, k3, [sl1, k1] twice, k2; rep from * to last 2 sts, sl1, k1.

Row 9: Using B, k1, * k1, sl1, k7, sl1; rep from * to last 2 sts, k2.

Row 11: Using A, k1, * sl1, k1; rep from * to last 2 sts, sl1, k1.

Row 13: As Row 9.

Row 15: As Row 7.

Row 17: As Row 5.

Row 19: As Row 3.

Row 21: Using B, k all sts.

Rep Rows 3 to 22. To finish, work Rows 23 to 24.

Row 23: Using A, k all sts.

Row 24: As Row 2.

Yarn A = Cream

Yarn B = Blue

MOSAIC CHART

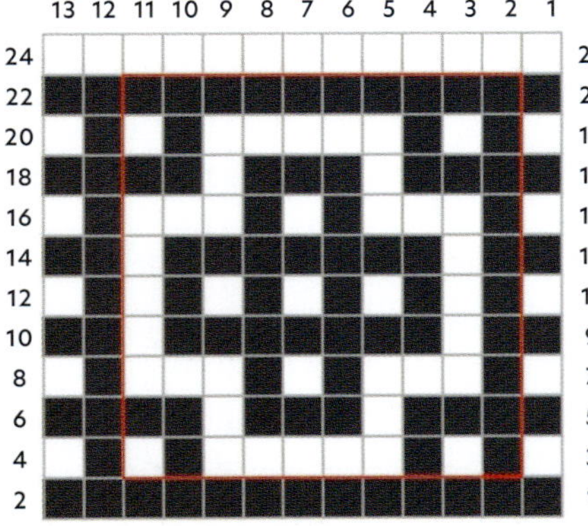

10 sts

Crochet Instructions

Multiple of 10 sts + 3

Using A, make desired number of chainless sc.

Row 1 (RS): Using B, 1 ch, 1 sc in every st, turn.

Row 2 and all WS rows: 1 ch, 1 sc in sts, ch and skip ch-sps, turn.

Row 3: Using A, 1 ch, 1 sc, * [2 ch, skip st, 1 sc] twice, 4 sc, 2 ch, skip st, 1 sc; rep from * to last 2 sts, 2 ch, skip st, 1 sc, turn.

Row 5: Using B, 1 ch, 1 sc, * 1 Mdc, 1 sc, 1 Mdc, 2 ch, skip st, 3 sc, 2 ch, skip st, 1 Mdc, 1 sc; rep from * to last 2 sts, 1 Mdc, 1 sc, turn.

Row 7: Using A, 1 ch, 1 sc, * 2 ch, skip st, 2 sc, 1 Mdc, 2 ch, skip st, 1 sc, 2 ch, skip st, 1 Mdc, 2 sc; rep from * to last 2 sts, 2 ch, skip st, 1 sc, turn.

Row 9: Using B, 1 ch, 1 sc, * 1 Mdc, 2 ch, skip st, 2 sc, 1 Mdc, 1 sc, 1 Mdc, 2 sc, 2 ch, skip st; rep from * to last 2 sts, 1 Mdc, 1 sc, turn.

Row 11: Using A, 1 ch, 1 sc, * 2 ch, skip st, 1 Mdc, [2 ch, skip st, 1 sc] 3 times, 2 ch, skip st, 1 Mdc; rep from * to last 2 sts, 2 ch, skip st, 1 sc, turn.

Row 13: Using B, 1 ch, 1 sc, * 1 Mdc, 2 ch, skip st, [1 Mdc, 1 sc] 3 times, 1 Mdc, 2 ch, skip st; rep from * to last 2 sts, 1 Mdc, 1 sc, turn.

Row 15: Using A, 1 ch, 1 sc, * 2 ch, skip st, 1 Mdc, 2 sc, [2 ch, skip st, 1 sc] twice, 1 sc, 1 Mdc; rep from * to last 2 sts, 2 ch, skip st, 1 sc, turn.

Row 17: Using B, 1 ch, 1 sc, * 1 Mdc, 2 sc, 2 ch, skip st, 1 Mdc, 1 sc, 1 Mdc, 2 ch, skip st, 2 sc; rep from * to last 2 sts, 1 Mdc, 1 sc, turn.

Row 19: Using A, 1 ch, 1 sc, * 2 ch, skip st, 1 sc, 2 ch, skip st, 1 Mdc, 3 sc, 1 Mdc, 2 ch, skip st, 1 sc; rep from * to last 2 sts, 2 ch, skip st, 1 sc, turn.

Row 21: Using B, 1 ch, 1 sc, * [1 Mdc, 1 sc] twice, 4 sc, 1 Mdc, 1 sc; rep from * to last 2 sts, 1 Mdc, 1 sc, turn.

Rep Rows 3 to 22. To finish, work Row 23.

Row 23: Using A, 1 sc in every st, turn.

Cubic Chevron

This delicate-looking pattern would work very well on a garment—it can be used as repeats or a panel. A darker Yarn B would give a bolder effect.

Knit Instructions

Multiple of 8 sts + 3

On RS rows, slip the sts purlwise with yarn in the back.

Cast on using A, k one row and p one row.

Row 1 (RS): Using B, k all sts.

Row 2 and all WS rows: P the knitted sts and sl the slipped sts purlwise with yarn in the front.

Row 3: Using A, k1, * [sl1, k1] twice, k2, sl1, k1; rep from * to last 2 sts, sl1, k1.

Row 5: Using B, k1, * k3, [sl1, k1] twice, k1; rep from * to last 2 sts, k2.

Row 7: Using A, k1, * sl1, k7; rep from * to last 2 sts, sl1, k1.

Row 9: Using B, k1, * k1, sl1; rep from * to last 2 sts, k2.

Row 11: Using A, k all sts.

Row 13: Using B, k1, * [sl1, k1] twice, k2, sl1, k1; rep from * to last 2 sts, sl1, k1.

Row 15: Using A, k1, * k3, [sl1, k1] twice, k1; rep from * to last 2 sts, k2.

Row 17: Using B, k1, * sl1, k7; rep from * to last 2 sts, sl1, k1.

Row 19: Using A, k1, * k1, sl; rep from * to last 2 sts, k2.

Row 21: Using B, k all sts.

Rep Rows 3 to 22. To finish, work Rows 23 to 24.

Row 23: Using A, k all sts.

Row 24: As Row 2.

Crochet Instructions

Multiple of 8 sts + 3

Using A, make desired number of chainless sc.

Row 1 (RS): Using B, 1 ch, 1 sc in every st, turn.

Row 2 and all WS rows: 1 ch, 1 sc in sts, ch and skip ch-sps, turn.

Row 3: Using A, 1 ch, 1 sc, * [2 ch, skip st, 1 sc] twice, 2 sc, 2 ch, skip st, 1 sc; rep from * to last 2 sts, 2 ch, skip st, 1 sc, turn.

Row 5: Using B, 1 ch, 1 sc, * 1 Mdc, 1 sc, 1 Mdc, 2 ch, skip st, 1 sc, 2 ch, skip st, 1 Mdc, 1 sc; rep from * to last 2 sts, 1 Mdc, 1 sc, turn.

Row 7: Using A, 1 ch, 1 sc, * 2 ch, skip st, 2 sc, [1 Mdc, 1 sc] twice, 1 sc; rep from * to last 2 sts, 2 ch, skip st, 1 sc, turn.

Row 9: Using B, 1 ch, 1 sc, * 1 Mdc, [2 ch, skip st, 1 sc] 3 times, 2 ch, skip st; rep from * to last 2 sts, 1 Mdc, 1 sc, turn.

Row 11: Using A, 1 ch, 1 sc, * [1 sc, 1 Mdc] 4 times; rep from * to last 2 sts, 2 sc, turn.

Row 13: Using B, 1 ch, 1 sc, * [2 ch, skip st, 1 sc] twice, 2 sc, 2 ch, skip st, 1 sc; rep from * to last 2 sts, 2 ch, skip st, 1 sc, turn.

Row 15: Using A, 1 ch, 1 sc, * 1 Mdc, 1 sc, 1 Mdc, 2 ch, skip st, 1 sc, 2 ch, skip st, 1 Mdc, 1 sc; rep from * to last 2 sts, 1 Mdc, 1 sc, turn.

Row 17: Using B, 1 ch, 1 sc, * 2 ch, skip st, 2 sc, [1 Mdc, 1 sc] twice, 1 sc; rep from * to last 2 sts, 2 ch, skip st, 1 sc, turn.

Row 19: Using A, 1 ch, 1 sc, * 1 Mdc, [2 ch, skip st, 1 sc] 3 times, 2 ch, skip st; rep from * to last 2 sts, 1 Mdc, 1 sc, turn.

Row 21: Using B, 1 ch, 1 sc, * [1 sc, 1 Mdc] 4 times; rep from * to last 2 sts, 2 sc, turn.

Rep Rows 3 to 22. To finish, work Row 23.

Row 23: Using A, 1 ch, 1 sc in every st, turn.

Yarn A = Cream

Yarn B = Pale pink

MOSAIC CHART

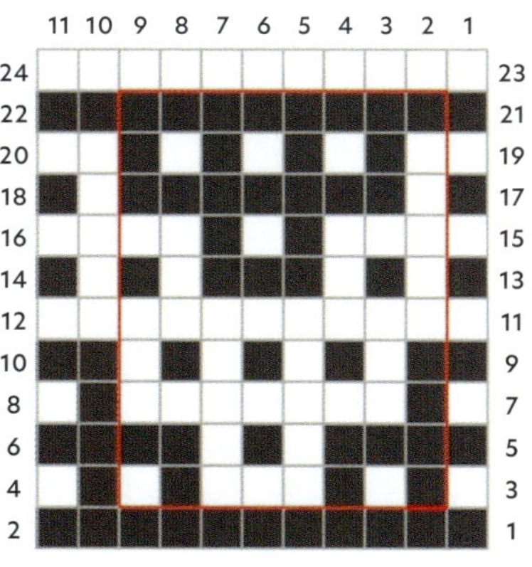

8 sts

Chevron

This is a bold design that can be used as a continuous repeat or as a single panel. It would look stunning on a cardigan or as a trim on a bag. For a continuous repeat, remove the first stitch of repeat.

Knit Instructions

Multiple of 24 sts + 3

On RS rows, slip the sts purlwise with yarn in the back.

Cast on using A, k one row and p one row.

Row 1 (RS): Using B, k1, * sl1, k6, sl2, [k1, sl2] 3 times, k6; rep from * to last 2 sts, sl1, k1.

Row 2 and all WS rows: P the knitted sts and sl the slipped sts purlwise with yarn in the front.

Row 3: Using A, k1, * k1, sl1, k1, sl1, k8, sl1, k8, sl1, k1, sl1; rep from * to last 2 sts, k2.

Row 5: Using B, k1, * sl1, k3, sl1, k1, sl2, k1, sl1, k5, sl1, k1, sl2, k1, sl1, k3; rep from * to last 2 sts, sl1, k1.

Row 7: Using A, k1, * k10, [sl1, k1] twice, sl1, k9; rep from * to last 2 sts, k2.

Row 9: Using B, k1, * sl2, k1, sl2, k1, sl1, k11, sl1, k1, sl2, k1, sl1; rep from * to last 2 sts, sl1, k1.

Row 11: Using A, k1, * k7, sl1, k1, sl1, k5, sl1, k1, sl1, k6; rep from * to last 2 sts, k2.

Row 13: Using B, k1, * sl2, k1, sl1, k6, sl2, k1, sl2, k6, sl1, k1, sl1; * rep from * to last 2 sts, sl1, k1.

Row 15: Using A, k1, * k4, sl1, k1, sl1, k11, sl1, k1, sl1, k3; rep from * to last 2 sts, k2.

Rep Rows 1 to 16. To finish, work Rows 17 to 24.

Row 17: As Row 1.

Row 19: As Row 3.

Row 21: As Row 5.

Row 23: Using A, k all sts.

Row 24: As Row 2.

Crochet Instructions

Multiple of 24 sts + 3

Pattern note: The repeat in the written instructions differs from the chart on Rows 9 and 15.

Using A, make desired number of chainless sc.

Row 1 (RS): Using B, 1 ch, 1 sc, 2 ch, skip st, * 6 sc, [3 ch, skip 2 sts, 1 sc] 3 times, 3 ch, skip 2 sts, 6 sc, 2 ch, skip st; rep from * to last st, 1 sc, turn.

Row 2 and all WS rows: 1 ch, 1 sc in sts, ch and skip ch-sps, turn.

Row 3: Using A, 1 ch, 1 sc, * 1 Mdc, 2 ch, skip st, 1 sc, 2 ch, skip st, 3 sc, 2 Mdc, 1 sc, 2 Mdc, 2 ch, skip st, 2 Mdc, 1 sc, 2 Mdc, 3 sc, 2 ch, skip st, 1 sc, 2 ch, skip st; rep from * to last 2 sts, 1 Mdc, 1 sc, turn.

Row 5: Using B, 1 ch, 1 sc, 2 ch, skip st, * 1 Mdc, 1 sc, 1 Mdc, 2 ch, skip st, 1 sc, 3 ch, skip 2 sts, 1 sc, 2 ch, skip st, 2 sc, 1 Mdc, 2 sc, 2 ch, skip st, 1 sc, 3 ch, skip 2 sts, 1 sc, 2 ch, skip st, 1 Mdc, 1 sc, 1 Mdc, 2 ch, skip st; rep from * to last st, 1 sc, turn.

Row 7: Using A, 1 ch, 1 sc, 1 Mdc, * 3 sc, 1 Mdc, 1 sc, 2 Mdc, 1 sc, 1 Mdc, [2 ch, skip st, 1 sc] twice, 2 ch, skip st, 1 Mdc, 1 sc, 2 Mdc, 1 sc, 1 Mdc, 3 sc, 1 Mdc; rep from * to last st, 1 sc, turn.

Row 9: Using B, 1 ch, 1 sc, 3 ch, skip 2 sts, * 1 sc, 3 ch, skip 2 sts, 1 sc, 2 ch, skip st, 3 sc, [1 Mdc, 1 sc] twice, 1 Mdc, 3 sc, 2 ch, skip st, 1 sc, 3 ch, skip 2 sts, 1 sc, ** 4 ch, skip 3 sts; rep from * to

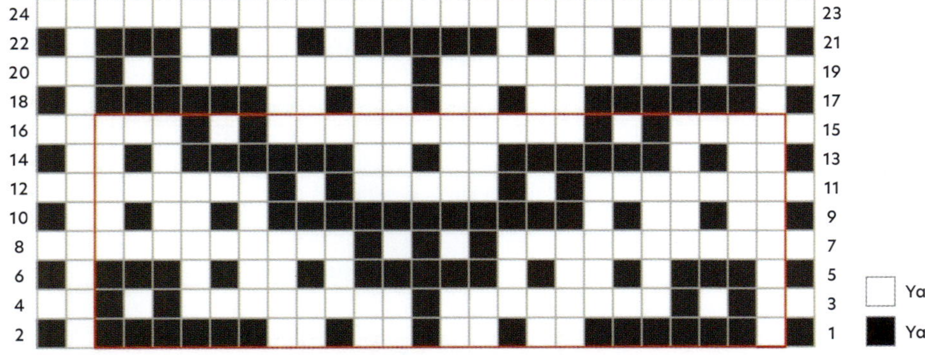

last 3 sts, ending last rep at **, 3 ch, skip 2 sts, 1 sc, turn.

Row 11: Using A, 1 ch, 1 sc, 1 Mdc, * 1 Mdc, 1 sc, 2 Mdc, 1 sc, 1 Mdc, 2 ch, skip st, 1 sc, 2 ch, skip st, 5 sc, 2 ch, skip st, 1 sc, 2 ch, skip st, 1 Mdc, 1 sc, 2 Mdc, 1 sc, 2 Mdc; rep from * to last st, 1 sc, turn.

Row 13: Using B, 1 ch, 1 sc, 3 ch, skip 2 sts, * 1 sc, 2 ch, skip st, 3 sc, 1 Mdc, 1 sc, 1 Mdc, 3 ch, skip 2 sts, 1 sc, 3 ch, skip 2 sts, 1 Mdc, 1 sc, 1 Mdc, 3 sc, 2 ch, skip st, 1 sc, ** 4 ch, skip 3 sts; rep from * to last 3 sts, ending last rep at **, 3 ch, skip 2 sts, 1 sc, turn.

Row 15: Using A, 1 ch, 1 sc, 1 Mdc, * 1 Mdc, 1 sc, 1 Mdc, 2 ch, skip st, 1 sc, 2 ch, skip st, 3 sc, 2 Mdc, 1 sc, 2 Mdc, 3 sc, 2 ch skip st, 1 sc, 2 ch, skip st, 1 Mdc, 1 sc, 2 Mdc; rep from * to last st, 1 sc, turn.

Rep Rows 1 to 16, placing 1 Mdc in sps as required on Row 1. To finish, work Rows 17 to 23.

Row 17: Using B, 1 ch, 1 sc, 2 ch, skip st, * 3 sc, 1 Mdc, 1 sc, 1 Mdc, [3 ch, skip 2 sts, 1 sc] 3 times, 3 ch, skip 2 sts, 1 Mdc, 1 sc, 1 Mdc, 3 sc, 2 ch, skip st; rep from * to last st, 1 sc, turn.

Row 19: Using A, 1 ch, 1 sc, 1 Mdc, * 2 ch, skip st, 1 sc, 2 ch, skip st, 3 sc, 2 Mdc, 1 sc, 2 Mdc, 2 ch, skip st, 2 Mdc, 1 sc, 2 Mdc, 3 sc, 2 ch, skip st, 1 sc, 2 ch, skip st, 1 Mdc; rep from * to last st, 1 sc, turn.

Row 21: Using B, 1 ch, 1 sc, 2 ch, skip st, * 1 Mdc, 1 sc, 1 Mdc, 2 ch, skip st, 1 sc, 3 ch, skip 2 sts, 1 sc, 2 ch, skip st, 2 sc, 1 Mdc, 2 sc, 1 Mdc, 2 sc, 2 ch, skip st, 1 sc, 3 ch, skip 2 sts, 1 sc, 2 ch, skip st, 1 Mdc, 1 sc, 1 Mdc, 2 ch, skip st; rep from * to last st, 1 sc, turn.

Row 23: Using A, 1 ch, 1 sc in every st and 1 Mdc in every sp, turn.

CROCHET

Arrowhead

The crochet version of this design is a little more defined and eye-catching than the knit. This pattern will work best as a large section with few repeats.

Knit Instructions

Multiple of 20 sts + 5

On RS rows, slip the sts purlwise with yarn in the back.

Cast on using B, k one row and p one row.

Row 1 (RS): Using A, k2, * [sl1, k1] twice, k1, [sl1, k4] twice, sl1, k2, sl1, k1; rep from * to last 3 sts, sl1, k2.

Row 2 and all WS rows: P the knitted sts and sl the slipped sts purlwise with yarn in the front.

Row 3: Using B, k2 * k4, [sl1, k1] twice, k6, [sl1, k1] twice, k2; rep from * to last 3 sts, k3.

Row 5: Using A, k2, * sl1, k4, sl1, k2, [sl1, k1] 3 times, k1, sl1, k4; rep from * to last 3 sts, sl1, k2.

Row 7: Using B, k1, sl1, * k1, sl1, [k5, sl1] 3 times; rep from * to last 3 sts, k1, sl1, k1.

Row 9: Using A, k2, * sl1, k3, sl3, k2, [sl1, k1] twice, k1, sl3, k3; rep from * to last 3 sts, sl1, k2.

Row 11: Using B, k1, sl1, * [k1, sl1] twice, k4, sl1, k3, sl1, k4, sl1, k1, sl1; rep from * to last 3 sts, k1, sl1, k1.

Row 13: Using A, k2, * sl1, k5, sl2, k2, sl1, k2, sl2, k5; rep from * to last 3 sts, sl1, k2.

Row 15: Using B, k2, * k3, [sl1, k1] twice, k2, [sl1, k1] twice, k2, [sl1, k1] twice, k1; rep from * to last 3 sts, k3.

Row 17: Using A, k2, * k2, sl1, k5, sl1, k3, sl1, k5, sl1, k1; rep from * to last 3 sts, k3.

Row 19: Using B, k1, sl1, * k1, sl1, k3, [sl1, k1] twice, k4, [sl1, k1] twice, k2, sl1; rep from * to last 3 sts, k1, sl1, k1.

Row 21: Using A, k2, * sl1, k2, sl2, [k5, sl1] twice, sl1, k2; rep from * to last 3 sts, sl1, k2.

Row 23: Using B, k2, * k2, sl1, k4, [sl1, k1] 4 times, k3, sl1, k1; rep from * to last 3 sts, k3.

Row 25: Using A, k1, sl1, * k1, sl1, k2, sl3, [k3, sl1] twice, sl2, k2, sl1; rep from * to last 3 sts, k1, sl1, k1.

Row 27: Using B, k2, * k3, sl1, k5, sl1, k1, sl1, k5, sl1, k2; rep from * to last 3 sts, k3.

Row 29: Using A, k2, * sl1, k1, sl1, k2, sl1, [k4, sl1] twice, k2, sl1, k1; rep from * to last 3 sts, sl1, k2.

Rep Rows 3 to 30. To finish, work Rows 31 to 32.

Row 31: Using B, k all sts.

Row 32: As Row 2.

Crochet Instructions

Multiple of 20 sts + 5

Using B, make desired number of chainless sc.

Row 1 (RS): Using A, 1 ch, 2 sc, * [2 ch, skip st, 1 sc] twice, 1 sc, [2 ch, skip st, 4 sc] twice, 2 ch, skip st, 2 sc, 2 ch, skip st, 1 sc; rep from * to last 3 sts, ending last rep with 2 ch, skip 1 st, 2 sc, turn.

Row 2 and all WS rows: 1 ch, 1 sc in sts, ch and skip ch-sps, turn.

Row 3: Using B, 1 ch, 2 sc, * [1 Mdc, 1 sc] twice, 2 ch, skip st, 1 Mdc, 2 ch, skip st, 3 sc, 1 Mdc, 3 sc, 2 ch, skip st, 1 Mdc, 2 ch, skip st, 1 sc, 1 Mdc, 1 sc; rep from * to last 3 sts, 1 Mdc, 2 sc, turn.

Row 5: Using A, 1 ch, 2 sc, * 2 ch, skip st, 3 sc, 1 Mdc, 2 ch, skip st, 1 Mdc, [1 sc, 2 ch, skip st] 3 times, 1 sc, 1 Mdc, 2 ch, skip st, 1 Mdc, 3 sc; rep from * to last 3 sts, 2 ch, skip st, 2 sc, turn.

Row 7: Using B, 1 ch, 1 sc, 2 ch, skip st, * 1 Mdc, 2 ch, skip st, 3 sc, 1 Mdc, 1 sc, 2 ch, skip st, [1 Mdc, 1 sc] twice, 1 Mdc, 2 ch, skip st, 1 sc, 1 Mdc, 3 sc, 2 ch, skip st; rep from * to last 3 sts, 1 Mdc, 2 ch, skip st, 1 sc, turn.

Row 9: Using A, 1 ch, 1 sc, 1 Mdc, * 2 ch, skip st, 1 Mdc, 2 sc, 4 ch, skip 3 sts, 1 Mdc, [1 sc, 2 ch, skip st] twice,

MOSAIC CHART

Yarn A = Cream

Yarn B = Pale pink

KNIT

CROCHET

1 sc, 1 Mdc, 4 ch, skip 3 sts, 2 sc, 1 Mdc; rep from * to last 3 sts, 2 ch, skip st, 1 Mdc, 1 sc, turn.

Row 11: Using B, 1 ch, 1 sc, 2 ch, skip st, * 1 Mdc, 2 ch, skip st, 1 sc, 2 ch, skip st, 3 Mdc, 1 sc, 2 ch, skip st, 1 Mdc, 1 sc, 1 Mdc, 2 ch, skip st, 1 sc, 3 Mdc, 2 ch, skip st, 1 sc, 2 ch, skip st; rep from * to last 3 sts, 1 Mdc, 2 ch, skip st, 1 sc, turn.

Row 13: Using A, 1 ch, 1 sc, 1 Mdc, * 2 ch, skip st, [1 Mdc, 1 sc] twice, 1 sc, 3 ch, skip 2 sts, 1 Mdc, 1 sc, 2 ch, skip st, 1 sc, 1 Mdc, 3 ch, skip 2 sts, 2 sc, 1 Mdc, 1 sc, 1 Mdc; rep from * to last 3 sts, 2 ch, skip st, 1 Mdc, 1 sc, turn.

Row 15: Using B, 1 ch, 2 sc, * 1 Mdc, 2 sc, 2 ch, skip st, 1 sc, 2 ch, skip st, 2 Mdc, 1 sc, 2 ch, skip st, 1 Mdc, 2 ch, skip st, 1 sc, 2 Mdc, [2 ch, skip st, 1 sc] twice, 1 sc; rep from * to last 3 sts, 1 Mdc, 2 sc, turn.

Row 17: Using A, 1 ch, 2 sc, * 2 sc, 2 ch, skip st, [1 Mdc, 1 sc] twice, 1 sc, 2 ch, skip st, 1 Mdc, 1 sc, 1 Mdc, 2 ch, skip st, 2 sc, 1 Mdc, 1 sc, 1 Mdc, 2 ch, skip st, 1 sc; rep from * to last 3 sts, 3 sc, turn.

Row 19: Using B, 1 ch, 1 sc, 2 ch, skip st, * 1 sc, 2 ch, skip st, 1 Mdc, 2 sc, 2 ch, skip st, 1 sc, 2 ch, skip st, 1 Mdc, 3 sc, 1 Mdc, 2 ch, skip st, 1 sc, 2 ch, skip st, 2 sc, 1 Mdc, 2 ch, skip st; rep from * to last 3 sts, 1 sc, 2 ch, skip st, 1 sc, turn.

Row 21: Using A, 1 ch, 1 sc, 1 Mdc, * 2 ch, skip st, 1 Mdc, 1 sc, 3 ch, skip 2 sts, [1 Mdc, 1 sc] twice, 1 sc, 2 ch, skip st, 2 sc, 1 Mdc, 1 sc, 1 Mdc, 3 ch, skip 2 sts, 1 sc, 1 Mdc; rep from * to last 3 sts, 2 ch, skip st, 1 Mdc, 1 sc, turn.

Row 23: Using B, 1 ch, 2 sc, * 1 Mdc, 1 sc, 2 ch, skip st, 2 Mdc, 2 sc, 2 ch, skip st, 1 sc, 2 ch, skip st, 1 Mdc, 2 ch, skip st, 1 sc, 2 ch, skip st, 2 sc, 2 Mdc, 2 ch, skip st, 1 sc; rep from * to last 3 sts, 1 Mdc, 2 sc, turn.

Row 25: Using A, 1 ch, 1 sc, 2 ch, skip st, * 1 sc, 2 ch, skip st, 1 Mdc, 1 sc, 4 ch, skip 3 sts, 1 Mdc, 1 sc, 1 Mdc, 2 ch, skip st, 1 Mdc, 1 sc, 1 Mdc, 4 ch, skip 3 sts, 1 sc, 1 Mdc, 2 ch, skip st; rep from * to last 3 sts, 1 sc, 2 ch, skip st, 1 sc, turn.

Row 27: Using B, 1 ch, 1 sc, 1 Mdc, * 1 sc, 1 Mdc, 1 sc, 2 ch, skip st, 3 Mdc, 2 sc, 2 ch, skip st, 1 Mdc, 2 ch, skip st, 2 sc, 3 Mdc, 2 ch, skip st, 1 sc, 1 Mdc; rep from * to last 3 sts, 1 sc, 1 Mdc, 1 sc, turn.

Row 29: Using A, 1 ch, 2 sc, * 2 ch, skip st, 1 sc, 2 ch, skip st, 1 Mdc, 1 sc, 2 ch, skip st, 3 sc, 1 Mdc, 2 ch, skip st, 1 Mdc, 3 sc, 2 ch, skip st, 1 sc, 1 Mdc, 2 ch, skip st, 1 sc; rep from * to last 3 sts, 2 ch, skip st, 2 sc, turn.

Rep Rows 3 to 30. To finish, work Row 31.

Row 31: Using B, 1 ch, 2 sc, * [1 Mdc, 1 sc] twice, 1 sc, 1 Mdc, [4 sc, 1 Mdc] twice, 2 sc, 1 Mdc, 1 sc; rep from * to last 3 sts, 1 Mdc, 2 sc, turn.

Diagonal Squares

This geometric design would really suit home accessories. It would well on a pillow or blanket, and a more contrasting Yarn B would give a stronger effect.

Knit Instructions

Multiple of 24 sts + 2

On RS rows, slip the sts purlwise with yarn in the back.

Cast on using A, k one row and p one row.

Row 1 (RS): Using B, k1, * k9, sl1, k3, [sl1, k1] 3 times, sl1, k3, sl1; rep from * to last st, k1.

Row 2 and all WS rows: P the knitted sts and sl the slipped sts purlwise with yarn in the front.

Row 3: Using A, k1, * k4, sl1, k3, sl1, k1, [sl1, k1] 3 times, k2, sl1, k5; rep from * to last st, k1.

Row 5: Using B, k1, * k3, [sl1, k1] 4 times, k2, sl1, k9, sl1; rep from * to last st, k1.

Row 7: Using A, k1, * [sl1, k1] 3 times, k2, sl1, k9, sl1, k3, sl1, k1; rep from * to last st, k1.

Row 9: Using B, k1, * k3, sl1, k9, sl1, k3, [sl1, k1] 3 times, sl1; rep from * to last st, k1.

Row 11: Using A, k1, * k8, sl1, k3, [sl1, k1] 4 times, k2, sl1, k1; rep from * to last st, k1.

Row 13: Using B, k1, * [k3, sl1] twice, [k1, sl1] 3 times, k3, sl1, k6; rep from * to last st, k1.

Row 15: Using A, k1, * k2, [sl1, k1] 4 times, k2, sl1, k9, sl1, k1; rep from * to last st, k1.

Row 17: Using B, k1, * [k1, sl1] twice, k3, sl1, k9, sl1, k3, sl1, k1, sl1; rep from * to last st, k1.

Row 19: Using A, k1, * k2, sl1, k9, sl1, k3, [sl1, k1] 4 times; rep from * to last st, k1.

Row 21: Using B, k1, * k7, sl1, k3, [sl1, k1] 4 times, k2, sl1, k2; rep from * to last st, k1.

Row 23: Using A, k1, * k2, sl1, k3, [sl1, k1] 4 times, k2, sl1, k7; rep from * to last st, k1.

Row 25: Using B, k1, * [k1, sl1] 4 times, k3, sl1, k9, sl1, k2; rep from * to last st, k1.

Row 27: Using A, k1, * sl1, k1, sl1, k3, sl1, k9, sl1, k3, [sl1, k1] twice; rep from * to last st, k1.

Row 29: Using B, k1, * k1, sl1, k9, sl1, k3,

MOSAIC CHART

24 sts

Yarn A = Cream

Yarn B = Gray

[sl1, k1] 4 times, k1; rep from * to last st, k1.
Row 31: Using A, k1, * k6, sl1, k3, [sl1, k1] 4 times, k2, sl1, k3; rep from * to last st, k1.
Row 33: Using B, k1, * k1, sl1, k3, [sl1, k1] 4 times, k2, sl1, k8; rep from * to last st, k1.
Row 35: Using A, k1, * [sl1, k1] 4 times, k2, sl1, k9, sl1, k3; rep from * to last st, k1.
Row 37: Using B, k1, * k1, sl1, k3, sl1, k9, sl1, k3, [sl1, k1] twice, sl1; rep from * to last st, k1.
Row 39: Using A, k1, * sl1, k9, sl1, k3, [sl1, k1] 4 times, k2; rep from * to last st, k1.
Row 41: Using B, k1, * k5, sl1, k3, [sl1, k1] 4 times, k2, sl1, k4; rep from * to last st, k1.
Row 43: Using A, k1, * sl1, k3, [sl1, k1] 4 times, k2, sl1, k9; rep from * to last st, k1.
Row 45: Using B, k1, * [k1, sl1] 3 times, k3, sl1, k9, sl1, k3, sl1; rep from * to last st, k1.
Row 47: Using A, k1, * sl1, k3, sl1, k9, sl1, k3, [sl1, k1] 3 times; rep from * to last st, k1.
Rep Rows 1 to 48. To finish, work Rows 49 to 52.
Row 49: Using B, k1, * k9, sl1, k3, [sl1, k1] 3 times, sl1, k3, sl1; rep from * to last st, k1.
Row 51: Using A, k all sts.
Row 52: As Row 2.

KNIT

Crochet Instructions

Multiple of 24 sts + 2
Using A, make desired number of chainless sc.
Row 1 (RS): Using B, 1 ch, 1 sc, * 9 sc, 2 ch, skip st, 3 sc, [2 ch, skip st, 1 sc] 3 times, 2 ch, skip st, 3 sc, 2 ch, skip st; rep from * to last st, 1 sc, turn.
Row 2 and all WS rows: 1 ch, 1 sc in sts, ch and skip ch-sps, turn.
Row 3: Using A, 1 ch, 1 sc, * 4 sc, 2 ch, skip st, 3 sc, 2 ch, skip st, 1 Mdc, 2 ch, skip st, 1 sc, 2 ch, skip st, 1 Mdc, 2 ch, skip st, 1 Mdc, 1 sc, 1 Mdc, 2 ch, skip st, 1 Mdc, 3 sc, 1 Mdc; rep from * to last st, 1 sc, turn.
Row 5: Using B, 1 ch, 1 sc, * 3 sc, 2 ch, skip st, 1 Mdc, 2 ch, skip st, 1 sc, 2 ch, skip st, 1 Mdc, 2 ch, skip st, 1 Mdc, 1 sc, 1 Mdc, 2 ch, skip st, 1 Mdc, 3 sc, 1 Mdc, 4 sc, 2 ch, skip st; rep from * to last st, 1 sc, turn.
Row 7: Using A, 1 ch, 1 sc, * 2 ch, skip st, 1 sc, 2 ch, skip st, 1 Mdc, 2 ch, skip st, 1 Mdc, 1 sc, 1 Mdc, 2 ch, skip st, 1 Mdc, 3 sc, 1 Mdc, 4 sc, 2 ch, skip st, 3 sc, 2 ch, skip st, 1 Mdc; rep from * to last st, 1 sc, turn.
Row 9: Using B, 1 ch, 1 sc, * 1 Mdc, 1 sc, 1 Mdc, 2 ch, skip st, 1 Mdc, 3 sc, 1 Mdc, 4 sc, 2 ch, skip st, 3 sc, 2 ch, skip st, 1 Mdc, 2 ch, skip st, 1 sc, 2 ch, skip st, 1 Mdc, 2 ch, skip st; rep from * to last st, 1 sc, turn.
Row 11: Using A, 1 ch, 1 sc, * 3 sc, 1 Mdc, 4 sc, 2 ch, skip st, 3 sc, 2 ch, skip st, 1 Mdc, 2 ch, skip st, 1 sc, 2 ch, skip st, 1 Mdc, 2 ch, skip st, 1 Mdc, 1 sc, 1 Mdc, 2 ch, skip st, 1 Mdc; rep from * to last st, 1 sc, turn.
Row 13: Using B, 1 ch, 1 sc, * [3 sc, 2 ch, skip st] twice, 1 Mdc, 2 ch, skip st, 1 sc, 2 ch, skip st, 1 Mdc, 2 ch, skip st, 1 Mdc, 1 sc, 1 Mdc, 2 ch, skip st, 1 Mdc, 3 sc, 1 Mdc, 1 sc; rep from * to last st, 1 sc, turn.
Row 15: Using A, 1 ch, 1 sc, * 2 sc, 2 ch, skip st, 1 Mdc, 2 ch, skip st, 1 sc, 2 ch, skip st, 1 Mdc, 2 ch, skip st, 1 Mdc, 1 sc, 1 Mdc, 2 ch, skip st, 1 Mdc, 3 sc, 1 Mdc, 4 sc, 2 ch, skip st, 1 sc; rep from * to last st, 1 sc, turn.
Row 17: Using B, 1 ch, 1 sc, * 1 sc, 2 ch, skip st, 1 Mdc, 2 ch, skip st, 1 Mdc, 1 sc, 1 Mdc, 2 ch, skip st, 1 Mdc, 3 sc, 1 Mdc, 4 sc, 2 ch, skip st, 3 sc, 2 ch, skip st, 1 Mdc, 2 ch, skip st; rep from * to last st, 1 sc, turn.
Row 19: Using A, 1 ch, 1 sc, * 1 sc, 1 Mdc, 2 ch, skip st, 1 Mdc, 3 sc, 1 Mdc, 4 sc, 2 ch, skip st, 3 sc, 2 ch, skip st, 1 Mdc, 2 ch, skip st, 1 sc, 2 ch, skip st, 1 Mdc, 2 ch, skip st, 1 Mdc; rep from * to last st, 1 sc, turn.
Row 21: Using B, 1 ch, 1 sc, * 2 sc, 1 Mdc, 4 sc, 2 ch, skip st, 3 sc, 2 ch, skip st, 1 Mdc, 2 ch, skip st, 1 sc, 2 ch, skip st, 1 Mdc, 2 ch, skip st, 1 Mdc, 1 sc, 1 Mdc, 2 ch, skip st, 1 Mdc, 1 sc; rep from * to last st, 1 sc, turn.
Row 23: Using A, 1 ch, 1 sc, * 2 sc, 2 ch, skip st, 3 sc, 2 ch, skip st, 1 Mdc, 2 ch, skip st, 1 sc, 2 ch, skip st, 1 Mdc, 2 ch, skip st, 1 Mdc, 1 sc, 1 Mdc, 2 ch, skip st, 1 Mdc, 3 sc, 1 Mdc, 2 sc; rep from * to last st, 1 sc, turn.

>>>

Row 25: Using B, 1 ch, 1 sc, * 1 sc, 2 ch, skip st, 1 Mdc, 2 ch, skip st, 1 sc, 2 ch, skip st, 1 Mdc, 2 ch, skip st, 1 Mdc, 1 sc, 1 Mdc, 2 ch, skip st, 1 Mdc, 3 sc, 1 Mdc, 4 sc, 2 ch, skip st, 2 sc; rep from * to last st, 1 sc, turn.

Row 27: Using A, 1 ch, 1 sc, * 2 ch, skip st, 1 Mdc, 2 ch, skip st, 1 Mdc, 1 sc, 1 Mdc, 2 ch, skip st, 1 Mdc, 3 sc, 1 Mdc, 4 sc, 2 ch, skip st, 3 sc, 2 ch, skip st, 1 Mdc, 2 ch, skip st, 1 sc; rep from * to last st, 1 sc, turn.

Row 29: Using B, 1 ch, 1 sc, * 1 Mdc, 2 ch, skip st, 1 Mdc, 3 sc, 1 Mdc, 4 sc, 2 ch, skip st, 3 sc, 2 ch, skip st, 1 Mdc, 2 ch, skip st, 1 sc, 2 ch, skip st, 1 Mdc, 2 ch, skip st, 1 Mdc, 1 sc; rep from * to last st, 1 sc, turn.

Row 31: Using A, 1 ch, 1 sc, * 1 sc, 1 Mdc, 4 sc, 2 ch, skip st, 3 sc, 2 ch, skip st, 1 Mdc, 2 ch, skip st, 1 sc, 2 ch, skip st, 1 Mdc, 2 ch, skip st, 1 Mdc, 1 sc, 1 Mdc, 2 ch, skip st, 1 Mdc, 2 sc; rep from * to last st, 1 sc, turn.

Row 33: Using B, 1 ch, 1 sc, * 1 sc, 2 ch, skip st, 3 sc, 2 ch, skip st, 1 Mdc, 2 ch, skip st, 1 sc, 2 ch, skip st, 1 Mdc, 2 ch, skip st, 1 Mdc, 1 sc, 1 Mdc, 2 ch, skip st, [1 Mdc, 3 sc] twice; rep from * to last st, 1 sc, turn.

Row 35: Using A, 1 ch, 1 sc, * 2 ch, skip st, 1 Mdc, 2 ch, skip st, 1 sc, 2 ch, skip st, 1 Mdc, 2 ch, skip st, 1 Mdc, 1 sc, 1 Mdc, 2 ch, skip st, 1 Mdc, 3 sc, 1 Mdc, 4 sc, 2 ch, skip st, 3 sc; rep from * to last st, 1 sc, turn.

Row 37: Using B, 1 ch, 1 sc, * 1 Mdc, 2 ch, skip st, 1 Mdc, 1 sc, 1 Mdc, 2 ch, skip st, 1 Mdc, 3 sc, 1 Mdc, 4 sc, 2 ch, skip st, 3 sc, 2 ch, skip st, 1 Mdc, 2 ch, skip st, 1 sc, 2 ch, skip st; rep from * to last st, 1 sc, turn.

Row 39: Using A, 1 ch, 1 sc, * 2 ch, skip st, 1 Mdc, 3 sc, 1 Mdc, 4 sc, 2 ch, skip st, 3 sc, 2 ch, skip st, 1 Mdc, 2 ch, skip st, 1 sc, 2 ch, skip st, 1 Mdc, 2 ch, skip st, 1 Mdc, 1 sc, 1 Mdc; rep from * to last st, 1 sc, turn.

Row 41: Using B, 1 ch, 1 sc, * 1 Mdc, 4 sc, 2 ch, skip st, 3 sc, 2 ch, skip st, 1 Mdc, 2 ch, skip st, 1 sc, 2 ch, skip st, 1 Mdc, 2 ch, skip st, 1 Mdc, 1 sc, 1 Mdc, 2 ch, skip st, 1 Mdc, 3 sc; rep from * to last st, 1 sc, turn.

Row 43: Using A, 1 ch, 1 sc, * 2 ch, skip st, 3 sc, 2 ch, skip st, 1 Mdc, 2 ch, skip st, 1 sc, 2 ch, skip st, 1 Mdc, 2 ch, skip st, 1 Mdc, 1 sc, 1 Mdc, 2 ch, skip st, 1 Mdc, 3 sc, 1 Mdc, 4 sc; rep from * to last st, 1 sc, turn.

Row 45: Using B, 1 ch, 1 sc, * 1 Mdc, 2 ch, skip st, 1 sc, 2 ch, skip st, 1 Mdc, 2 ch, skip st, 1 Mdc, 1 sc, 1 Mdc, 2 ch, skip st, 1 Mdc, 3 sc, 1 Mdc, 4 sc, 2 ch, skip st, 3 sc, 2 ch, skip st; rep from * to last st, 1 sc, turn.

Row 47: Using A, 1 ch, 1 sc, * 2 ch, skip st, 1 Mdc, 1 sc, 1 Mdc, 2 ch, skip st, 1 Mdc, 3 sc, 1 Mdc, 4 sc, 2 ch, skip st, 3 sc, 2 ch, skip st, 1 Mdc, 2 ch, skip st, 1 sc, 2 ch, skip st, 1 Mdc; rep from * to last st, 1 sc, turn.

Rep Rows 1 to 48, placing 1 Mdc in sps as required on Row 1. To finish, work Rows 49 to 51.

Row 49: Using B, 1 ch, 1 sc, * 1 Mdc, 3 sc, 1 Mdc, 4 sc, 2 ch, skip st, 3 sc, 2 ch, skip st, 1 Mdc, 2 ch, skip st, 1 sc, 2 ch, skip st, 1 Mdc, 2 ch, skip st, 1 Mdc, 1 sc, 1 Mdc, 2 ch, skip st; rep from * to last st, 1 sc, turn.

Row 51: Using A, 1 ch, 1 sc, * 9 sc, 1 Mdc, 3 sc, 1 Mdc, [1 sc, 1 Mdc] 3 times, 3 sc, 1 Mdc; rep from * to last st, 1 sc, turn.

Signature

This design will require concentration, make sure to follow the pattern carefully. You will be rewarded with an effective all-over pattern that would look great on a pillow or other homewares.

Knit Instructions

Multiple of 24 sts + 3

On RS rows, slip the sts purlwise with yarn in the back.

Cast on using A, k one row and p one row.

Row 1 (RS): Using B, k1, * k1, sl1, k3, [sl3, k1] twice, k2, sl1, k8; rep from * to last 2 sts, k2.

Row 2 and all WS rows: P the knitted sts and sl the slipped sts purlwise with yarn in the front.

Row 3: Using A, k1, * k8, sl1, k3, [sl1, k1] 4 times, k2, sl1, k1; rep from * to last 2 sts, k2.

Row 5: Using B, k1, * sl2, k3, sl1, k9, sl1, k3, sl3, k1, sl1; rep from * to last 2 sts, sl1, k1.

Row 7: Using A, k1, * k2, [sl1, k1] 4 times, k2, sl1, k9, sl1, k1; rep from * to last 2 sts, k2.

Row 9: Using B, k1, * k5, sl1, k3, sl3, k1, sl3, k3, sl1, k4; rep from * to last 2 sts, k2.

Row 11: Using A, k1, * k2, sl1, k9, sl1, k3, [sl1, k1] 4 times; rep from * to last 2 sts, k2.

Row 13: Using B, k1, * sl2, k1, sl3, k3, sl1, k9, sl1, k3, sl1; rep from * to last 2 sts, sl1, k1.

Row 15: Using A, k1, * k2, sl1, k3, [sl1, k1] 4 times, k2, sl1, k7; rep from * to last 2 sts, k2.

Row 17: Using B, k1, * k9, sl1, k3, sl3, k1, sl3, k3, sl1; rep from * to last 2 sts, k2.

Row 19: Using A, k1, * sl1, k1, sl1, k3, sl1, k9, sl1, k3, [sl1, k1] twice; rep from * to last 2 sts, sl1, k1.

Row 21: Using B, k1, * k3, sl3, k1, sl3, k3, sl1, k9, sl1; rep from * to last 2 sts, k2.

Row 23: Using A, k1, * k6, sl1, k3, [sl1, k1] 4 times, k2, sl1, k3; rep from * to last 2 sts, k2.

Row 25: Using B, k1, * k3, sl1, k9, sl1, k3, sl3, k1, sl3; rep from * to last 2 sts, k2.

Row 27: Using A, k1, * [sl1, k1] 4 times, k2, sl1, k9, sl1, k3; rep from * to last 2 sts, sl1, k1.

Row 29: Using B, k1, * [k3, sl1] twice, sl2, k1, sl3, k3, sl1, k6; rep from * to last 2 sts, k2.

Row 31: Using A, k1, * sl1, k9, sl1, k3, [sl1, k1] 4 times, k2; rep from * to last 2 sts, sl1, k1.

Row 33: Using B, k1, * k1, sl3, k3, sl1, k9, sl1, k3, sl3; rep from * to last 2 sts, k2.

Row 35: Using A, k1, * sl1, k3, [sl1, k1] 4 times, k2, sl1, k9; rep from * to last 2 sts, sl1, k1.

Row 37: Using B, k1, * k7, sl1, k3, sl3, k1, sl3, k3, sl1, k2; rep from * to last 2 sts, k2.

Row 39: Using A, k1, * sl1, k3, sl1, k9, sl1, k3, [sl1, k1] 3 times; rep from * to last 2 sts, sl1, k1.

Row 41: Using B, k1, * [k1, sl3] twice, k3, sl1, k9, sl1, k2; rep from * to last 2 sts, k2.

Row 43: Using A, k1, * [sl1, k3] twice, [sl1, k1] 4 times, k2, sl1, k5; rep from * to last 2 sts, k2.

Row 45: Using B, k1, * k1, sl1, k9, sl1, k3, [sl3, k1] twice, k1; rep from * to last 2 sts, k2.

>>>

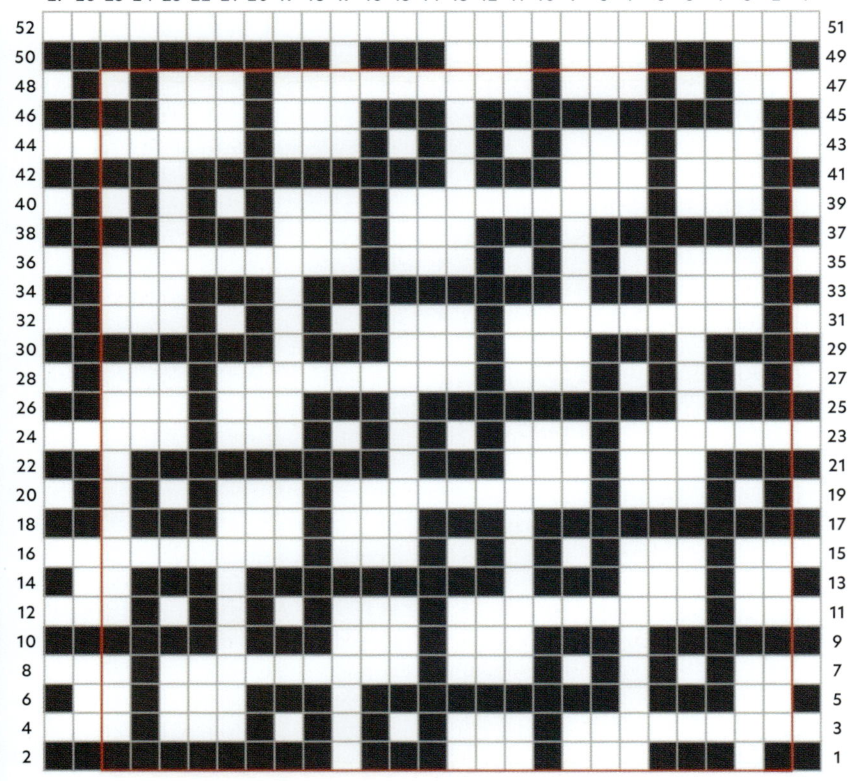

Yarn A = Cream

Yarn B = Pale pink

Row 47: Using A, k1, * k2, sl1, k1, sl1, k3, sl1, k9, sl1, k3, sl1, k1; rep from * to last 2 sts, sl1, k1.
Rep Rows 1 to 48. To finish, work Rows 49 to 52.
Row 49: Using B, k1, * sl2, k3, sl3, k1, sl3, k3, sl1, k8; rep from * to last 2 sts, k2.
Row 51: Using A, k all sts.
Row 52: As Row 2.

Crochet Instructions

Multiple of 24 sts + 3
Pattern note: The repeat in the written instructions differs from the chart on Rows 5 and 13.
Using A, make desired number of chainless sc.
Row 1 (RS): Using B, 1 ch, 1 sc, * 1 sc, 2 ch, skip st, 3 sc, 4 ch, skip 3 sts, 1 sc, 4 ch, skip 3 sts, 3 sc, 2 ch, skip st, 8 sc; rep from * to last 2 sts, 2 sc, turn.
Row 2 and all WS rows: 1 ch, 1 sc in sts, ch and skip ch-sps, turn.
Row 3: Using A, 1 ch, 1 sc, * 1 sc, 1 Mdc, 3 sc, [3 Mdc, 2 ch, skip st] twice, 1 sc, 2 ch, skip st, 1 Mdc, 2 ch, skip st, 1 sc, 2 ch, skip st, 3 sc, 2 ch, skip st, 1 sc; rep from * to last 2 sts, 2 sc, turn.
Row 5: Using B, 1 ch, 1 sc, 3 ch, skip 2 sts, * 3 sc, 2 ch, skip st, 2 sc, 1 Mdc, 3 sc, 1 Mdc, 1 sc, 1 Mdc, 2 ch, skip st, 1 Mdc, 1 sc, 1 Mdc, 4 ch, skip 3 sts, 1 Mdc, ** 4 ch, skip 3 sts; rep from * to last st, ending last rep at **, 3 ch, skip 2 sts, 1 sc, turn.
Row 7: Using A, 1 ch, 1 sc, * 2 Mdc, 2 ch, skip st, 1 sc, 2 ch, skip st, 1 Mdc, 2 ch, skip st, 1 sc, 2 ch, skip st, 3 sc, 2 ch, skip st, 2 sc, 1 Mdc, 3 sc, 3 Mdc, 2 ch, skip st, 1 Mdc; rep from * to last 2 sts, 1 Mdc, 1 sc, turn.
Row 9: Using B, 1 ch, 1 sc, * 2 sc, 1 Mdc, 1 sc, 1 Mdc, 2 ch, skip st, 1 Mdc, 1 sc, 1 Mdc, 4 ch, skip 3 sts, 1 Mdc, 4 ch, skip 3 sts, 3 sc, 2 ch, skip st, 2 sc, 1 Mdc, 1 sc; rep from * to last 2 sts, 2 sc, turn.
Row 11: Using A, 1 ch, 1 sc, * 2 sc, 2 ch, skip st, 2 sc, 1 Mdc, 3 sc, [3 Mdc, 2 ch, skip st] twice, 1 sc, 2 ch, skip st, 1 Mdc, [2 ch, skip st, 1 sc] twice; rep from * to last 2 sts, 2 sc, turn.
Row 13: Using B, 1 ch, 1 sc, 3 ch, skip 2 sts, * 1 Mdc, 4 ch, skip 3 sts, 3 sc, 2 ch, skip st, 2 sc, 1 Mdc, 3 sc, 1 Mdc, 1 sc, 1 Mdc, 2 ch, skip st, 1 Mdc, 1 sc, 1 Mdc, ** 4 ch, skip 3 sts; rep from * to last st, ending last rep at **, 3 ch, skip 2 sts, 1 sc, turn.
Row 15: Using A, 1 ch, 1 sc, * 2 Mdc, 2 ch, skip st, 2 Mdc, [1 Mdc, 2 ch, skip st, 1 sc, 2 ch, skip st] twice, 3 sc, 2 ch, skip st, 2 sc, 1 Mdc, 3 sc, 1 Mdc; rep from * to last 2 sts, 1 Mdc, 1 sc, turn.
Row 17: Using B, 1 ch, 1 sc, * 2 sc, 1 Mdc, 3 sc, 1 Mdc, 1 sc, 1 Mdc, 2 ch, skip st, 1 Mdc, 1 sc, [1 Mdc, 4 ch, skip 3 sts] twice, 3 sc, 2 ch, skip st; rep from * to last 2 sts, 2 sc, turn.
Row 19: Using A, 1 ch, 1 sc, * [2 ch, skip st, 1 sc] twice, 2 sc, 2 ch, skip st, 2 sc, 1 Mdc, 3 sc, [3 Mdc, 2 ch, skip st] twice, 1 sc, 2 ch, skip st, 1 Mdc; rep from * to last 2 sts, 2 ch, skip st, 1 sc, turn.
Row 21: Using B, 1 ch, 1 sc, * 1 Mdc, 1 sc, [1 Mdc, 4 ch, skip 3 sts] twice, 3 sc, 2 ch, skip st, 2 sc, 1 Mdc, 3 sc, 1 Mdc, 1 sc, 1 Mdc, 2 ch, skip st; rep from * to last 2 sts, 1 Mdc, 1 sc, turn.
Row 23: Using A, 1 ch, 1 sc, * 3 sc, [3 Mdc, 2 ch, skip st] twice, 1 sc, 2 ch, skip st, 1 Mdc, 2 ch, skip st, 1 sc, 2 ch, skip st, 3 sc, 2 ch, skip st, 2 sc, 1 Mdc; rep from * to last 2 sts, 2 sc, turn.
Row 25: Using B, 1 ch, 1 sc, * 3 sc, 2 ch, skip st, 2 sc, 1 Mdc, 3 sc, 1 Mdc, 1 sc, 1 Mdc, 2 ch, skip st, 1 Mdc, 1 sc, [1 Mdc, 4 ch, skip 3 sts] twice; rep from * to last 2 sts, 2 sc, turn.
Row 27: Using A, 1 ch, 1 sc, * 2 ch, skip st, 1 sc, 2 ch, skip st, 1 Mdc, 2 ch, skip st, 1 sc, 2 ch, skip st, 3 sc, 2 ch, skip st, 2 sc, 1 Mdc, 3 sc, 3 Mdc, 2 ch, skip st, 3 Mdc; rep from * to last 2 sts, 2 ch, skip st, 1 sc, turn.
Row 29: Using B, 1 ch, 1 sc, * 1 Mdc, 1 sc, 1 Mdc, 2 ch, skip st, 1 Mdc, 1 sc, 1 Mdc, 4 ch, skip 3 sts, 1 Mdc, 4 ch, skip 3 sts, 3 sc, 2 ch, skip st, 2 sc, 1 Mdc, 3 sc; rep from * to last 2 sts, 1 Mdc, 1 sc, turn.
Row 31: Using A, 1 ch, 1 sc, * 2 ch, skip st, 2 sc, 1 Mdc, 3 sc, [3 Mdc, 2 ch, skip st] twice, 1 sc, 2 ch, skip st, 1 Mdc, [2 ch, skip st, 1 sc] twice, 2 sc; rep from * to last 2 sts, 2 ch, skip st, 1 sc, turn.
Row 33: Using B, 1 ch, 1 sc, * 1 Mdc, 4 ch, skip 3 sts, 3 sc, 2 ch, skip st, 2 sc, 1 Mdc, 3 sc, 1 Mdc, 1 sc, 1 Mdc, 2 ch, skip st, 1 Mdc, 1 sc, 1 Mdc, 4 ch, skip 3 sts; rep from * to last 2 sts, 1 Mdc, 1 sc, turn.
Row 35: Using A, 1 ch, 1 sc, * 2 ch, skip st, 2 Mdc, [1 Mdc, 2 ch, skip st, 1 sc, 2 ch, skip st] twice, 3 sc, 2 ch, skip st, 2 sc, 1 Mdc, 3 sc, 3 Mdc; rep from * to last 2 sts, 2 ch, skip st, 1 sc, turn.
Row 37: Using B, 1 ch, 1 sc, * 1 Mdc,

TIP: For the knit version: Mosaic knitting usually creates a fabric that can be tighter as the slip stitches pull the fabric in. Use needles that are one or even two sizes bigger to create looser fabric.

3 sc, 1 Mdc, 1 sc, 1 Mdc, 2 ch, skip st, 1 Mdc, 1 sc, 1 Mdc, 4 ch, skip 3 sts, 1 Mdc, 4 ch, skip 3 sts, 3 sc, 2 ch, skip st, 2 sc; rep from * to last 2 sts, 1 Mdc, 1 sc, turn.

Row 39: Using A, 1 ch, 1 sc, * 2 ch, skip st, 3 sc, 2 ch, skip st, 2 sc, 1 Mdc, 3 sc, [3 Mdc, 2 ch, skip st] twice, 1 sc, 2 ch, skip st, 1 Mdc, 2 ch, skip st, 1 sc; rep from * to last 2 sts, 2 ch, skip st, 1 sc, turn.

Row 41: Using B, 1 ch, 1 sc, * [1 Mdc, 4 ch, skip 3 sts] twice, 3 sc, 2 ch, skip st, 2 sc, 1 Mdc, 3 sc, 1 Mdc, 1 sc, 1 Mdc, 2 ch, skip st, 1 Mdc, 1 sc; rep from * to last 2 sts, 1 Mdc, 1 sc, turn.

Row 43: Using A, 1 ch, 1 sc, * [2 ch, skip st, 3 Mdc] twice, 2 ch, skip st, 1 sc, 2 ch, skip st, 1 Mdc, 2 ch, skip st, 1 sc, 2 ch, skip st, 3 sc, 2 ch, skip st, 2 sc, 1 Mdc, 2 sc; rep from * to last 2 sts, 2 sc, turn.

Row 45: Using B, 1 ch, 1 sc, * 1 Mdc, 2 ch, skip st, 2 sc, 1 Mdc, 3 sc, 1 Mdc, 1 sc, 1 Mdc, 2 ch, skip st, 1 Mdc, 1 sc, [1 Mdc, 4 ch, skip 3 sts] twice, 2 sc; rep from * to last 2 sts, 2 sc, turn.

Row 47: Using A, 1 ch, 1 sc, * 1 sc, 1 Mdc, [2 ch, skip st, 1 sc] twice, 2 sc, 2 ch, skip st, 2 sc, 1 Mdc, 3 sc, [3 Mdc, 2 ch, skip st] twice, 1 sc; rep from * to last 2 sts, 2 ch, skip st, 1 sc, turn.

Rep Rows 1 to 48, placing 1 Mdc in sps as required on Row 1. To finish, work Rows 49 to 51.

Row 49: Using B, 1 ch, 1 sc, * 3 ch, skip 2 sts, 1 Mdc, 1 sc, [1 Mdc, 4 ch, skip 3 sts] twice, 3 sc, 2 ch, skip st, 2 sc, 1 Mdc, 3 sc, 1 Mdc, 1 sc; rep from * to last 2 sts, 1 Mdc, 1 sc, turn.

Row 51: Using A, 1 ch, 1 sc, * 2 Mdc, 3 sc, 3 Mdc, 1 sc, 3 Mdc, 3 sc, 1 Mdc, 8 sc; rep from * to last 2 sts, 2 sc, turn.

KNIT

CROCHET

Diamonds

This bold design is perfect for larger projects such as blankets, which will showcase the pattern to full effect. The knitted version produces fabric with a slightly tight gauge.

Knit Instructions

Multiple of 12 sts + 3

On RS rows, slip the sts purlwise with yarn in the back.

Cast on using A, k one row and p one row.

Row 1 (RS): Using B, k2, * sl1, k2, sl2, k1, sl2, k2, sl1, k1; rep from * to last st, k1.

Row 2 and all WS rows: P the knitted sts and sl the slipped sts purlwise with yarn in the front.

Row 3: Using A, k2, * k1, [sl1, k3] twice, sl1, k2; rep from * to last st, k1.

Row 5: Using B, k1, sl1, * k2, sl2, k3, sl2, k2, sl1; rep from * to last st, k1.

Row 7: Using A, k2, * sl1, k3, sl1, k1, sl1, k3, sl1, k1; rep from * to last st, k1.

Row 9: Using B, k2, * k1, sl2, k2, sl1, k2, sl2, k2; * rep from * to last st, k1.

Row 11: Using A, k1, sl1, * [k3, sl1] three times; rep from * to last st, k1.

Row 13: Using B, k2, * sl2, k2, sl1, k1, sl1, k2, sl2, k1; rep from * to last st, k1.

Row 15: Using A, k2, * [k2, sl1] 3 times, k3; rep from * to last st, k1.

Row 17: Using B, k1, sl1, * sl1, k2, sl1, k3, sl1, k2, sl2; rep from * to last st, k1.

Row 19: As Row 15.

Row 21: As Row 13.

Row 23: As Row 11.

Row 25: As Row 9.

Row 27: As Row 7.

Row 29: As Row 5.

Row 31: As Row 3.

Row 33: As Row 1.

Row 35: Using A, k1, sl1, * k2, sl1, k5, sl1, k2, sl1; rep from * to last st, k1.

Row 37: Using B, k2, * k1, sl1, k2, sl3, k2, sl1, k2; rep from * to last st, k1.

Row 39: Using A, k1, sl1, * k2, sl1, k5, sl1, k2, sl1; rep from * to last st, k1.

Row 40: As Row 2.

Rep Rows 1 to 40. To finish, work Rows 39 and 40 by k on RS and p on WS all sts using A.

MOSAIC CHART

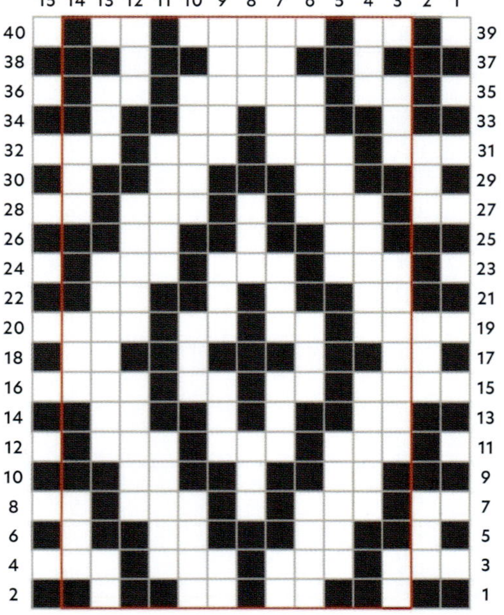

12 sts

Yarn A = Cream

Yarn B = Dark pink

Crochet Instructions

Multiple of 12 sts + 3

Pattern note: The repeat in the written instructions differs from the chart on Row 17.

Using A, make desired number of chainless sc.

Row 1 (RS): Using B, 1 ch, 2 sc, * 2 ch, skip st, 2 sc, 3 ch, skip 2 sts, 1 sc, 3 ch, skip 2 sts, 2 sc, 2 ch, skip st, 1 sc; rep from * to last st, 1 sc, turn.

Row 2 and all WS rows: 1 ch, 1 sc in sts, ch and skip ch-sps, turn.

Row 3: Using A, 1 ch, 2 sc, * 1 Mdc, 2 ch, skip st, 1 sc, 2 Mdc, 2 ch, skip st, 2 Mdc, 1 sc, 2 ch, skip st, 1 Mdc, 1 sc; rep from * to last st, 1 sc, turn.

Row 5: Using B, 1 ch, 1 sc, 2 ch, skip st, * 1 sc, 1 Mdc, 3 ch, skip 2 sts, 1 sc, 1 Mdc, 1 sc, 3 ch, skip 2 sts, 1 Mdc, 1 sc, 2 ch, skip st; rep from * to last st, 1 sc, turn.

Row 7: Using A, 1 ch, 1 sc, 1 Mdc,* 2 ch, skip st, 1 sc, 2 Mdc, 2 ch, skip st, 1 sc, 2 ch, skip st, 2 Mdc, 1 sc, 2 ch, skip st, 1 Mdc; rep from * to last st, 1 sc, turn.

Row 9: Using B, 1 ch, 2 sc, * 1 Mdc, 3 ch, skip 2 sts, 1 sc, 1 Mdc, 2 ch, skip st, 1 Mdc, 1 sc, 3 ch, skip 2 sts, 1 Mdc, 1 sc; rep from * to last st, 1 sc, turn.

Row 11: Using A, 1 ch, 1 sc, 2 ch, skip st, * 1 sc, 2 Mdc, 2 ch, skip st, 1 sc, 1 Mdc, 1 sc, 2 ch, skip st, 2 Mdc, 1 sc, 2 ch, skip st; rep from * to last st, 1 sc, turn.

Row 13: Using B, 1 ch, 1 sc, 1 Mdc, * 3 ch, skip 2 sts, 1 sc, 1 Mdc, 2 ch, skip st, 1 sc, 2 ch, skip st, 1 Mdc, 1 sc, 3 ch, skip 2 sts, 1 Mdc; rep from * to last st, 1 sc, turn.

Row 15: Using A, 1 ch, 2 sc, * 2 Mdc, 2 ch, skip st, 1 sc, 1 Mdc, 2 ch, skip st, 1 Mdc, 1 sc, 2 ch, skip st, 2 Mdc, 1 sc; rep from * to last st, 1 sc, turn.

Row 17: Using B, 1 ch, 1 sc, 3 ch, skip 2 sts, * 1 sc, 1 Mdc, 2 ch, skip st, 1 sc, 1 Mdc, 1 sc, 2 ch, skip st, 1 Mdc, 1 sc,

** 4 ch, skip 3 sts; rep from * to last st, ending last rep at **, 3 ch, skip 2 sts, 1 sc, turn.

Row 19: Using A, 1 ch, 1 sc, 1 Mdc, * 1 Mdc, 1 sc, 2 ch, skip st, 1 Mdc, 1 sc, 2 ch, skip st, 1 sc, 1 Mdc, 2 ch, skip st, 1 sc, 2 Mdc; rep; from * to last st, 1 sc, turn.

Row 21: Using B, 1 ch, 2 sc, * 3 ch, skip 2 sts, 1 Mdc, 1 sc, 2 ch, skip st, 1 Mdc, 2 ch, skip st, 1 sc, 1 Mdc, 3 ch, skip 2 sts, 1 sc; rep from * to last st, 1 sc, turn.

Row 23: Using A, 1 ch, 1 sc, 2 ch, skip st, * 2 Mdc, 1 sc, 2 ch, skip st, 1 Mdc, 1 sc, 1 Mdc, 2 ch, skip st, 1 sc, 2 Mdc, 2 ch, skip st; rep from * to last st, 1 sc, turn.

Row 25: Using B, 1 ch, 1 sc, 1 Mdc, * 1 sc, 3 ch, skip 2 sts, 1 Mdc, 1 sc, 2 ch, skip st, 1 sc, 1 Mdc, 3 ch, skip 2 sts, 1 sc, 1 Mdc; rep from * to last st, 1 sc, turn.

Row 27: Using A, 1 ch, 2 sc, * 2 ch, skip st, 2 Mdc, 1 sc, 2 ch, skip st, 1 Mdc, 2 ch, skip st, 1 sc, 2 Mdc, 2 ch, skip st, 1 sc; rep from * to last st, 1 sc, turn.

Row 29: Using B, 1 ch, 1 sc, 2 ch, skip st, * 1 Mdc, 1 sc, 3 ch, skip 2 sts, 1 Mdc, 1 sc, 1 Mdc, 3 ch, skip 2 sts, 1 sc, 1 Mdc, 2 ch, skip st; rep from * to last st, 1 sc, turn.

Row 31: Using A, 1 ch, 1 sc, 1 Mdc, * 1 sc, 2 ch, skip st, 2 Mdc, 1 sc, 2 ch, skip st, 1 sc, 2 Mdc, 2 ch, skip st, 1 sc, 1 Mdc; rep from * to last st, 1 sc, turn.

Row 33: Using B, 1 ch, 2 sc, * 2 ch, skip st, 1 Mdc, 1 sc, 3 ch, skip 2 sts, 1 Mdc, 3 ch, skip 2 sts, 1 sc, 1 Mdc, 2 ch, skip st, 1 sc; rep from * to last st, 1 sc, turn.

Row 35: Using A, 1 ch, 1 sc, 2 ch, skip st, * 1 Mdc, 1 sc, 2 ch, skip st, 2 Mdc, 1 sc, 2 Mdc, 2 ch, skip st, 1 sc, 1 Mdc, 2 ch, skip st; rep from * to last st, 1 sc, turn.

Row 37: Using B, 1 ch, 1 sc, 1 Mdc, * 1 sc, 2 ch, skip st, 1 Mdc, 1 sc, 4 ch, skip 3 sts, 1 sc, 1 Mdc, 2 ch, skip st, 1 sc, 1 Mdc; rep from * to last st, 1 sc, turn.

Row 39: Using A, 1 ch, 1 sc, 2 ch, skip st, * 1 sc, 1 Mdc, 2 ch, skip st, 1 sc, 3 Mdc, 1 sc, 2 ch, skip st, 1 Mdc, 1 sc, 2 ch, skip st; rep from * to last st, 1 sc, turn.

Row 40: As Row 2.

Rep Rows 1 to 40, placing 1 Mdc in sps as required on Row 1. End last rep with Row 39 as follows: Using A, 1 ch, 1 sc in every st and Mdc in every sp.

KNIT

CROCHET

Illusion

On the knit version, the stripe background is worked in a stockinette stitch which produces a looser fabric than the motif itself. Knitting the background in garter stitch will even it out a bit.

Knit Instructions

Multiple of 24 sts + 3

On RS rows, slip the sts purlwise with yarn in the back.

Cast on using A, k one row and p one row.

Row 1 (RS): Using B, k2, * k6, sl1, k7, sl1, k9; rep from * to last st, k1.

Row 2 and all WS rows: P the knitted sts and sl the slipped sts purlwise with yarn in the front.

Row 3: Using A, k2, * k7, sl1, k5, sl1, k10; rep from * to last st, k1.

Row 5: Using B, k2, * k2, sl1, k5, sl1, k3, sl1, k1, sl1, k9; rep from * to last st, k1.

Row 7: Using A, k2, * k3, sl1, k3, [sl1, k1] 4 times, k9; rep from * to last st, k1.

Row 9: Using B, k2, * k2, sl1, k1, [sl1, k3] twice, sl1, k1, sl1, k9; rep from * to last st, k1.

Row 11: Using A, k2, * k3, [sl1, k1] 3 times, k4, sl1, k10; rep from * to last st, k1.

Row 13: Using B, k2, * sl1, k13, sl1, k9; rep from * to last st, k1.

Row 15: Using A, k2, * k1, sl1, k5, [sl1, k1] 3 times, k11; rep from * to last st, k1.

Row 17: Using B, k2, * sl1, k1, [sl1, k3] 3 times, sl1, k7, sl1, k1; rep from * to last st, k1.

Row 19: Using A, k2, * [k1, sl1] 4 times, k3, [sl1, k1] 3 times, k4, sl1, k2; rep from * to last st, k1.

Row 21: Using B, k2, * sl1, k1, sl1, k3, sl1, k9, sl1, k3, [sl1, k1] twice; rep from * to last st, k1.

Row 23: Using A, k2, * k1, sl1, k5, [sl1, k1] 3 times, k2, [sl1, k1] 4 times, k1; rep from * to last st, k1.

Row 25: Using B, k2, * sl1, k7, [sl1, k3] 3 times, [sl1, k1] twice; rep from * to last st, k1.

Row 27: Using A, k2, * k11, [sl1, k1] 3 times, k4, sl1, k2; rep from * to last st, k1.

Row 29: Using B, k2, * k8, sl1, k13, sl1, k1; rep from * to last st, k1.

Row 31: Using A, k2, * k9, sl1, k5, [sl1, k1] 3 times, k3; rep from * to last st, k1.

Row 33: Using B, k2, * k8, sl1, k1, [sl1, k3] twice, [sl1, k1] twice, k2; rep from * to last st, k1.

Row 35: Using A, k2, * k9, [sl1, k1] 4 times, k2, sl1, k4; rep from * to last st, k1.

Row 37: Using B, k2, * k8, sl1, k1, sl1, k3, sl1, k5, sl1, k3; rep from * to last st, k1.

Row 39: Using A, k2, * k9, [sl1, k5] twice, k3; rep from * to last st, k1.

Row 41: Using B, k2, * k8, [sl1, k7] twice; rep from * to last st, k1.

Row 43: Using A, k all sts,

Row 44: As Row 2.

Rep Rows 1 to 44.

Crochet Instructions

Multiple of 24 sts + 3

Using A, make desired number of chainless sc.

Row 1 (RS): Using B, 1 ch, 2 sc, * 6 sc, 2 ch, skip st, 7 sc, 2 ch, skip st, 9 sc; rep from * to last st, 1 sc,

Row 2 and all WS rows: 1 ch, 1 sc in sts, ch and skip ch-sps, turn.

Row 3: Using A, 1 ch, 2 sc, * 6 sc, 1 Mdc, 2 ch, skip st, 5 sc, 2 ch, skip st, 1 Mdc, 9 sc; rep from * to last st, 1 sc, turn.

Row 5: Using B, 1 ch, 2 sc, * 2 sc, 2 ch, skip st, 4 sc, 1 Mdc, 2 ch, skip st, 3 sc, 2 ch, skip st, 1 Mdc, 2 ch, skip st, 9 sc; rep from * to last st, 1 sc, turn.

Row 7: Using A, 1 ch, 2 sc, * 2 sc, 1 Mdc, 2 ch, skip st, 3 sc, 2 ch, skip st, 1 Mdc, 2 ch, skip st, 1 sc, 2 ch, skip st, 1 Mdc, 2 ch, skip st, 1 Mdc, 9 sc; rep from * to last st, 1 sc, turn.

MOSAIC CHART

24 sts

Yarn A = Cream

Yarn B = Blue

KNIT

CROCHET

Row 9: Using B, 1 ch, 2 sc, * 2 sc, 2 ch, skip st, 1 Mdc, 2 ch, skip st, 2 sc, 1 Mdc, 2 ch, skip st, 1 Mdc, 1 sc, 1 Mdc, 2 ch, skip st, 1 Mdc, 2 ch, skip st, 9 sc; rep from * to last st, 1 sc, turn.
Row 11: Using A, 1 ch, 2 sc, * 2 sc, 1 Mdc, 2 ch, skip st, 1 Mdc, 2 ch, skip st, 1 sc, 2 ch, skip st, 1 Mdc, 3 sc, 1 Mdc, 2 ch, skip st, 1 Mdc, 9 sc; rep from * to last st, 1 sc, turn.
Row 13: Using B, 1 ch, 2 sc, * 2 ch, skip st, 2 sc, [1 Mdc, 1 sc] 3 times, 4 sc, 1 Mdc, 2 ch, skip st, 9 sc; rep from * to last st, 1 sc, turn.
Row 15: Using A, 1 ch, 2 sc, * 1 Mdc, 2 ch, skip st, 5 sc, [2 ch, skip st, 1 sc] 3 times, 1 sc, 1 Mdc, 9 sc; rep from * to last st, 1 sc, turn.
Row 17: Using B, 1 ch, 2 sc, * 2 ch, skip st, 1 Mdc, 2 ch, skip st, 3 sc, 2 ch, skip st, 1 Mdc, 1 sc, 1 Mdc, 2 ch, skip st, 1 Mdc, 2 sc, 2 ch, skip st, 7 sc, 2 ch, skip st, 1 sc; rep from * to last st, 1 sc, turn.
Row 19: Using A, 1 ch, 2 sc, * [1 Mdc, 2 ch, skip st] twice, 1 sc, 2 ch, skip st, 1 Mdc, 2 ch, skip st, 2 sc, 1 Mdc, 2 ch, skip st, 1 sc, 2 ch, skip st, 1 Mdc, 2 ch, skip st, 5 sc, 2 ch, skip st, 1 Mdc, 1 sc; rep from * to last st, 1 sc, turn.
Row 21: Using B, 1 ch, 2 sc, * [2 ch, skip st, 1 Mdc] twice, 1 sc, 1 Mdc, 2 ch, skip st, 1 Mdc, 3 sc, 1 Mdc, [1 sc, 1 Mdc] twice, 2 ch, skip st, 3 sc, 2 ch, skip st, 1 Mdc, 2 ch, skip st, 1 sc; rep from * to last st, 1 sc, turn.
Row 23: Using A, 1 ch, 2 sc, * 1 Mdc, 2 ch, skip st, 1 Mdc, 3 sc, 1 Mdc, [2 ch, skip st, 1 sc] 3 times, 2 sc, 2 ch, skip st, 1 Mdc, 2 ch, skip st, 1 sc, [2 ch, skip st, 1 Mdc] twice, 1 sc; rep from * to last st, 1 sc, turn.
Row 25: Using B, 1 ch, 2 sc, * 2 ch, skip st, 1 Mdc, 5 sc, 1 Mdc, 2 ch, skip st, 1 Mdc, 1 sc, 1 Mdc, 2 ch, skip st, 2 sc, 1 Mdc, 2 ch, skip st, 1 Mdc, 1 sc, [1 Mdc, 2 ch, skip st] twice, 1 sc; rep from * to last st, 1 sc, turn.
Row 27: Using A, 1 ch, 2 sc, * 1 Mdc, 7 sc, 1 Mdc, 2 sc, 2 ch, skip st, 1 Mdc, 2 ch, skip st, 1 sc, 2 ch, skip st, 1 Mdc, 3 sc, 1 Mdc, 2 ch, skip st, 1 Mdc, 1 sc; rep from * to last st, 1 sc, turn.
Row 29: Using B, 1 ch, 2 sc, * 8 sc, 2 ch, skip st, 2 sc, [1 Mdc, 1 sc] 3 times, 4 sc, 1 Mdc, 2 ch, skip st, 1 sc; rep from * to last st, 1 sc, turn.
Row 31: Using A, 1 ch, 2 sc, * 8 sc, 1 Mdc, 2 ch, skip st, 5 sc, [2 ch, skip st, 1 sc] 3 times, 1 sc, 1 Mdc, 1 sc; rep from * to last st, 1 sc, turn.
Row 33: Using B, 1 ch, 2 sc, * 8 sc, 2 ch, skip st, 1 Mdc, 2 ch, skip st, 3 sc, 2 ch, skip st, 1 Mdc, 1 sc, 1 Mdc, 2 ch, skip st, 1 Mdc, 2 ch, skip st, 3 sc; rep from * to last st, 1 sc, turn.
Row 35: Using A, 1 ch, 2 sc, * 8 sc, 1 Mdc, 2 ch, skip st, 1 Mdc, 2 ch, skip st, 1 sc, 2 ch, skip st, 1 Mdc, 2 ch, skip st, 2 sc, 1 Mdc, 2 ch, skip st, 1 Mdc, 3 sc; rep from * to last st, 1 sc, turn.
Row 37: Using B, 1 ch, 2 sc, * 8 sc, [2 ch, skip st, 1 Mdc] twice, 1 sc, 1 Mdc, 2 ch, skip st, 1 Mdc, 3 sc, 1 Mdc, 2 ch, skip st, 3 sc; rep from * to last st, 1 sc, turn.
Row 39: Using A, 1 ch, 2 sc, * 8 sc, 1 Mdc, 2 ch, skip st, 1 Mdc, 3 sc, 1 Mdc, 2 ch, skip st, 4 sc, 1 Mdc, 3 sc; rep from * to last st, 1 sc, turn.
Row 41: Using B, 1 ch, 2 sc, * 8 sc, 2 ch, skip st, 1 Mdc, 5 sc, 1 Mdc, 2 ch, skip st, 7 sc; rep from * to last st, 1 sc, turn.
Row 43: Using A, 1 ch, 2 sc, * 8 sc, 1 Mdc, 7 sc, 1 Mdc, 7 sc; rep from * to last st, 1 sc, turn.
Row 44: As Row 2.
Rep Rows 1 to 44, ending last rep with Row 43.

Links

This is a modern pattern with many uses. It can be used as panels or repeats and would be ideal for borders or large sections of blankets.

Knit Instructions

Multiple of 12 sts + 3

On RS rows, slip the sts purlwise with yarn in the back.

Cast on using B, k one row and p one row.

Row 1 (RS): Using A, k2, * k4, sl3, k5; rep from * to last st, k1.

Row 2 and all WS rows: P the knitted sts and sl the slipped sts purlwise with yarn in the front.

Row 3: Using B, k2 * [k3, sl1] twice, k4; rep from * to last st, k1.

Row 5: Using A, k1, sl1, * k11, sl1; rep from * to last st, k1.

Row 7: Using B, k2, * sl1, k2, sl1, k3, sl1, k2, sl1, k1; rep from * to last st, k1.

Row 9: As Row 5.

Row 11: As Row 3.

Row 13: As Row 1.

Row 15: Using B, k all sts.

Row 17: Using A, k1, sl1, * sl1, k9, sl2; rep from * to last st, k1.

Row 19: Using B, k2, * k1, sl1, k7, sl1, k2; rep from * to last st, k1.

Row 21: Using A, k2, * k5, sl1, k6; rep from * to last st, k1.

Row 23: Using B, k2, * [k1, sl1, k2, sl1] twice, k2; rep from * to last st, k1.

Row 25: As Row 21.

Row 27: As Row 19.

Row 29: As Row 17.

Row 31: Using B, k all sts.

Row 32: As Row 2.

Rep Rows 1 to 32.

Crochet Instructions

Multiple of 12 sts + 3

Pattern note: The repeat in the written instructions differs from the chart on Rows 17 and 29.

Using B, make desired number of chainless sc.

Row 1 (RS): Using A, 1 ch, 2 sc, * 4 sc, 4 ch, skip 3 sts, 5 sc; rep from * to last st, 1 sc, turn.

Row 2 and all WS rows: 1 ch, 1 sc in sts, ch and skip ch-sps, turn.

Row 3: Using B, 1 ch, 2 sc, * 3 sc, 2 ch, skip st, 3 Mdc, 2 ch, skip st, 4 sc; rep from * to last st, 1 sc, turn.

Row 5: Using A, 1 ch, 1 sc, 2 ch, skip st, * [3 sc, 1 Mdc] twice, 3 sc, 2 ch, skip st; rep from * to last st, 1 sc, turn.

Row 7: Using B, 1 ch, 1 sc, 1 Mdc * 2 ch, skip st, 2 sc, 2 ch, skip st, 3 sc, 2 ch, skip st, 2 sc, 2 ch, skip st, 1 Mdc; rep from * to last st, 1 sc, turn.

Row 9: Using A, 1 ch, 1 sc, 2 ch, skip st, * 1 Mdc, 2 sc, 1 Mdc, 3 sc, 1 Mdc, 2 sc, 1 Mdc, 2 ch, skip st; rep from * to last st, 1 sc, turn.

Row 11: Using B, 1 ch, 1 sc, 1 Mdc * [3 sc, 2 ch, skip st] twice, 3 sc, 1 Mdc; rep from * to last st, 1 sc, turn.

Row 13: Using A, 1 ch, 2 sc, * 3 sc, 1 Mdc, 4 ch, skip 3 sts, 1 Mdc, 4 sc; rep from * to last st, 1 sc, turn.

MOSAIC CHART

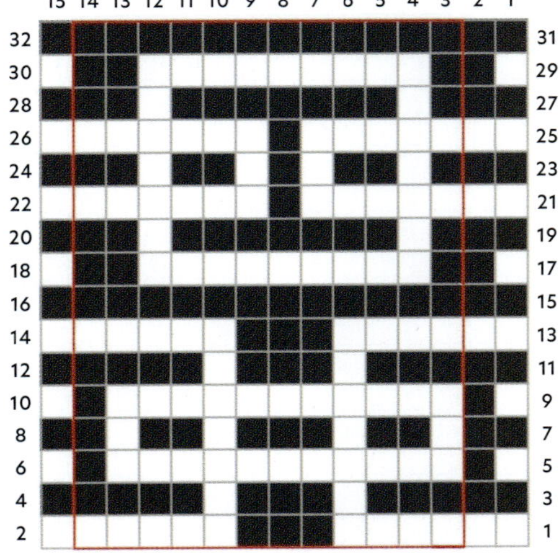

12 sts

Yarn A = Cream

Yarn B = Gray

Row 15: Using B, 1 ch, 2 sc, * 4 sc, 3 Mdc, 5 sc; rep from * to last st, 1 sc, turn.
Row 17: Using A, 1 ch, 1 sc, 3 ch, skip 2 sts, * 9 sc, ** 4 ch, skip 3 sts; rep from * to last 3 sts ending last rep at **, 3 ch, skip 2 sts, 1 sc, turn.
Row 19: Using B, 1 ch, 1 sc, 1 Mdc, * 1 Mdc, 2 ch, skip st, 7 sc, 2 ch, skip st, 2 Mdc; rep from * to last st, 1 sc, turn.
Row 21: Using A, 1 ch, 2 sc, * 1 sc, 1 Mdc, 3 sc, 2 ch, skip st, 3 sc, 1 Mdc, 2 sc; rep from * to last st, 1 sc, turn.
Row 23: Using B, 1 ch, 2 sc, * 1 sc, 2 ch, skip st, 2 sc, 2 ch, skip st, 1 Mdc, [2 ch, skip st, 2 sc] twice; rep from * to last st, 1 sc, turn.
Row 25: Using A, 1 ch, 2 sc, * 1 sc, 1 Mdc, 2 sc, 1 Mdc, 2 ch, skip st, 1 Mdc, 2 sc, 1 Mdc, 2 sc; rep from * to last st, 1 sc, turn.
Row 27: Using B, 1 ch, 2 sc, * 1 sc, 2 ch, skip st, 3 sc, 1 Mdc, 3 sc, 2 ch, skip st, 2 sc; rep from * to last st, 1 sc, turn.
Row 29: Using A, 1 ch, 1 sc, 3 ch, skip 2 sts, * 1 Mdc, 7 sc, 1 Mdc, ** 4 ch, skip 3 sts; rep from * to last 3 sts ending last rep at **, 3 ch, skip 2 sts, 1 sc, turn.
Row 31: Using B, 1 ch, 1 sc, 1 Mdc * 1 Mdc, 9 sc, 2 Mdc; rep from * to last st, 1 sc, turn.
Row 32: As Row 2.
Rep Rows 1 to 32, placing 1 Mdc in sps as required on Row 1. End last rep with Row 31.

KNIT

CROCHET

Gems

A very sweet pattern that creates large and small diamonds when repeated. The small squares within the diamonds look like hearts on the crochet swatch and circles on the knitted swatch, but it is the same pattern!

Knit Instructions

Multiple of 6 sts + 3

On RS rows, slip the sts purlwise with yarn in the back.

Cast on using A, k one row and p one row.

Row 1 (RS): Using B, k1, * sl1, k1; rep from * to last 2 sts, sl1, k1.

Row 2 and all WS rows: P the knitted sts and sl the slipped sts purlwise with yarn in the front.

Row 3: Using A, k1, * k3, sl1, k2; rep from * to last 2 sts, k2.

Row 5: Using B, k1, * k1, sl1, k3, sl1; rep from * to last 2 sts, k2.

Row 7: Using A, k1, * k2, [sl1, k1] twice; rep from * to last 2 sts, k2.

Row 9: Using B, k1, * [sl1, k2] twice; rep from * to last 2 sts, sl1, k1.

Row 11: Using A, k1, * k1, sl1, k3, sl1; rep from * to last 2 sts, k2.

Row 13: Using B, k1, * k2, [sl1, k1] twice; rep from * to last 2 sts, k2.

Row 15: As Row 11.

Row 17: As Row 9.

Row 19: As Row 7.

Row 21: As Row 5.

Row 23: As Row 3.

Rep Rows 1 to 24. To finish, work Rows 25 to 28.

Row 25: As Row 1.

Row 27: Using A, k all sts.

Row 28: As Row 2.

Crochet Instructions

Multiple of 6 sts + 3

Pattern note: The repeat in the written instructions differs from the chart on Row 17.

Using A, make desired number of chainless sc.

Row 1 (RS): Using B, 1 ch, 1 sc, * [2 ch, skip st, 1 sc] 3 times; rep from * to last 2 sts, 2 ch, skip st, 1 sc, turn.

Row 2 and all WS rows: 1 ch, 1 sc in sts, ch and skip ch-sps, turn.

Row 3: Using A, 1 ch, 1 sc, * 1 Mdc, 1 sc, 1 Mdc, 2 ch, skip st, 1 Mdc, 1 sc; rep from * to last 2 sts, 1 Mdc, 1 sc, turn.

Row 5: Using B, 1 ch, 1 sc, * 1 sc, 2 ch, skip st, 1 sc, 1 Mdc, 1 sc, 2 ch, skip st; rep from * to last 2 sts, 2 sc, turn.

Row 7: Using A, 1 ch, 1 sc, * 1 sc, 1 Mdc, 2 ch, skip st, 1 sc, 2 ch, skip st, 1 Mdc; rep from * to last 2 sts, 2 sc, turn.

Row 9: Using B, 1 ch, 1 sc, * 2 ch, skip st, 1 sc, 1 Mdc, 2 ch, skip st, 1 Mdc, 1 sc; rep from * to last 2 sts, 2 ch, skip st, 1 sc, turn.

Row 11: Using A, 1 ch, 1 sc, * 1 Mdc, 2 ch, skip st, 1 sc, 1 Mdc, 1 sc, 2 ch, skip st; rep from * to last 2 sts, 1 Mdc, 1 sc, turn.

Row 13: Using B, 1 ch, 1 sc, * 1 sc, 1 Mdc, 2 ch, skip st, 1 sc, 2 ch, skip st, 1 Mdc; rep from * to last 2 sts, 2 sc, turn.

Row 15: Using A, 1 ch, 1 sc, * 1 sc, 2 ch,

skip st, 1 Mdc, 1 sc, 1 Mdc, 2 ch, skip st; rep from * to last 2 sts, 2 sc, turn.

Row 17: Using B, 1 ch, 1 sc, * 2 ch, skip st, 1 Mdc, 1 sc, 2 ch, skip st, 1 sc, 1 Mdc; rep from * to last 2 sts, 2 ch, skip st, 1 sc, turn.

Row 19: Using A, 1 ch, 1 sc, * 1 Mdc, 1 sc, 2 ch, skip st, 1 Mdc, 2 ch, skip st, 1 sc; rep from * to last 2 sts, 1 Mdc, 1 sc, turn.

Row 21: Using B, 1 ch, 1 sc, * 1 sc, 2 ch, skip st, 1 Mdc, 1 sc, 1 Mdc, 2 ch, skip st; rep from * to last 2 sts, 2 sc, turn.

Row 23: Using A, 1 ch, 1 sc, * 1 sc, 1 Mdc, 1 sc, 2 ch, skip st, 1 sc, 1 Mdc; rep from * to last 2 sts, 2 sc, turn.

Rep Rows 1 to 24, placing 1 Mdc in sps as required on Row 1. To finish, work Rows 25 to 27.

Row 25: Using B, 1 ch, 1 sc, * 2 ch, skip st, 1 sc, 2 ch, skip st, 1 Mdc, 2 ch, skip st, 1 sc; rep from * to last 2 sts, 2 ch, skip st, 1 sc, turn.

Row 27: Using A, 1 ch, 1 sc, * [1 Mdc, 1 sc] 3 times; rep from * to last 2 sts, 1 Mdc, 1 sc, turn.

CROCHET

TIP: This design would look great as a cowl for winter. Choose a wool mix that is soft to touch, so it doesn't irritate the skin while also keeping you warm. You can create this cowl by knitting or crocheting a large panel and sewing the sides together, or you can knit or crochet in the round. Learn more about this on page 25.

Waves

A very simple but effective pattern, creating vertical waves. Work several repeats to allow the design to shine. This would look amazing on a stroller blanket or could be made into a charming bag.

Knit Instructions

Multiple of 5 sts + 4

On RS rows, slip the sts purlwise with yarn in the back.

Cast on using A, k one row and p one row.

Row 1 (RS): Using B, k1, sl2, * sl1, k2, sl2; rep from * to last st, k1.

Row 2 and all WS rows: P the knitted sts and sl the slipped sts purlwise with yarn in the front.

Row 3: Using A, k3, * k1, sl2, k2; rep from * to last st, k1.

Row 5: Using B, k1, sl2, * k3, sl2; rep from * to last st, k1.

Row 7: Using A, k3, * sl2, k3; rep from * to last st, k1.

Row 9: Using B, k1, sl1, k1, * k2, sl2, k1; rep from * to last st, k1.

Row 11: Using A, k2, sl1, * sl1, k3, sl1; rep from * to last st, k1.

Row 13: Using B, k3, * k1, sl2, k2; rep from * to last st, k1.

Row 15: Using A, k1, sl2, * k3, sl2; rep from * to last st, k1.

Row 17: Using B, k3, * k1, sl2, k2; rep from * to last st, k1.

Row 19: As Row 11.

Row 21: As Row 9.

Row 23: As Row 7.

Row 25: As Row 5.

Row 27: As Row 3.

Row 29: Using B, k2, sl1, * sl1, k3, sl1; rep from * to last st, k1.

Row 31: Using A, k1, sl1, k1, * k2, sl2, k1; rep from * to last st, k1.

Row 33: Using B, k2, sl1, * sl1, k3, sl1; rep from * to last st, k1.

Row 35: As Row 3.

Rep Rows 1 to 36. To finish, work Rows 37 to 40.

Row 37: As Row 1.

Row 39: Using A, k all sts.

Row 40: As Row 2.

MOSAIC CHART

5 sts

Yarn A = Cream

Yarn B = Gray

Crochet Instructions

Multiple of 5 sts + 4

Pattern note: The repeat in the written instructions differs from the chart on Rows 1, 11, 19, 29, and 33.

Using A, make desired number of chainless sc.

Row 1 (RS): Using B, 1 ch, 1 sc, 4 ch, skip 3 sts, * 2 sc, ** 4 ch, skip 3 sts; rep from * to last 3 sts, ending last rep at **, 3 ch, skip 2 sts, 1 sc, turn.

Row 2 and all WS rows: 1 ch, 1 sc in sts, ch and skip ch-sps, turn.

Row 3: Using A, 1 ch, 1 sc, 2 Mdc, * 1 Mdc, 3 ch, skip 2 sts, 2 Mdc; rep from * to last st, 1 sc, turn.

Row 5: Using B, 1 ch, 1 sc, 3 ch, skip 2 sts, * 1 sc, 2 Mdc, 3 ch, skip 2 sts; rep from * to last st, 1 sc, turn.

Row 7: Using A, 1 ch, 1 sc, 2 Mdc, * 3 ch, skip 2 sts, 1 sc, 2 Mdc; rep from * to last st, 1 sc, turn.

Row 9: Using B, 1 ch, 1 sc, 2 ch, skip st, 1 sc, * 2 Mdc, 3 ch, skip 2 sts, 1 sc; rep from * to last st, 1 sc, turn.

Row 11: Using A, 1 ch, 1 sc, 1 Mdc, 3 ch, skip 2 sts, * 1 sc, 2 Mdc, ** 3 ch skip 2 sts; rep from * to last 3 sts, ending last rep at **, 2 ch, skip st, 1 sc, turn.

Row 13: Using B, 1 ch, 2 sc, 1 Mdc, * 1 Mdc, 3 ch, skip 2 sts, 1 sc, 1 Mdc; rep from * to last st, 1 sc, turn.

Row 15: Using A, 1 ch, 1 sc, 3 ch, skip 2 sts, * 1 sc, 2 Mdc, 3 ch, skip 2 sts; rep from * to last st, 1 sc, turn.

Row 17: Using B, 1 ch, 1 sc, 2 Mdc, * 1 sc, 3 ch, skip 2 sts, 2 Mdc; rep from * to last st, 1 sc, turn.

Row 19: Using A, 1 ch, 2 sc, 3 ch, skip 2 sts, * 2 Mdc, 1 sc, ** 3 ch, skip 2 sts; rep from * to last 2 sts, ending last rep at **, 2 ch, skip st, 1 sc, turn.

Row 21: Using B, 1 ch, 1 sc, 2 ch, skip st, 1 Mdc, * 1 Mdc, 1 sc, 3 ch, skip 2 sts, 1 Mdc; rep from * to last st, 1 sc, turn.

Row 23: Using A, 1 ch, 1 sc, 1 Mdc, 1 sc, * 3 ch, skip 2 sts, 2 Mdc, 1 sc; rep from * to last st, 1 sc, turn.

Row 25: Using B, 1 ch, 1 sc, 3 ch, skip 2 sts, * 2 Mdc, 1 sc, 3 ch, skip 2 sts; rep from * to last st, 1 sc, turn.

Row 27: Using A, 1 ch, 1 sc, 2 Mdc, * 1 sc, 3 ch, skip 2 sts, 2 Mdc; rep from * to last st, 1 sc, turn.

Row 29: Using B, 1 ch, 2 sc, 3 ch, skip 2 sts, * 2 Mdc, 1 sc, ** 3 ch, skip 2 sts; rep from * to last 2 sts, ending last rep at **, 2 ch, skip st, 1 sc, turn.

Row 31: Using A, 1 ch, 1 sc, 2 ch, skip st, 1 Mdc, * 1 Mdc, 1 sc, 3 ch, skip 2 sts, 1 Mdc; rep from * to last st, 1 sc, turn.

Row 33: Using B, 1 ch, 1 sc, 1 Mdc, 3 ch, skip 2 sts, * 1 sc, 2 Mdc, ** 3 ch, skip 2 sts; rep from * to last 2 sts, ending last rep at **, 2 ch, skip st, 1 sc, turn.

Row 35: Using A, 1 ch, 2 sc, 1 Mdc, * 1 Mdc, 3 ch, skip 2 sts, 1 sc, 1 Mdc; rep from * to last st, 1 sc, turn.

Rep Rows 1 to 36, placing 1 Mdc in sps as required on Row 1. To finish, work Rows 37 to 39.

Row 37: Using B, 1 ch, 1 sc, 4 ch, skip 3 sts, * 2 Mdc, ** 4 ch, skip 3 sts; rep from * to last 3 sts, ending last rep at **, 3 ch, skip 2 sts, 1 sc, turn.

Row 39: Using A, 1 ch, 1 sc, 2 Mdc, *1 Mdc, 2 sc, 2 Mdc; rep from * to last st, 1 sc, turn.

KNIT

CROCHET

Pippin

Pippin is really versatile; it will work vertically or horizontally in small or large repeats. The knit version of this design is slightly more defined.

Knit Instructions

Multiple of 6 sts + 3

On RS rows, slip the sts purlwise with yarn in the back.

Cast on using A, k one row and p one row.

Row 1 (RS): Using B, k1, * k3, sl1, k2; rep from * to last 2 sts, k2.

Row 2 and all WS rows: P the knitted sts and sl the slipped sts purlwise with yarn in the front.

Row 3: Using A, k all sts.

Row 5: Using B, k1, * k2, [sl1, k1] twice; rep from * to last 2 sts, k2.

Row 7: Using A, k all sts.

Row 9: Using B, k1, * k1, [sl1, k1] twice, sl1; rep from * to last 2 sts, k2.

Row 11: Using A, k all sts.

Row 13: As Row 5.

Row 15: Using A, k all sts.

Rep Rows 1 to 16. To finish, work Rows 17 to 20.

Row 17: As Row 1.

Row 19: Using A, k all sts.

Row 20: As Row 2.

Crochet Instructions

Multiple of 6 sts + 3

Using A, make desired number of chainless sc.

Row 1 (RS): Using B, 1 ch, 1 sc, * 3 sc, 2 ch, skip st, 2 sc; rep from * to last 2 sts, 2 sc, turn.

Row 2 and all WS rows: 1 ch, 1 sc in sts, ch and skip ch-sps, turn.

Row 3: Using A, 1 ch, 1 sc, * 3 sc, 1 Mdc, 2 sc; rep from * to last 2 sts, 2 sc, turn.

Row 5: Using B, 1 ch, 1 sc, * 2 sc, [2 ch, skip st, 1 sc] twice; rep from * to last 2 sts, 2 sc, turn.

Row 7: Using A, 1 ch, 1 sc, * 2 sc, [1 Mdc, 1 sc] twice; rep from * to last 2 sts, 2 sc, turn.

Row 9: Using B, 1 ch, 1 sc, * 1 sc, [2 ch, skip st, 1 sc] twice, 2 ch, skip st; rep from * to last 2 sts, 2 sc, turn.

Row 11: Using A, 1 ch, 1 sc, * 1 sc, [1 Mdc, 1 sc] twice, 1 Mdc; rep from * to last 2 sts, 2 sc, turn.

Row 13: As Row 5.

Row 15: Using A, 1 ch, 1 sc, * 2 sc, [1 Mdc, 1 sc] twice; rep from * to last 2 sts, 2 sc, turn.

Rep Rows 1 to 16. To finish, work Rows 17 to 19.

Row 17: Using B, 1 ch, 1 sc, * 3 sc, 2 ch, skip st, 2 sc; rep from * to last 2 sts, 2 sc, turn.

Row 19: Using A, 1 ch, 1 sc, * 3 sc, 1 Mdc, 2 sc; rep from * to last 2 sts, 2 sc, turn.

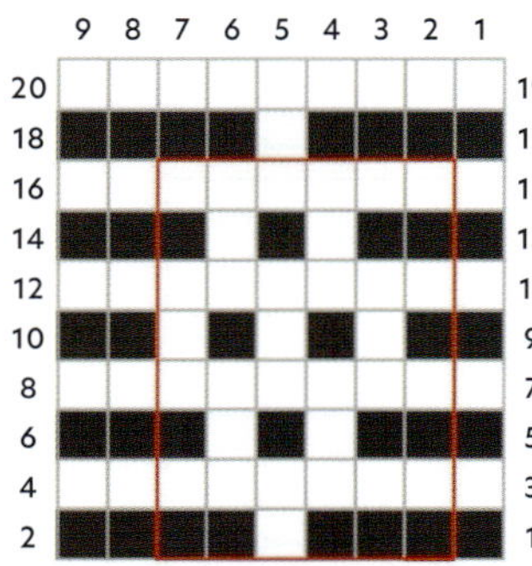

Yarn A = Cream

Yarn B = Dark pink

KNIT

CROCHET

Thick and Thin

This stunning pattern is best worked in a large section with few repeats; this will show off the design beautifully. This pattern is perfect for garments, accessories, and home decorations.

Knit Instructions

Multiple of 10 sts + 3

On RS rows, slip the sts purlwise with yarn in the back.

Cast on using A, k one row and p one row.

Row 1 (RS): Using B, k1, * [k1, sl1] twice, k3, sl1, k1, sl1; rep from * to last 2 sts, k2.

Row 2 and all WS rows: P the knitted sts and sl the slipped sts purlwise with yarn in the front.

Row 3: Using A, k1, * k4, sl1, k1, sl1, k3; rep from * to last 2 sts, k2.

Row 5: Using B, k1, * [sl1, k1] twice, k4, sl1, k1; rep from * to last 2 sts, sl1, k1.

Row 7: Using A, k1, * k3, [sl1, k1] 3 times, k1; rep from * to last 2 sts, k2.

Row 9: Using B, k1, * k1, sl1, k7, sl1; rep from * to last 2 sts, k2.

Row 11: Using A, k1, * k2, [sl1, k1] 4 times; rep from * to last 2 sts, k2.

Row 13: As Row 9.

Row 15: As Row 7.

Row 17: As Row 5.

Row 19: As Row 3.

Rep Rows 1 to 20. To finish, work Rows 21 to 24.

Row 21: As Row 1.

Row 23: Using A, k all sts.

Row 24: As Row 2.

Crochet Instructions

Multiple of 10 sts + 3

Using A, make desired number of chainless sc.

Row 1 (RS): Using B, 1 ch, 1 sc, * [1 sc, 2 ch, skip st] twice, 3 sc, 2 ch, skip st, 1 sc, 2 ch, skip st; rep from * to last 2 sts, 2 sc, turn.

Row 2 and all WS rows: 1 ch, 1 sc in sts, ch and skip ch-sps, turn.

Row 3: Using A, 1 ch, 1 sc, * [1 sc, 1 Mdc] twice, 2 ch, skip st, 1 sc, 2 ch, skip st, 1 Mdc, 1 sc, 1 Mdc; rep from * to last 2 sts, 2 sc, turn.

Row 5: Using B, 1 ch, 1 sc, * [2 ch, skip st, 1 sc] twice, [1 Mdc, 1 sc] twice, 2 ch, skip st, 1 sc; rep from * to last 2 sts, 2 ch, skip st, 1 sc, turn.

Row 7: Using A, 1 ch, 1 sc, * 1 Mdc, 1 sc, 1 Mdc, [2 ch, skip st, 1 sc] twice, 2 ch, skip st, 1 Mdc, 1 sc; rep from * to last 2 sts, 1 Mdc, 1 sc, turn.

Row 9: Using B, 1 ch, 1 sc, * 1 sc, 2 ch, skip st, [1 sc, 1 Mdc] 3 times, 1 sc, 2 ch, skip st; rep from * to last 2 sts, 2 sc, turn.

Row 11: Using A, 1 ch, 1 sc, * 1 sc, 1 Mdc, [2 ch, skip st, 1 sc] 3 times, 2 ch, skip st, 1 Mdc; rep from * to last 2 sts, 2 sc, turn.

Row 13: Using B, 1 ch, 1 sc, * 1 sc, 2 ch, skip st, [1 Mdc, 1 sc] 3 times, 1 Mdc, 2 ch, skip st; rep from * to last 2 sts, 2 sc, turn.

Row 15: Using A, 1 ch, 1 sc, * 1 sc, 1 Mdc, 1 sc, [2 ch, skip st, 1 sc] 3 times, 1 Mdc; rep from * to last 2 sts, 2 sc, turn.

Row 17: Using B, 1 ch, 1 sc, * 2 ch, skip st, 1 sc, 2 ch, skip st, [1 Mdc, 1 sc] twice, 1 Mdc, 2 ch, skip st, 1 sc; rep from * to last 2 sts, 2 ch, skip st, 1 sc, turn.

Row 19: Using A, 1 ch, 1 sc, * [1 Mdc, 1 sc] twice, [2 ch, skip st, 1 sc] twice, 1 Mdc, 1 sc; rep from * to last 2 sts, 1 Mdc, 1 sc, turn.

Rep Rows 1 to 20, placing 1 Mdc in sps as required on Row 1. To finish, work Rows 21 to 23.

Row 21: Using B, 1 ch, 1 sc, * [1 sc, 2 ch, skip st] twice, 1 Mdc, 1 sc, 1 Mdc, 2 ch, skip st, 1 sc, 2 ch, skip st; rep from * to last 2 sts, 2 sc, turn.

Row 23: Using A, 1 ch, 1 sc, * [1 sc, 1 Mdc] twice, 3 sc, 1 Mdc, 1 sc, 1 Mdc; rep from * to last 2 sts, 2 sc, turn.

Yarn A = Cream

Yarn B = Pale pink

MOSAIC CHART

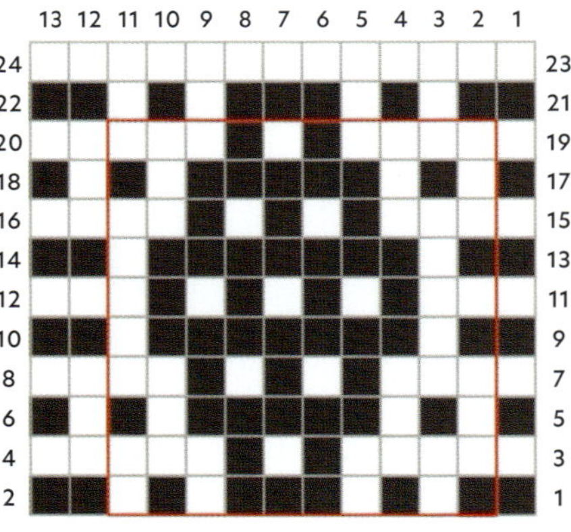

10 sts

KNIT

CROCHET

Cubes

This is one of the patterns that will work best in a large section with few repeats. This will allow the design to really shine. Perfect for larger projects such as shawls and wraps.

Knit Instructions

Multiple of 6 sts + 3

On RS rows, slip the sts purlwise with yarn in the back.

Cast on using B, k one row and p one row.

Row 1 (RS): Using A, k1, * [k1, sl1] twice, k2; rep from * to last 2 sts, k2.

Row 2 and all WS rows: P the knitted sts and sl the slipped sts purlwise with yarn in the front.

Row 3: Using B, k1, * sl1, k3, sl1, k1; rep from * to last 2 sts, sl1, k1.

Row 5: Using A, k1, * k5, sl1; rep from * to last 2 sts, k2.

Row 7: Using B, as Row 3.

Row 9: Using A, as Row 1.

Row 11: Using B, k1, * k2, sl1, k3; rep from * to last 2 sts, k2.

Rep Rows 1 to 12. To finish, work Rows 13 to 16.

Row 13: Using A, as Row 1.

Row 15: Using B, k all sts.

Row 16: As Row 2.

Crochet Instructions

Multiple of 6 sts + 3

Using B, make desired number of chainless sc.

Row 1 (RS): Using A, 1 ch, 1 sc, * [1 sc, 2 ch, skip st] twice, 2 sc; rep from * to last 2 sts, 2 sc, turn.

Row 2 and all WS rows: 1 ch, 1 sc in sts, ch and skip ch-sps, turn.

Row 3: Using B, 1 ch, 1 sc, * 2 ch, skip st, 1 Mdc, 1 sc, 1 Mdc, 2 ch, skip st, 1 sc; rep from * to last 2 sts, 2 ch, skip st, 1 sc, turn.

Row 5: Using A, 1 ch, 1 sc, * 1 Mdc, 3 sc, 1 Mdc, 2 ch, skip st; rep from * to last 2 sts, 1 Mdc, 1 sc, turn.

Row 7: Using B, 1 ch, 1 sc, * 2 ch, skip st, 3 sc, 2 ch, skip st, 1 Mdc; rep from * to last 2 sts, 2 ch, skip st, 1 sc, turn.

Row 9: Using A, 1 ch, 1 sc, * 1 Mdc, 2 ch, skip st, 1 sc, 2 ch, skip st, 1 Mdc, 1 sc; rep from * to last 2 sts, 1 Mdc, 1 sc, turn.

Row 11: Using B, 1 ch, 1 sc, * 1 sc, 1 Mdc, 2 ch, skip st, 1 Mdc, 2 sc; rep from * to last 2 sts, 2 sc, turn.

Rep Rows 1 to 12, placing 1 Mdc in sps as required on Row 1. To finish, work Rows 13 to 15.

Row 13: Using A, 1 ch, 1 sc, * 1 sc, 2 ch, skip st, 1 Mdc, 2 ch, skip st, 2 sc; rep from * to last 2 sts, 2 sc, turn.

Row 15: Using B, 1 ch, 1 sc, * 1 sc, 1 Mdc, 1 sc, 1 Mdc, 2 sc; rep from * to last 2 sts, 2 sc, turn.

MOSAIC CHART

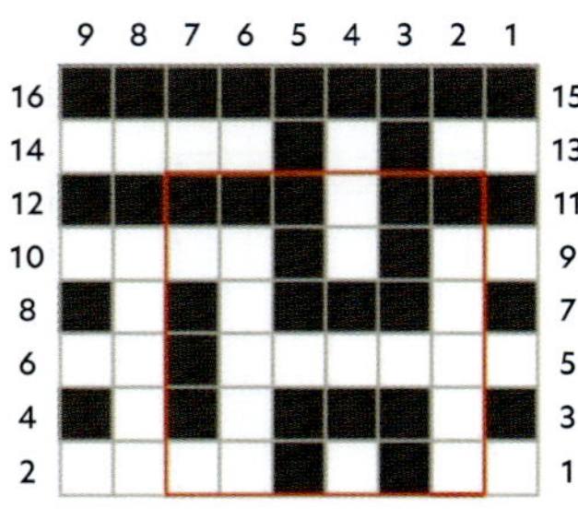

6 sts

Yarn A = Cream

Yarn B = Gray

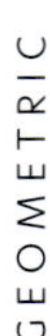

Ripple

A small, sweet pattern that will work equally wonderfully with small or large repeats. This would look great on a sweater or cardigan.

Knit Instructions

Multiple of 8 sts + 3

On RS rows, slip the sts purlwise with yarn in the back.

Cast on using A, k one row and p one row.

Row 1 (RS): Using B, k1, * k2, [sl1, k1] twice, k2; rep from * to last 2 sts, k2.

Row 2 and all WS rows: P the knitted sts and sl the slipped sts purlwise with yarn in the front.

Row 3: Using A, k1, * k1, sl1, k3, sl1, k2; rep from * to last 2 sts, k2.

Row 5: Using B, k1, * sl1, k5, sl1, k1; rep from * to last 2 sts, sl1, k1.

Row 7: Using A, k1, * k3, sl1; rep from * to last 2 sts, k2.

Rep Rows 1 to 8. To finish, work Rows 9 to 12.

Row 9: As Row 1.

Row 11: Using A, k all sts.

Row 12: As Row 2.

Crochet Instructions

Multiple of 8 sts + 3

Using A, make desired number of chainless sc.

Row 1 (RS): Using B, 1 ch, 1 sc, * 2 sc, [2 ch, skip st, 1 sc] twice, 2 sc; rep from * to last 2 sts, 2 sc, turn.

Row 2 and all WS rows: 1 ch, 1 sc in sts, ch and skip ch-sps, turn.

Row 3: Using A, 1 ch, 1 sc, * 1 sc, 2 ch, skip st, 1 Mdc, 1 sc, 1 Mdc, 2 ch, skip st, 2 sc; rep from * to last 2 sts, 2 sc, turn.

Row 5: Using B, 1 ch, 1 sc, * 2 ch, skip st, 1 Mdc, 3 sc, 1 Mdc, 2 ch, skip st, 1 sc; rep from * to last 2 sts, 2 ch, skip st, 1 sc, turn.

Row 7: Using A, 1 ch, 1 sc, * 1 Mdc, 2 sc, 2 ch, skip st, 2 sc, 1 Mdc, 2 ch, skip st; rep from * to last 2 sts, 1 Mdc, 1 sc, turn.

Rep Rows 1 to 8, placing 1 Mdc in sps as required on Row 1. To finish, work Rows 9 to 11.

Row 9: Using B, 1 ch, 1 sc, * 2 sc, 2 ch, skip st, 1 Mdc, 2 ch, skip st, 2 sc, 1 Mdc; rep from * to last 2 sts, 2 sc, turn.

Row 11: Using A, 1 ch, 1 sc, * 2 sc, 1 Mdc, 1 sc, 1 Mdc, 3 sc; rep from * to last 2 sts, 2 sc, turn.

MOSAIC CHART

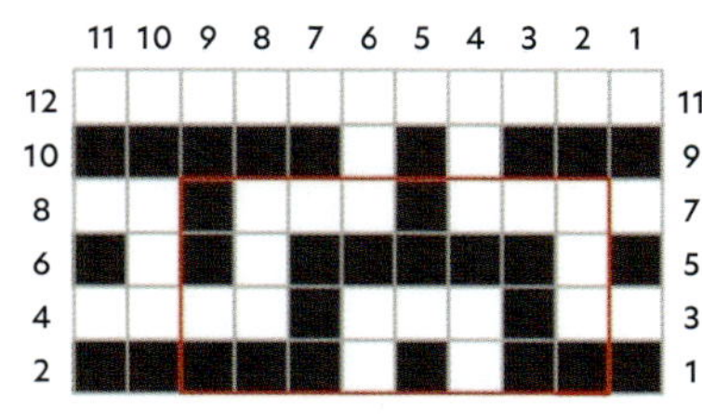

8 sts

Marvel

This stunning pattern requires a minimum of two repeats horizontally and vertically. It would look beautiful on any project: dress, sweater, or home accessory.

Knit Instructions

Multiple of 12 sts + 5

On RS rows, slip the sts purlwise with yarn in the back.

Cast on using A, k one row and p one row.

Row 1 (RS): Using B, k2, * k3, [sl1, k1] 4 times, k1; rep from * to last 3 sts, k3.

Row 2 and all WS rows: P the knitted sts and sl the slipped sts purlwise with yarn in the front.

Row 3: Using A, k2, * k2, sl1, [k3, sl1] twice, k1; rep from * to last 3 sts, k3.

Row 5: Using B, k1, sl1, * k1, sl1, k3, sl1, k1, sl1, k3, sl1; rep from * to last 3 sts, k1, sl1, k1.

Row 7: Using A, k2, * sl1, k3; rep from * to last 3 sts, sl1, k2.

Row 9: Using B, k1, sl1, * [k1, sl1] twice, k5, sl1, k1, sl1; rep from * to last 3 sts, k1, sl1, k1.

Row 11: Using A, k2, * sl1, k5; rep from * to last 3 sts, sl1, k2.

Row 13: Using B, k2, * k5, sl1, k1, sl1, k4; rep from * to last 3 sts, k3.

Row 15: As Row 11.

Row 17: As Row 9.

Row 19: As Row 7.

Row 21: As Row 5.

Row 23: As Row 3.

Row 25: As Row 1.

Row 27: As Row 11.

Row 29: Using B, k1, sl1, * k1, sl1, k9, sl1; rep from * to last 3 sts, k1, sl1, k1.

Row 31: As Row 11.

Rep Rows 1 to 32. To finish, work Rows 33 to 36.

Row 33: As Row 1.

Row 35: Using A, k all sts.

Row 36: As Row 2.

MOSAIC CHART

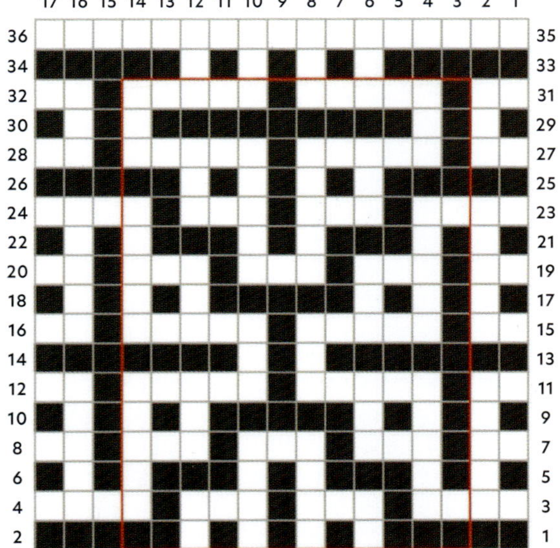

Yarn A = Cream

Yarn B = Dark pink

12 sts

Crochet Instructions

Multiple of 12 sts + 5

Using A, make desired number of chainless sc.

Row 1 (RS): Using B, 1 ch, 2 sc, * 3 sc, [2 ch, skip st, 1 sc] 4 times, 1 sc; rep from * to last 3 sts, 3 sc, turn.

Row 2 and all WS rows: 1 ch, 1 sc in sts, ch and skip ch-sps, turn.

Row 3: Using A, 1 ch, 2 sc, * 2 sc, [2 ch, skip st, 1 Mdc, 1 sc, 1 Mdc] twice, 2 ch, skip st, 1 sc; rep from * to last 3 sts, 3 sc, turn.

Row 5: Using B, 1 ch, 1 sc, 2 ch, skip st, * 1 sc, 2 ch, skip st, 1 Mdc, 2 sc, 2 ch, skip st, 1 Mdc, 2 ch, skip st, 2 sc, 1 Mdc, 2 ch, skip st; rep from * to last 3 sts, 1 sc, 2 ch, skip st, 1 sc, turn.

Row 7: Using A, 1 ch, 1 sc, 1 Mdc, * 2 ch, skip st, 1 Mdc, 2 sc, 2 ch, skip st, 1 Mdc, 1 sc, 1 Mdc, 2 ch, skip st, 2 sc, 1 Mdc; rep from * to last 3 sts, 2 ch, skip st, 1 Mdc, 1 sc, turn.

Row 9: Using B, 1 ch, 1 sc, 2 ch, skip st, * 1 Mdc, 2 ch, skip st, 1 sc, 2 ch, skip st, 1 Mdc, 3 sc, 1 Mdc, 2 ch, skip st, 1 sc, 2 ch, skip st; rep from * to last 3 sts, 1 Mdc, 2 ch, skip st, 1 sc, turn.

Row 11: Using A, 1 ch, 1 sc, 1 Mdc, * 2 ch, skip st, 1 Mdc, 1 sc, 1 Mdc, 2 sc, 2 ch, skip st, 2 sc, 1 Mdc, 1 sc, 1 Mdc; rep from * to last 3 sts, 2 ch, skip st, 1 Mdc, 1 sc, turn.

Row 13: Using B, 1 ch, 2 sc, * 1 Mdc, 4 sc, 2 ch, skip st, 1 Mdc, 2 ch, skip st, 4 sc; rep from * to last 3 sts, 1 Mdc, 2 sc, turn.

Row 15: Using A, 1 ch, 2 sc, * 2 ch, skip st, 4 sc, 1 Mdc, 2 ch, skip st, 1 Mdc, 4 sc; rep from * to last 3 sts, 2 ch, skip st, 2 sc, turn.

Row 17: Using B, 1 ch, 1 sc, 2 ch, skip st, * 1 Mdc, 2 ch, skip st, 1 sc, 2 ch, skip st, 2 sc, 1 Mdc, 2 sc, 2 ch, skip st, 1 sc, 2 ch,

KNIT

CROCHET

skip st; rep from * to last 3 sts, 1 Mdc, 2 ch, skip st, 1 sc, turn.

Row 19: Using A, 1 ch, 1 sc, 1 Mdc, * 2 ch, skip st, 1 Mdc, 1 sc, 1 Mdc, 2 ch, skip st, 3 sc, 2 ch, skip st, 1 Mdc, 1 sc, 1 Mdc; rep from * to last 3 sts, 2 ch, skip st, 1 Mdc, 1 sc, turn.

Row 21: Using B, 1 ch, 1 sc, 2 ch, skip st, * 1 Mdc, 2 ch, skip st, 2 sc, 1 Mdc, 2 ch, skip st, 1 sc, 2 ch, skip st, 1 Mdc, 2 sc, 2 ch, skip st; rep from * to last 3 sts, 1 Mdc, 2 ch, skip st, 1 sc, turn.

Row 23: Using A, 1 ch, 1 sc, 1 Mdc, * 1 sc, 1 Mdc, 2 ch, skip st, 2 sc, 1 Mdc, 2 ch, skip st, 1 Mdc, 2 sc, 2 ch, skip st, 1 Mdc; rep from * to last 3 sts, 1 sc, 1 Mdc, 1 sc, turn.

Row 25: Using B, 1 ch, 2 sc, * 2 sc, [1 Mdc, 2 ch, skip st, 1 sc, 2 ch, skip st] twice, 1 Mdc, 1 sc; rep from * to last 3 sts, 3 sc, turn.

Row 27: Using A, 1 ch, 2 sc, * 2 ch, skip st, 2 sc, 1 Mdc, 1 sc, 1 Mdc, 2 ch, skip st, 1 Mdc, 1 sc, 1 Mdc, 2 sc; rep from * to last 3 sts, 2 ch, skip st, 2 sc, turn.

Row 29: Using B, 1 ch, 1 sc, 2 ch, skip st, * 1 Mdc, 2 ch, skip st, 4 sc, 1 Mdc, 4 sc, 2 ch, skip st; rep from * to last 3 sts, 1 Mdc, 2 ch, skip st, 1 sc, turn.

Row 31: Using A, 1 ch, 1 sc, 1 Mdc, * 2 ch, skip st, 1 Mdc, 4 sc, 2 ch, skip st, 4 sc, 1 Mdc; rep from * to last 3 sts, 2 ch, skip st, 1 Mdc, 1 sc, turn.

Rep Rows 1 to 32, placing 1 Mdc in sps as required on Row 1. To finish, work Rows 33 to 35.

Row 33: Using B, 1 ch, 2 sc, * 1 Mdc, 2 sc, 2 ch, skip st, 1 sc, 2 ch, skip st, 1 Mdc, 2 ch, skip st, 1 sc, 2 ch, skip st, 2 sc; rep from * to last 3 sts, 1 Mdc, 2 sc, turn.

Row 35: Using A, 1 ch, 2 sc, * 3 sc, [1 Mdc, 1 sc] 4 times, 1 sc; rep from * to last 3 sts, 3 sc, turn.

Stripe Diamond

A very interesting pattern, which is a combination of half horizontal stripes and half vertical stripes that creates diamond shapes over the fabric. Give it space so that you can see the pattern.

Knit Instructions

Multiple of 12 sts + 3

On RS rows, slip the sts purlwise with yarn in the back.

Cast on using B, k one row and p one row.

Row 1 (RS): Using A, k1, * [sl1, k1] 4 times, sl1, k3; rep from * to last 2 sts, sl1, k1.

Row 2 and all WS rows: P the knitted sts and sl the slipped sts purlwise with yarn in the front.

Row 3: Using B, k1, * k1, sl1, k5, sl1, k4; rep from * to last 2 sts, k2.

Row 5: Using A, k1, * sl1, k1, sl1, k3, [sl1, k1] 3 times; rep from * to last 2 sts, sl1, k1.

Row 7: Using B, k1, * k7, [sl1, k1] twice, k1; rep from * to last 2 sts, k2.

Row 9: Using A, k1, * sl1, k5, [sl1, k1] 3 times; rep from * to last 2 sts, sl1, k1.

Row 11: Using B, k1, * k7, [sl1, k1] twice, k1; rep from * to last 2 sts, k2.

Row 13: Using A, k1, * sl1, k1, sl1, k3, [sl1, k1] 3 times; rep from * to last 2 sts, sl1, k1.

Row 15: Using B, k1, * k1, sl1, k5, sl1, k4; rep from * to last 2 sts, k2.

Row 17: Using A, k1, * [sl1, k1] 4 times, sl1, k3; rep from * to last 2 sts, sl1, k1.

Row 19: Using B, k1, * [k1, sl1] twice, k8; rep from * to last2 sts, k2.

Row 21: Using A, k1, * [sl1, k1] 3 times, sl1, k5; rep from * to last 2 sts, sl1, k1.

Row 23: Using B, k1, * [k1, sl1] twice, k8; rep from * to last 2 sts, k2.

Rep Rows 1 to 24. To finish, work Rows 25 to 28.

Row 25: As Row 1.

Row 27: Using B, k all sts.

Row 28: As Row 2.

Crochet Instructions

Multiple of 12 sts + 3

Using B, make desired number of chainless sc.

Row 1 (RS): Using A, 1 ch, 1 sc, * [2 ch, skip st, 1 sc] 4 times, 2 ch, skip st, 3 sc; rep from * to last 2 sts, 2 ch, skip st, 1 sc, turn.

Row 2 and all WS rows: 1 ch, 1 sc in sts, ch and skip ch-sps, turn.

Row 3: Using B, 1 ch, 1 sc, * 1 Mdc, 2 ch, skip st, [1 Mdc, 1 sc] twice, 1 Mdc, 2 ch, skip st, 1 Mdc, 3 sc; rep from * to last 2 sts, 1 Mdc, 1 sc, turn.

Row 5: Using A, 1 ch, 1 sc, * 2 ch, skip st, 1 Mdc, 2 ch, skip st, 3 sc, 2 ch, skip st, 1 Mdc, [2 ch, skip st, 1 sc] twice; rep from * to last 2 sts, 2 ch, skip st, 1 sc, turn.

Row 7: Using B, 1 ch, 1 sc, * [1 Mdc, 1 sc] twice, 2 sc, [1 Mdc, 2 ch, skip st] twice, 1 Mdc, 1 sc; rep from * to last 2 sts, 1 Mdc, 1 sc, turn.

Row 9: Using A, 1 ch, 1 sc, * 2 ch, skip st, 5 sc, [2 ch, skip st, 1 Mdc] twice, 2 ch, skip st, 1 sc; rep from * to last 2 sts, 2 ch, skip st, 1 sc, turn.

Row 11: Using B, 1 ch, 1 sc, * 1 Mdc, 5 sc, [1 Mdc, 2 ch, skip st] twice, 1 Mdc, 1 sc; rep from * to last 2 sts, 1 Mdc, 1 sc, turn.

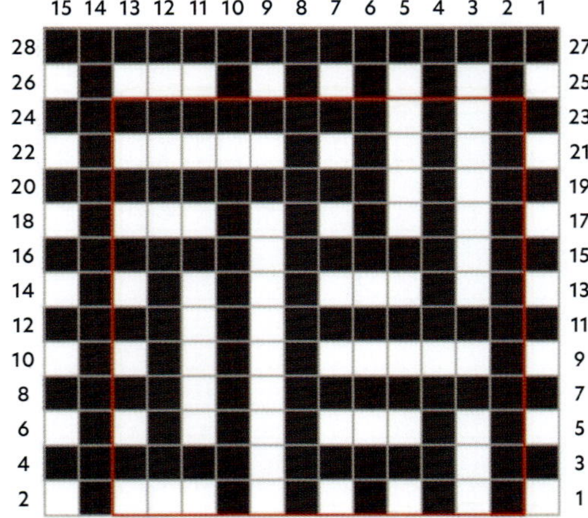

Yarn A = Cream

Yarn B = Gray

TIP: For the crochet version: Crochet stitches are significantly larger than knit ones, resulting in mosaic crochet being a lot bigger. If you would like the design to be smaller, try converting it to overlay mosaic crochet (see page 24) or crochet it in the round, omitting WS rows.

KNIT

CROCHET

Row 13: Using A, 1 ch, 1 sc, * 2 ch, skip st, 1 sc, 2 ch, skip st, 3 sc, [2 ch, skip st, 1 Mdc] twice, 2 ch, skip st, 1 sc; rep from * to last 2 sts, 2 ch, skip st, 1 sc, turn.
Row 15: Using B, 1 ch, 1 sc, * 1 Mdc, 2 ch, skip st, 1 Mdc, 3 sc, 1 Mdc, 2 ch, skip st, [1 Mdc, 1 sc] twice; rep from * to last 2 sts, 1 Mdc, 1 sc, turn.
Row 17: Using A, 1 ch, 1 sc, * 2 ch, skip st, 1 Mdc, [2 ch, skip st, 1 sc] twice, 2 ch, skip st, 1 Mdc, 2 ch, skip st, 3 sc; rep from * to last 2 sts, 2 ch, skip st, 1 sc, turn.
Row 19: Using B, 1 ch, 1 sc, * [1 Mdc, 2 ch, skip st] twice, [1 Mdc, 1 sc] twice, 1 Mdc, 3 sc; rep from * to last 2 sts, 1 Mdc, 1 sc, turn.
Row 21: Using A, 1 ch, 1 sc, * [2 ch, skip st, 1 Mdc] twice, 2 ch, skip st, 1 sc, 2 ch, skip st, 5 sc; rep from * to last 2 sts, 2 ch, skip st, 1 sc, turn.
Row 23: Using B, 1 ch, 1 sc, * [1 Mdc, 2 ch, skip st] twice, 1 Mdc, 1 sc, 1 Mdc, 5 sc; rep from * to last 2 sts, 1 Mdc, 1 sc, turn.
Rep Rows 1 to 24, placing 1 Mdc in sps as required on Row 1. To finish, work Rows 25 to 27.
Row 25: Using A, 1 ch, 1 sc, * [2 ch, skip st, 1 Mdc] twice, [2 ch, skip st, 1 sc] twice, 2 ch, skip st, 3 sc; rep from * to last 2 sts, 2 ch, skip st, 1 sc, turn.
Row 27: Using B, 1 ch, 1 sc, * [1 Mdc, 1 dc] 5 times, 2 sc; rep from * to last 2 sts, 1 Mdc, 1 sc, turn.

Wonder

An eye-catching design that creates an optical illusion. Ideal for a panel, but it will also look beautiful in vertical repeats. Great for adding interest to plain garments.

Knit Instructions

Multiple of 12 sts + 5

On RS rows, slip the sts purlwise with yarn in the back.

Cast on using B, k one row and p one row.

Row 1 (RS): Using A, k1, sl1, k1, * sl1, k3, sl3, k3, sl1, k1; rep from * to last 2 sts, sl1, k1.

Row 2 and all WS rows: P the knitted sts and sl the slipped sts purlwise with yarn in the front.

Row 3: Using B, k3, * k1, sl1, k7, sl1, k2; rep from * to last 2 sts, k2.

Row 5: Using A, k2, sl1, * k2, sl1, k5, sl1, k2, sl1; rep from * to last 2 sts, k2.

Row 7: Using B, k1, sl1, k1, * sl1, k2, sl1, k3, sl1, k2, sl1, k1; rep from * to last 2 sts, sl1, k1.

Row 9: Using A, k3, * k1, sl1, k2, sl1, k1, [sl1, k2] twice; rep from * to last 2 sts, k2.

Row 11: Using B, k2, sl1, * [k2, sl1] 4 times; rep from * to last 2 sts, k2.

Row 13: Using A, k1, sl1, k1, * [sl1, k2] twice, k1, sl1, k2, sl1, k1; rep from * to last 2 sts, sl1, k1.

Row 15: Using B, k2, sl1, * k1, sl1, k2, sl1, k1, sl1, k2, sl1, k1, sl1; rep from * to last 2 sts, k2.

Row 17: Using A, k1, sl1, k1, * [sl1, k1] twice, k1, sl1, k2, [sl1, k1] twice; rep from * to last 2 sts, sl1, k1.

Row 19: Using B, k2, sl1, * [k1, sl1] twice, k3, [sl1, k1] twice, sl1; rep from * to last 2 sts, k2.

Row 21: Using A, k1, sl1, k1, * sl1, k1; rep from * to last 2 sts, sl1, k1.

Row 23: Using B, k2, sl1, * k1, sl1; rep from * to last 2 sts, k2.

Row 25: As Row 21.

Row 27: As Row 19.

Row 29: As Row 17.

Row 31: As Row 15.

Row 33: As Row 13.

Row 35: As Row 11.

Row 37: As Row 9.

Row 39: As Row 7.

Row 41: As Row 5.

Row 43: As Row 3.

Rep Rows 1 to 44. To finish, work Rows 45 to 48.

Row 45: As Row 1.

Row 47: Using B, k all sts.

Row 48: As Row 2.

MOSAIC CHART

17 16 15 14 13 12 11 10 9 8 7 6 5 4 3 2 1

12 sts

Yarn A = Cream

Yarn B = Dark pink

Crochet Instructions

Multiple of 12 sts + 5

Using B, make desired number of chainless sc.

Row 1 (RS): Using A, 1 ch, 1 sc, 2 ch, skip st, 1 sc, * 2 ch, skip st, 3 sc, 4 ch, skip 3 sts, 3 sc, 2 ch, skip st, 1 sc; rep from * to last 2 sts, 2 ch, skip st, 1 sc, turn.

Row 2 and all WS rows: 1 ch, 1 sc in sts, ch and skip ch-sps, turn.

Row 3: Using B, 1 ch, 1 sc, 1 Mdc, 1 sc, * 1 Mdc, 2 ch, skip st, 2 sc, 3 Mdc, 2 sc, 2 ch, skip st, 1 Mdc, 1 sc; rep from * to last 2 sts, 1 Mdc, 1 sc, turn.

Row 5: Using A, 1 ch, 2 sc, 2 ch, skip st, * 1 sc, 1 Mdc, 2 ch, skip st, 5 sc, 2 ch, skip st, 1 Mdc, 1 sc, 2 ch, skip st; rep from * to last 2 sts, 2 sc, turn.

Row 7: Using B, 1 ch, 1 sc, 2 ch, skip st, 1 Mdc, * 2 ch, skip st, 1 sc, 1 Mdc, 2 ch, skip st, 3 sc, 2 ch, skip st, 1 Mdc, 1 sc, 2 ch, skip st, 1 Mdc; rep from * to last 2 sts, 2 ch, skip st, 1 sc, turn.

Row 9: Using A, 1 ch, 1 sc, 1 Mdc, 1 sc, * 1 Mdc, 2 ch, skip st, 1 sc, 1 Mdc, 2 ch,

KNIT

CROCHET

skip st, 1 sc, [2 ch, skip st, 1 Mdc, 1 sc] twice; rep from * to last 2 sts, 1 Mdc, 1 sc, turn.
Row 11: Using B, 1 ch, 2 sc, 2 ch, skip st, * [1 sc, 1 Mdc, 2 ch, skip st] twice, [1 Mdc, 1 sc, 2 ch, skip st] twice; rep from * to last 2 sts, 2 sc, turn.
Row 13: Using A, 1 ch, 1 sc, 2 ch, skip st, 1 Mdc, * [2 ch, skip st, 1 sc, 1 Mdc] twice, [1 sc, 2 ch, skip st, 1 Mdc] twice; rep from * to last 2 sts, 2 ch, skip st, 1 sc, turn.
Row 15: Using B, 1 ch, 1 sc, 1 Mdc, 2 ch, skip st, * 1 Mdc, 2 ch, skip st, 1 sc, 1 Mdc, 2 ch, skip st, 1 sc, 2 ch, skip st, 1 Mdc, 1 sc, 2 ch, skip st, 1 Mdc, 2 ch, skip st; rep from * to last 2 sts, 1 Mdc, 1 sc, turn.
Row 17: Using A, 1 ch, 1 sc, 2 ch, skip st, 1 Mdc, * 2 ch, skip st, 1 Mdc, 2 ch, skip st, 1 sc, 1 Mdc, 2 ch, skip st, 1 Mdc, 1 sc, [2 ch, skip st, 1 Mdc] twice; rep from * to last 2 sts, 2 ch, skip st, 1 sc, turn.
Row 19: Using B, 1 ch, 1 sc, 1 Mdc, 2 ch, skip st, * [1 Mdc, 2 ch, skip st] twice, 1 sc, 1 Mdc, 1 sc, [2 ch, skip st, 1 Mdc] twice, 2 ch, skip st; rep from * to last 2 sts, 1 Mdc, 1 sc, turn.
Row 21: Using A, 1 ch, 1 sc, 2 ch, skip st, 1 Mdc, * [2 ch, skip st, 1 Mdc] twice, 2 ch, skip st, 1 sc, [2 ch, skip st, 1 Mdc] 3 times; rep from * to last 2 sts, 2 ch, skip st, 1 sc, turn.
Row 23: Using B, 1 ch, 1 sc, 1 Mdc, 2 ch, skip st, * [1 Mdc, 2 ch, skip st] 6 times; rep from * to last 2 sts, 1 Mdc, 1 sc, turn.
Row 25: Using A, 1 ch, 1 sc, 2 ch, skip st, 1 Mdc, * [2 ch, skip st, 1 Mdc] 6 times; rep from * to last 2 sts, 2 ch, skip st, 1 sc, turn.
Row 27: Using B, 1 ch, 1 sc, 1 Mdc, 2 ch, skip st, * [1 Mdc, 2 ch, skip st] twice, 1 Mdc, 1 sc, 1 Mdc, [2 ch, skip st, 1 Mdc] twice, 2 ch, skip st; rep from * to last 2 sts, 1 Mdc, 1 sc, turn.
Row 29: Using A, 1 ch, 1 sc, 2 ch, skip st, 1 Mdc, * [2 ch, skip st, 1 Mdc] twice, 1 sc, 2 ch, skip st, 1 sc, 1 Mdc, [2 ch, skip st, 1 Mdc] twice; rep from * to last 2 sts, 2 ch, skip st, 1 sc, turn.
Row 31: Using B, 1 ch, 1 sc, 1 Mdc, 2 ch, skip st, * 1 Mdc, 2 ch, skip st, 1 Mdc, 1 sc, 2 ch, skip st, 1 Mdc, 2 ch, skip st, 1 sc, [1 Mdc, 2 ch, skip st] twice; rep from * to last 2 sts, 1 Mdc, 1 sc, turn.
Row 33: Using A, 1 ch, 1 sc, 2 ch, skip st, 1 Mdc, * [2 ch, skip st, 1 Mdc, 1 sc] twice, 1 Mdc, 2 ch, skip st, 1 sc, 1 Mdc, 2 ch, skip st, 1 Mdc; rep from * to last 2 sts, 2 ch, skip st, 1 sc, turn.
Row 35: Using B, 1 ch, 1 sc, 1 Mdc, 2 ch, skip st, * [1 Mdc, 1 sc, 2 ch, skip st] twice, [1 sc, 1 Mdc, 2 ch, skip st] twice; rep from * to last 2 sts, 1 Mdc, 1 sc, turn.
Row 37: Using A, 1 ch, 2 sc, 1 Mdc, * 1 sc, 2 ch, skip st, 1 Mdc, 1 sc, 2 ch, skip st, 1 Mdc, [2 ch, skip st, 1 sc, 1 Mdc] twice; rep from * to last 2 sts, 2 sc, turn.
Row 39: Using B, 1 ch, 1 sc, 2 ch, skip st, 1 sc, * [2 ch, skip st, 1 Mdc, 1 sc] twice, [1 Mdc, 2 ch, skip st, 1 sc] twice; rep from * to last 2 sts, 2 ch, skip st, 1 sc, turn.
Row 41: Using A, 1 ch, 1 sc, 1 Mdc, 2 ch, skip st, * 1 Mdc, 1 sc, 2 ch, skip st, 1 Mdc, 3 sc, 1 Mdc, 2 ch, skip st, 1 sc, 1 Mdc, 2 ch, skip st; rep from * to last 2 sts, 1 Mdc, 1 sc, turn.
Row 43: Using B, 1 ch, 2 sc, 1 Mdc, * 1 sc, 2 ch, skip st, 1 Mdc, 5 sc, 1 Mdc, 2 ch, skip st, 1 sc, 1 Mdc; rep from * to last 2 sts, 2 sc, turn.
Rep Rows 1 to 44, placing 1 Mdc in sps as required on Row 1. To finish, work Rows 45 to 47.
Row 45: Using A, 1 ch, 1 sc, 2 ch, skip st, 1 sc, * 2 ch, skip st, 1 Mdc, 2 sc, 4 ch, skip 3 sts, 2 sc, 1 Mdc, 2 ch, skip st, 1 sc; rep from * to last 2 sts, 2 ch, skip st, 1 sc, turn.
Row 47: Using B, 1 ch, 1 sc, 1 Mdc, 1 sc, * 1 Mdc, 3 sc, 3 Mdc, 3 sc, 1 Mdc, 1 sc; rep from * to last 2 sts, 1 Mdc, 1 sc, turn.

Sweetheart

A striking pattern that requires a minimum of two repeats horizontally and vertically. This pattern will work well on a number of projects, particularly a garment large enough to showcase it.

Knit Instructions

Multiple of 16 sts + 5

On RS rows, slip the sts purlwise with yarn in the back.

Cast on using A, k one row and p one row.

Row 1 (RS): Using B, k1, sl1, * sl1, k15; rep from * to last 3 sts, sl2, k1.

Row 2 and all WS rows: P the knitted sts and sl the slipped sts purlwise with yarn in the front.

Row 3: Using A, k2, * k3, [sl1, k1] 6 times, k1; rep from * to last 3 sts, k3.

Row 5: Using B, k2, * k2, sl1, k11, sl1, k1; rep from * to last 3 sts, k3.

Row 7: Using A, k1, sl1, * k1, sl1, k3, [sl1, k1] 4 times, k2, sl1; rep from * to last 3 sts, k1, sl1, k1.

Row 9: Using B, k2, * k4, sl1, k7, sl1, k3; rep from * to last 3 sts, k3.

Row 11: Using A, k1, sl1, * [k1, sl1] twice, k3, [sl1, k1] twice, k2, sl1, k1, sl1; rep from * to last 3 sts, k1, sl1, k1.

Row 13: Using B, k2, * k6, sl1, k3, sl1, k5; rep from * to last 3 sts, k3.

Row 15: Using A, k1, sl1, * [k1, sl1] 3 times, k5, [sl1, k1] twice, sl1; rep from * to last 3 sts, k1, sl1, k1.

Row 17: Using B, k2, * k8, sl1, k7; rep from * to last 3 sts, k3.

Row 19: As Row 15.

Row 21: As Row 13.

Row 23: As Row 11.

Row 25: As Row 9.

Row 27: As Row 7.

Row 29: As Row 5.

Row 31: As Row 3.

Rep Rows 1 to 32. To finish, work Rows 33 to 36.

Row 33: As Row 1.

Row 35: Using A, k all sts.

Row 36: As Row 2.

Crochet Instructions

Multiple of 16 sts + 5

Pattern note: The repeat in the written instructions differs from the chart on Rows 1 and 33.

Using A, make desired number of chainless sc.

Row 1 (RS): Using B, 1 ch, 1 sc, 3 ch, skip 2 sts, * 15 sc, ** 2 ch, skip st; rep from * to last st, ending last rep at **, 3 ch, skip 2 sts, 1 sc, turn.

Row 2 and all WS rows: 1 ch, 1 sc in sts, ch and skip ch-sps, turn.

Row 3: Using A, 1 ch, 1 sc, 1 Mdc, * 1 Mdc, 2 sc, [2 ch, skip st, 1 sc] 6 times, 1 sc; rep from * to last 3 sts, 2 Mdc, 1 sc, turn.

Row 5: Using B, 1 ch, 2 sc, * 2 sc, 2 ch, skip st, [1 Mdc, 1 sc] 5 times, 1 Mdc, 2 ch, skip st, 1 sc; rep from * to last 3 sts, 3 sc, turn.

Row 7: Using A, 1 ch, 1 sc, 2 ch, skip st, * 1 sc, 2 ch, skip st, 1 Mdc, 2 sc, [2 ch, skip st, 1 sc] 4 times, 1 sc, 1 Mdc, 2 ch, skip st; rep from * to last 3 sts, 1 sc, 2 ch, skip st, 1 sc, turn.

Row 9: Using B, 1 ch, 1 sc, 1 Mdc, * 1 sc, 1 Mdc, 2 sc, 2 ch, skip st, [1 Mdc, 1 sc] 3 times, 1 Mdc, 2 ch, skip st, 2 sc, 1 Mdc; rep from * to last 3 sts, 1 sc, 1 Mdc, 1 sc, turn.

Row 11: Using A, 1 ch, 1 sc, 2 ch, skip st, * [1 sc, 2 ch, skip st] twice, 1 Mdc, 2 sc, [2 ch, skip st, 1 sc] twice, 1 sc, 1 Mdc, 2 ch, skip st, 1 sc, 2 ch, skip st; rep from * to last 3 sts, 1 sc, 2 ch, skip st, 1 sc, turn.

Row 13: Using B, 1 ch, 1 sc, 1 Mdc, * [1 sc, 1 Mdc] twice, 2 sc, 2 ch, skip st, 1 Mdc, 1 sc, 1 Mdc, 2 ch, skip st, 2 sc, 1 Mdc, 1 sc, 1 Mdc; rep from * to last 3 sts, 1 sc, 1 Mdc, 1 sc, turn.

Row 15: Using A, 1 ch, 1 sc, 2 ch, skip st,

MOSAIC CHART

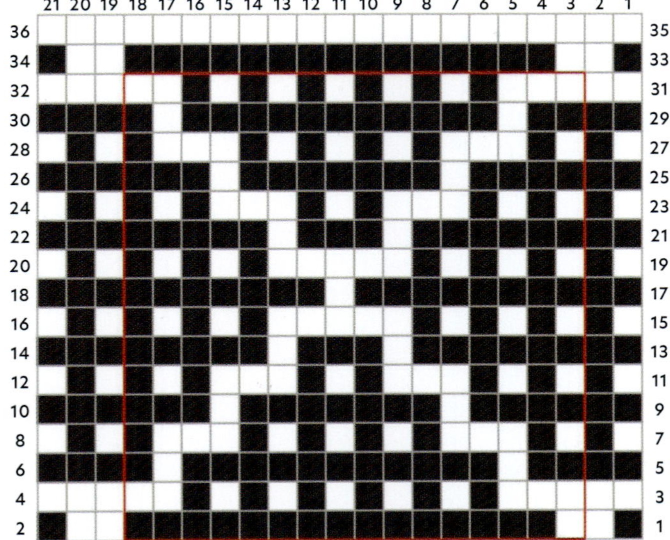

Yarn A = Cream

Yarn B = Pale pink

16 sts

* [1 sc, 2 ch, skip st] 3 times, 1 Mdc, 3 sc, 1 Mdc, [2 ch, skip st, 1 sc] twice, 2 ch, skip st; rep from * to last 3 sts, 1 sc, 2 ch, skip st, 1 sc, turn.

Row 17: Using B, 1 ch, 1 sc, 1 Mdc, * [1 sc, 1 Mdc] 3 times, 2 sc, 2 ch, skip st, 2 sc, [1 Mdc, 1 sc] twice, 1 Mdc; rep from * to last 3 sts, 1 sc, 1 Mdc, 1 sc, turn.

Row 19: Using A, 1 ch, 1 sc, 2 ch, skip st, * [1 sc, 2 ch, skip st] 3 times, 2 sc, 1 Mdc, 2 sc, [2 ch, skip st, 1 sc] twice, 2 ch, skip st; rep from * to last 3 sts, 1 sc, 2 ch, skip st, 1 sc, turn.

Row 21: Using B, 1 ch, 1 sc, 1 Mdc, * [1 sc, 1 Mdc] 3 times, 2 ch, skip st, 3 sc, 2 ch, skip st, [1 Mdc, 1 sc] twice, 1 Mdc; rep from * to last 3 sts, 1 sc, 1 Mdc, 1 sc, turn.

Row 23: Using A, 1 ch, 1 sc, 2 ch, skip st, * [1 sc, 2 ch, skip st] twice, 2 sc, 1 Mdc, 2 ch, skip st, 1 sc, 2 ch, skip st, 1 Mdc, 2 sc, 2 ch, skip st, 1 sc, 2 ch, skip st; rep from * to last 3 sts, 1 sc, 2 ch, skip st, 1 sc, turn.

Row 25: Using B, 1 ch, 1 sc, 1 Mdc, * [1 sc, 1 Mdc] twice, 2 ch, skip st, 2 sc, 1 Mdc, 1 sc, 1 Mdc, 2 sc, 2 ch, skip st, 1 Mdc, 1 sc, 1 Mdc; rep from * to last 3 sts, 1 sc, 1 Mdc, 1 sc, turn.

Row 27: Using A, 1 ch, 1 sc, 2 ch, skip st, * 1 sc, 2 ch, skip st, 2 sc, 1 Mdc, [2 ch, skip st, 1 sc] 3 times, 2 ch, skip st, 1 Mdc, 2 sc, 2 ch, skip st; rep from * to last 3 sts, 1 sc, 2 ch, skip st, 1 sc, turn.

Row 29: Using B, 1 ch, 1 sc, 1 Mdc, * 1 sc, 1 Mdc, 2 ch, skip st, 2 sc, [1 Mdc, 1 sc] 4 times, 1 sc, 2 ch, skip st, 1 Mdc; rep from * to last 3 sts, 1 sc, 1 Mdc, 1 sc, turn.

Row 31: Using A, 1 ch, 2 sc, * 2 sc, 1 Mdc, [2 ch, skip st, 1 sc] 5 times, 2 ch, skip st, 1 Mdc, 1 sc; rep from * to last 3 sts, 3 sc, turn.

Rep Rows 1 to 32, placing 1 Mdc in sps as required on Row 1. To finish, work Rows 33 to 35.

Row 33: Using B, 1 ch, 1 sc, 3 ch, skip 2 sts, * 2 sc, [1 Mdc, 1 sc] 6 times, 1 sc, ** 2 ch, skip st; rep from * to last 3 sts, ending last rep at **, 3 ch, skip 2 sts, 1 sc, turn.

Row 35: Using A, 1 ch, 1 sc, 1 Mdc, * 1 Mdc, 15 sc; rep from * to last 3 sts, 2 Mdc, 1 sc, turn.

KNIT

CROCHET

Spike

This simple but effective design would work on a small accessory like a hat but also over a large surface on a blanket. It would also look great on a pillow; the choice is yours.

Knit Instructions

Multiple of 2 sts + 3

On RS rows, slip the sts purlwise with yarn in the back.

Cast on with A, k one row and p one row.

Row 1 (RS): Using B, k1, * k1, sl1; rep from * to last 2 sts, k2.

Row 2 and all WS rows: P the knitted sts and sl the slipped sts purlwise with yarn in the front.

Row 3: Using A, k1, * sl1, k1; rep from * to last 2 sts, sl1, k1.

Row 5: Using B, k all sts.

Row 7: As Row 3.

Row 9: Using B, k all sts.

Row 11: As Row 3.

Row 13: As Row 1.

Rep Rows 3 to 14. To finish, work Rows 15 to 16.

Row 15: Using A, k all sts.

Row 16: As Row 2.

Crochet Instructions

Multiple of 2 sts + 3

Using A, make desired number of chainless sc.

Row 1 (RS): Using B, 1 ch, 1 sc, * 1 sc, 2 ch, skip st; rep from * to last 2 sts, 2 sc, turn.

Row 2 and all WS rows: 1 ch, 1 sc in sts, ch and skip ch-sps, turn.

Row 3: Using A, 1 ch, 1 sc, * 2 ch, skip st, 1 Mdc; rep from * to last 2 sts, 2 ch, skip st, 1 sc, turn.

Row 5: Using B, 1 ch, 1 sc, * 1 Mdc, 1 sc; rep from * to last 2 sts, 1 Mdc, 1 sc, turn.

Row 7: Using A, 1 ch, 1 sc, * 2 ch, skip st, 1 sc; rep from * to last 2 sts, 2 ch, skip st, 1 sc, turn.

Row 9: Using B, 1 ch, 1 sc, * 1 Mdc, 1 sc; rep from * to last 2 sts, 1 Mdc, 1 sc, turn.

Row 11: Using A, 1 ch, 1 sc, * 2 ch, skip st, 1 sc; rep from * to last 2 sts, 2 ch, skip st, 1 sc, turn.

Row 13: Using B, 1 ch, 1 sc, * 1 Mdc, 2 ch, skip st; rep from * to last 2 sts, 1 Mdc, 1 sc, turn.

Rep Rows 3 to 14. To finish, work Row 15.

Row 15: Using A, 1 ch, 1 sc, * 1 sc, 1 Mdc; rep from * to last 2 sts, 2 sc, turn.

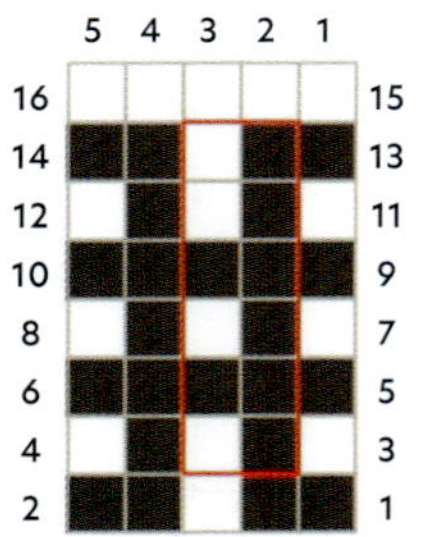

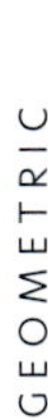

Lines

Another versatile pattern that could be featured on a dress or a home accessory. It will work with both small and large repeats.

Knit Instructions

Multiple of 4 sts + 3

On RS rows, slip the sts purlwise with yarn in the back.

Cast on using A, k one row and p one row.

Row 1 (RS): Using B, k1, sl1, * k3, sl1; rep from * to last st, k1.

Row 2 and all WS rows: P the knitted sts and sl the slipped sts purlwise with yarn in the front.

Row 3: Using A, k2, * k1, sl1, k2; rep from * to last st, k1.

Row 5: Using B, k1, sl1, * k3, sl1; rep from * to last st, k1.

Row 7: Using A, k2, * k1, sl1, k2; rep from * to last st, k1.

Row 8: As Row 2.

Rep Rows 1 to 8. To finish, using A, work Row 7 by k all sts, and Row 8 by p all sts.

Crochet Instructions

Multiple of 4 sts + 3

Using A, make desired number of chainless sc.

Row 1 (RS): Using B, 1 ch, 1 sc, 2 ch, skip st, * 3 sc, 2 ch, skip st; rep from * to last st, 1 sc, turn.

Row 2 and all WS rows: 1 ch, 1 sc in sts, ch and skip ch-sps, turn.

Row 3: Using A, 1 ch, 1 sc, 1 Mdc, * 1 sc, 2 ch, skip st, 1 sc, 1 Mdc; rep from * to last st, 1 sc, turn.

Row 5: Using B, 1 ch, 1 sc, 2 ch, skip st, * 1 sc, 1 Mdc, 1 sc, 2 ch, skip st; rep from * to last st, 1 sc, turn.

Row 7: Using A, 1 ch, 1 sc, 1 Mdc, * 1 sc, 2 ch, skip st, 1 sc, 1 Mdc; rep from * to last st, 1 sc, turn.

Row 8: As Row 2.

Rep Rows 1 to 8, placing 1 Mdc in sps as required on Row 1. End last rep with Row 7 as follows: Using A, sc in every st and Mdc in every ch-sp.

MOSAIC CHART

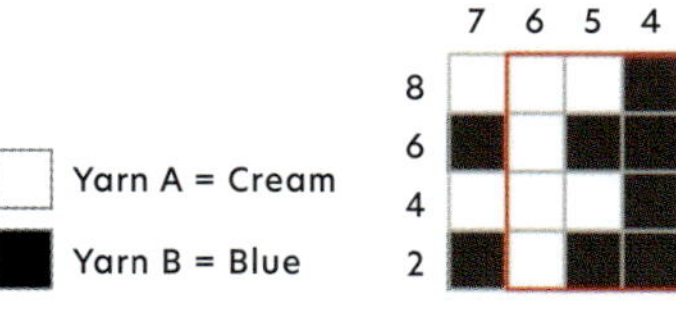

Aztec

Aztec 1

The Aztec designs in this chapter are designed to be stacked on top of one another. You could use this spiral with a selection of others from the chapter to make a blanket or Afghan.

Knit Instructions

Multiple of 5 sts +3

On RS rows, slip the sts purlwise with yarn in the back.

Cast on using A, k one row and p one row.

Row 1 (RS): Using B, k all sts.

Row 2 and all WS rows: P the knitted sts and sl the slipped sts purlwise with yarn in the front.

Row 3: Using A, k2, * sl1, k4; rep from * to last st, k1.

Row 5: Using B, k1, sl1, * k1, sl1, k2, sl1; rep from * to last st, k1.

Row 7: Using A, k2, * sl1, k2, sl1, k1; rep from * to last st, k1.

Row 9: Using B, k1, sl1, * k4, sl1; rep from * to last st, k1.

Row 11: Using A, k all sts.

Row 12: As Row 2.

Rep Rows 1 to 12.

MOSAIC CHART

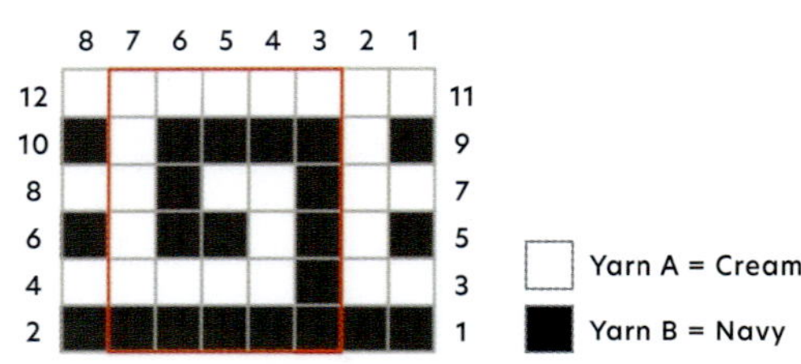

5 sts

Crochet Instructions

Multiple of 5 sts + 3

Using A, make desired number of chainless sc.

Row 1 (RS): Using B, 1 ch, 1 sc in every st to end, turn.

Row 2 and all WS rows: 1 ch, 1 sc in sts, ch and skip ch-sps, turn.

Row 3: Using A, 1 ch, 2 sc, * 2 ch, skip st, 4 sc; rep from * to last st, 1 sc, turn.

Row 5: Using B, 1 ch, 1 sc, 2 ch, skip st, * 1 Mdc, 2 ch, skip st, 2 sc, 2 ch, skip st; rep from * to last st, 1 sc, turn.

Row 7: Using A, 1 ch, 1 sc, 1 Mdc, * 2 ch, skip st, 1 Mdc, 1 sc, 2 ch, skip st, 1 Mdc; rep from * to last st, 1 sc, turn.

Row 9: Using B, 1 ch, 1 sc, 2 ch, skip st, * 1 Mdc, 2 sc, 1 Mdc, 2 ch, skip st; rep from * to last st, 1 sc, turn.

Row 11: Using A, 1 ch, 1 sc, 1 Mdc, * 4 sc, 1 Mdc; rep from * to last st, 1 sc, turn.

Row 12: As Row 2.

Rep Rows 1 to 12, ending last rep with Row 11.

Aztec 2

Aztec designs are typically geometric shapes, recurring in long, symmetrical lines. As well as being stackable they could be used in decorative borders. This spiral would be perfect for a blanket border.

Knit Instructions

Multiple of 8 sts +3

On RS rows, slip the sts purlwise with yarn in the back.

Cast on using A, k one row and p one row.

Row 1 (RS): Using B, k2, * k6, sl1, k1; rep from * to last st, k1.

Row 2 and all WS rows: P the knitted sts and sl the slipped sts purlwise with yarn in the front.

Row 3: Using A, k1, sl1, * k5, sl1, k1, sl1; rep from * to last st, k1.

Row 5: Using B, k2, * sl1, k3, [sl1, k1] twice; rep from * to last st, k1.

Row 7: Using A, k1, sl1, * k1, sl; rep from * to last st, k1.

Row 9: Using B, k2, * [sl1, k1] twice, k2, sl1, k1; rep from * to last st, k1.

Row 11: Using A, k1, sl1, * k1, sl1, k5, sl1; rep from * to last st, k1.

Row 13: Using B, k2, * sl1, k7; rep from * to last st, k1.

Row 15: Using A, k all sts.

Row 16: As Row 2.

Rep Rows 1 to 16.

Crochet Instructions

Multiple of 8 sts + 3

Using A, make desired number of chainless sc.

Row 1 (RS): Using B, 1 ch, 2 sc, * 6 sc, 2 ch, skip st, 1 sc; rep from * to last st, 1 sc, turn.

Row 2 and all WS rows: 1 ch, 1 sc in sts, ch and skip ch-sps, turn.

Row 3: Using A, 1 ch, 1 sc, 2 ch, skip st, * 5 sc, 2 ch, skip st, 1 Mdc, 2 ch, skip st; rep from * to last st, 1 sc, turn.

Row 5: Using B, 1 ch, 1 sc, 1 Mdc, * 2 ch, skip st, 3 sc, [2 ch, skip st, 1 Mdc] twice; rep from * to last st, 1 sc, turn.

Row 7: Using A, 1 ch, 1 sc, 2 ch, skip st, * 1 Mdc, 2 ch, skip st, 1 sc, [2 ch, skip st, 1 Mdc] twice, 2 ch, skip st; rep from * to last st, 1 sc, turn.

Row 9: Using B, 1 ch, 1 sc, 1 Mdc, * [2 ch, skip st, 1 Mdc] twice, 1 sc, 1 Mdc, 2 ch, skip st, 1 Mdc; rep from * to last st, 1 sc, turn.

Row 11: Using A, 1 ch, 1 sc, 2 ch, skip st, * 1 Mdc, 2 ch, skip st, 1 Mdc, 3 sc, 1 Mdc, 2 ch, skip st; rep from * to last st, 1 sc, turn.

Row 13: Using B, 1 ch, 1 sc, 1 Mdc, * 2 ch, skip st, 1 Mdc, 5 sc, 1 Mdc; rep from * to last st, 1 sc, turn.

Row 15: Using A, 1 ch, 2 sc, * 1 Mdc, 7 sc; rep from * to last st, 1 sc, turn.

Row 16: As Row 2.

Rep Rows 1 to 16, ending last rep with Row 15.

Yarn A = Cream

Yarn B = Navy

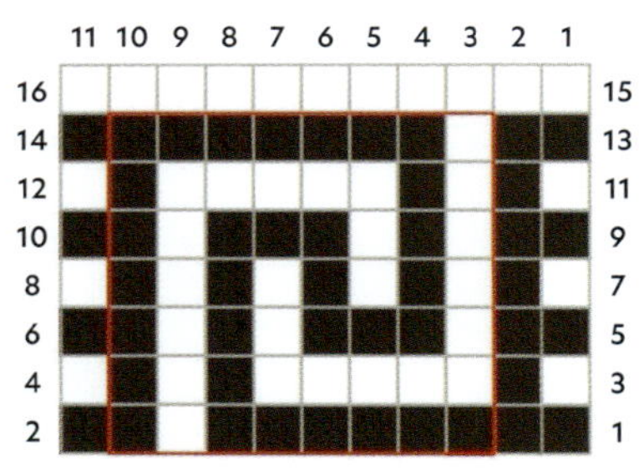

Aztec 3

The knit version of this pattern is less elongated than the crochet, but both would combine beautifully with the spiral patterns (Aztec 1 and 2).

Knit Instructions

Multiple of 10 sts + 2
On RS rows, slip the sts purlwise with yarn in the back.
Cast on using A, k one row and p one row.
Row 1 (RS): Using B, k1, * k2, sl1, k2, sl2, k1, sl2; rep from * to last st, k1.
Row 2 and all WS rows: P the knitted sts and sl the slipped sts purlwise with yarn in the front.
Row 3: Using A, k1, * sl2, k1, sl2, k2, sl1, k2; rep from * to last st, k1.
Row 5: Using B, k1, * k5, sl1, k3, sl1; rep from * to last st, k1.
Row 7: Using A, k1, * k1, sl3, k2, sl3, k1; rep from * to last st, k1.
Row 9: Using B, k1, * sl1, k3, sl1, k5; rep from * to last st, k1.
Row 11: Using A, k1, * k2, sl1, k2, sl2, k1, sl2; rep from * to last st, k1.
Row 13: Using B, k1, * sl2, k1, sl2, k2, sl1, k2; rep from * to last st, k1.
Row 15: Using A, k all sts.
Row 17: Using B, k1, * k1, sl3, k1, sl2, k1, sl2; rep from * to last st, k1.
Row 19: As Row 15.
Row 21: As Row 13.
Row 23: As Row 11.
Row 25: As Row 9.
Row 27: As Row 7.
Row 29: As Row 5.
Row 31: As Row 3.
Row 33: As Row 1.
Row 35: Using A, k all sts.
Row 36: As Row 2.
Rep Rows 1 to 36.

Crochet Instructions

Multiple of 10 sts + 2
Using A, make desired number of chainless sc.
Row 1 (RS): Using B, 1 ch, 1 sc, * 2 sc, 2 ch, skip st, 2 sc, 3 ch, skip 2 sts, 1 sc, 3 ch, skip 2 sts; rep from * to last st, 1 sc, turn.
Row 2 and all WS rows: 1 ch, 1 sc in sts, ch and skip ch-sps, turn.
Row 3: Using A, 1 ch, 1 sc, * 3 ch, skip 2 sts, 1 Mdc, 3 ch, skip 2 sts, 2 Mdc, 2 ch, skip st, 2 Mdc; rep from * to last st, 1 sc, turn.
Row 5: Using B, 1 ch, 1 sc, * 2 Mdc, 1 sc, 2 Mdc, 2 ch, skip st, 1 sc, 1 Mdc, 1 sc, 2 ch, skip st; rep from * to last st, 1 sc, turn.
Row 7: Using A, 1 ch, 1 sc, * 1 sc, 4 ch, skip 3 sts, 1 sc, 1 Mdc, 4 ch, skip 3 sts, 1 Mdc; rep from * to last st, 1 sc, turn.
Row 9: Using B, 1 ch, 1 sc, * 2 ch, skip st, 3 Mdc, 2 ch, skip st, 1 sc, 3 Mdc, 1 sc; rep from * to last st, 1 sc, turn.
Row 11: Using A, 1 ch, 1 sc, * 1 Mdc, 1 sc, 2 ch, skip st, 1 sc, 1 Mdc, 3 ch, skip 2 sts, 1 sc, 3 ch, skip 2 sts; rep from * to last st, 1 sc, turn.
Row 13: Using B, 1 ch, 1 sc, * 3 ch, skip 2 sts, 1 Mdc, 3 ch, skip 2 sts, 2 Mdc, 2 ch, skip st, 2 Mdc; rep from * to last st, 1 sc, turn.
Row 15: Using A, 1 ch, 1 sc, * 2 Mdc,

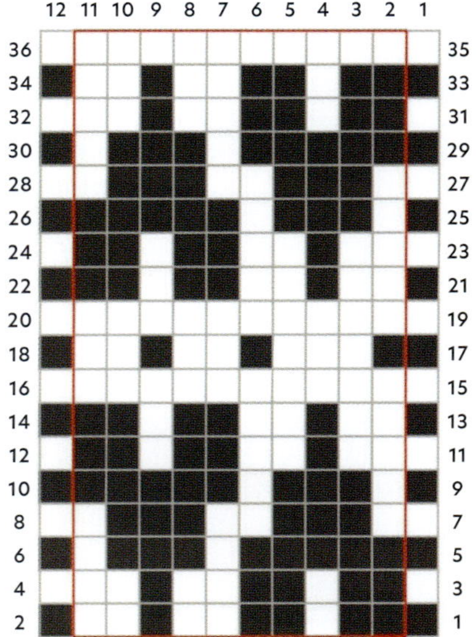

Yarn A = Cream
Yarn B = Burgundy

CROCHET

1 sc, 2 Mdc, 2 sc, 1 Mdc, 2 sc; rep from * to last st, 1 sc, turn.

Row 17: Using B, 1 ch, 1 sc, * 1 sc, 4 ch, skip 3 sts, 1 sc, 3 ch, skip 2 sts, 1 sc, 3 ch, skip 2 sts; rep from * to last st, 1 sc, turn.

Row 19: Using A, 1 ch, 1 sc, * 1 sc, 3 Mdc, 1 sc, 2 Mdc, 1 sc, 2 Mdc; rep from * to last st, 1 sc, turn.

Row 21: Using B, 1 ch, 1 sc, * 3 ch, skip 2 sts, 1 sc, 3 ch, skip 2 sts, 2 sc, 2 ch, skip st, 2 sc; rep from * to last st, 1 sc, turn.

Row 23: Using A, 1 ch, 1 sc, * 2 Mdc, 2 ch, skip st, 2 Mdc, 3 ch, skip 2 sts, 1 Mdc, 3 ch, skip 2 sts; rep from * to last st, 1 sc, turn.

Row 25: Using B, 1 ch, 1 sc, * 2 ch, skip st, 1 sc, 1 Mdc, 1 sc, 2 ch, skip st, 2 Mdc, 1 sc, 2 Mdc; rep from * to last st, 1 sc, turn.

Row 27: Using A, 1 ch, 1 sc, * 1 Mdc, 4 ch, skip 3 sts, 1 Mdc, 1 sc, 4 ch, skip 3 sts, 1 sc; rep from * to last st, 1 sc, turn.

Row 29: Using B, 1 ch, 1 sc, * 1 sc, 3 Mdc, 1 sc, 2 ch, skip st, 3 Mdc, 2 ch, skip st; rep from * to last st, 1 sc, turn.

Row 31: Using A, 1 ch, 1 sc, * 3 ch, skip 2 sts, 1 sc, 3 ch, skip 2 sts, 1 Mdc, 1 sc, 2 ch, skip st, 1 sc, 1 Mdc; rep from * to last st, 1 sc, turn.

Row 33: Using B, 1 ch, 1 sc, * 2 Mdc, 2 ch, skip st, 2 Mdc, 3 ch, skip 2 sts, 1 Mdc, 3 ch, skip 2 sts; rep from * to last st, 1 sc, turn.

Row 35: Using A, 1 ch, 1 sc, * 2 sc, 1 Mdc, 2 sc, 2 Mdc, 1 sc, 2 Mdc; rep from * to last st, 1 sc, turn.

Row 36: As Row 2.

Rep Rows 1 to 36, ending last rep with Row 35.

Aztec 4

The crochet version of this pattern makes for a more elongated and slightly crisper tower. Mix and match with other Aztec motifs in horizontal panels.

Knit Instructions

Multiple of 6 sts + 3

On RS rows, slip the sts purlwise with yarn in the back.

Cast on using B, k one row and p one row.

Row 1 (RS): Using A, k all sts.

Row 2 and all WS rows: P the knitted sts and sl the slipped sts purlwise with yarn in the front.

Row 3: Using B, k2, * sl1, k1; rep from * to last st, k1.

Row 5: Using A, k1, sl1, * k5, sl1; rep from * to last st, k1.

Row 7: Using B, k2, * [k1, sl1] twice, k2; rep from * to last st, k1.

Row 9: Using A, k2, * sl1, k3, sl1, k1; rep from * to last st, k1.

Row 11: Using B, k2, * k2, sl1, k3; rep from * to last st, k1.

Row 13: Using A, k1, sl1, * k1, sl1; rep from * to last st, k1.

Row 15: Using B, k all sts.

Row 16: As Row 2.

Rep Rows 1 to 16.

Crochet Instructions

Multiple of 6 sts + 3

Using B, make desired number of chainless sc.

Row 1 (RS): Using A, 1 ch, 1 sc in every st to end, turn.

Row 2 and all WS rows: 1 ch, 1 sc in sts, ch and skip ch-sps, turn.

Row 3: Using B, 1 ch, 2 sc, * [2 ch, skip st, 1 sc] 3 times; rep from * to last st, 1 sc, turn.

Row 5: Using A, 1 ch, 1 sc, 2 ch, skip st, * [1 Mdc, 1 sc] twice, 1 Mdc, 2 ch, skip st; rep from * to last st, 1 sc, turn.

Row 7: Using B, 1 ch, 1 sc, 1 Mdc, * [1 sc, 2 ch, skip st] twice, 1 sc, 1 Mdc; rep from * to last st, 1 sc, turn.

Row 9: Using A, 1 ch, 2 sc, * 2 ch, skip st, 1 Mdc, 1 sc, 1 Mdc, 2 ch, skip st, 1 sc; rep from * to last st, 1 sc, turn.

Row 11: Using B, 1 ch, 2 sc, * 1 Mdc, 1 sc, 2 ch, skip st, 1 sc, 1 Mdc, 1 sc; rep from * to last st, 1 sc, turn.

Row 13: Using A, 1 ch, 1 sc, 2 ch, skip st, * 1 sc, 2 ch, skip st, 1 Mdc, 2 ch, skip st, 1 sc, 2 ch, skip st; rep from * to last st, 1 sc, turn.

Row 15: Using B, 1 ch, 1 sc, 1 Mdc, * [1 sc, 1 Mdc] 3 times; rep from * to last st, 1 sc, turn.

Row 16: As Row 2.

Rep Rows 1 to 16, ending last rep with Row 15.

MOSAIC CHART

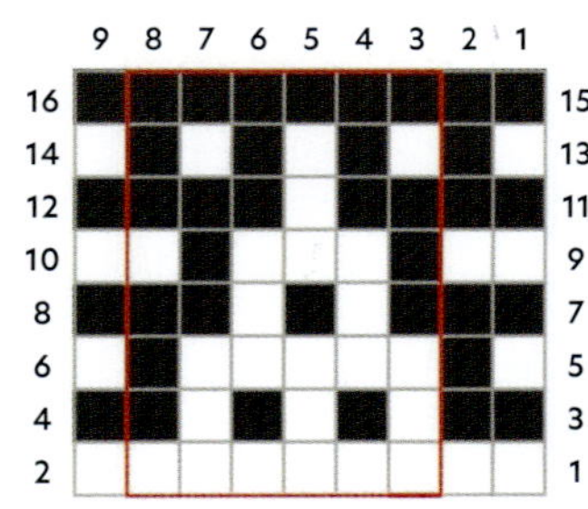

6 sts

Yarn A = Cream

Yarn B = Navy

Aztec 5

Perfect for use in panels or rows, this simple but bold pattern would look great on pillows, bags, or any home accessories.

Knit Instructions

Multiple of 6 sts +3

On RS rows, slip the sts purlwise with yarn in the back.

Cast on using A, k one row and p one row.

Row 1 (RS): Using B, k2, * sl3, k3; rep from * to last st, k1.

Row 2 and all WS rows: P the knitted sts and sl the slipped sts purlwise with yarn in the front.

Row 3: Using A, k1, sl1, * k5, sl1; rep from * to last st, k1.

Row 5: Using B, k2, * k1, sl1, k4; rep from * to last st, k1.

Row 7: Using A, k2, * sl1, k3, sl1, k1; rep from * to last st, k1.

Row 9: Using B, k1, sl1, * k2, sl1; rep from * to last st, k1.

Row 11: Using A, k2, * [k1, sl1] twice, k2; rep from * to last st, k1.

Row 13: Using B, k2, * k4, sl1, k1; rep from * to last st, k1.

Row 15: Using A, k2, * k2, sl1, k3; rep from * to last st, k1.

Row 17: Using B, k1, sl1, * k3, sl3; rep from * to last st, k1.

Row 19: Using A, k all sts.

Row 20: As Row 2.

Rep Rows 1 to 20.

Crochet Instructions

Multiple of 6 sts + 3

Using A, make desired number of chainless sc.

Row 1 (RS): Using B, 1 ch, 2 sc, * 4 ch, skip 3 sts, 3 sc; rep from * to last st, 1 sc, turn.

Row 2 and all WS rows: 1 ch, 1 sc in sts, ch and skip ch-sps, turn.

Row 3: Using A, 1 ch, 1 sc, 2 ch, skip st, * 3 Mdc, 2 sc, 2 ch, skip st; rep from * to last st, 1 sc, turn.

Row 5: Using B, 1 ch, 1 sc, 1 Mdc, * 1 sc, 2 ch, skip st, 3 sc, 1 Mdc; rep from * to last st, 1 sc, turn.

Row 7: Using A, 1 ch, 2 sc, * 2 ch, skip st, 1 Mdc, 2 sc, 2 ch, skip st, 1 sc; rep from * to last st, 1 sc, turn.

Row 9: Using B, 1 ch, 1 sc, 2 ch, skip st, * 1 Mdc, 1 sc, 2 ch, skip st, 1 sc, 1 Mdc, 2 ch, skip st; rep from * to last st, 1 sc, turn.

Row 11: Using A, 1 ch, 1 sc, 1 Mdc, * 1 sc, 2 ch, skip st, 1 Mdc, 2 ch, skip st, 1 sc, 1 Mdc; rep from * to last st, 1 sc, turn.

Row 13: Using B, 1 ch, 2 sc, * [1 sc, 1 Mdc] twice, 2 ch, skip st, 1 sc; rep from * to last st, 1 sc, turn.

Row 15: Using A, 1 ch, 2 sc, * 2 sc, 2 ch, skip st, 1 sc, 1 Mdc, 1 sc; rep from * to last st, 1 sc, turn.

Row 17: Using B, 1 ch, 1 sc, 2 ch, skip st * 2 sc, 1 Mdc, 4 ch, skip 3 sts; rep from * to last st, 1 sc, turn.

Row 19: Using A, 1 ch, 1 sc, 1 Mdc, * 3 sc, 3 Mdc; rep from * to last st, 1 sc, turn.

Row 20: As Row 2.

Rep Rows 1 to 20, ending last rep with Row 19.

MOSAIC CHART

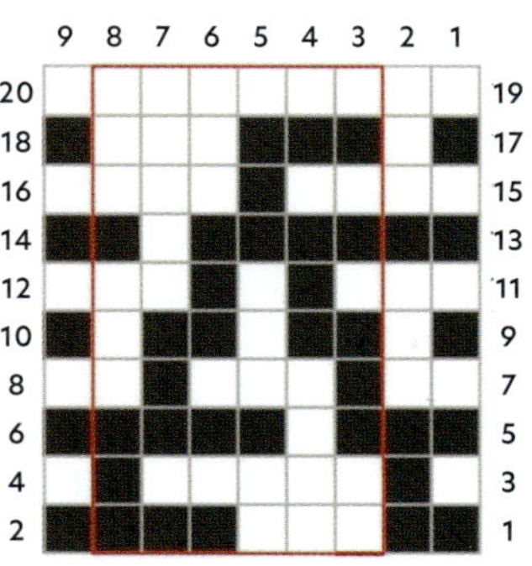

6 sts

Yarn A = Cream

Yarn B = Burgundy

Aztec 6

This bold repeat is larger and more complex than some of the others. It would work well as a stand-alone or in repeats as a panel or large section on a wrap or broad scarf.

Knit Instructions

Multiple of 20 sts + 3

On RS rows, slip the sts purlwise with yarn in the back.

Cast on using A, k one row and p one row.

Row 1 (RS): Using B, k1, * sl1, k1; rep from * to last 2 sts, sl1, k1.

Row 2 and all WS rows: P the knitted sts and sl the slipped sts purlwise with yarn in the front.

Row 3: Using A, k all sts.

Row 5: Using B, k1, * sl1, k9; rep from * to last 2 sts, sl1, k1.

Row 7: Using A, k1, * [k1, sl1] twice, k5, [sl1, k1] twice, k4, sl1, k1, sl1; rep from * to last 2 sts, k2.

Row 9: Using B, k1, * k6, [sl1, k1] twice, k2, [sl1, k1] twice, k4; rep from * to last 2 sts, k2.

Row 11: Using A, k1, * [k1, sl1] 3 times, k3, [sl1, k1] twice, k1, [k1, sl1] 3 times; rep from * to last 2 sts, k2.

Row 13: Using B, k1, * k2, sl1, k5, sl1, k3, sl1, k5, sl1, k1; rep from * to last 2 sts, k2.

Row 15: Using A, k1, * k1, sl1, k3, [sl1, k1] 6 times, k2, sl1; rep from * to last 2 sts, k2.

Row 17: Using B, k1, * k2, sl1, k1, sl1, k11, sl1, k1, sl1, k1; rep from * to last 2 sts, k2.

Row 19: Using A, k1, * k1, sl1, k5, [sl1, k1] 4 times, k4, sl1; rep from * to last 2 sts, k2.

Row 21: As Row 5.

Row 23: As Row 3.

Row 25: As Row 1.

Row 27: Using A, k all sts.

Row 28: As Row 2.

Rep Rows 5 to 28.

Crochet Instructions

Multiple of 20 sts + 3

Using A, make desired number of chainless sc.

Row 1 (RS): Using B, 1 ch, 1 sc, * [2 ch, skip st, 1 sc] 10 times; rep from * to last 2 sts, 2 ch, skip st, 1 sc, turn.

Row 2 and all WS rows: 1 ch, 1 sc in sts, ch and skip ch-sps, turn.

Row 3: Using A, 1 ch, 1 sc, * [1 Mdc, 1 sc] 10 times; rep from * to last 2 sts, 1 Mdc, 1 sc, turn.

Row 5: Using B, 1 ch, 1 sc, * [2 ch, skip st, 9 sc] twice; rep from * to last 2 sts, 2 ch, skip st, 1 sc, turn.

Row 7: Using A, 1 ch, 1 sc, * 1 Mdc, [2 ch, skip st, 1 sc] twice, 4 sc, 2 ch, skip st, 1 Mdc, 2 ch, skip st, 4 sc, [1 sc, 2 ch, skip st] twice; rep from * to last 2 sts, 1 Mdc, 1 sc, turn.

Row 9: Using B, 1 ch, 1 sc, * [1 sc, 1 Mdc] twice, 1 sc, [1 sc, 2 ch, skip st] twice, 1 Mdc, 1 sc, 1 Mdc, [2 ch, skip st, 1 sc] twice, [1 sc, 1 Mdc] twice; rep from * to last 2 sts, 2 sc, turn.

Row 11: Using A, 1 ch, 1 sc, * [1 sc, 2 ch, skip st] 3 times, 1 Mdc, 1 sc, 1 Mdc, 2 ch, skip st, 1 sc, 2 ch, skip st, 1 Mdc, 1 sc,

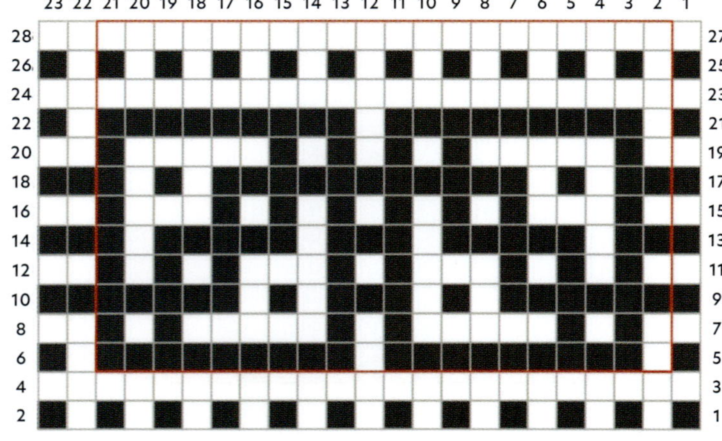

1 Mdc, [2 ch, skip st, 1 sc] twice, 2 ch, skip st; rep from * to last 2 sts, 2 sc, turn.

Row 13: Using B, 1 ch, 1 sc, * 1 sc, 1 Mdc, 2 ch, skip st, [1 Mdc, 1 sc] twice, 1 sc, 2 ch, skip st, 1 Mdc, 1 sc, 1 Mdc, 2 ch, skip st, 1 sc, [1 sc, 1 Mdc] twice, 2 ch, skip st, 1 Mdc; rep from * to last 2 sts, 2 sc, turn.

Row 15: Using A, 1 ch, 1 sc, * 1 sc, 2 ch, skip st, 1 Mdc, 1 sc, [1 sc, 2 ch, skip st] twice, 1 Mdc, 2 ch, skip st, 1 sc, 2 ch, skip st, 1 Mdc, [2 ch, skip st, 1 sc] twice, 1 sc, 1 Mdc, 2 ch, skip st; rep from * to last 2 sts, 2 sc, turn.

Row 17: Using B, 1 ch, 1 sc, * 1 sc, 1 Mdc, 2 ch, skip st, 1 sc, 2 ch, skip st, [1 Mdc, 1 sc] 5 times, 1 Mdc, 2 ch, skip st, 1 sc, 2 ch, skip st, 1 Mdc; rep from * to last 2 sts, 2 sc, turn.

Row 19: Using A, 1 ch, 1 sc, * 1 sc, 2 ch, skip st, 1 Mdc, 1 sc, 1 Mdc, 2 sc, [2 ch, skip st, 1 sc] 4 times, [1 sc, 1 Mdc] twice, 2 ch, skip st; rep from * to last 2 sts, 2 sc, turn.

Row 21: Using B, 1 ch, 1 sc, * 2 ch, skip st, 1 Mdc, 4 sc, [1 sc, 1 Mdc] twice, 2 ch, skip st, [1 Mdc, 1 sc] twice, 4 sc, 1 Mdc; rep from * to last 2 sts, 2 ch, skip st, 1 sc, turn.

Row 23: Using A, 1 ch, 1 sc, * [1 Mdc, 9 sc] twice; rep from * to last 2 sts, 1 Mdc, 1 sc, turn.

Row 25: As Row 1.

Row 27: As Row 3.

Row 28: As Row 2.

Rep Rows 1 to 28, ending last rep with Row 27.

CROCHET

Aztec 7

This crisp, geometric repeat will look best if repeated several times, perhaps on a table runner or other home accessory.

Knit Instructions

Multiple of 10 sts + 5

On RS rows, slip the sts purlwise with yarn in the back.

Cast on using A, k one row and p one row.

Row 1 (RS): Using B, k1, sl1, k1, * sl1, k7, sl1, k1; rep from * to last 2 sts, sl1, k1.

Row 2 and all WS rows: P the knitted sts and sl the slipped sts purlwise with yarn in the front.

Row 3: Using A, k2, sl1, * k1, sl1, k5, sl1, k1, sl1; rep from * to last 2 sts, k2.

Row 5: Using B, k3, * k2, sl1, k3, sl1, k3; rep from * to last 2 sts, k2.

Row 7: Using A, k2, sl1, * k3, sl1, k1, sl1, k3, sl1; rep from * to last 2 sts, k2.

Row 9: Using B, k1, sl1, k1, * [sl1, k3] twice, sl1, k1; rep from * to last 2 sts, sl1, k1.

Row 11: Using A, k3, * k1, sl1, k5, sl1, k2; rep from * to last 2 sts, k2.

Row 13: Using B, k3, * k2, [sl1, k3] twice; rep from * to last 2 sts, k2.

Row 15: Using A, k all sts.

Row 17: As Row 13.

Row 19: As Row 11.

Row 21: As Row 9.

Row 23: As Row 7.

Row 25: As Row 5.

Row 27: As Row 3.

Row 29: As Row 1.

Row 31: Using A, k all sts.

Row 32: As Row 2.

Rep Rows 1 to 32.

Crochet Instructions

Multiple of 10 sts + 5

Using A, make desired number of chainless sc.

Row 1 (RS): Using B, 1 ch, 1 sc, 2 ch, skip st, 1 sc, * 2 ch, skip st, 7 sc, 2 ch, skip st, 1 sc; rep from * to last 2 sts, 2 ch, skip st, 1 sc, turn.

Row 2 and all WS rows: 1 ch, 1 sc in sts, ch and skip ch-sps, turn.

Row 3: Using A, 1 ch, 1 sc, 1 Mdc, 2 ch, skip st, * 1 Mdc, 2 ch, skip st, 5 sc, 2 ch, skip st, 1 Mdc, 2 ch, skip st; rep from * to last 2 sts, 1 Mdc, 1 sc, turn.

Row 5: Using B, 1 ch, 2 sc, 1 Mdc, * 1 sc, 1 Mdc, 2 ch, skip st, 3 sc, 2 ch, skip st, 1 Mdc, 1 sc, 1 Mdc; rep from * to last 2 sts, 2 sc, turn.

Row 7: Using A, 1 ch, 2 sc, 2 ch, skip st, * 2 sc, 1 Mdc, 2 ch, skip st, 1 sc, 2 ch, skip st, 1 Mdc, 2 sc, 2 ch, skip st; rep from * to last 2 sts, 2 sc, turn.

Row 9: Using B, 1 ch, 1 sc, 2 ch, skip st, 1 Mdc, * 2 ch, skip st, 2 sc, 1 Mdc, 2 ch, skip st, 1 Mdc, 2 sc, 2 ch, skip st, 1 Mdc; rep from * to last 2 sts, 2 ch, skip st, 1 sc, turn.

Row 11: Using A, 1 ch, 1 sc, 1 Mdc, 1 sc * 1 Mdc, 2 ch, skip st, 2 sc, 1 Mdc, 2 sc, 2 ch, skip st, 1 Mdc, 1 sc; rep from * to last 2 sts, 1 Mdc, 1 sc, turn.

Row 13: Using B, 1 ch, 3 sc, * 1 sc,

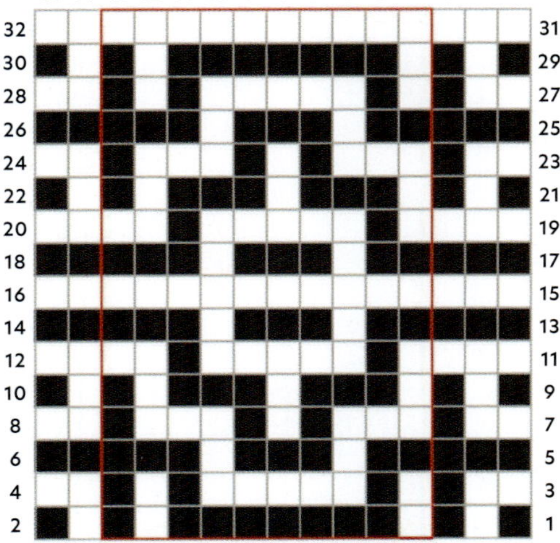

1 Mdc, 2 ch, skip st, 3 sc, 2 ch, skip st, 1 Mdc, 2 sc; rep from * to last 2 sts, 2 sc, turn.

Row 15: Using A, 1 ch, 3 sc, * 2 sc, [1 Mdc, 3 sc] twice; rep from * to last 2 sts, 2 sc, turn.

Row 17: Using B, 1 ch, 3 sc, * 2 sc, [2 ch, skip st, 3 sc] twice; rep from * to last 2 sts, 2 sc, turn.

Row 19: Using A, 1 ch, 3 sc, * 1 sc, 2 ch, skip st, 1 Mdc, 3 sc, 1 Mdc, 2 ch, skip st, 2 sc; rep from * to last 2 sts, 2 sc, turn.

Row 21: Using B, 1 ch, 1 sc, 2 ch, skip st, 1 sc, * 2 ch, skip st, 1 Mdc, 2 sc, 2 ch, skip st, 2 sc, 1 Mdc, 2 ch, skip st, 1 sc; rep from * to last 2 sts, 2 ch, skip st, 1 sc, turn.

Row 23: Using A, 1 ch, 1 sc, 1 Mdc, 2 ch, skip st, * 1 Mdc, 2 sc, 2 ch, skip st, 1 Mdc, 2 ch, skip st, 2 sc, 1 Mdc, 2 ch, skip st; rep from * to last 2 sts, 1 Mdc, 1 sc, turn.

Row 25: Using B, 1 ch, 2 sc, 1 Mdc, * 2 sc, 2 ch, skip st, 1 Mdc, 1 sc, 1 Mdc, 2 ch, skip st, 2 sc, 1 Mdc; rep from * to last 2 sts, 2 sc, turn.

Row 27: Using A, 1 ch, 2 sc, 2 ch, skip st, * 1 sc, 2 ch, skip st, 1 Mdc, 3 sc, 1 Mdc, 2 ch, skip st, 1 sc, 2 ch, skip st; rep from * to last 2 sts, 2 sc, turn.

Row 29: Using B, 1 ch, 1 sc, 2 ch, skip st, 1 Mdc, * 2 ch, skip st, 1 Mdc, 5 sc, 1 Mdc, 2 ch, skip st, 1 Mdc; rep from * to last 2 sts, 2 ch, skip st, 1 sc, turn.

Row 31: Using A, 1 ch, 1 sc, 1 Mdc, 1 sc, * 1 Mdc, 7 sc, 1 Mdc, 1 sc; rep from * to last 2 sts, 1 Mdc, 1 sc, turn.

Row 32: As Row 2.

Rep Rows 1 to 32, ending last rep with Row 31.

KNIT

CROCHET

Aztec 8

This pattern does require concentration, but if you follow the instructions closely, the results are stunning. This would work well as a panel on a sweater or perhaps a shawl.

Knit Instructions

Multiple of 24 sts + 3

On RS rows, slip the sts purlwise with yarn in the back.

Cast on using B, k one row and p one row.

Row 1 (RS): Using A, k1, sl1, * k1, sl2, k1, sl1, k2, sl1, k7, sl1, k2, sl1, k1, sl2, k1, sl1; rep from * to last st, k1.

Row 2 and all WS rows: P the knitted sts and sl the slipped sts purlwise with yarn in the front.

Row 3: Using B, k2, * k5, sl1, k4, [sl1, k1] twice, k3, sl1, k6; rep from * to last st, k1.

Row 5: Using A, k1, sl1, * k4, sl1, k13, sl1, k4, sl1; rep from * to last st, k1.

Row 7: Using B, k2, * sl1, k2, sl1, k4, [sl1, k1] 4 times, k3, sl1, k2, sl1, k1; rep from * to last st, k1.

Row 9: Using A, k1, sl1, * k2, sl1, k17, sl1, k2, sl1; rep from * to last st, k1.

Row 11: Using B, k2, * k6, [sl1, k1] 6 times, k6; rep from * to last st, k1.

Row 13: As Row 9.

Row 15: As Row 7.

Row 17: As Row 5.

Row 19: As Row 3.

Row 21: As Row 1.

Row 23: Using B, k all sts.

Row 24: As Row 2.

Rep Rows 1 to 24.

Crochet Instructions

Multiple of 24 sts + 3

Using B, make desired number of chainless sc.

Row 1 (RS): Using A, 1 ch, 1 sc, 2 ch, skip st, * 1 sc, 3 ch, skip 2 sts, 1 sc, 2 ch, skip st, 2 sc, 2 ch, skip st, 7 sc, 2 ch, skip st, 2 sc, 2 ch, skip st, 1 sc, 3 ch, skip 2 sts, 1 sc, 2 ch, skip st; rep from * to last st, 1 sc, turn.

Row 2 and all WS rows: 1 ch, 1 sc in sts, ch and skip ch-sps, turn.

Row 3: Using B, 1 ch, 1 sc, 1 Mdc, * 1 sc, 2 Mdc, 1 sc, 1 Mdc, 2 ch, skip st, 1 sc, 1 Mdc, 2 sc, [2 ch, skip st, 1 sc] twice, 1 sc, 1 Mdc, 1 sc, 2 ch, skip st, 1 Mdc, 1 sc, 2 Mdc, 1 sc, 1 Mdc; rep from * to last st, 1 sc, turn.

Row 5: Using A, 1 ch, 1 sc, 2 ch, skip st, * 4 sc, 2 ch, skip st, 1 Mdc, 4 sc, [1 Mdc, 1 sc] twice, 3 sc, 1 Mdc, 2 ch, skip st, 4 sc, 2 ch, skip st; rep from * to last st, 1 sc, turn.

Row 7: Using B, 1 ch, 1 sc, 1 Mdc, * 2 ch, skip st, 2 sc, 2 ch, skip st, 1 Mdc, 3 sc, [2 ch, skip st, 1 sc] 4 times, 2 sc, 1 Mdc, 2 ch, skip st, 2 sc, 2 ch, skip st, 1 Mdc; rep from * to last st, 1 sc, turn.

Row 9: Using A, 1 ch, 1 sc, 2 ch, skip st, * 1 Mdc, 1 sc, 2 ch, skip st, 1 Mdc, 4 sc, [1 Mdc, 1 sc] 4 times, 3 sc, 1 Mdc, 2 ch, skip st, 1 sc, 1 Mdc, 2 ch, skip st; rep from * to last st, 1 sc, turn.

MOSAIC CHART

Row 11: Using B, 1 ch, 1 sc, 1 Mdc, * 2 sc, 1 Mdc, 3 sc, [2 ch, skip st, 1 sc] 6 times, 2 sc, 1 Mdc, 2 sc, 1 Mdc; rep from * to last st, 1 sc, turn.
Row 13: Using A, 1 ch, 1 sc, 2 ch, skip st, * 2 sc, 2 ch, skip st, 3 sc, [1 Mdc, 1 sc] 6 times, 2 sc, 2 ch, skip st, 2 sc, 2 ch, skip st; rep from * to last st, 1 sc, turn.
Row 15: Using B, 1 ch, 1 sc, 1 Mdc, * 2 ch, skip st, 1 sc, 1 Mdc, 2 ch, skip st, 4 sc, [2 ch, skip st, 1 sc] 4 times, 3 sc, 2 ch, skip st, 1 Mdc, 1 sc, 2 ch, skip st, 1 Mdc; rep from * to last st, 1 sc, turn.
Row 17: Using A, 1 ch, 1 sc, 2 ch, skip st, * 1 Mdc, 2 sc, 1 Mdc, 2 ch, skip st, 3 sc, [1 Mdc, 1 sc] 4 times, 2 sc, 2 ch, skip st, 1 Mdc, 2 sc, 1 Mdc, 2 ch, skip st; rep from * to last st, 1 sc, turn.
Row 19: Using B, 1 ch, 1 sc, 1 Mdc, * 4 sc, 1 Mdc, 2 ch, skip st, 4 sc, [2 ch, skip st, 1 sc] twice, 3 sc, 2 ch, skip st, 1 Mdc, 4 sc, 1 Mdc; rep from * to last st, 1 sc, turn.
Row 21: Using A, 1 ch, 1 sc, 2 ch, skip st, * 1 sc, 3 ch, skip 2 sts, 1 sc, 2 ch, skip st, 1 Mdc, 1 sc, 2 ch, skip st, 2 sc, [1 Mdc, 1 sc] twice, 1 sc, 2 ch, skip st, 1 sc, 1 Mdc, 2 ch, skip st, 1 sc, 3 ch, skip 2 sts, 1 sc, 2 ch, skip st; rep from * to last st, 1 sc, turn.
Row 23: Using B, 1 ch, 1 sc, 1 Mdc, * 1 sc, 2 Mdc, 1 sc, 1 Mdc, 2 sc, 1 Mdc, 7 sc, 1 Mdc, 2 sc, 1 Mdc, 1 sc, 2 Mdc, 1 sc, 1 Mdc; rep from * to last st, 1 sc, turn.
Row 24: As Row 2.
Rep Rows 1 to 24, ending last rep with Row 23.

KNIT

CROCHET

Aztec 9

This is another design that would benefit from being used as a panel on a large item, so that it can really stand out.

Knit Instructions

Multiple of 20 sts + 3

On RS rows, slip the sts purlwise with yarn in the back.

Cast on using B, k one row and p one row.

Row 1 (RS): Using A, k1, sl1, * k5, [sl1, k1] 4 times, sl1, k5, sl1; rep from * to last st, k1.

Row 2 and all WS rows: P the knitted sts and sl the slipped sts purlwise with yarn in the front.

Row 3: Using B, k2, * sl1, k3, sl1, k9, sl1, k3, sl1, k1; rep from * to last st, k1.

Row 5: Using A, k1, sl1, * k1, sl1, k5, [sl1, k1] 3 times, k4, sl1, k1, sl1; rep from * to last st, k1.

Row 7: Using B, k2, * k2, sl1, k3, sl1, k5, [sl1, k3] twice; rep from * to last st, k1.

Row 9: Using A, k1, sl1, * [k1, sl1] twice, [k5, sl1] twice, [k1, sl1] twice; rep from * to last st, k1.

Row 11: Using B, k2, * [sl1, k3] twice, sl1, k1, [sl1, k3] twice, sl1, k1; rep from * to last st, k1.

Row 13: Using A, k1, sl1, * [k1, sl1] 3 times, k7, sl1, [k1, sl1] 3 times; rep from * to last st, k1.

Row 15: Using B, k2, * [sl1, k1] twice, [k2, sl1] 3 times, k3, [sl1, k1] twice; rep from * to last st, k1.

Row 17: Using A, k1, sl1, * [k1, sl1] 3 times, [k1, sl2] twice, [k1, sl1] 4 times; rep from * to last st, k1.

Row 19: Using B, k all sts.

Row 20: As Row 2.

Rep Rows 1 to 20.

Crochet Instructions

Multiple of 20 sts + 3

Using B, make desired number of chainless sc.

Row 1 (RS): Using A, 1 ch, 1 sc, 2 ch, skip st, * 5 sc, [2 ch, skip st, 1 sc] 5 times, 4 sc, 2 ch, skip st; rep from * to last st, 1 sc, turn.

Row 2 and all WS rows: 1 sc in sts, ch and skip ch-sps, turn.

Row 3: Using B, 1 ch, 1 sc, 1 Mdc, * 2 ch, skip st, 3 sc, 2 ch, skip st, [1 Mdc, 1 sc] 4 times, 1 Mdc, 2 ch, skip st, 3 sc, 2 ch, skip st, 1 Mdc; rep from * to last st, 1 sc, turn.

Row 5: Using A, 1 ch, 1 sc, 2 ch, skip st, * 1 Mdc, 2 ch, skip st, 2 sc, 1 Mdc, 2 sc, [2 ch, skip st, 1 sc] 3 times, 1 sc, 1 Mdc, 2 sc, 2 ch, skip st, 1 Mdc, 2 ch, skip st; rep from * to last st, 1 sc, turn.

Row 7: Using B, 1 ch, 1 sc, 1 Mdc, * 1 sc, 1 Mdc, 2 ch, skip st, 3 sc, 2 ch, skip st, [1 Mdc, 1 sc] twice, 1 Mdc, 2 ch, skip st, 3 sc, 2 ch, skip st, 1 Mdc, 1 sc, 1 Mdc; rep from * to last st, 1 sc, turn.

Row 9: Using A, 1 ch, 1 sc, 2 ch, skip st, * 1 sc, 2 ch, skip st, 1 Mdc, 2 ch, skip st, 2 sc, 1 Mdc, 2 sc, 2 ch, skip st, 2 sc, 1 Mdc, 2 sc, 2 ch, skip st, 1 Mdc, 2 ch, skip st, 1 sc, 2 ch, skip st; rep from * to last st, 1 sc, turn.

Row 11: Using B, 1 ch, 1 sc, 1 Mdc, * 2 ch, skip st, 1 Mdc, 1 sc, 1 Mdc, 2 ch, skip st, 3 sc, 2 ch, skip st, 1 Mdc, 2 ch, skip st, 3 sc, 2 ch, skip st, 1 Mdc, 1 sc, 1 Mdc, 2 ch, skip st, 1 Mdc; rep from

MOSAIC CHART

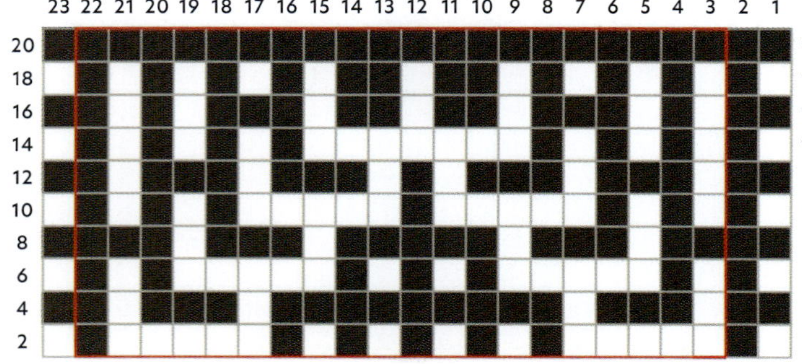

* to last st, 1 sc, turn.

Row 13: Using A, 1 ch, 1 sc, 2 ch, skip st, * 1 Mdc, 2 ch, skip st, 1 sc, 2 ch, skip st, 1 Mdc, 2 ch, skip st, 2 sc, 1 Mdc, 1 sc, 1 Mdc, 2 sc, 2 ch, skip st, 1 Mdc, 2 ch, skip st, 1 sc, 2 ch, skip st, 1 Mdc, 2 ch, skip st; rep from * to last st, 1 sc, turn.

Row 15: Using B, 1 ch, 1 sc, 1 Mdc, * [2 ch, skip st, 1 Mdc] twice, 1 sc, 1 Mdc, [2 ch, skip st, 2 sc] twice, 2 ch, skip st, 1 Mdc, 1 sc, [1 Mdc, 2 ch, skip st] twice, 1 Mdc; rep from * to last st, 1 sc, turn.

Row 17: Using A, 1 ch, 1 sc, 2 ch, skip st, * [1 Mdc, 2 ch, skip st] twice, 1 sc, 2 ch, skip st, [1 Mdc, 3 ch, skip 2 sts] twice, 1 Mdc, 2 ch, skip st, 1 sc, [2 ch, skip st, 1 Mdc] twice, 2 ch, skip st; rep from * to last st, 1 sc, turn.

Row 19: Using B, 1 ch, 1 sc, 1 Mdc, * [1 sc, 1 Mdc] 3 times, [1 sc, 2 Mdc] twice, [1 sc, 1 Mdc] 4 times; rep from * to last st, 1 sc, turn.

Row 20: As Row 2.

Rep Rows 1 to 20, ending last rep with Row 19.

KNIT

CROCHET

Aztec 10

This simple pattern works up quickly and creates a dipping path. Stack this pattern with Aztec 4 on page 74 and Aztec 12 on page 86. Note that every two repeats of Aztec 10, will only need one repeat of Aztec 12.

Knit Instructions

Multiple of 6 sts + 4

On RS rows, slip the sts purlwise with yarn in the back.

Cast on using A, k one row and p one row.

Row 1 (RS): Using B, k1, * k3, sl2, k1; rep from * to last 3 sts, k3.

Row 2 and all WS rows: P the knitted sts and sl the slipped sts purlwise with yarn in the front.

Row 3: Using A, k1, * k2, sl1, k2, sl1; rep from * to last 3 sts, k3.

Row 5: Using B, k1, * sl2, k4; rep from * to last 3 sts, sl2, k1.

Row 7: Using A, k all sts.

Row 8: As Row 2.

Rep Rows 1 to 8.

Crochet Instructions

Multiple of 6 sts + 4

Using A, make desired number of chainless sc.

Row 1 (RS): Using B, 1 ch, 1 sc, * 3 sc, 3 ch, skip 2 sts, 1 sc; rep from * to last 3 sts, 3 sc, turn.

Row 2 and all WS rows: 1 ch, 1 sc in sts, ch and skip ch-sps, turn.

Row 3: Using A, 1 ch, 1 sc, * 2 sc, 2 ch, skip st, 2 Mdc, 2 ch, skip st; rep from * to last 3 sts, 3 sc, turn.

Row 5: Using B, 1 ch, 1 sc, * 3 ch, skip 2 sts, 1 Mdc, 2 sc, 1 Mdc; rep from * to last 3 sts, 3 ch, skip 2 sts, 1 sc, turn.

Row 7: Using A, 1 ch, 1 sc, * 2 Mdc, 4 sc; rep from * to last 3 sts, 2 Mdc, 1 sc, turn.

Row 8: As Row 2.

Rep Rows 1 to 8, ending last rep with Row 7.

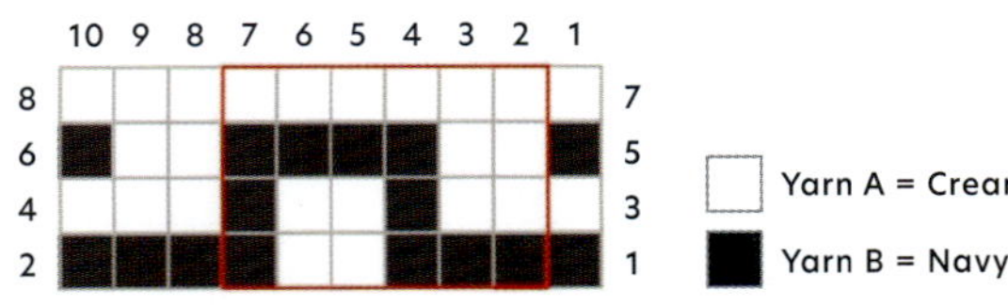

Aztec 11

The triangular shape of this pattern resembles a mountain in a valley. Stack this with Aztec 4 or 5 in alternating rows.

Knit Instructions

Multiple of 6 sts + 3

On RS rows, slip the sts purlwise with yarn in the back.

Cast on using B, k one row and p one row.

Row 1 (RS): Using A, k1, sl1, * k5, sl1; rep from * to last st, k1.

Row 2 and all WS rows: P the knitted sts and sl the slipped sts purlwise with yarn in the front.

Row 3: Using B, k2, * k1, sl3, k2; rep from * to last st, k1.

Row 5: Using A, k1, sl1, * sl1, k3, sl2; rep from * to last st, k1.

Row 7: Using B, k2, * k2, sl1, k3; rep from * to last st, k1.

Row 9: Using A, k2, * sl2, k1; rep from * to last st, k1.

Row 11: Using B, k all sts.

Row 12: As Row 2.

Rep Rows 1 to 12.

Crochet Instructions

Multiple of 6 sts + 3

Pattern note: The repeat in the written instructions differs from chart on Row 5.

Using B, make desired number of chainless sc.

Row 1 (RS): Using A, 1 ch, 1 sc, 2 ch, skip st, * 5 sc, 2 ch, skip st; rep from * to last st, 1 sc, turn.

Row 2 and all WS rows: 1 ch, 1 sc in sts, ch and skip ch-sps, turn.

Row 3: Using B, 1 ch, 1 sc, 1 Mdc, * 1 sc, 4 ch, skip 3 sts, 1 sc, 1 Mdc; rep from * to last st, 1 sc, turn.

Row 5: Using A, 1 ch, 1 sc, 3 ch, skip 2 sts, * 3Mdc, ** 4 ch, skip 3 sts; rep from * to last 3 sts, ending last rep at **, 3 ch, skip 2 sts, 1 sc, turn.

Row 7: Using B, 1 ch, 1 sc, 1 Mdc, * 1 Mdc, 1 sc, 2 ch, skip st, 1 sc, 2 Mdc; rep from * to last st, 1 sc, turn.

Row 9: Using A, 1 ch, 2 sc, * 3 ch, skip 2 sts, 1 Mdc, 3 ch, skip 2 sts, 1 sc; rep from * to last st, 1 sc, turn.

Row 11: Using B, 1 ch, 2 sc, * [2 Mdc, 1 sc] twice; rep from * to last st, 1 sc, turn.

Row 12: As Row 2.

Rep Rows 1 to 12, ending last rep with Row 11.

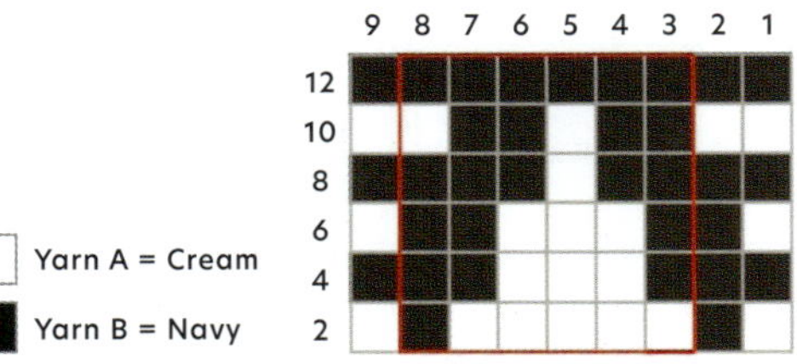

Aztec 12

This design looks crisp in both crochet and knit and will look best if worked in a panel, as a border on accessories, or at the bottom and top of blankets.

Knitting Instructions

Multiple of 12 sts + 3

On RS rows, slip the sts purlwise with yarn in the back.

Cast on using A, k one row and p one row.

Row 1 (RS): Using B, k2, * k1, sl2, k5, sl2, k2; rep from * to last st, k1.

Row 2 and all WS rows: P the knitted sts and sl the slipped sts purlwise with yarn in the front.

Row 3: Using A, k2, * sl1, k2, sl1, k3, sl1, k2, sl1, k1; rep from * to last st, k1.

Row 5: Using B, k1, sl1, * k2, sl1; rep from * to last st, k1.

Row 7: Using A, k2, * k1, sl1, k2, sl1, k1, [sl1, k2] twice; rep from * to last st, k1.

Row 9: Using B, k2, * [k3, sl1] twice, k4; rep from * to last st, k1.

Row 11: Using A, k2, * [k2, sl1] 3 times, k3; rep from * to last st, k1.

Row 13: Using B, k all sts.

Row 15: As Row 11.

Row 17: As Row 9.

Row 19: As Row 7.

Row 21: As Row 5.

Row 23: As Row 3.

Row 25: As Row 1.

Row 27: Using A, k all sts.

Row 28: As Row 2.

Rep Rows 1 to 28.

Crochet Instructions

Multiple of 12 sts + 3

Using A, make desired number of chainless sc.

Row 1 (RS): Using B, 1 ch, 2 sc, * 1 sc, 3 ch, skip 2 sts, 5 sc, 3 ch, skip 2 sts, 2 sc; rep from * to last st, 1 sc, turn.

Row 2 and all WS rows: 1 ch, 1 sc in sts, ch and skip ch-sps, turn.

Row 3: Using A, 1 ch, 2 sc, * 2 ch, skip st, 2 Mdc, 2 ch, skip st, 3 sc, 2 ch, skip st, 2 Mdc, 2 ch, skip st, 1 sc; rep from * to last st, 1 sc, turn.

Row 5: Using B, 1 ch, 1 sc, 2 ch, skip st, * 1 Mdc, 1 sc, 2 ch, skip st, 1 Mdc, 1 sc, [2 ch, skip st, 1 sc, 1 Mdc] twice, 2 ch, skip st; rep from * to last st, 1 sc, turn.

Row 7: Using A, 1 ch, 1 sc, 1 Mdc, * 1 sc, 2 ch, skip st, 1 Mdc, 1 sc, 2 ch, skip st, 1 Mdc, [2 ch, skip st, 1 sc, 1 Mdc] twice; rep from * to last st, 1 sc, turn.

Row 9: Using B, 1 ch, 2 sc, * 1 sc, 1 Mdc, 1 sc, 2 ch, skip st, 1 Mdc, 1 sc, 1 Mdc, 2 ch, skip st, 1 sc, 1 Mdc, 2 sc; rep from * to last st, 1 sc, turn.

Row 11: Using A, 1 ch, 2 sc, * 2 sc, 2 ch, skip st, 1 Mdc, 1 sc, 2 ch, skip st, 1 sc, 1 Mdc, 2 ch, skip st, 3 sc; rep from * to last st, 1 sc, turn.

Row 13: Using B, 1 ch, 2 sc, * [2 sc, 1 Mdc] 3 times, 3 sc; rep from * to last st, 1 sc, turn.

Row 15: Using A, 1 ch, 2 sc, * [2 sc, 2 ch, skip st] 3 times, 3 sc; rep from * to last st, 1 sc, turn.

Row 17: Using B, 1 ch, 2 sc, * 2 sc, 1 Mdc,

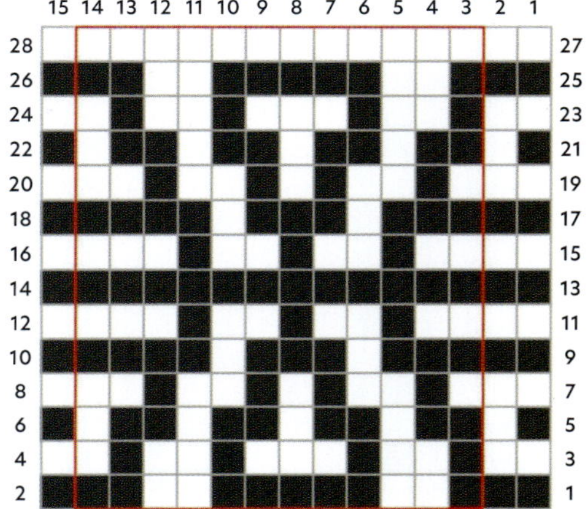

2 ch, skip st, 1 sc, 1 Mdc, 1 sc, 2 ch, skip st, 1 Mdc, 3 sc; rep from * to last st, 1 sc, turn.
Row 19: Using A, 1 ch, 2 sc, * 1 sc, 2 ch, skip st, 1 sc, 1 Mdc, 2 ch, skip st, 1 sc, 2 ch, skip st, 1 Mdc, 1 sc, 2 ch, skip st, 2 sc; rep from * to last st, 1 sc, turn.
Row 21: Using B, 1 ch, 1 sc, 2 ch, skip st, * [1 sc, 1 Mdc, 2 ch, skip st] twice, [1 Mdc, 1 sc, 2 ch, skip st] twice; rep from * to last st, 1 sc, turn.
Row 23: Using A, 1 ch, 1 sc, 1 Mdc, * [2 ch, skip st, 1 sc, 1 Mdc] twice, 1 sc, 2 ch, skip st, 1 Mdc, 1 sc, 2 ch, skip st, 1 Mdc; rep from * to last st, 1 sc, turn.
Row 25: Using B, 1 ch, 2 sc, * 1 Mdc, 3 ch, skip 2 sts, 1 Mdc, 3 sc, 1 Mdc, 3 ch, skip 2 sts, 1 Mdc, 1 sc; rep from * to last st, 1 sc, turn.
Row 27: Using A, 1 ch, 2 sc, * 1 sc, 2 Mdc, 5 sc, 2 Mdc, 2 sc; rep from * to last st, 1 sc, turn.
Row 28: As Row 2.
Rep rows 1 to 28, ending last rep with Row 27.

KNIT

CROCHET

Aztec 13

This bold and impressive pattern would be eye-catching as a stand-alone design or used as a vertical or horizontal panel, perfect for a bag or for the back of a sweater or cardigan.

Knit Instructions

Multiple of 16 sts + 3

On RS rows, slip the sts purlwise with yarn in the back.

Cast on using A, k one row and p one row.

Row 1 (RS): Using B, k all sts.

Row 2 and all WS rows: P the knitted sts and sl the slipped sts purlwise with yarn in the front.

Row 3: Using A, k1, * sl1, [k3, sl3] twice, k3; rep from * to last 2 sts, sl1, k1.

Row 5: Using B, k1, * k1, sl1, k5, sl1, k1, sl1, k5, sl1; rep from * to last 2 sts, k2.

Row 7: Using A, k1, * k2, sl2, k4, sl1, k4, sl2, k1; rep from * to last 2 sts, k2.

Row 9: Using B, k1, * sl1, k3, [sl1, k1, sl1, k3] twice, k3; rep from * to last 2 sts, sl1, k1.

Row 11: Using A, k1, * k1, sl1, k3, [sl1, k1] 4 times, k2, sl1; rep from * to last 2 sts, k2.

Row 13: Using B, k1, * k2, sl1, k1, [sl1, k3] twice; [sl1, k1] twice; rep from * to last 2 sts, k2.

Row 15: Using A, k1, * k3, [sl1, k1] twice, k4, [sl1, k1] twice, k1; rep from * to last 2 sts, k2.

Row 17: Using B, k1, * sl1, k1, [sl1, k3] 3 times, sl1, k1; rep from * to last 2 sts, sl1, k1.

Row 19: Using A, k1, * k1, [sl1, k1, sl1, k3] twice, sl1, k1, sl1; rep from * to last 2 sts, k2.

Row 21: Using B, k1, * k4, sl1, k7, sl1, k3; rep from * to last 2 sts, k2.

Row 23: As Row 19.

Row 25: As Row 17.

Row 27: As Row 15.

Row 29: As Row 13.

Row 31: As Row 11.

Row 33: As Row 9.

Row 35: As Row 7.

Row 37: As Row 5.

Row 39: As Row 3.

Row 41: As Row 1.

Row 42: As Row 2.

Row 43: Using A, k all sts.

Row 44: As Row 2.

Rep Rows 1 to 44.

MOSAIC CHART

16 sts

Yarn A = Cream

Yarn B = Blue

Crochet Instructions

Multiple of 16 sts + 3

Using A, make desired number of chainless sc.

Row 1 (RS): Using B, 1 ch, 1 sc in every st, turn.

Row 2 and all WS rows: 1 ch, 1 sc in sts, ch and skip ch-sps, turn.

Row 3: Using A, 1 ch, 1 sc, * 2 ch, skip st, [3 sc, 4 ch, skip 3 sts] twice, 3 sc; rep from * to last 2 sts, 2 ch, skip st, 1 sc, turn.

Row 5: Using B, 1 ch, 1 sc, * 1 Mdc, 2 ch, skip st, 2 sc, 3 Mdc, 2 ch, skip st, 1 sc, 2 ch, skip st, 3 Mdc, 2 sc, 2 ch, skip st; rep from * to last 2 sts, 1 Mdc, 1 sc, turn.

Row 7: Using A, 1 ch, 1 sc, * 1 sc, 1 Mdc, 3 ch, skip 2 sts, 3 sc, 1 Mdc, 2 ch, skip st, 1 Mdc, 3 sc, 3 ch, skip 2 sts, 1 Mdc; rep from * to last 2 sts, 2 sc, turn.

Row 9: Using B, 1 ch, 1 sc, * 2 ch, skip st, 1 sc, 2 Mdc, [2 ch, skip st, 1 sc] twice, 1 Mdc, [1 sc, 2 ch, skip st] twice, 2 Mdc, 1 sc; rep from * to last 2 sts, 2 ch, skip st, 1 sc, turn.

Row 11: Using A, 1 ch, 1 sc, * 1 Mdc, 2 ch, skip st, 2 sc, 1 Mdc, 2 ch, skip st, 1 Mdc, 2 ch, skip st, 1 sc, [2 ch, skip st,

KNIT

CROCHET

1 Mdc] twice, 2 sc, 2 ch, skip st; rep from * to last 2 sts, 1 Mdc, 1 sc, turn.

Row 13: Using B, 1 ch, 1 sc, * 1 sc, 1 Mdc, 2 ch, skip st, 1 sc, [2 ch, skip st, 1 Mdc, 1 sc, 1 Mdc] twice, 2 ch, skip st, 1 sc, 2 ch, skip st, 1 Mdc; rep from * to last 2 sts, 2 sc, turn.

Row 15: Using A, 1 ch, 1 sc, * 2 sc, [1 Mdc, 2 ch, skip st] twice, 2 sc, 1 Mdc, 2 sc, [2 ch, skip st, 1 Mdc] twice, 1 sc; rep from * to last 2 sts, 2 sc, turn.

Row 17: Using B, 1 ch, 1 sc, * 2 ch, skip st, 1 sc, 2 ch, skip st, 1 Mdc, 1 sc, 1 Mdc, 2 ch, skip st, 3 sc, 2 ch, skip st, 1 Mdc, 1 sc, 1 Mdc, 2 ch, skip st, 1 sc; rep from * to last 2 sts, 2 ch, skip st, 1 sc, turn.

Row 19: Using A, 1 ch, 1 sc, * [1 Mdc, 2 ch, skip st] twice, 2 sc, 1 Mdc, 2 ch, skip st, 1 sc, 2 ch, skip st, 1 Mdc, 2 sc, 2 ch, skip st, 1 Mdc, 2 ch, skip st; rep from * to last 2 sts, 1 Mdc, 1 sc, turn.

Row 21: Using B, 1 ch, 1 sc, * [1 sc, 1 Mdc] twice, 2 ch, skip st, 2 sc, 1 Mdc, 1 sc, 1 Mdc, 2 sc, 2 ch, skip st, 1 Mdc, 1 sc, 1 Mdc; rep from * to last 2 sts, 2 sc, turn.

Row 23: Using A, 1 ch, 1 sc, * [1 sc, 2 ch, skip st] twice, 1 Mdc, 2 sc, 2 ch, skip st, 1 sc, 2 ch, skip st, 2 sc, 1 Mdc, 2 ch, skip st, 1 sc, 2 ch, skip st; rep from * to last 2 sts, 2 sc, turn.

Row 25: Using B, 1 ch, 1 sc, * [2 ch, skip st, 1 Mdc] twice, 2 sc, 2 ch, skip st, 1 Mdc, 1 sc, 1 Mdc, 2 ch, skip st, 2 sc, 1 Mdc, 2 ch, skip st, 1 Mdc; rep from * to last 2 sts, 2 ch, skip st, 1 sc, turn.

Row 27: Using A, 1 ch, 1 sc, * 1 Mdc, 1 sc, 1 Mdc, 2 ch, skip st, 1 sc, 2 ch, skip st, 1 Mdc, 3 sc, 1 Mdc, 2 ch, skip st, 1 sc, 2 ch, skip st, 1 Mdc, 1 sc; rep from * to last 2 sts, 1 Mdc, 1 sc, turn.

Row 29: Using B, 1 ch, 1 sc, * 2 sc, [2 ch, skip st, 1 Mdc] twice, 2 sc, 2 ch, skip st, 2 sc, [1 Mdc, 2 ch, skip st] twice, 1 sc; rep from * to last 2 sts, 2 sc, turn.

Row 31: Using A, 1 ch, 1 sc, * 1 sc, 2 ch, skip st, 1 Mdc, 1 sc, [1 Mdc, 2 ch, skip st, 1 sc, 2 ch, skip st] twice, 1 Mdc, 1 sc, 1 Mdc, 2 ch, skip st; rep from * to last 2 sts, 2 sc, turn.

Row 33: Using B, 1 ch, 1 sc, * 2 ch, skip st, 1 Mdc, 2 sc, [2 ch, skip st, 1 Mdc] twice, 1 sc, [1 Mdc, 2 ch, skip st] twice, 2 sc, 1 Mdc; rep from * to last 2 sts, 2 ch, skip st, 1 sc, turn.

Row 35: Using A, 1 ch, 1 sc, * 1 Mdc, 1 sc, 3 ch, skip 2 sts, [1 Mdc, 1 sc] twice, 2 ch, skip st, [1 sc, 1 Mdc] twice, 3 ch, skip 2 sts, 1 sc; rep from * to last 2 sts, 1 Mdc, 1 sc, turn.

Row 37: Using B, 1 ch, 1 sc, * 1 sc, 2 ch, skip st, 2 Mdc, 3 sc, 2 ch, skip st, 1 Mdc, 2 ch, skip st, 3 sc, 2 Mdc, 2 ch, skip st; rep from * to last 2 sts, 2 sc, turn.

Row 39: Using A, 1 ch, 1 sc, * 2 ch, skip st, 1 Mdc, 2 sc, 4 ch, skip 3 sts, 1 Mdc, 1 sc, 1 Mdc, 4 ch, skip 3 sts, 2 sc, 1 Mdc; rep from * to last 2 sts, 2 ch, skip st, 1 sc, turn.

Row 41: Using B, 1 ch, 1 sc, * 1 Mdc, [3 sc, 3 Mdc] twice, 3 sc; rep from * to last 2 sts, 1 Mdc, 1 sc, turn.

Row 43: Using A, 1 ch, 1 sc in every st, turn.

Row 44: As Row 2.

Rep Rows 1 to 44, ending last rep with Row 43.

Aztec 14

This design is quite easy to work but looks impressive. It would be stunning combined with the spirals (Aztec 1 and 2 on pages 70–71) or something bold like Aztec 11 (page 85).

Knit Instructions

Multiple of 12 sts + 3

On RS rows, slip the sts purlwise with yarn in the back.

Cast on using A, k one row and p one row.

Row 1 (RS): Using B, k1, * sl1, k5, [sl1, k1] 3 times; rep from * to last 2 sts, sl1, k1.

Row 2 and all WS rows: P the knitted sts and sl the slipped sts purlwise with yarn in the front.

Row 3: Using A, k1, * k7, [sl1, k1] twice, sl1; rep from * to last 2 sts, k2.

Rows 5 to 8: As Rows 1 to 4.

Rows 9 and 10: As Rows 1 and 2.

Row 11: Using A, k all sts.

Row 12: As Row 2.

Rep Rows 1 to 12.

MOSAIC CHART

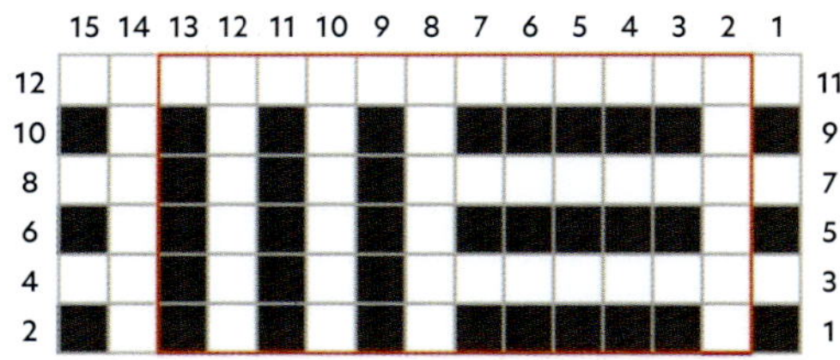

Yarn A = Cream

Yarn B = Blue

Crochet Instructions

Multiple of 12 sts + 3

Using A, make desired number of chainless sc.

Row 1 (RS): Using B, 1 ch, 1 sc, * 2 ch, skip st, 5 sc, [2 ch, skip st, 1 sc] 3 times; rep from * to last 2 sts, 2 ch, skip st, 1 sc, turn.

Row 2 and all WS rows: 1 ch, 1 sc in sts, ch and skip ch-sps, turn.

Row 3: Using A, 1 ch, 1 sc, * 1 Mdc, 5 sc, [1 Mdc, 2 ch, skip st] 3 times; rep from * to last 2 sts, 1 Mdc, 1 sc, turn.

Row 5: Using B, 1 ch, 1 sc, * 2 ch, skip st, 5 sc, [2 ch, skip st, 1 Mdc] 3 times; rep from * to last 2 sts, 2 ch, skip st, 1 sc, turn.

Rows 7 to 10: As Rows 3 to 6.

Row 11: Using A, 1 ch, 1 sc, * 1 Mdc, 5 sc, [1 Mdc, 1 sc] 3 times; rep from * to last 2 sts, 1 Mdc, 1 sc, turn.

Row 12: As Row 2.

Rep Rows 1 to 12, ending last rep with Row 11.

Aztec 15

This slightly more complex design would work well in a panel used as a border on a garment or at the bottom and top of a blanket.

Knit Instructions

Multiple of 8 sts + 3

On RS rows, slip the sts purlwise with yarn in the back.

Cast on using A, k one row and p one row.

Row 1 (RS): Using B, k1, * sl1, k7; rep from * to last 2 sts, sl1, k1.

Row 2 and all WS rows: P the knitted sts and sl the slipped sts purlwise with yarn in the front.

Row 3: Using A, k1, * k2, sl1, k3, sl1, k1; rep from * to last 2 sts, k2.

Row 5: Using B, k all sts.

Row 7: Using A, k1, * sl1, k1; rep from * to last 2 sts, sl1, k1.

Row 9: As Row 5.

Row 11: As Row 3.

Row 13: As Row 1.

Row 15: Using A, k all sts.

Row 16: As Row 2.

Rep Rows 1 to 16.

Crochet Instructions

Multiple of 8 sts + 3

Using A, make desired number of chainless sc.

Row 1 (RS): Using B, 1 ch, 1 sc, * 2 ch, skip st, 7 sc; rep from * to last 2 sts, 2 ch, skip st, 1 sc, turn.

Row 2 and all WS rows: 1 ch, 1 sc in sts, ch and skip ch-sps, turn.

Row 3: Using A, 1 ch, 1 sc, * 1 Mdc, 1 sc, 2 ch, skip st, 3 sc, 2 ch, skip st, 1 sc; rep from * to last 2 sts, 1 Mdc, 1 sc, turn.

Row 5: Using B, 1 ch, 1 sc, * 2 sc, 1 Mdc, 3 sc, 1 Mdc, 1 sc; rep from * to last 2 sts, 2 sc, turn.

Row 7: Using A, 1 ch, 1 sc, * [2 ch, skip st, 1 sc] 4 times; rep from * to last 2 sts, 2 ch, skip st, 1 sc, turn.

Row 9: Using B, 1 ch, 1 sc, * [1 Mdc, 1 sc] 4 times; rep from * to last 2 sts, 1 Mdc, 1 sc, turn.

Row 11: Using A, 1 ch, 1 sc, * 2 sc, 2 ch, skip st, 3 sc, 2 ch, skip st, 1 sc; rep from * to last 2 sts, 2 sc, turn.

Row 13: Using B, 1 ch, 1 sc, * 2 ch, skip st, 1 sc, 1 Mdc, 3 sc, 1 Mdc, 1 sc; rep from * to last 2 sts, 2 ch, skip st, 1 sc, turn.

Row 15: Using A, 1 ch, 1 sc, * 1 Mdc, 7 sc; rep from * to last 2 sts, 1 Mdc, 1 sc, turn.

Row 16: As Row 2.

Rep Rows 1 to 16, ending last rep with Row 15.

MOSAIC CHART

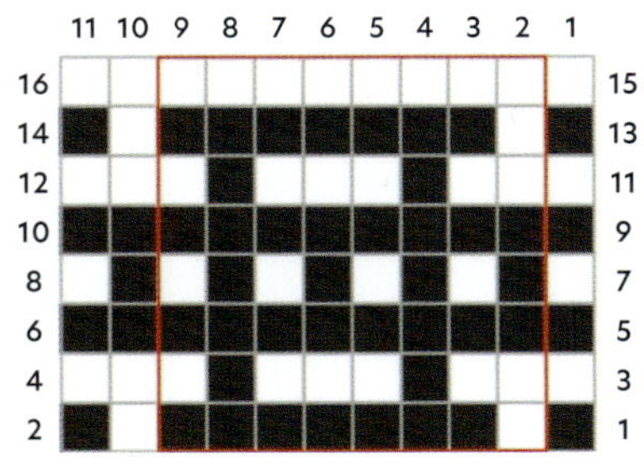

General

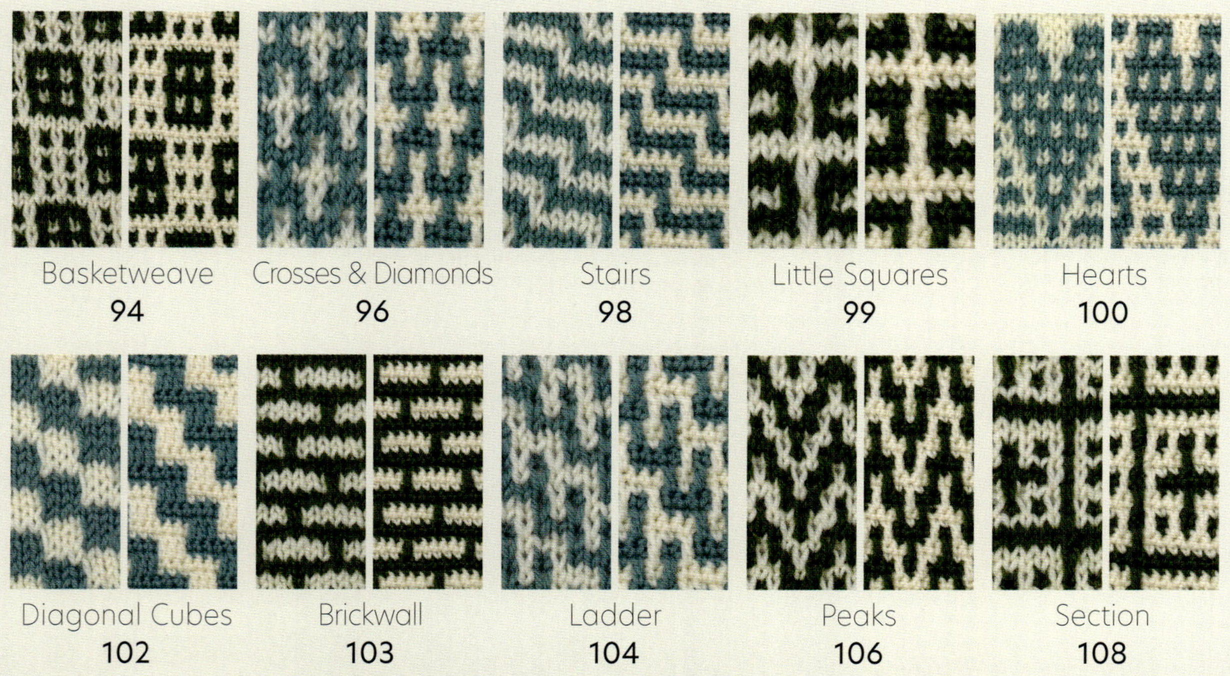

Starry Night
110

Square in a Square
112

Triangles
114

Candy Corn
116

Chains
117

Basketweave

This "easy to remember" repeat pattern is fun to work on. Use it on a large make so that you can really see the design.

Knit Instructions

Multiple of 10 sts + 4

On RS rows, slip the sts purlwise with yarn in the back.

Cast on using A, k one row and p one row.

Row 1 (RS): Using B, k1, sl1, * [sl1, k1] twice, sl1, k5; rep from * to last 2 sts, sl1, k1.

Row 2 and all WS rows: P the knitted sts and sl the slipped sts purlwise with yarn in the front.

Row 3: Using A, k2, * k5, [sl1, k1] twice, sl1; rep from * to last 2 sts, k2.

Rows 5 to 8: As Rows 1 to 4.

Rows 9 and 10: As Rows 1 and 2.

Row 11: Using A, k all sts.

Row 13: Using B, k1, sl1, * k5, [sl1, k1] twice, sl1; rep from * to last 2 sts, sl1, k1.

Row 15: Using A, k2, * [sl1, k1] twice, sl1, k5; rep from * to last 2 sts, k2.

Rows 17 to 20: As Rows 13 to 16.

Rows 21 and 22: As Rows 13 and 14.

Row 23: Using A, k all sts.

Row 24: As Row 2.

Rep Rows 1 to 24.

Crochet Instructions

Multiple of 10 sts + 4

Pattern note: The repeat in the written instructions differs from chart on Rows 1, 5, 13, and 17.

Using A, make desired number of chainless sc.

Row 1 (RS): Using B, 1 ch, 1 sc, 3 ch, skip 2 sts, * [1 sc, 2 ch, skip st] twice, 5 sc, 2 ch, skip st; rep from * to last st, 1 sc, turn.

Row 2 and all WS rows: 1 ch, 1 sc in sts, ch and skip ch-sps, turn.

Row 3: Using A, 1 ch, 1 sc, 1 Mdc, * 1 Mdc, [1 sc, 1 Mdc] twice, [2 ch, skip st, 1 sc] twice, 2 ch, skip st; rep from * to last 2 sts, 1 Mdc, 1 sc, turn.

Row 5: Using B, 1 ch, 1 sc, 3 ch, skip 2 sts, * [1 sc, 2 ch, skip st] twice, [1 Mdc, 1 sc] twice, 1 Mdc, 2 ch, skip st; rep from * to last st, 1 sc, turn.

Rows 7 to 10: As Rows 3 to 6.

Row 11: Using A, 1 ch, 1 sc, 1 Mdc, * 1 Mdc, [1 sc, 1 Mdc] twice, 5 sc; rep from * to last 2 sts, 1 Mdc, 1 sc, turn.

Row 13: Using B, 1 ch, 1 sc, 2 ch, skip st, * 5 sc, [2 ch, skip st, 1 sc] twice, ** 2 ch, skip st; rep from * to last 3 sts, ending last rep at **, 3 ch, skip 2 sts, 1 sc, turn.

Row 15: Using A, 1 ch, 1 sc, 1 Mdc, * [2 ch, skip st, 1 sc] twice, 2 ch, skip st, [1 Mdc, 1 sc] twice, 1 Mdc; rep from * to

MOSAIC CHART

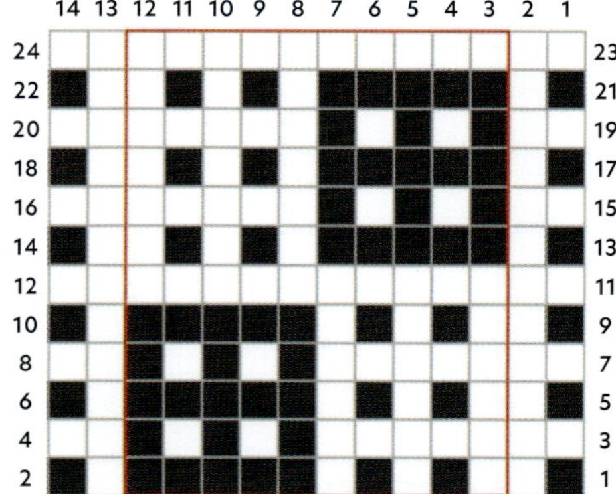

last 2 sts, 1 Mdc, 1 sc, turn.
Row 17: Using B, 1 ch, 1 sc, 2 ch, skip st, * [1 Mdc, 1 sc] twice, 1 Mdc, [2 ch, skip st, 1 sc] twice, ** 2 ch, skip st; rep from * to last 3 sts, ending last rep at **, 3 ch, skip 2 sts, 1 sc, turn.
Rows 19 to 22: As Rows 15 to 18.
Row 23: Using A, 1 ch, 1 sc, 1 Mdc, * 5 sc, [1 Mdc, 1 sc] twice, 1 Mdc; rep from * to last 2 sts, 1 Mdc, 1 sc, turn.
Row 24: As Row 2.
Rep Rows 1 to 24, ending last rep with Row 23.

CROCHET

TIP: For the knit version: Try slip stitching the first stitch at the beginning of a row to tighten the edges.

Crosses & Diamonds

The crochet version of this pattern makes for a more elongated cross. Mix and match with other motifs for unique designs.

Knit Instructions

Multiple of 4 sts + 7

On RS rows, slip the sts purlwise with yarn in the back.

Cast on using B, k one row and p one row.

Row 1 (RS): Using A, k1, sl2, k1, * sl1, k1; rep from * to last 3 sts, sl2, k1.

Row 2 and all WS rows: P the knitted sts and sl the slipped sts purlwise with yarn in the front.

Row 3: Using B, k4, * k1, sl1, k2; rep from * to last 3 sts, k3.

Row 5: Using A, [k1, sl1] twice, * k3, sl1; rep from * to last 3 sts, k1, sl1, k1.

Row 7: Using B, k4, * k1, sl1, k2; rep from * to last 3 sts, k3.

Row 9: Using A, k1, sl2, k1, * sl1, k1; rep from * to last 3 sts, sl2, k1.

Row 11: Using B, k3, sl1, * k3, sl1; rep from * to last 3 sts, k3.

Row 13: Using A, k1, sl1, k2, * k1, sl1, k2; rep from * to last 3 sts, k1, sl1, k1.

Row 15: Using B, As Row 11.

Rep Rows 1 to 16. To finish, work Rows 17 to 20.

Row 17: As Row 9.

Row 19: Using B, k all sts.

Row 20: As Row 2.

Crochet Instructions

Multiple of 4 sts + 7

Using B, make desired number of chainless sc.

Row 1 (RS): Using A, 1 ch, 1 sc, 3 ch, skip 2 sts, 1 sc, * [2 ch, skip st, 1 sc] twice; rep from * to last 3 sts, 3 ch, skip 2 sts, 1 sc, turn.

Row 2 and all WS rows: 1 ch, 1 sc in sts, ch and skip ch-sps, turn.

Row 3: Using B, 1 ch, 1 sc, 2 Mdc, 1 sc, * 1 Mdc, 2 ch, skip st, 1 Mdc, 1 sc; rep from * to last 3 sts, 2 Mdc, 1 sc, turn.

Row 5: Using A, 1 ch, [1 sc, 2 ch, skip st] twice, * 1 sc, 1 Mdc, 1 sc, 2 ch, skip st; rep from * to last 3 sts, 1 sc, 2 ch, skip st, 1 sc, turn.

Row 7: Using B, 1 ch, [1 sc, 1 Mdc] twice, * 1 sc, 2 ch, skip st, 1 sc, 1 Mdc; rep from * to last 3 sts, 1 sc, 1 Mdc, 1 sc, turn.

Row 9: Using A, 1 ch, 1 sc, 3 ch, skip 2 sts, 1 sc, * 2 ch, skip st, 1 Mdc, 2 ch, skip st, 1 sc; rep from * to last 3 sts, 3 ch, skip 2 sts, 1 sc, turn.

Row 11: Using B, 1 ch, 1 sc, 2 Mdc, 2 ch, skip st, * 1 Mdc, 1 sc, 1 Mdc, 2 ch, skip st; rep from * to last 3 sts, 2 Mdc, 1 sc, turn.

Row 13: Using A, 1 ch, 1 sc, 2 ch, skip st, 1 sc, 1 Mdc, * 1 sc, 2 ch, skip st, 1 sc, 1 Mdc; rep from * to last 3 sts, 1 sc, 2 ch, skip st, 1 sc, turn.

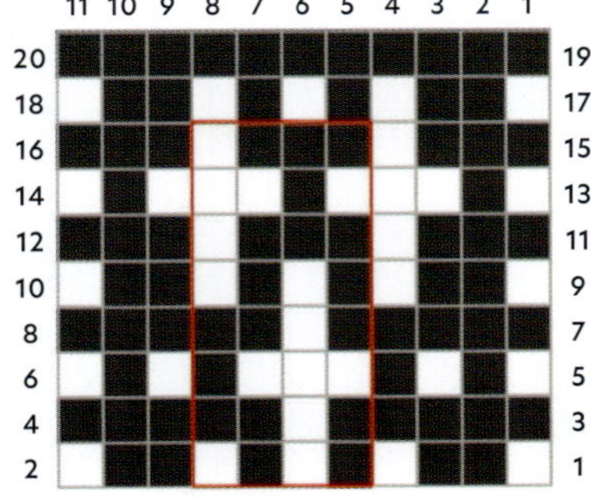

Yarn A = Cream

Yarn B = Teal

Row 15: Using B, 1 ch, 1 sc, 1 Mdc, 1 sc, 2 ch, skip st, * 1 sc, 1 Mdc, 1 sc, 2 ch, skip st; rep from * to last 3 sts, 1 sc, 1 Mdc, 1 sc, turn.

Rep rows 1 to 16, placing 1 Mdc in sps as required on Row 1. To finish, work Rows 17 to 19.

Row 17: Using A, 1 ch, 1 sc, 3 ch, skip 2 sts, 1 Mdc, * 2 ch, skip st, 1 sc, 2 ch, skip st, 1 Mdc; rep from * to last 3 sts, 3 ch, skip 2 sts, 1 sc, turn.

Row 19: Using B, 1 ch, 1 sc in every st and Mdc in every sp.

CROCHET

Stairs

Most designs in this section are perfect for beginners, the stairs pattern included. If you have never tried mosaic knit or crochet, this is the perfect place to start.

Knit Instructions

Multiple of 6 sts + 5

On RS rows, slip the sts purlwise with yarn in the back.

Cast on using A, k one row and p one row.

Row 1 (RS): Using B, k1, sl1, * k5, sl1; rep from * to last 3 sts, k1, sl1, k1.

Row 2 and all WS rows: P the knitted sts and sl the slipped sts purlwise with yarn in the front.

Row 3: Using A, k2, * k4, sl1, k1; rep from * to last 3 sts, k3.

Row 5: Using B, k1, sl1, * k3, sl1, k2; rep from * to last 3 sts, k1, sl1, k1.

Row 7: Using A, k2, * k2, sl1, k3; rep from * to last 3 sts, k3.

Row 9: Using B, k1, sl1, * k1, sl1, k4; rep from * to last 3 sts, k1, sl1, k1.

Row 11: Using A, k2, * sl1, k5; rep from * to last 3 sts, sl1, k2.

Rep Rows 1 to 12. To finish, work Rows 13 to 16.

Row 13: Using B, k1, sl1, * k5, sl1; rep from * to last 3 sts, k1, sl1, k1.

Row 15: Using A, k all sts.

Row 16: As Row 2.

Crochet Instructions

Multiple of 6 sts + 5

Using A, make desired number of chainless sc.

Row 1 (RS): Using B, 1 ch, 1 sc, 2 ch, skip st, * 5 sc, 2 ch, skip st; rep from * to last 3 sts, 1 sc, 2 ch, skip st, 1 sc, turn.

Row 2 and all WS rows: 1 ch, 1 sc in sts, ch and skip ch-sps, turn.

Row 3: Using A, 1 ch, 1 sc, 1 Mdc, * 4 sc, 2 ch, skip st, 1 Mdc; rep from * to last 3 sts, 1 sc, 1 Mdc 1 sc, turn.

Row 5: Using B, 1 ch, 1 sc, 2 ch, skip st, * 3 sc, 2 ch, skip st, 1 Mdc, 1 sc; rep from * to last 3 sts, 1 sc, 2 ch, skip st, 1 sc, turn.

Row 7: Using A, 1 ch, 1 sc, 1 Mdc, * 2 sc, 2 ch, skip st, 1 Mdc, 2 sc; rep from * to last 3 sts, 1 sc, 1 Mdc, 1 sc, turn.

Row 9: Using B, 1 ch, 1 sc, 2 ch, skip st, * 1 sc, 2 ch, skip st, 1 Mdc, 3 sc; rep from * to last 3 sts, 1 sc, 2 ch, skip st, 1 sc, turn.

Row 11: Using A, 1 ch, 1 sc, 1 Mdc, * 2 ch, skip st, 1 Mdc, 4 sc; rep from * to last 3 sts, 2 ch, skip st, 1 Mdc, 1 sc, turn.

Rep Rows 1 to 12, placing 1 Mdc in sps as required on Row 1. To finish, work Rows 13 to 15.

Row 13: Using B, 1 ch, 1 sc, 2 ch, skip st, * 1 Mdc, 4 sc, 2 ch, skip st; rep from * to last 3 sts, 1 Mdc, 2 ch, skip st, 1 sc, turn.

Row 15: Using A, 1 ch, 1 sc, 1 Mdc, * 5 sc, 1 Mdc; rep from * to last 3 sts, 1 sc, 1 Mdc, 1 sc, turn.

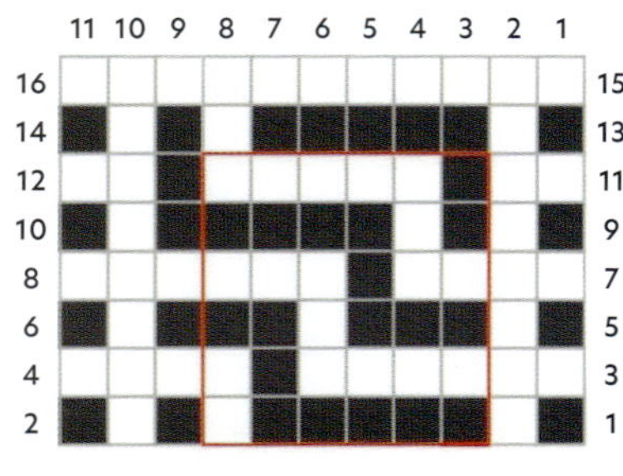

6 sts

Yarn A = Cream

Yarn B = Teal

Little Squares

The crochet version of this pattern is crisper than the knit because the slip stitches slightly distort the lines, but the designs still look just as charming.

Knit Instructions

Multiple of 5 sts + 3

On RS rows, slip the sts purlwise with yarn in the back.

Cast on using A, k one row and p one row.

Row 1 (RS): Using B, k1, sl1, * k4, sl1; rep from * to last st, k1.

Row 2 and all WS rows: P the knitted sts and sl the slipped sts purlwise with yarn in the front.

Row 3: Using A, k2, * sl1, k2, sl1, k1; rep from * to last st, k1.

Row 5: Using B, k1, sl 1, * k4, sl1; rep from * to last st, k1.

Row 7: Using A, k all sts.

Row 8: As Row 2.

Rep Rows 1 to 8.

Crochet Instructions

Multiple of 5 sts + 3

Using A, make desired number of chainless sc.

Row 1 (RS): Using B, 1 ch, 1 sc, 2 ch, skip st, * 4 sc, 2 ch, skip st; rep from * to last st, 1 sc, turn.

Row 2 and all WS rows: 1 ch, 1 sc in sts, ch and skip ch-sps, turn.

Row 3: Using A, 1 ch, 1 sc, 1 Mdc, * 2 ch, skip st, 2 sc, 2 ch, skip st, 1 Mdc; rep from * to last st, 1 sc, turn.

Row 5: Using B, 1 ch, 1 sc, 2 ch, skip st, * 1 Mdc, 2 sc, 1 Mdc, 2 ch, skip st; rep from * to last st, 1 sc, turn.

Row 7: Using A, 1 ch, 1 sc, 1 Mdc, * 4 sc, 1 Mdc; rep from * to last st, 1 sc, turn.

Row 8: As Row 2.

Rep Rows 1 to 8, ending last rep with Row 7.

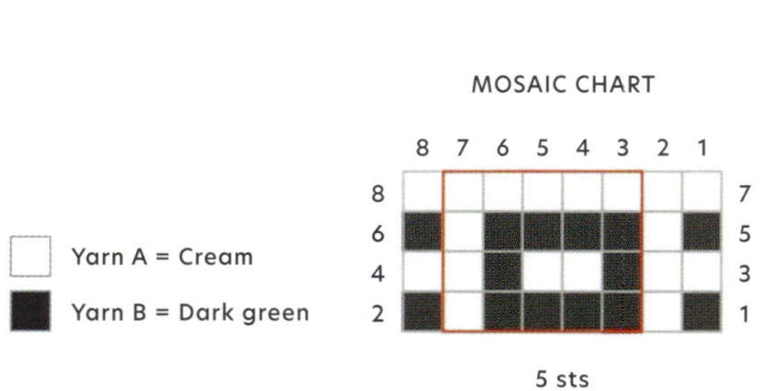

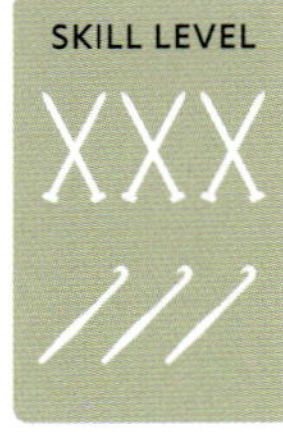

Hearts

A beautiful horizontal repeat that is ideal for adding a touch of charm to any project. Will make perfect table mats, or any home accessory.

Knit Instructions

Multiple of 22 sts + 3

On RS rows, slip the sts purlwise with yarn in the back.

Cast on using A, k one row and p one row.

Row 1 (RS): Using B, k all sts.

Row 2 and all WS rows: P the knitted sts and sl the slipped sts purlwise with yarn in the front.

Row 3: Using A, k all sts.

Row 5: Using B, k2, * sl1, k4, sl1, k3, sl3, k3, sl1, k4, sl1, k1; rep from * to last st, k1.

Row 7: Using A, k1, sl1, * k6, sl1, k1, sl1, k3, sl1, k1, sl1, k6, sl1; rep from * to last st, k1.

Row 9: Using B, k2, * k1, sl1, k2, sl1, k5, sl1, k5, sl1, k2, sl1, k2; rep from * to last st, k1.

Row 11: Using A, k2, * sl1, k4, [sl1, k1] 6 times, k3, sl1, k1; rep from * to last st, k1.

Row 13: Using B, k2, * k2, sl1, k1, sl1, k11, sl1, k1, sl1, k3; rep from * to last st, k1.

Row 15: Using A, k1, sl1, * k1, sl1, k4, [sl1, k1] 5 times, k3, sl1, k1, sl1; rep from * to last st, k1.

Row 17: Using B, k2, * k3, sl1, k1, sl1, k9, sl1, k1, sl1, k4; rep from * to last st, k1.

Row 19: Using A, k2, * sl1, k1, sl1, k4, [sl1, k1] 4 times, k3, [sl1, k1] twice; rep from * to last st, k1.

Row 21: Using B, k2, * k4, sl1, k1, sl1, k7, sl1, k1, sl1, k5; rep from * to last st, k1.

Row 23: Using A, k1, sl1, * [k1, sl1] twice, k4, [sl1, k1] 3 times, k3, [sl1, k1] twice, sl1; rep from * to last st, k1.

Row 25: Using B, k2, * k5, sl1, k1, sl1, k5, sl1, k1, sl1, k6; rep from * to last st, k1.

Row 27: Using A, k2, * sl1, [k1, sl1] twice, k4, [sl1, k1] twice, k3, [sl1, k1] 3 times; rep from * to last st, k1.

Row 29: Using B, k1, sl1, * k5, sl1, k2, sl1, k3, sl1, k2, sl1, k5, sl1; rep from * to last st, k1.

Row 31: Using A, k2, * [k1, sl1] twice, k6, sl1, k6, [sl1, k1] twice, k1; rep from * to last st, k1.

Row 33: Using B, k1, sl1, * sl1, k3, sl1, k4, sl1, k1, sl1, k4, sl1, k3, sl2; rep from * to last st, k1.

Row 35: Using A, k all sts.

Row 37: Using B, k all sts.

Row 39: Using A, k all sts.

Row 40: As Row 2.

Crochet Instructions

Multiple of 22 sts + 3

Pattern note: The repeat in written instructions differs from chart on Row 33.

Using A, make desired number of chainless sc.

Row 1 (RS): Using B, 1 ch, 1 sc in every st, turn.

Row 2 and all WS rows: 1 ch, 1 sc in sts, ch and skip ch-sps, turn.

Row 3: Using A, 1 ch, 1 sc in every st, turn.

Row 5: Using B, 1 ch, 2 sc, * 2 ch, skip st, 4 sc, 2 ch, skip st, 3 sc, 4 ch, skip 3 sts, 3 sc, 2 ch, skip st, 4 sc, 2 ch, skip st, 1 sc; rep from * to last st, 1 sc, turn.

Row 7: Using A, 1 ch, 1 sc, 2 ch, skip st, * 1 Mdc, 4 sc, 1 Mdc, 2 ch, skip st, 1 sc, 2 ch, skip st, 3 Mdc, 2 ch, skip st, 1 sc, 2 ch, skip st, 1 Mdc, 4 sc, 1 Mdc, 2 ch, skip st; rep from * to last 1 st, 1 sc, turn.

Row 9: Using B, 1 ch, 1 sc, 1 Mdc, * 1 sc, 2 ch, skip st, 2 sc, 2 ch, skip st, [1 sc, 1 Mdc] twice, 1 sc, 2 ch, skip st [1 sc, 1 Mdc] twice, 1 sc, 2 ch, skip st, 2 sc, 2 ch, skip st, 1 sc, 1 Mdc; rep from * to last st, 1 sc, turn.

Yarn A = Cream

Yarn B = Teal

MOSAIC CHART

22 sts

Row 11: Using A, 1 ch, 2 sc, * 2 ch, skip st, 1 Mdc, 2 sc, 1 Mdc, [2 ch, skip st, 1 sc] twice, 2 ch, skip st, 1 Mdc, [2 ch, skip st, 1 sc] twice, 2 ch, skip st, 1 Mdc, 2 sc, 1 Mdc, 2 ch, skip st, 1 sc; rep from * to last 1 st, 1 sc, turn.
Row 13: Using B, 1 ch, 2 sc, * 1 Mdc, 1 sc, 2 ch, skip st, 1 sc, 2 ch, skip st, [1 Mdc, 1 sc] 5 times, 1 Mdc, 2 ch, skip st, 1 sc, 2 ch, skip st, 1 sc, 1 Mdc, 1 sc; rep from * to last st, 1 sc, turn.
Row 15: Using A, 1 ch, 1 sc, 2 ch, skip st, * 1 sc, 2 ch, skip st, [1 Mdc, 1 sc] twice, [2 ch, skip st, 1 sc] 5 times, 1 Mdc, 1 sc, 1 Mdc, 2 ch, skip st, 1 sc, 2 ch, skip st; rep from * to last 1 st, 1 sc, turn.
Row 17: Using B, 1 ch, 1 sc, 1 Mdc, * 1 sc, 1 Mdc, 1 sc, 2 ch, skip st, 1 sc, 2 ch, skip st, [1 Mdc, 1 sc] 4 times, 1 Mdc, 2 ch, skip st, 1 sc, 2 ch, skip st, [1 sc, 1 Mdc] twice; rep from * to last st, 1 sc, turn.
Row 19: Using A, 1 ch, 2 sc, * 2 ch, skip st, 1 sc, 2 ch, skip st, [1 Mdc, 1 sc] twice, [2 ch, skip st, 1 sc] 4 times, 1 Mdc, 1 sc, 1 Mdc, [2 ch, skip st, 1 sc] twice; rep from * to last 1 st, 1 sc, turn.
Row 21: Using B, 1 ch, 2 sc, * [1 Mdc, 1 sc] twice, 2 ch, skip st, 1 sc, 2 ch, skip st, [1 Mdc, 1 sc] 3 times, 1 Mdc, 2 ch, skip st, 1 sc, 2 ch, skip st, [1 sc, 1 Mdc] twice, 1 sc; rep from * to last st, 1 sc, turn.
Row 23: Using A, 1 ch, 1 sc, 2 ch, skip st, * [1 sc, 2 ch, skip st] twice, [1 Mdc, 1 sc] twice, [2 ch, skip st, 1 sc] twice, 2 ch, skip st, [1 sc, 1 Mdc] twice, [2 ch, skip st, 1 sc] twice, 2 ch, skip st; rep from * to last 1 st, 1 sc, turn.
Row 25: Using B, 1 ch, 1 sc, 1 Mdc, * [1 sc, 1 Mdc] twice, 1 sc, 2 ch, skip st, 1 sc, 2 ch, skip st, [1 Mdc, 1 sc] twice, 1 Mdc, 2 ch, skip st, 1 sc, 2 ch, skip st, [1 sc, 1 Mdc] 3 times; rep from * to last st, 1 sc, turn.
Row 27: Using A, 1 ch, 2 sc, * [2 ch, skip st, 1 sc] twice, 2 ch, skip st, [1 Mdc, 1 sc] twice, [2 ch, skip st, 1 sc] twice, 1 Mdc, 1 sc, 1 Mdc, [2 ch, skip st, 1 sc] 3 times; rep from * to last 1 st, 1 sc, turn.
Row 29: Using B, 1 ch, 1 sc, 2 ch, skip st, * [1 Mdc, 1 sc] twice, 1 Mdc, 2 ch, skip st, 2 sc, 2 ch, skip st, 1 Mdc, 1 sc, 1 Mdc, 2 ch, skip st, 2 sc, 2 ch, skip st, [1 Mdc, 1 sc] twice, 1 Mdc, 2 ch, skip st; rep from * to last st, 1 sc, turn.
Row 31: Using A, 1 ch, 1 sc, 1 Mdc, * [1 sc, 2 ch, skip st] twice, 1 sc, 1 Mdc, 2 sc, 1 Mdc, 1 sc, 2 ch, skip st, 1 sc, 1 Mdc, 2 sc, 1 Mdc, 1 sc, [2 ch, skip st, 1 sc] twice, 1 Mdc; rep from * to last 1 st, 1 Mdc, turn.
Row 33: Using B, 1 ch, 1 sc, 3 ch, skip 2sts, * 1 Mdc, 1 sc, 1 Mdc, 2 ch, skip st, 4 sc, 2 ch, skip st, 1 Mdc, 2 ch, skip st, 4 sc, 2 ch, skip st, 1 Mdc, 1 sc. 1 Mdc **, 4 ch, skip 3 sts; rep from * to last 3 sts, ending last rep at **, 3 ch, skip 2 sts, 1 sc, turn.
Row 35: Using A, 1 ch, 1 sc, 1 Mdc, * 1 Mdc, 3 sc, 1 Mdc, 4 sc, 1 Mdc, 1 sc, 1 Mdc, 4 sc, 1 Mdc, 3 sc, 2 Mdc; rep from * to last 1 st, 1 sc, turn.
Row 37: Using B, 1 ch, 1 sc in every st, turn.
To finish, work Row 39.
Row 39: Using A, 1 ch, 1 sc in every st.

Diagonal Cubes

This is another one of the simple-to-work designs that will really benefit from being worked over a large area, to make the most of the visual effect of the repeat.

Knit Instructions

Multiple of 9 sts + 5

On RS rows, slip the sts purlwise with yarn in the back.

Cast on using A, k one row and p one row.

Row 1 (RS): Using B, k1, * k3, sl3, k3; rep from * to last 4 sts, k4.

Row 2 and all WS rows: P the knitted sts and sl the slipped sts purlwise with yarn in the front.

Row 3: Using A, k1, * sl3, k6; rep from * to last 4 sts, sl3, k1.

Row 5: Using B, k1, * k6, sl3; rep from * to last 4 sts, k4.

Row 7: Using A, k1, * k3, sl3, k3; rep from * to last 4 sts, k4.

Row 9: Using B, k1, * sl3, k6; rep from * to last 4 sts, sl3, k1.

Row 11: Using A, k1, * k6, sl3; rep from * to last 4 sts, k4.

Row 12: As Row 2.

Rep Rows 1 to 12. To finish, work Row 11 by k all sts and Row 12 by p all sts.

Crochet Instructions

Multiple of 9 sts + 5

Using A, make desired number of chainless sc.

Row 1 (RS): Using B, 1 ch, 1 sc, * 3 sc, 4 ch, skip 3 sts, 3 sc; rep from * to last 4 sts, 4 sc, turn.

Row 2 and all WS rows: 1 ch, 1 sc in sts, ch and skip ch-sps, turn.

Row 3: Using A, 1 ch, 1 sc, * 4 ch, skip 3 sts, 3 Mdc, 3 sc; rep from * to last 4 sts, 4 ch, skip 3 sts, 1 sc, turn.

Row 5: Using B, 1 ch, 1 sc, * 3 Mdc, 3 sc, 4 ch, skip 3 sts; rep from * to last 4 sts, 3 Mdc, 1 sc, turn.

Row 7: Using A, 1 ch, 1 sc, * 3 sc, 4 ch, skip 3 sts, 3 Mdc; rep from * to last 4 sts, 4 sc, turn.

Row 9: Using B, 1 ch, 1 sc, * 4 ch, skip 3 sts, 3 Mdc, 3 sc; rep from * to last 4 sts, 4 ch, skip 3 sts, 1 sc, turn.

Row 11: Using A, 1 ch, 1 sc, * 3 Mdc, 3 sc, 4 ch, skip 3 sts; rep from * to last 4 sts, 3 Mdc, 1 sc, turn.

Row 12: As Row 2.

Rep Rows 1 to 12, placing 1 Mdc in sps as required on Row 1. End last rep with Row 11 as follows: Using A, work 1 sc in every st and 1 Mdc in every sp.

MOSAIC CHART

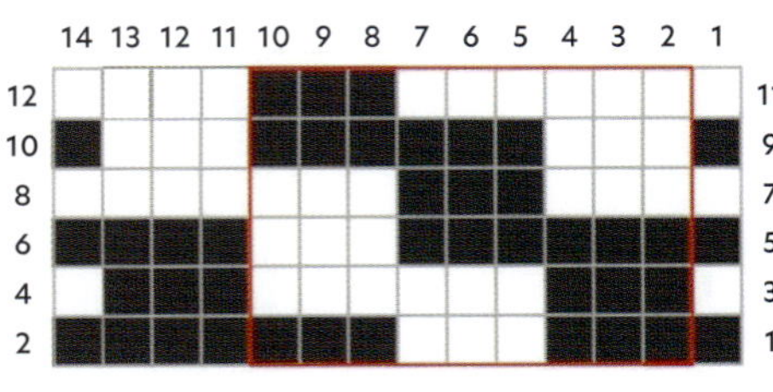

Yarn A = Cream

Yarn B = Teal

Brickwall

The simplicity of the repeat in this pattern means you'll soon get the hang of it—a very relaxing and satisfying design to work on.

Knit Instructions

Multiple of 6 sts + 5

On RS rows, slip the sts purlwise with yarn in the back.

Cast on using A, k one row and p one row.

Row 1 (RS): Using B, k all sts.

Row 2 and all WS rows: P the knitted sts and sl the slipped sts purlwise with yarn in the front.

Row 3: Using A, k2, * sl1, k5; rep from * to last 3 sts, sl1, k2.

Row 5: Using B, k all sts.

Row 7: Using A, k2, * k3, sl1, k2; rep from * to last 3 sts, k3.

Row 9: Using B, k all sts.

Row 11: Using A, as Row 3.

Row 12: As Row 4.

Rep Rows 5 to 12. To finish, work Row 11 by k all sts and Row 12 by p all sts.

Crochet Instructions

Multiple of 6 sts + 5

Using A, make desired number of chainless sc.

Row 1 (RS): Using B, 1 ch, 1 sc in every st to end, turn.

Row 2 and all WS rows: 1 ch, 1 sc in sts, ch and skip ch-sps, turn.

Row 3: Using A, 1 ch, 2 sc, * 2 ch, skip st, 5 sc; rep from * to last 3 sts, 2 ch, skip st, 2 sc, turn.

Row 5: Using B, 1 ch, 2 sc, * 1 Mdc, 5 sc; rep from * to last 3 sts, 1 Mdc, 2 sc, turn.

Row 7: Using A, 1 ch, 2 sc, * 3 sc, 2 ch, skip st, 2 sc; rep from * to last 3 sts, 3 sc, turn.

Row 9: Using B, 1 ch, 2 sc, * 3 sc, 1 Mdc, 2 sc; rep from * to last 3 sts, 3 sc, turn.

Row 11: Using A, as Row 3.

Row 12: Using A, as Row 2.

Rep Rows 5 to 12, ending last rep with Row 11 as follows: Using A, work 1 sc in every st and 1 Mdc in every sp.

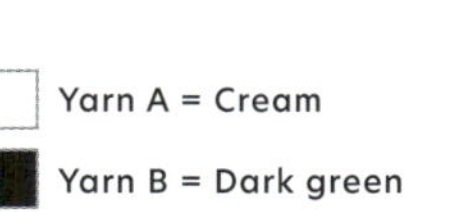

MOSAIC CHART

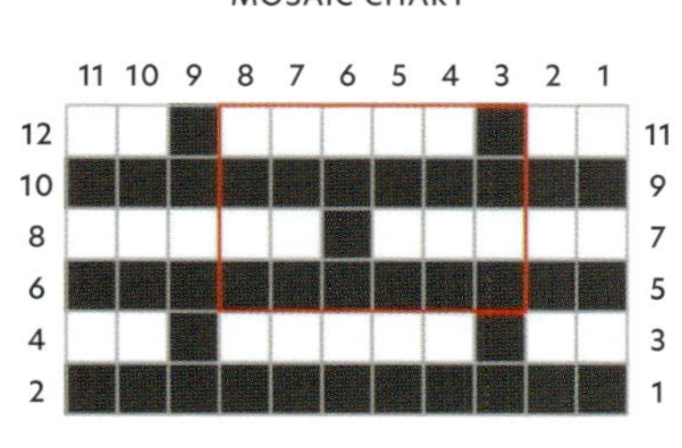

Ladder

Perfect for larger projects such as pillows, blankets, scarves, and table runners, this pattern will give a diagonal striped effect.

Knit Instructions

Multiple of 6 sts + 5

On RS rows, slip the sts purlwise with yarn in the back.

Cast on using A, k one row and p one row.

Row 1 (RS): Using B, k1, sl1, * k1, sl3, k1, sl1; rep from * to last 3 sts, k1, sl1, k1.

Row 2 and all WS rows: P the knitted sts and sl the slipped sts purlwise with yarn in the front.

Row 3: Using A, k2, * sl1, k3, sl1, k1; rep from * to last 3 sts, sl1, k2.

Row 5: Using B, k1, sl1, * k3, sl1, k1, sl1; rep from * to last 3 sts, k1, sl1, k1.

Row 7: Using A, k2, * [sl1, k1] twice, k2; rep from * to last 3 sts, sl1, k2.

Row 9: Using B, k1, sl1, * k1, sl1, k3, sl1; rep from * to last 3 sts, k1, sl1, k1.

Row 11: Using A, k2, * k2, [sl1, k1] twice; rep from * to last 3 sts, k3.

Row 13: Using B, k1, sl1, * [k1, sl1] twice, k2; rep from * to last 3 sts, k1, sl1, k1.

Row 15: Using A, k2, * sl1, k3, sl1, k1; rep from * to last 3 sts, sl1, k2.

Row 16: As Row 2.

Rep Rows 5 to 16. To finish, work Row 15 by k all sts and Row 16 by p all sts.

Crochet Instructions

Multiple of 6 sts + 5

Using A, make desired number of chainless sc.

Row 1 (RS): Using B, 1 ch, 1 sc, 2 ch, skip st, * 1 sc, 4 ch, skip 3 sts, 1 sc, 2 ch, skip st; rep from * to last 3 sts, 1 sc, 2 ch, skip st, 1 sc, turn.

Row 2 and all WS rows: 1 ch, 1 sc in sts, ch and skip ch-sps, turn.

Row 3: Using A, 1 ch, 1 sc, 1 Mdc, * 2 ch, skip st, 3 Mdc, 2 ch, skip st, 1 Mdc; rep from * to last 3 sts, 2 ch, skip st, 1 Mdc, 1 sc, turn.

Row 5: Using B, 1 ch, 1 sc, 2 ch, skip st, * 1 Mdc, 2 sc, 2 ch, skip st, 1 Mdc, 2 ch, skip st; rep from * to last 3 sts, 1 Mdc, 2 ch, skip st, 1 sc, turn.

Row 7: Using A, 1 ch, 1 sc, 1 Mdc, * 2 ch, skip st, 1 sc, 2 ch, skip st, 1 Mdc, 1 sc, 1 Mdc; rep from * to last 3 sts, 2 ch, skip st, 1 Mdc, 1 sc, turn.

Row 9: Using B, 1 ch, 1 sc, 2 ch, skip st, * 1 Mdc, 2 ch, skip st, 1 Mdc, 2 sc, 2 ch, skip st; rep from * to last 3 sts, 1 Mdc, 2 ch, skip st, 1 sc, turn.

Row 11: Using A, 1 ch, 1 sc, 1 Mdc, * 1 sc, 1 Mdc, 2 ch, skip st, 1 sc, 2 ch, skip st, 1 Mdc; rep from * to last 3 sts, 1 sc, 1 Mdc, 1 sc, turn.

Row 13: Using B, 1 ch, 1 sc, 2 ch, skip st, * 1 sc, 2 ch, skip st, 1 Mdc, 2 ch, skip st, 1 Mdc, 1 sc; rep from * to last 3 sts, 1 sc, 2 ch, skip st, 1 sc, turn.

Row 15: Using A, 1 ch, 1 sc, 1 Mdc, * 2 ch, skip st, 1 Mdc, 1 sc, 1 Mdc, 2 ch,

MOSAIC CHART

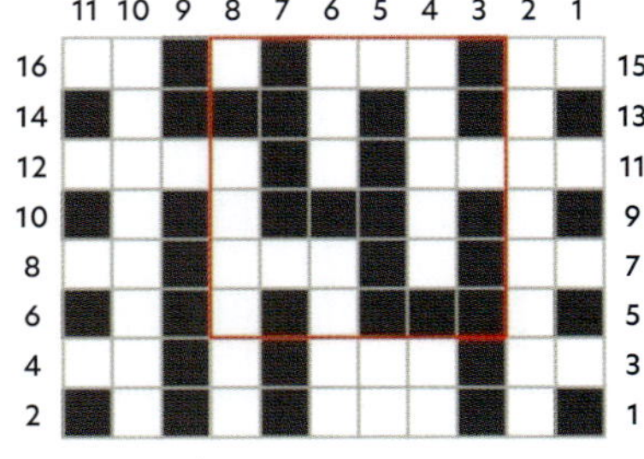

6 sts

Yarn A = Cream

Yarn B = Teal

skip st, 1 sc; rep from * to last 3 sts, 2 ch, skip st, 1 Mdc, 1 sc, turn.

Row 16: As Row 2.

Rep Rows 5 to 16, placing 1 Mdc in sps as required on Row 1. End last rep with Row 15 as follows: Using A, 1 sc in every st and 1 Mdc in every sp.

KNIT

CROCHET

Peaks

This simple repeat will make for a stunning patterned fabric when worked over a large area, but it would also work on a smaller scale as a patch pocket or hat.

Knit Instructions

Multiple of 6 sts + 3

On RS rows, slip the sts purlwise with yarn in the back.

Cast on using A, k one row and p one row.

Row 1 (RS): Using B, k2, * k1, sl1, k1, sl1, k2; rep from * to last st, k1.

Row 2 and all WS rows: P the knitted sts and sl the slipped sts purlwise with yarn in the front.

Row 3: Using A, k1, sl1, * k2, sl1, k2, sl1; rep from * to last st, k1.

Row 5: Using B, k2, * sl1, k3, sl1, k1; rep from * to last st, k1.

Row 7: Using A, k2, * k1, sl1, k1, sl1, k2; rep from * to last st, k1.

Row 9: Using B, k1, sl1, * k2, sl1, k2, sl1; rep from * to last st, k1.

Row 11: Using A, k2, * sl1, k3, sl1, k1; rep from * to last st, k1.

Rep Rows 1 to 12. To finish, work Rows 13 to 20.

Row 13: Using B, k2, * k1, sl1, k1, sl1, k2; rep from * to last st, k1.

Row 15: Using A, k1, sl1, * k2, sl1, k2, sl1; rep from * to last st, k1.

Row 17: Using B, k2, * sl1, k3, sl1, k1; rep from * to last st, k1.

Row 19: Using A, k all sts.

Row 20: As Row 19.

Crochet Instructions

Multiple of 6 sts + 3

Using A, make desired number of chainless sc.

Row 1 (RS): Using B, 1 ch, 2 sc, * 1 sc, 2 ch, skip st, 1 sc, 2 ch, skip st, 2 sc; rep from * to last st, 1 sc, turn.

Row 2 and all WS rows: 1 ch, 1 sc in sts, ch and skip ch-sps, turn. **Row 3:** Using A, 1 ch, 1 sc, 2 ch, skip st, * 1 sc, 1 Mdc, 2 ch, skip st, 1 Mdc, 1 sc, 2 ch, skip st; rep from * to last st, 1 sc, turn.

Row 5: Using B, 1 ch, 1 sc, 1 Mdc, * 2 ch, skip st, 1 sc, 1 Mdc, 1 sc, 2 ch, skip st, 1 Mdc; rep from * to last st, 1 sc, turn.

Row 7: Using A, 1 ch, 2 sc, * 1 Mdc, 2 ch, skip st, 1 sc, 2 ch, skip st, 1 Mdc, 1 sc; rep from * to last st, 1 sc, turn.

Row 9: Using B, 1 ch, 1 sc, 2 ch, skip st, * 1 sc, 1 Mdc, 2 ch, skip st, 1 Mdc, 1 sc, 2 ch, skip st; rep from * to last st, 1 sc, turn.

Row 11: Using A, 1 ch, 1 sc, 1 Mdc, * 2 ch, skip st, 1 sc, 1 Mdc, 1 sc, 2 ch, skip st, 1 Mdc; rep from * to last st, 1 sc, turn.

Rep Rows 1 to 12, placing 1 Mdc in sps as required on Row 1. To finish, work Rows 13 to 19.

Row 13: Using B, 1 ch, 2 sc, * 1 Mdc, 2 ch, skip st, 1 sc, 2 ch, skip st, 1 Mdc, 1 sc; rep from * to last st, 1 sc, turn.

Row 15: Using A, 1 ch, 1 sc, 2 ch, skip st, * 1 sc, 1 Mdc, 2 ch, skip st, 1 Mdc, 1 sc,

MOSAIC CHART

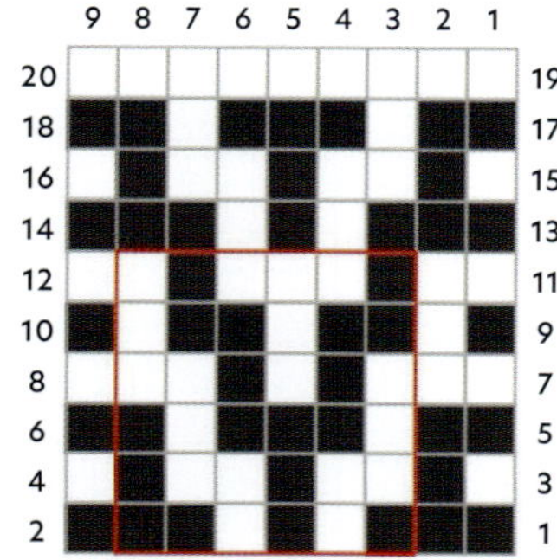

2 ch, skip st; rep from * to last st, 1 sc, turn.

Row 17: Using B, 1 ch, 1 sc, 1 Mdc, * 2 ch, skip st, 1 sc, 1 Mdc, 1 sc, 2 ch, skip st, 1 Mdc; rep from * to last st, 1 sc, turn.

Row 19: Using A, 1 ch, 2 sc, * 1 Mdc, 3 sc, 1 Mdc, 1 sc; rep from * to last st, 1 sc.

KNIT

CROCHET

Section

The lines of the crochet version of Section are a lot more defined, but the knit design produces a squarer shape—both give charming results.

Knit Instructions

Multiple of 8 sts + 3

On RS rows, slip the sts purlwise with yarn in the back.

Cast on using A, k one row and p one row.

Row 1 (RS): Using B, k2, * k2, [sl1, k1] twice, k2; rep from * to last st, k1.

Row 2 and all WS rows: P the knitted sts and sl the slipped sts purlwise with yarn in the front.

Row 3: Using A, k1, sl1, * [k3, sl1] twice; rep from * to last st, k1.

Row 5: Using B, k2, * sl1, k1; rep from * to last st, k1.

Row 7: Using A, k2, * k3, sl1, k4; rep from * to last st, k1.

Row 9: Using B, k all sts.

Row 11: Using A, as Row 7.

Row 13: Using B, as Row 5.

Row 15: Using A, as Row 3.

Rep Rows 1 to 16. To finish, work Rows 17 to 20.

Row 17: Using B, as Row 1.

Row 19: Using A, k2, * k3, sl1, k4; rep from * to last st, k1.

Row 20: As Row 2.

Crochet Instructions

Multiple of 8 sts + 3

Using A, make desired number of chainless sc.

Row 1 (RS): Using B, 1 ch, 2 sc, * 2 sc, [2 ch, skip st, 1 sc] twice, 2 sc; rep from * to last st, 1 sc, turn.

Row 2 and all WS rows: 1 ch, 1 sc in sts, ch and skip ch-sps, turn.

Row 3: Using A, 1 ch, 1 sc, 2 ch, skip st, * 2 sc, 1 Mdc, 2 ch, skip st, 1 Mdc, 2 sc, 2 ch, skip st; rep from * to last st, 1 sc, turn.

Row 5: Using B, 1 ch, 1 sc, 1 Mdc, * [2 ch, skip st, 1 sc, 2 ch, skip st, 1 Mdc] twice ; rep from * to last st, 1 sc, turn.

Row 7: Using A, 1 ch, 2 sc, * 1 Mdc, 1 sc, 1 Mdc, 2 ch, skip st, [1 Mdc, 1 sc] twice; rep from * to last st, 1 sc, turn.

Row 9: Using B, 1 ch, 2 sc, * 3 sc, 1 Mdc, 4 sc; rep from * to last st, 1 sc, turn.

Row 11: Using A, 1 ch, 2 sc, * 3 sc, 2 ch, skip st, 4 sc; rep from * to last st, 1 sc, turn.

Row 13: Using B, 1 ch, 2 sc, * 2 ch, skip

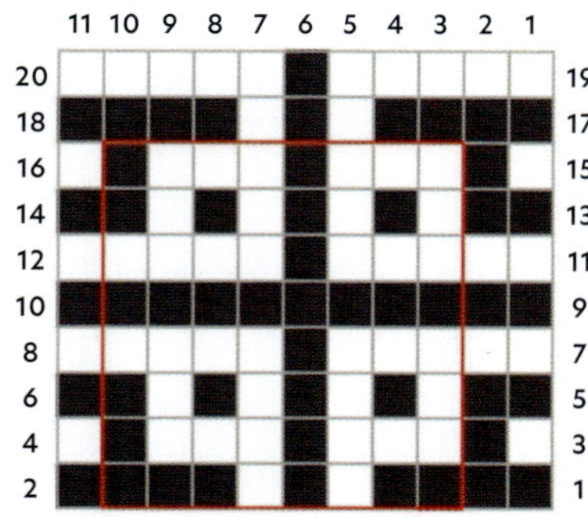

st, 1 sc, 2 ch, skip st, 1 Mdc, 2 ch, skip st, 1 sc, 2 ch, skip st, 1 sc; rep from * to last st, 1 sc, turn.

Row 15: Using A, 1 ch, 1 sc, 2 ch, skip st, * 1 Mdc, 1 sc, 1 Mdc, 2 ch, skip st, 1 Mdc, 1 sc, 1 Mdc, 2 ch, skip st; rep from * to last st, 1 sc, turn.

Rep Rows 1 to 16, placing 1 Mdc in spaces as required on Row 1. To finish, work Rows 17 to 19.

Row 17: Using B, 1 ch, 1 sc, 1 Mdc, * 2 sc, 2 ch, skip st, 1 Mdc, 2 ch, skip st, 2 sc, 1 Mdc; rep from * to last st, 1 sc, turn.

Row 19: Using A, 1 ch, 1 sc in every st and 1 Mdc in every sp.

CROCHET

Starry Night

Inspired by the sparkling stars in the night sky, this pattern would also look beautiful with a navy background. Perfect for bags and accessories.

Knit Instructions

Multiple of 8 sts + 5

On RS rows, slip the sts purlwise with yarn in the back.

Cast on using B, k one row and p one row.

Row 1 (RS): Using A, k1, sl1, * k1, sl1; rep from * to last 3 sts, k1, sl1, k1.

Row 2 and all WS rows: P the knitted sts and sl the slipped sts purlwise with yarn in the front.

Row 3: Using B, k2, * sl1, k7; rep from * to last 3 sts, sl1, k2.

Row 5: Using A, k1, sl1, * k3, [sl1, k1] twice, k1; rep from * to last 3 sts, k1, sl1, k1.

Row 7: As Row 3.

Row 9: As Row 1.

Row 11: Using B, k2, * k4, sl1, k3; rep from * to last 3 sts, k3.

Row 13: Using A, k1, sl1, * k1, sl1, k5, sl1; rep from * to last 3 sts, k1, sl1, k1.

Row 15: As Row 11.

Rep Rows 1 to 16. To finish, work Rows 17 to 20.

Row 17: As Row 1.

Row 19: Using B, k all sts.

Row 20: As Row 2.

Crochet Instructions

Multiple of 8 sts + 5

Using B, make desired number of chainless sc.

Row 1 (RS): Using A, 1 ch, 1 sc, 2 ch, skip st, * [1 sc, 2 ch, skip st] 4 times; rep from * to last 3 sts, 1 sc, 2 ch, skip st, 1 sc, turn.

Row 2 and all WS rows: 1 ch, 1 sc in sts, ch and skip ch-sps, turn.

Row 3: Using B, 1 ch, 1 sc, 1 Mdc, * 2 ch, skip st, [1 Mdc, 1 sc] 3 times, 1 Mdc; rep from * to last 3 sts, 2 ch, skip st, 1 Mdc, 1 sc, turn.

Row 5: Using A, 1 ch, 1 sc, 2 ch, skip st, * 1 Mdc, 2 sc, [2 ch, skip st, 1 sc] twice, 1 sc; rep from * to last 3 sts, 1 Mdc, 2 ch, skip st, 1 sc, turn.

Row 7: Using B, 1 ch, 1 sc, 1 Mdc, * 2 ch, skip st, 2 sc, [1 Mdc, 1 sc] twice, 1 sc; rep from * to last 3 sts, 2 ch, skip st, 1 Mdc, 1 sc, turn.

Row 9: Using A, 1 ch, 1 sc, 2 ch, skip st, * 1 Mdc, [2 ch, skip st, 1 sc] 3 times, 2 ch, skip st; rep from * to last 3 sts, 1 Mdc, 2 ch, skip st, 1 sc, turn.

Row 11: Using B, 1 ch, 1 sc, 1 Mdc, * [1 sc, 1 Mdc] twice, 2 ch, skip st, 1 Mdc, 1 sc, 1 Mdc; rep from * to last 3 sts, 1 sc, 1 Mdc, 1 sc, turn.

Row 13: Using A, 1 ch, 1 sc, 2 ch, skip st, * 1 sc, 2 ch, skip st, 2 sc, 1 Mdc, 2 sc, 2 ch, skip st; rep from * to last 3 sts, 1 sc, 2 ch, skip st, 1 sc, turn.

Row 15: Using B, 1 ch, 1 sc, 1 Mdc, * 1 sc, 1 Mdc, 2 sc, 2 ch, skip st, 2 sc, 1 Mdc; rep from * to last 3 sts, 1 sc, 1 Mdc, 1 sc, turn.

Rep Rows 1 to 16, placing 1 Mdc in sps

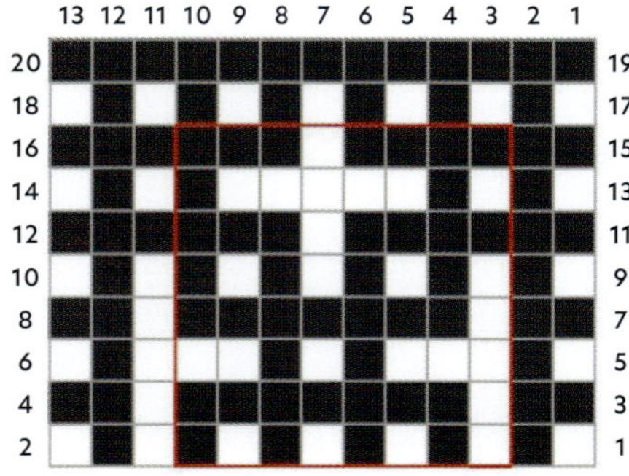

Yarn A = Cream

Yarn B = Teal

as required on Row 1. To finish, work Rows 17 to 19.

Row 17: Using A, 1 ch, 1 sc, 2 ch, skip st, * [1 sc, 2 ch, skip st] twice, 1 Mdc, 2 ch, skip st, 1 sc, 2 ch, skip st; rep from * to last 3 sts, 1 sc, 2 ch, skip st, 1 sc, turn.

Row 19: Using B, 1 ch, 1 sc, 1 Mdc, * [1 sc, 1 Mdc] 4 times; rep from * to last 3 sts, 1 sc, 1 Mdc, 1 sc, turn.

KNIT

CROCHET

Square in a Square

This design is fantastic for mixing and matching with other designs in this chapter. Use a few rows of each pattern to create a unique effect.

Knit Instructions

Multiple of 10 sts + 3

On RS rows, slip the sts purlwise with yarn in the back.

Cast on using A, k one row and p one row.

Row 1 (RS): Using B, k1, * sl1, k9; rep from * to last 2 sts, sl1, k1.

Row 2 and all WS rows: P the knitted sts and sl the slipped sts purlwise with yarn in the front.

Row 3: Using A, k1, * k1, sl1, k7, sl1; rep from * to last 2 sts, k2.

Row 5: Using B, k1, * [sl1, k1] twice, k4, sl1, k1; rep from * to last 2 sts, sl1, k1.

Row 7: Using A, k1, * [k1, sl1] twice, k3, sl1, k1, sl1; rep from * to last 2 sts, k2.

Row 9: Using B, k1, * sl1, k1; rep from * to last 2 sts, sl1, k1.

Row 11: Using A, as Row 7.

Row 13: Using B, as Row 5.

Row 15: Using A, as Row 3.

Row 17: Using B, as Row 1.

Row 19: Using A, k all sts.

Row 20: As Row 2.

Rep Rows 1 to 20.

Crochet Instructions

Multiple of 10 sts + 3

Using A, make desired number of chainless sc.

Row 1 (RS): Using B, 1 ch, 1 sc, * 2 ch, skip st, 9 sc; rep from * to last 2 sts, 2 ch, skip st, 1 sc, turn.

Row 2 and all WS rows: 1 ch, 1 sc in sts, ch and skip ch-sps, turn. **Row 3:** Using A, 1 ch, 1 sc, * 1 Mdc, 2 ch, skip st, 7 sc, 2 ch, skip st; rep from * to last 2 sts, 1 Mdc, 1 sc, turn.

Row 5: Using B, 1 ch, 1 sc, * 2 ch, skip st, 1 Mdc, 2 ch, skip st, 5 sc, 2 ch, skip st, 1 Mdc; rep from * to last 2 sts, 2 ch, skip st, 1 sc, turn.

Row 7: Using A, 1 ch, 1 sc, * [1 Mdc, 2 ch, skip st] twice, 3 sc, 2 ch, skip st, 1 Mdc, 2 ch, skip st; rep from * to last 2 sts, 1 Mdc, 1 sc, turn.

Row 9: Using B, 1 ch, 1 sc, * [2 ch, skip st, 1 Mdc] twice, 2 ch, skip st, 1 sc, [2 ch, skip st, 1 Mdc] twice; rep from * to last 2 sts, 2 ch, skip st, 1 sc, turn.

Row 11: Using A, 1 ch, 1 sc, * [1 Mdc, 2 ch, skip st] twice, 1 Mdc, 1 sc, [1 Mdc, 2 ch, skip st] twice; rep from * to last 2 sts, 1 Mdc, 1 sc, turn.

Row 13: Using B, 1 ch, 1 sc, * [2 ch, skip st, 1 Mdc] twice, 3 sc, 1 Mdc, 2 ch, skip st, 1 Mdc; rep from * to last 2 sts, 2 ch, skip st, 1 sc, turn.

Row 15: Using A, 1 ch, 1 sc, * 1 Mdc, 2 ch, skip st, 1 Mdc, 5 sc, 1 Mdc, 2 ch, skip st; rep from * to last 2 sts, 1 Mdc, 1 sc, turn.

Row 17: Using B, 1 ch, 1 sc, * 2 ch, skip st, 1 Mdc, 7 sc, 1 Mdc; rep from * to last

MOSAIC CHART

2 sts, 2 ch, skip st, 1 sc, turn.

Row 19: Using A, 1 ch, 1 sc, * 1 Mdc, 9 sc; rep from * to last 2 sts, 1 Mdc, 1 sc, turn.

Row 20: As Row 2.

Rep Rows 1 to 20, ending last rep with Row 19.

CROCHET

Triangles

To really showcase the pattern, a few repeats need to be worked. The triangles look gentle but are very effective when showcased on a larger section.

Knit Instructions

Multiple of 12 sts + 3

On RS rows, slip the sts purlwise with yarn in the back.

Cast on using A, k one row and p one row.

Row 1 (RS): Using B, k1, * k5, sl1, k1, sl1, k4; rep from * to last 2 sts, k2.

Row 2 and all WS rows: P the knitted sts and sl the slipped sts purlwise with yarn in the front.

Row 3: Using A, k1, * k3, [sl1, k2] 3 times; rep from * to last 2 sts, k2.

Row 5: Using B, k1, * sl2, k2, sl1, k3, sl1, k2, sl1; rep from * to last 2 sts, sl1, k1.

Row 7: Using A, k1, * [k2, sl1] twice, k1, sl1, k2, sl1, k1; rep from * to last 2 sts, k2.

Row 9: Using B, k1, * sl1, k2; rep from * to last 2 sts, sl1, k1.

Row 11: Using A, k1, * k1, sl1, k2, sl1, k3, sl1, k2, sl1; rep from * to last 2 sts, k2.

Row 13: Using B, k1, * [k2, sl1] twice, sl2, k2, sl1, k1; rep from * to last 2 sts, k2.

Row 15: Using A, k1, * sl1, k2, sl1, k5, sl1, k2; rep from * to last 2 sts, sl1, k1.

Row 17: Using B, k1, * k1, sl1, k9, sl1; rep from * to last 2 sts, k2.

Row 19: Using A, k all sts.

Row 20: As Row 2.

Rep Rows 1 to 20.

Crochet Instructions

Multiple of 12 sts + 3

Pattern note: The repeat in written instructions differs from chart on Row 5.

Using A, make desired number of chainless sc.

Row 1 (RS): Using B, 1 ch, 1 sc, * 5 sc, [2 ch, skip st, 1 sc] twice, 3 sc; rep from * to last 2 sts, 2 sc, turn.

Row 2 and all WS rows: 1 ch, 1 sc in sts, ch and skip ch-sps, turn. **Row 3:** Using A, 1 ch, 1 sc, * 3 sc, 2 ch, skip st, 1 sc, 1 Mdc, 2 ch, skip st, 1 Mdc, 1 sc, 2 ch, skip st, 2 sc; rep from * to last 2 sts, 2 sc, turn.

Row 5: Using B, 1 ch, 1 sc, 3 ch, skip 2 sts, * 1 sc, 1 Mdc, 2 ch, skip st, 1 sc, 1 Mdc, 1 sc, 2 ch, skip st, 1 Mdc, 1 sc **, 4 ch, skip 3 sts; rep from * to last 3 sts, ending last rep at **, 3 ch, skip 2 sts, 1 sc, turn.

Row 7: Using A, 1 ch, 1 sc, * 2 Mdc, 2 ch, skip st, 1 sc, 1 Mdc, 2 ch, skip st, 1 sc, 2 ch, skip st, 1 Mdc, 1 sc, 2 ch, skip st, 1 Mdc; rep from * to last 2 sts, 1 Mdc, 1 sc, turn.

Row 9: Using B, 1 ch, 1 sc, * [2 ch, skip st, 1 sc, 1 Mdc] twice, [2 ch, skip st, 1 Mdc, 1 sc] twice; rep from * to last 2 sts, 2 ch, skip st, 1 sc, turn.

Row 11: Using A, 1 ch, 1 sc, * 1 Mdc, 2 ch, skip st, 1 sc, 1 Mdc, 2 ch, skip st, 1 sc, 1 Mdc, 1 sc, 2 ch, skip st, 1 Mdc, 1 sc, 2 ch, skip st; rep from * to last 2 sts, 1 Mdc, 1 sc, turn.

Row 13: Using B, 1 ch, 1 sc, * 1 sc, 1 Mdc, 2 ch, skip st, 1 sc, 1 Mdc, 4 ch, skip 3 sts, 1 Mdc, 1 sc, 2 ch, skip st, 1 Mdc; rep from * to last 2 sts, 2 sc, turn.

MOSAIC CHART

12 sts

Yarn A = Cream

Yarn B = Teal

Row 15: Using A, 1 ch, 1 sc, * [2 ch, skip st, 1 sc, 1 Mdc] twice, 2 Mdc, 1 sc, 2 ch, skip st, 1 Mdc, 1 sc; rep from * to last 2 sts, 2 ch, skip st, 1 sc, turn.
Row 17: Using B, 1 ch, 1 sc, * 1 Mdc, 2 ch, skip st, 1 sc, 1 Mdc, 5 sc, 1 Mdc, 1 sc, 2 ch, skip st; rep from * to last 2 sts, 1 Mdc, 1 sc, turn.
Row 19: Using A, 1 ch, 1 sc, * 1 sc, 1 Mdc, 9 sc, 1 Mdc; rep from * to last 2 sts, 2 sc, turn.
Row 20: As Row 2.
Rep Rows 1 to 20, ending last rep with Row 19.

CROCHET

TIP: For the knit version: Because of the closeness of slip stitches in the knit version, the slip stitches might get elongated and stitches next to them will burrow. To avoid this and for neater finish, work a garter stitch: knit on the wrong side rows and slip stitches with your yarn in the front.

Candy Corn

This pattern will work perfectly in a single horizontal repeat, but is also rather gorgeous in vertical ones. The knitted version produces fabric with a slightly tight gauge.

Knit Instructions

Multiple of 8 sts + 5

On RS rows, slip the sts purlwise with yarn in the back.

Cast on using B, k one row and p one row.

Row 1 (RS): Using A, k1, sl1, * k3, sl3, k2; rep from * to last 3 sts, k1, sl1, k1.

Row 2 and all WS rows: P the knitted sts and sl the slipped sts purlwise with yarn in the front.

Row 3: Using B, k all sts.

Row 5: Using A, k1, sl1, * k2, [sl2, k1] twice; rep from * to last 3 sts, k1, sl1, k1.

Row 7: Using B, k all sts.

Row 9: Using A, k1, sl1, * k1, sl2, k3, sl2; rep from * to last 3 sts, k1, sl1, k1.

Row 11: Using B, k all sts.

Row 13: Using A, k1, sl1, * sl2, k5, sl1; rep from * to last 3 sts, sl2, k1.

Row 15: Using B, k all sts.

Row 16: As Row 2.

Rep Rows 1 to 16.

Crochet Instructions

Multiple of 8 sts + 5

Pattern note: The repeat in the written instructions differs from chart on Row 13.

Using B, make desired number of chainless sc.

Row 1 (RS): Using A, 1 ch, 1 sc, 2 ch, skip st, * 3 sc, 4 ch, skip 3 sts, 2 sc; rep from * to last 3 sts, 1 sc, 2 ch, skip st, 1 sc, turn.

Row 2 and all WS rows: 1 ch, 1 sc in sts, ch and skip ch-sps, turn.

Row 3: Using B, 1 ch, 1 sc, 1 Mdc, * 3 sc, 3 Mdc, 2 sc; rep from * to last 3 sts, 1 sc, 1 Mdc, 1 sc, turn.

Row 5: Using A, 1 ch, 1 sc, 2 ch, skip st, * 2 sc, [3 ch, skip 2 sts, 1 sc] twice; rep from * to last 3 sts, 1 sc, 2 ch, skip st, 1 sc, turn.

Row 7: Using B, 1 ch, 1 sc, 1 Mdc, * 2 sc, [2 Mdc, 1 sc] twice; rep from * to last 3 sts, 1 sc, 1 Mdc, 1 sc, turn.

Row 9: Using A, 1 ch, 1 sc, 2 ch, skip st, * 1 sc, 3 ch, skip 2 sts, 3 sc, 3 ch, skip 2 sts; rep from * to last 3 sts, 1 sc, 2 ch, skip st, 1 sc, turn.

Row 11: Using B, 1 ch, 1 sc, 1 Mdc, * 1 sc, 2 Mdc, 3 sc, 2 Mdc; rep from * to last 3 sts, 1 sc, 1 Mdc, 1 sc, turn.

Row 13: Using A, 1 ch, 1 sc, * 4 ch, skip 3 sts, 5 sc; rep from * to last 4 sts, 4 ch, skip 3 sts, 1 sc, turn.

Row 15: Using B, 1 ch, 1 sc, 1 Mdc, * 2 Mdc, 5 sc, 1 Mdc; rep from * to last 3 sts, 2 Mdc, 1 sc, turn.

Row 16: As Row 2.

Rep Rows 1 to 16, ending last rep with Row 15.

MOSAIC CHART

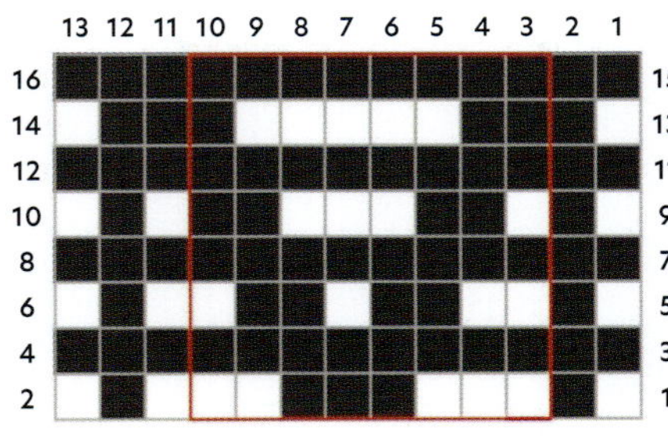

8 sts

Yarn A = Cream

Yarn B = Teal

Chains

This design is best worked with a few repeats that will showcase the pattern to its full beauty.

Knit Instructions

Multiple of 6 sts + 7

On RS rows, slip the sts purlwise with yarn in the back.

Cast on using B, k one row and p one row.

Row 1 (RS): Using A, k1, sl1, k2, * k1, sl1, k4; rep from * to last 3 sts, k1, sl1, k1.

Row 2 and all WS rows: P the knitted sts and sl the slipped sts purlwise with yarn in the front.

Row 3: Using B, k2, sl1, k1, * k2, [sl1, k1] twice; rep from * to last 3 sts, k3.

Row 5: Using A, [k1, sl1] twice, * k5, sl1; rep from * to last 3 sts, k1, sl1, k1.

Row 7: Using B, k4, * [sl1, k1] twice, k2; rep from * to last 3 sts, sl1, k2.

Row 9: Using A, k1, sl1, k2, * k3, sl1, k2; rep from * to last 3 sts, k1, sl1, k1.

Row 11: Using B, k2, sl1, k1, * sl1, k3, sl1, k1; rep from * to last 3 sts, sl1, k2.

Row 12: As Row 2.

Rep Rows 1 to 12. To finish, work Row 11 by k all sts and Row 12 by p all sts.

Crochet Instructions

Multiple of 6 sts + 7

Using B, make desired number of chainless sc.

Row 1 (RS): Using A, 1 ch, 1 sc, 2 ch, skip st, 2 sc, * 1 sc, 2 ch, skip st, 4 sc; rep from * to last 3 sts, 1 sc, 2 ch, skip st, 1 sc, turn.

Row 2 and all WS rows: 1 ch, 1 sc in sts, ch and skip ch-sps, turn.

Row 3: Using B, 1 ch, 1 sc, 1 Mdc, 2 ch, skip st, 1 sc, * 1 sc, 1 Mdc, [2 ch, skip st, 1 sc] twice; rep from * to last 3 sts, 1 sc, 1 Mdc, 1 sc, turn.

Row 5: Using A, 1 ch, 1 sc, 2 ch, skip st, 1 Mdc, 2 ch, skip st, * 2 sc, 1 Mdc, 1 sc, 1 Mdc, 2 ch, skip st; rep from * to last 3 sts, 1 sc, 2 ch, skip st, 1 sc, turn.

Row 7: Using B, 1 ch, [1 sc, 1 Mdc] twice, * [2 ch, skip st, 1 sc] twice, 1 sc, 1 Mdc; rep from * to last 3 sts, 2 ch, skip st, 1 Mdc, 1 sc, turn.

Row 9: Using A, 1 ch, 1 sc, 2 ch, skip st, 2 sc, * 1 Mdc, 1 sc, 1 Mdc, 2 ch, skip st, 2 sc; rep from * to last 3 sts, 1 Mdc, 2 ch, skip st, 1 sc, turn.

Row 11: Using B, 1 ch, 1 sc, 1 Mdc, 2 ch, skip st, 1 sc, * 2 ch, skip st, 2 sc, 1 Mdc, 2 ch, skip st, 1 sc; rep from * to last 3 sts, 2 ch, skip st, 1 Mdc, 1 sc, turn.

Row 12: As Row 2.

Rep Rows 1 to 12, placing 1 Mdc in sps as required on Row 1. End last rep with Row 11 as follows: Using A, work 1 sc in every st and 1 Mdc in every sp.

MOSAIC CHART

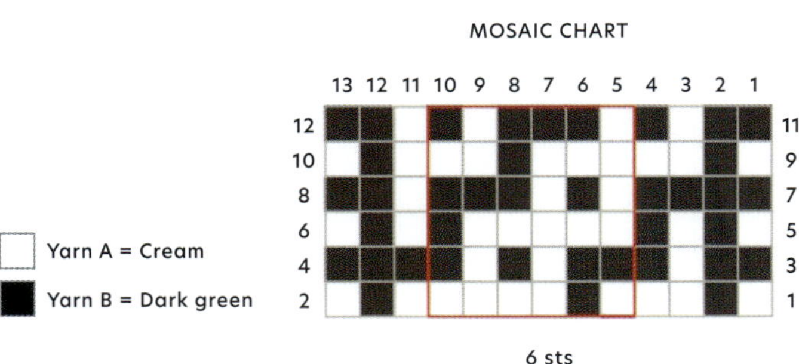

Nature

Bees

I had to include nature's super workers in the book. This bee design will look amazing on a blanket, a cardigan, or a shawl where the repeat pattern can shine.

Knit Instructions

Multiple of 12 sts + 5

On RS rows, slip the sts purlwise with yarn in the back.

Cast on using A, k one row and p one row.

Row 1 (RS): Using B, k1, sl1, k1, * sl1, k9, sl1, k1; rep from * to last 2 sts, sl1, k1.

Row 2 and all WS rows: P the knitted sts and sl the slipped sts purlwise with yarn in the front.

Row 3: Using A, k2, sl1, * k4, sl1, k1, sl1, k4, sl1; rep from * to last 2 sts, k2.

Row 5: Using B, k3, * k1, sl3, k3, sl3, k2; rep from * to last 2 sts, k2.

Row 7: Using A, k1, sl1, k1, * sl1, k4, sl1, k4, sl1, k1; rep from * to last 2 sts, sl1, k1.

Row 9: Using B, k3, * k4, sl1, k1, sl1, k5; rep from * to last 2 sts, k2.

Row 11: Using A, k1, sl1, k1, * sl1, k2, sl1, k3, sl1, k2, sl1, k1; rep from * to last 2 sts, sl1, k1.

Row 13: Using B, k3, * k5, sl1, k6; rep from * to last 2 sts, k2.

Row 15: Using A, k1, sl1, k1, * sl1, k3, sl1, k1, sl1, k3, sl1, k1; rep from * to last 2 sts, sl1, k1.

Row 17: Using B, k3, * k5, sl1, k6; rep from * to last 2 sts, k2.

Row 19: Using A, k1, sl2, * sl1, k9, sl2; rep from * to last 2 sts, sl1, k1.

Row 21: Using B, k3, * k1, sl2, k2, sl1, k2, sl2, k2; rep from * to last 2 sts, k2.

Row 23: Using A, k1, sl1, k1, * sl1, k3, sl1, k1, sl1, k3, sl1, k1; rep from * to last 2 sts, sl1; k1.

Row 25: Using B, k2, sl1, * k2, sl2, k3, sl2, k2, sl1; rep from * to last 2 sts, k2.

Row 27: Using A, k3, * k4, sl3, k5; rep from * to last 2 sts, k2.

Row 29: Using B, k2, sl1, * k11, sl1; rep from * to last 2 sts, k2.

Row 31: Using A, k1, sl1, k1, * sl1, k3, sl1, k1, sl1, k3, sl1, k1; rep from * to last 2 sts, sl1, k1.

Row 33: Using B, k2, sl1, * k11, sl1; rep from * to last 2 sts, k2.

Row 35: Using A, k3, * k1, sl1, k2, sl1, k1, sl1, k2, sl1, k2; rep from * to last 2 sts, k2.

Rep Rows 1 to 36. To finish, work Rows 37 to 40.

Row 37: Using B, k1, sl1, k1, * sl1, k9, sl1, k1; rep from * to last 2 sts, sl1, k1.

Row 39: Using A, k all sts.

Row 40: As Row 2.

MOSAIC CHART

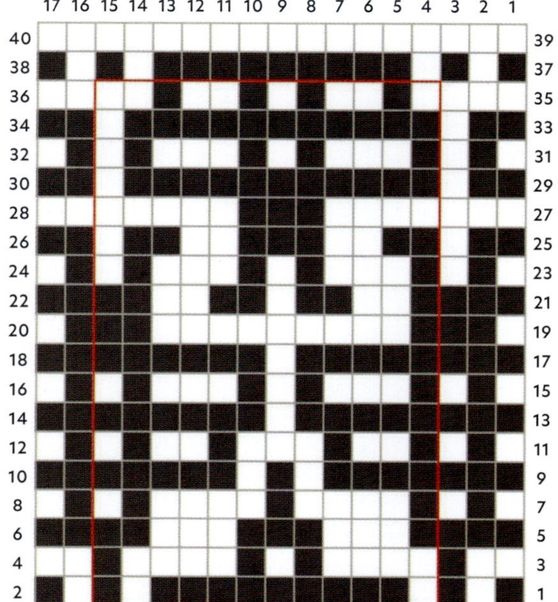

12 sts

Yarn A = Cream

Yarn B = Yellow

Crochet Instructions

Multiple of 12 sts + 5

Using A, make desired number of chainless sc.

Row 1 (RS): Using B, 1 ch, 1 sc, 2 ch, skip st, 1 sc, * 2 ch, skip st, 9 sc, 2 ch, skip st, 1 sc; rep from * to last 2 sts, 2 ch, skip st, 1 sc, turn.

Row 2 and all WS rows: 1 ch, 1 sc in sts, ch and skip ch-sps, turn.

Row 3: Using A, 1 ch, 1 sc, 1 Mdc, 2 ch, skip st, * 1 Mdc, 3 sc, 2 ch, skip st, 1 sc, 2 ch, skip st, 3 sc, 1 Mdc, 2 ch, skip st; rep from * to last 2 sts, 1 Mdc, 1 sc, turn.

Row 5: Using B, 1 ch, 2 sc, 1 Mdc, * 1 sc, 4 ch, skip 3 sts, 1 Mdc, 1 sc, 1 Mdc, 4 ch, skip 3 sts, 1 sc, 1 Mdc; rep from * to last 2 sts, 2 sc, turn.

Row 7: Using A, 1 ch, 1 sc, 2 ch, skip st, 1 sc, * 2 ch, skip st, 3 Mdc, 1 sc, 2 ch, skip st, 1 sc, 3 Mdc, 2 ch, skip st, 1 sc; rep from * to last 2 sts, 2 ch, skip st, 1 sc, turn.

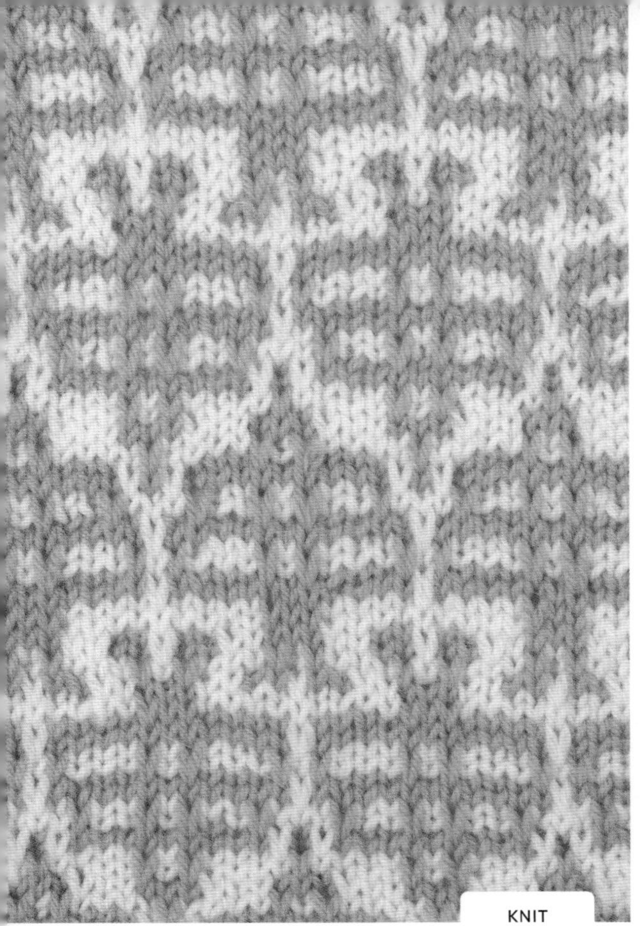
KNIT

CROCHET

Row 9: Using B, 1 ch, 1 sc, 1 Mdc, 1 sc, * 1 Mdc, 3 sc, 2 ch, skip st, 1 Mdc, 2 ch, skip st, 3 sc, 1 Mdc, 1 sc; rep from * to last 2 sts, 1 Mdc, 1 sc, turn.
Row 11: Using A, 1 ch, 1 sc, 2 ch, skip st, 1 sc, * 2 ch, skip st, 2 sc, 2 ch, skip st, 1 Mdc, 1 sc, 1 Mdc, 2 ch, skip st, 2 sc, 2 ch, skip st, 1 sc; rep from * to last 2 sts, 2 ch, skip st, 1 sc, turn.
Row 13: Using B, 1 ch, 1 sc, 1 Mdc, 1 sc, * 1 Mdc, 2 sc, 1 Mdc, 1 sc, 2 ch, skip st, 1 sc, 1 Mdc, 2 sc, 1 Mdc, 1 sc; rep from * to last 2 sts, 1 Mdc, 1 sc, turn.
Row 15: Using A, 1 ch, 1 sc, 2 ch, skip st, 1 sc, * 2 ch, skip st, 3 sc, 2 ch, skip st, 1 Mdc, 2 ch, skip st, 3 sc, 2 ch, skip st, 1 sc; rep from * to last 2 sts, 2 ch, skip st, 1 sc, turn.
Row 17: Using B, 1 ch, 1 sc, 1 Mdc, 1 sc, * 1 Mdc, 3 sc, 1 Mdc, 2 ch, skip st, 1 Mdc, 3 sc, 1 Mdc, 1 sc; rep from * to last 2 sts, 1 Mdc, 1 sc, turn.
Row 19: Using A, 1 ch, 1 sc, 4 ch, skip 3 sts, * 4 sc, 1 Mdc, 4 sc, 4 ch, skip 3 sts; rep from * to last st, 1 sc, turn.
Row 21: Using B, 1 ch, 1 sc, 2 Mdc, * 1 Mdc, 3 ch, skip 2 sts, 2 sc, 2 ch, skip st, 2 sc, 3 ch, skip 2 sts, 2 Mdc; rep from * to last 2 sts, 1 Mdc, 1 sc, turn.
Row 23: Using A, 1 ch, 1 sc, 2 ch, skip st, 1 sc, * 2 ch, skip st, 2 Mdc, 1 sc, 2 ch, skip st, 1 Mdc, 2 ch, skip st, 1 sc, 2 Mdc, 2 ch, skip st, 1 sc; rep from * to last 2 sts, 2 ch, skip st, 1 sc, turn.
Row 25: Using B, 1 ch, 1 sc, 1 Mdc, 2 ch, skip st, * 1 Mdc, 1 sc, 3 ch, skip 2 sts, 1 Mdc, 1 sc, 1 Mdc, 3 ch, skip 2 sts, 1 sc, 1 Mdc, 2 ch, skip st; rep from * to last 2 sts, 1 Mdc, 1 sc, turn.
Row 27: Using A, 1 ch, 2 sc, 1 Mdc, * 2 sc, 2 Mdc, 4 ch, skip 3 sts, 2 Mdc, 2 sc, 1 Mdc; rep from * to last 2 sts, 2 sc, turn.
Row 29: Using B, 1 ch, 2 sc, 2 ch, skip st, * 4 sc, 3 Mdc, 4 sc, 2 ch, skip st; rep from * to last 2 sts, 2 sc, turn.
Row 31: Using A, 1 ch, 1 sc, 2 ch, skip st, 1 Mdc, * 2 ch, skip st, 3 sc, 2 ch, skip st, 1 sc, 2 ch, skip st, 3 sc, 2 ch, skip st, 1 Mdc; rep from * to last 2 sts, 2 ch, skip st, 1 sc, turn.
Row 33: Using B, 1 ch, 1 sc, 1 Mdc, 2 ch, skip st, * 1 Mdc, 3 sc, 1 Mdc, 1 sc, 1 Mdc, 3 sc, 1 Mdc, 2 ch, skip st; rep from * to last 2 sts, 1 Mdc, 1 sc, turn.
Row 35: Using A, 1 ch, 2 sc, 1 Mdc * 1 sc, 2 ch, skip st, 2 sc, 2 ch, skip st, 1 sc, 2 ch, skip st, 2 sc, 2 ch, skip st, 1 sc, 1 Mdc; rep from * to last 2 sts, 2 sc, turn.
Rep Rows 1 to 36, placing 1 Mdc in sps as required on Row 1. To finish, work Rows 37 to 39.
Row 37: Using B, 1 ch, 1 sc, 2 ch, skip st, 1 sc, * 2 ch, skip st, 1 Mdc, 2 sc, 1 Mdc, 1 sc, 1 Mdc, 2 sc, 1 Mdc, 2 ch, skip st, 1 sc; rep from * to last 2 sts, 2 ch, skip st, 1 sc, turn.
Row 39: Using A, 1 ch, 1 sc in every st and Mdc in every sp.

Cactus

Perfect as a stand-alone design or used in panels or rows. The striped background on the knit cactus is worked in stockinette stitch which produces a looser fabric than the design itself. Place repeats close together to even out the fabric or work the background in garter stitch.

Knit Instructions

Multiple of 20 sts + 3

On RS rows, slip the sts purlwise with yarn in the back.

Cast on using B, k one row and p one row.

Row 1 (RS): Using A, k1, * k7, sl1, k5, sl1, k6; rep from * to last 2 sts, k2.

Row 2 and all WS rows: P the knitted sts and sl the slipped sts purlwise with yarn in the front.

Row 3: Using B, k1, * k8, [sl1, k1] twice, sl1, k7; rep from * to last 2 sts, k2.

Row 5: Using A, k1, * k7, sl1, k5, sl1, k6; rep from * to last 2 sts, k2.

Row 7: Using B, k1, * k8, sl2, k1, sl2, k7; rep from * to last 2 sts, k2.

Row 9: Using A, k1, * k3, sl1, k9, sl1, k6; rep from * to last 2 sts, k2.

Row 11: Using B, k1, * k4, [sl1, k1] 4 times, sl1, k7; rep from * to last 2 sts, k2.

Row 13: Using A, k1, * k1, sl1, k11, sl1, k6; rep from * to last 2 sts, k2.

Row 15: Using B, k1, * k2, [sl1, k1] twice, k2, sl2, k1, sl2, k7; rep from * to last 2 sts, k2.

Row 17: Using A, k1, * k1, sl1, k3, sl1, k1, sl1, k9, sl1, k2; rep from * to last 2 sts, k2.

Row 19: Using B, k1, * k2, [sl1, k1] twice, k2, [sl1, k1] 5 times, k2; rep from * to last 2 sts, k2.

Row 21: Using A, k1, * k1, sl1, k3, sl1, k1, sl1, k11, sl1; rep from * to last 2 sts, k2.

Row 23: Using B, k1, * k2, [sl1, k1] twice, k2, [sl2, k1] twice, k2, sl1, k1, sl1, k1; rep from * to last 2 sts, k2.

Row 25: Using A, k1, * k1, sl1, k3, sl1, k1, sl1, k5, sl1, k1, sl1, k3, sl1; rep from * to last 2 sts, k2.

Row 27: Using B, k1, * k8, [sl1, k1] 3 times, k2, [sl1, k1] twice; rep from * to last 2 sts, k2.

Row 29: Using A, k1, * k7, sl1, k5, sl1, k1, sl1, k3, sl1; rep from * to last 2 sts, k2.

Row 31: Using B, k1, * k8, [sl2, k1] twice, k6; rep from * to last 2 sts, k2.

Row 33: Using A, k1, * k7, sl1, k5, sl1, k6; rep from * to last 2 sts, k2.

Row 35: Using B, k1, * k9, [sl1, k1] twice, k7; rep from * to last 2 sts, k2.

Row 37: Using A, k1, * k8, sl1, k3, sl1, k7; rep from * to last 2 sts, k2.

Row 39: Using B, k1, * k10, sl1, k9; rep from * to last 2 sts, k2.

Row 41: Using A, k1, * k9, sl1, k1, sl1, k8; rep from * to last 2 sts, k2.

Row 43: Using B, k all sts.

Row 44: As Row 2.

Crochet Instructions

Multiple of 20 sts + 3

Using B, make desired number of chainless sc.

Row 1 (RS): Using A, 1 ch, 1 sc, * 7 sc, 2 ch, skip st, 5 sc, 2 ch, skip st, 6 sc; rep from * to last 2 sts, 2 sc, turn.

Row 2 and all WS rows: 1 ch, 1 sc in sts, ch and skip ch-sps, turn.

Row 3: Using B, 1 ch, 1 sc, * 7 sc, 1 Mdc, [2 ch, skip st, 1 sc] twice, 2 ch, skip st, 1 Mdc, 6 sc; rep from * to last 2 sts, 2 sc, turn.

Row 5: Using A, 1 ch, 1 sc, * 7 sc, 2 ch, skip st, [1 Mdc, 1 sc] twice, 1 Mdc, 2 ch, skip st, 6 sc; rep from * to last 2 sts, 2 sc, turn.

Row 7: Using B, 1 ch, 1 sc, * 7 sc, 1 Mdc, 3 ch, skip 2 sts, 1 sc, 3 ch, skip 2 sts, 1 Mdc, 6 sc; rep from * to last 2 sts, 2 sc, turn.

MOSAIC CHART

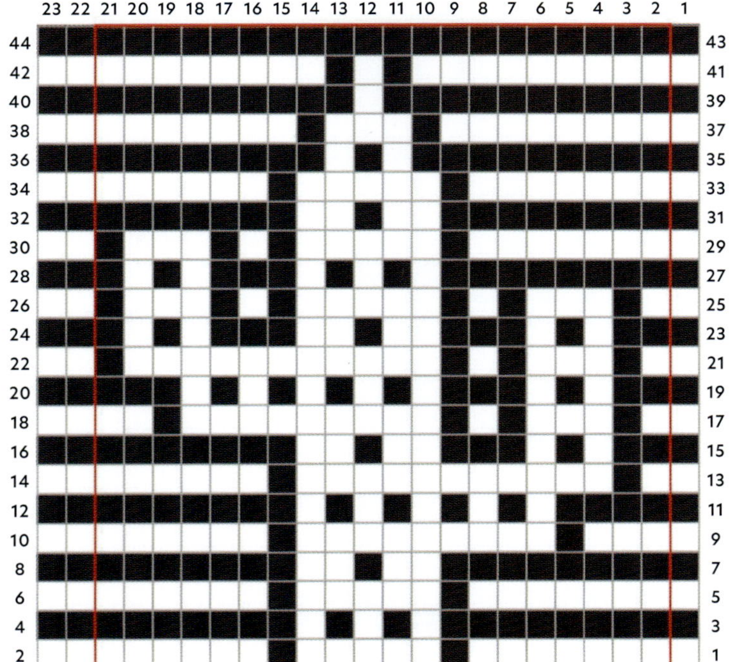

20 sts

Yarn A = Cream

Yarn B = Yellow

Row 9: Using A, 1 ch, 1 sc, * 3 sc, 2 ch, skip st, 4 sc, 2 Mdc, 1 sc, 2 Mdc, 2 ch, skip st, 6 sc; rep from * to last 2 sts, 2 sc, turn.
Row 11: Using B, 1 ch, 1 sc, * 3 sc, 1 Mdc, [2 ch, skip st, 1 sc] 4 times, 2 ch, skip st, 1 Mdc, 6 sc; rep from * to last 2 sts, 2 sc, turn.
Row 13: Using A, 1 ch, 1 sc, * 1 sc, 2 ch, skip st, 2 sc, [1 Mdc, 1 sc] 4 times, 1 Mdc, 2 ch, skip st, 6 sc; rep from * to last 2 sts, 2 sc, turn.
Row 15: Using B, 1 ch, 1 sc, * 1 sc, 1 Mdc, [2 ch, skip st, 1 sc] twice, 2 sc, 3 ch, skip 2 sts, 1 sc, 3 ch, skip 2 sts, 1 Mdc, 6 sc; rep from * to last 2 sts, 2 sc, turn.
Row 17: Using A, 1 ch, 1 sc, * 1 sc, 2 ch, skip st, 1 Mdc, 1 sc, 1 Mdc, 2 ch, skip st, 1 sc, 2 ch, skip st, 2 Mdc, 1 sc, 2 Mdc, 4 sc, 2 ch, skip st, 2 sc; rep from * to last 2 sts, 2 sc, turn.
Row 19: Using B, 1 ch, 1 sc, * 1 sc, 1 Mdc, 2 ch, skip st, 1 sc, 2 ch, skip st, 1 Mdc, 1 sc, 1 Mdc, [2 ch, skip st, 1 sc] 4 times, 2 ch, skip st, 1 Mdc, 2 sc; rep from * to last 2 sts, 2 sc, turn.
Row 21: Using A, 1 ch, 1 sc, * 1 sc, 2 ch, skip st, 1 Mdc, 1 sc, 1 Mdc, 2 ch, skip st, 1 sc, 2 ch, skip st, [1 Mdc, 1 sc] 4 times, 1 Mdc, 2 sc, 2 ch, skip st; rep from * to last 2 sts, 2 sc, turn.
Row 23: Using B, 1 ch, 1 sc, * 1 sc, 1 Mdc, 2 ch, skip st, 1 sc, 2 ch, skip st, 1Mdc, 1 sc, 1 Mdc, [3 ch, skip 2 sts, 1 sc] twice, 2 sc, 2 ch, skip st, 1 sc, 2 ch, skip st, 1 Mdc; rep from * to last 2 sts, 2 sc, turn.
Row 25: Using A, 1 ch, 1 sc, * 1 sc, 2 ch, skip st, 1 Mdc, 1 sc, 1 Mdc, 2 ch, skip st, 1 sc, 2 ch, skip st, 2 Mdc, 1 sc, 2 Mdc, 2ch, skip st, 1 sc, 2 ch, skip st, 1 Mdc, 1 sc, 1 Mdc, 2 ch, skip st; rep from * to last 2 sts, 2 sc, turn.
Row 27: Using B, 1 ch, 1 sc, * 1 sc, 1 Mdc, 3 sc, 1 Mdc, 1 sc, 1 Mdc, [2 ch, skip st, 1 sc] twice, 2 ch, skip st, 1 Mdc, 1 sc, 1 Mdc, 2 ch, skip st, 1 sc, 2 ch, skip st, 1 Mdc; rep from * to last 2 sts, 2 sc, turn.
Row 29: Using A, 1 ch, 1 sc, * 7 sc, 2 ch, skip st, [1 Mdc, 1 sc] twice, 1 Mdc, 2 ch, skip st, 1 sc, 2 ch, skip st, 1 Mdc, 1 sc, 1 Mdc, 2 ch, skip st; rep from * to last 2 sts, 2 sc, turn.
Row 31: Using B, 1 ch, 1 sc, * 7 sc, 1 Mdc, 3 ch, skip 2 sts, 1 sc, 3 ch, skip 2 sts, 1 Mdc, 1 sc, 1 Mdc, 3 sc, 1 Mdc; rep from * to last 2 sts, 2 sc, turn.
Row 33: Using A, 1 ch, 1 sc, * 7 sc, 2 ch, skip st, 2 Mdc, 1 sc, 2 Mdc, 2 ch, skip st, 6 sc; rep from * to last 2 sts, 2 sc, turn.
Row 35: Using B, 1 ch, 1 sc, * 7 sc, 1 Mdc, 1 sc, 2 ch, skip st, 1 sc, 2 ch, skip st, 1 sc, 1 Mdc, 6 sc; rep from * to last 2 sts, 2 sc, turn.
Row 37: Using A, 1 ch, 1 sc, * 8 sc, 2 ch, skip st, 1 Mdc, 1 sc, 1 Mdc, 2 ch, skip st, 7 sc; rep from * to last 2 sts, 2 sc, turn.
Row 39: Using B, 1 ch, 1 sc, * 8 sc, 1 Mdc, 1 sc, 2 ch, skip st, 1 sc, 1 Mdc, 7 sc; rep from * to last 2 sts, 2 sc, turn.
Row 41: Using A, 1 ch, 1 sc, * 9 sc, 2 ch, skip st, 1 Mdc, 2 ch, skip st, 8 sc; rep from * to last 2 sts, 2 sc, turn.
Row 43: Using B, 1 ch, 1 sc in every st and Mdc in every sp.
Row 44: As Row 2.

Falling Leaves

This pattern needs to be repeated at least once to showcase the motif and the pattern to its full effect. Consider using it for a bucket hat or winter beanie.

Knit Instructions

Multiple of 12 sts + 3

On RS rows, slip the sts purlwise with yarn in the back.

Cast on using B, k one row and p one row.

Row 1 (RS): Using A, k1, * k1, sl3, k2, sl1, k2, sl3; rep from * to last 2 sts, k2.

Row 2 and all WS rows: P the knitted sts and sl the slipped sts purlwise with yarn in the front.

Row 3: Using B, k1, * sl1, k4, sl1, k1, sl1, k4; rep from * to last 2 sts, sl1, k1.

Row 5: Using A, k1, * k3, sl2, k3, sl2, k2; rep from * to last 2 sts, k2.

Row 7: Using B, k1, * k2, sl1, k3, sl1, k3, sl1, k1; rep from * to last 2 sts, k2.

Row 9: Using A, k1, * k1, sl1, k2, sl2, k1, sl2, k2, sl1; rep from * to last 2 sts, k2.

Row 11: Using B, k1, * sl1, k2, sl1, k5, sl1, k2; rep from * to last 2 sts, sl1, k1.

Row 13: Using A, k1, * k1, sl1, k2, sl2, k1, sl2, k2, sl1; rep from * to last 2 sts, k2.

Row 15: Using B, k1, * k2, sl1, k3, sl1, k3, sl1, k1; rep from * to last 2 sts, k2.

Row 17: Using A, k1, * sl1, k2, sl1, k5, sl1, k2; rep from * to last 2 sts, sl1, k1.

Row 19: Using B, k1, * k1, sl1, k2, sl1, k3, sl1, k2, sl1; rep from * to last 2 sts, k2.

Row 21: Using A, k1, * k2, sl1, k2, sl1, k1, sl1, k2, sl1, k1; rep from * to last 2 sts, k2.

Row 23: Using B, k1, * sl1, k2, sl1, k2, sl1, k2, sl1, k2; rep from * to last 2 sts, sl1, k1.

Row 25: Using A, k1, * k1, sl2, k2, sl1, k1, sl1, k2, sl2; rep from * to last 2 sts, k2.

Row 27: Using B, k1, * k4, sl1, k3, sl1, k3; rep from * to last 2 sts, k2.

Row 28: Using B, as Row 2.

Rep Rows 1 to 27. To finish, using B, work Row 27 by k all sts and Row 28 by p all sts.

Crochet Instructions

Multiple of 12 sts + 3

Using B, make desired number of chainless sc.

Row 1 (RS): Using A, 1 ch, 1 sc, * 1 sc, 4 ch, skip 3 sts, 2 sc, 2 ch, skip st, 2 sc, 4 ch, skip 3 sts; rep from * to last 2 sts, 2 sc, turn.

Row 2 and all WS rows: 1 ch, 1 sc in sts, ch and skip ch-sps, turn.

Row 3: Using B, 1 ch, 1 sc, * 2 ch, skip st, 3 Mdc, 1 sc, 2 ch, skip st, 1 Mdc, 2 ch, skip st, 1 sc, 3 Mdc; rep from * to last 2 sts, 2 ch skip st, 1 sc, turn.

Row 5: Using A, 1 ch, 1 sc, * 1 Mdc, 2 sc, 3 ch, skip 2 sts, 1 Mdc, 1 sc, 1 Mdc, 3 ch, skip 2 sts, 2 sc; rep from * to last 2 sts, 1 Mdc, 1 sc, turn.

Row 7: Using B, 1 ch, 1 sc, * 2 sc, 2 ch, skip st, 2 Mdc, 1 sc, 2 ch, skip st, 1 sc, 2 Mdc, 2 ch, skip st, 1 sc; rep from * to last 2 sts, 2 sc, turn.

Row 9: Using A, 1 ch, 1 sc, * 1 sc, 2 ch, skip st, 1 Mdc, 1 sc, 3 ch, skip 2 sts, 1 Mdc, 3 ch, skip 2 sts, 1 sc, 1 Mdc, 2 ch, skip st; rep from * to last 2 sts, 2 sc, turn.

Row 11: Using B, 1 ch, 1 sc, * 2 ch, skip st, 1 Mdc, 1 sc, 2 ch, skip st, 2 Mdc, 1 sc, 2 Mdc, 2 ch, skip st, 1 sc, 1 Mdc;

MOSAIC CHART

12 sts

Yarn A = Cream

Yarn B = Green

rep from * to last 2 sts, 2 ch, skip st, 1 sc, turn.

Row 13: Using A, 1 ch, 1 sc, * 1 Mdc, 2 ch, skip st, 1 sc, 1 Mdc, 3 ch, skip 2 sts, 1 sc, 3 ch, skip 2 sts, 1 Mdc, 1 sc, 2 ch, skip st; rep from * to last 2 sts, 1 Mdc, 1 sc, turn.

Row 15: Using B, 1 ch, 1 sc, * 1 sc, 1 Mdc, 2 ch, skip st, 1 sc, 2 Mdc, 2 ch, skip st, 2 Mdc, 1 sc, 2 ch, skip st, 1 Mdc; rep from * to last 2 sts, 2 sc, turn.

Row 17: Using A, 1 ch, 1 sc, * 2 ch, skip st, 1 sc, 1 Mdc, 2 ch, skip st, 2 sc, 1 Mdc, 2 sc, 2 ch, skip st, 1 Mdc, 1 sc; rep from * to last 2 sts, 2 ch, skip st, 1 sc, turn.

Row 19: Using B, 1 ch, 1 sc, * 1 Mdc, 2 ch, skip st, 1 sc, 1 Mdc, 2 ch, skip st, 3 sc, 2 ch, skip st, 1 Mdc, 1 sc, 2 ch, skip st; rep from * to last 2 sts, 1 Mdc, 1 sc, turn.

Row 21: Using A, 1 ch, 1 sc, * 1 sc, 1 Mdc, 2 ch, skip st, 1 sc, 1 Mdc, 2 ch, skip st, 1 sc, 2 ch, skip st, 1 Mdc, 1 sc, 2 ch, skip st, 1 Mdc; rep from * to last 2 sts, 2 sc, turn.

Row 23: Using B, 1 ch, 1 sc, * 2 ch, skip st, 1 sc, 1 Mdc, 2 ch, skip st, 1 sc, 1 Mdc, 2 ch, skip st, 1 Mdc, 1 sc, 2 ch, skip st, 1 Mdc, 1 sc; rep from * to last 2 sts, 2 ch, skip st, 1 sc, turn.

Row 25: Using A, 1 ch, 1 sc, * 1 Mdc, 3 ch, skip 2 sts, 1 Mdc, 1 sc, 2 ch, skip st, 1 Mdc, 2 ch, skip st, 1 sc, 1 Mdc, 3 ch, skip 2 sts; rep from * to last 2 sts, 1 Mdc, 1 sc, turn.

Row 27: Using B, 1 ch, 1 sc, * 1 sc, 2 Mdc, 1 sc, 2 ch, skip st, 1 Mdc, 1 sc, 1 Mdc, 2 ch, skip st, 1 sc, 2 Mdc; rep from * to last 2 sts, 2 sc, turn.

Row 28: As Row 2.

Rep Rows 1 to 28, placing 1 Mdc in sps as required on Row 1. To finish, using B, work Row 27 as follows: 1 ch, 1 sc in every st and 1 Mdc in every sp.

CROCHET

Flower Field

This field of flowers will look best in large repeat sections, perfect for cardigans, dresses, and shawls. Use cotton yarn for summer outfits and a soft wool for winter.

Knit Instructions

Multiple of 10 sts + 5

On RS rows, slip the sts purlwise with yarn in the back.

Cast on using A, k one row and p one row.

Row 1 (RS): Using B, k1, sl1, * k1, sl2, k5, sl2; rep from * to last 3 sts, k1, sl1, k1.

Row 2 and all WS rows: P the knitted sts and sl the slipped sts purlwise with yarn in the front.

Row 3: Using A, k2, * sl1, k3, [sl1, k1] twice k2; rep from * to last 3 sts, sl1, k2.

Row 5: Using B, k1, sl1, * k3, sl1, k3, sl1, k2; rep from * to last 3 sts, k1, sl1, k1.

Row 7: Using A, k2, * sl1, k1, sl1, k5, sl1, k1; rep from * to last 3 sts, sl1, k2.

Row 9: Using B, k1, sl1, * k1, sl1, k2, sl1, k1, sl1, k2, sl1; rep from * to last 3 sts, k1, sl1, k1.

Row 11: Using A, k2, * sl1, k2, sl1, k3, sl1, k2; rep from * to last 3 sts, sl1, k2.

Row 13: Using B, k1, sl1, * k2, [sl1, k1] 4 times; rep from * to last 3 sts, k1, sl1, k1.

Row 15: Using A, k2, * k1, sl1, k7, sl1; rep from * to last 3 sts, k3.

Row 17: Using B, k1, sl1, * k3, [sl2, k1] twice, k1; rep from * to last 3 sts, k1, sl1, k1.

Row 19: Using A, k2, * sl1, k1, sl1, k5, sl1, k1; rep from * to last 3 sts, sl1, k2.

Row 21: Using B, k1, sl1, * k3, sl2, k1, sl2, k2; rep from * to last 3 sts, k1, sl1, k1.

Row 23: Using A, k2, * k1, sl1, [k3, sl1] twice; rep from * to last 3 sts, k3.

Row 25: Using B, k1, sl1, * k2, sl1, k5, sl1, k1; rep from * to last 3 sts, k1, sl1, k1.

Row 27: Using A, k2, * k3, [sl1, k1] 3 times, k1; rep from * to last 3 sts, k3.

Row 29: Using B, k1, sl1, * k1, sl1, k2, sl1, k1, sl1, k2, sl1; rep from * to last 3 sts, k1, sl1, k1.

Row 31: Using A, k2, * k2, [sl1, k2] twice, sl1, k1; rep from * to last 3 sts, k3.

Row 33: Using B, k1, sl1, * [k1, sl1] twice, k3, sl1, k1, sl1; rep from * to last 3 sts, k1, sl1, k1.

Row 35: Using A, k2, * k4, sl1, k1, sl1, k3; rep from * to last 3 sts, k3.

Row 37: Using B, k1, sl1, * k1, sl2, k5, sl2; rep from * to last 3 sts, k1, sl1, k1.

Row 39: Using A, k2, * k3, [sl1, k1] 3 times, k1; rep from * to last 3 sts, k3.

Rep Rows 1 to 40. To finish, work Rows 41 to 44.

Row 41: Using B, k1, sl1, * k1, sl2, k5, sl2; rep from * to last 3 sts, k1, sl1, k1.

Row 43: Using A, k all sts.

Row 44: As Row 2.

MOSAIC CHART

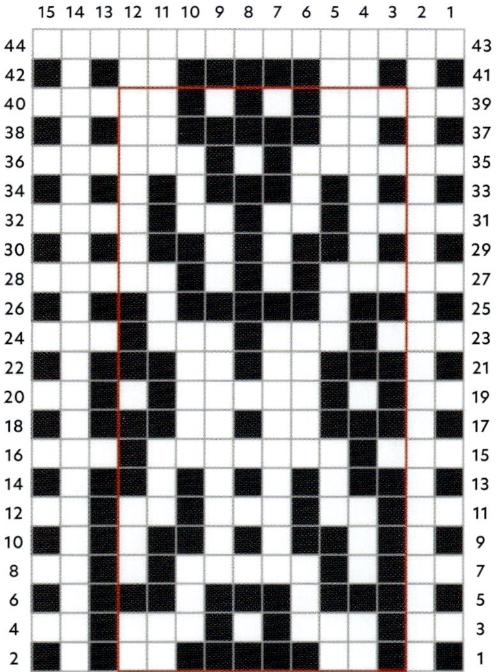

Yarn A = Cream

Yarn B = Red

Crochet Instructions

Multiple of 10 sts + 5

Using A, make desired number of chainless sc.

Row 1 (RS): Using B, 1 ch, 1 sc, 2 ch, skip st, * 1 sc, 3 ch, skip 2 sts, 5 sc, 3 ch, skip 2 sts; rep from * to last 3 sts, 1 sc, 2 ch, skip st, 1 sc, turn.

Row 2 and all WS rows: 1 ch, 1 sc in sts, ch and skip ch-sps, turn.

Row 3: Using A, 1 ch, 1 sc, 1 Mdc, * 2 ch, skip st, 2 Mdc, [1 sc, 2 ch, skip st] twice, 1 sc, 2 Mdc; rep from * to last 3 sts, 2 ch, skip st, 1 Mdc, 1 sc, turn.

Row 5: Using B, 1 ch, 1 sc, 2 ch, skip st, * 1 Mdc, 2 sc, 2 ch, skip st, 1 Mdc, 1 sc, 1 Mdc, 2 ch, skip st, 2 sc; rep from * to last 3 sts, 1 Mdc, 2 ch, skip st, 1 sc, turn.

Row 7: Using A, 1 ch, 1 sc, 1 Mdc, * 2 ch, skip st, 1 sc, 2 ch, skip st, 1 Mdc, 3 sc, 1 Mdc, 2 ch, skip st, 1 sc; rep from * to last 3 sts, 2 ch, skip st, 1 Mdc, 1 sc, turn.

Row 9: Using B, 1 ch, 1 sc, 2 ch, skip st, * 1 Mdc, 2 ch, skip st, 1 Mdc, 1 sc, [2

ch, skip st, 1 sc] twice, 1 Mdc, 2 ch, skip st; rep from * to last 3 sts, 1 Mdc, 2 ch, skip st, 1 sc, turn.

Row 11: Using A, 1 ch, 1 sc, 1 Mdc, * 2 ch, skip st, 1 Mdc, 1 sc, 2 ch, skip st, 1 Mdc, 1 sc, 1 Mdc, 2 ch, skip st, 1 sc, 1 Mdc; rep from * to last 3 sts, 2 ch, skip st, 1 Mdc, 1 sc, turn.

Row 13: Using B, 1 ch, 1 sc, 2 ch, skip st, * 1 Mdc, 1 sc, 2 ch, skip st, 1 Mdc, 2 ch, skip st, 1 sc, 2 ch, skip st, 1 Mdc, 2 ch, skip st, 1 sc; rep from * to last 3 sts, 1 Mdc, 2 ch, skip st, 1 sc, turn.

Row 15: Using A, 1 ch, 1 sc, 1 Mdc, * 1 sc, 2 ch, skip st, [1 Mdc, 1 sc] 3 times, 1 Mdc, 2 ch, skip st; rep from * to last 3 sts, 1 sc, 1 Mdc, 1 sc, turn.

Row 17: Using B, 1 ch, 1 sc, 2 ch, skip st, * 1 sc, 1 Mdc, [1 sc, 3 ch, skip 2 sts] twice, 1 sc, 1 Mdc; rep from * to last 3 sts, 1 sc, 2 ch, skip st, 1 sc, turn.

Row 19: Using A, 1 ch, 1 sc, 1 Mdc, * 2 ch, skip st, 1 sc, 2 ch, skip st, 2 Mdc, 1 sc, 2 Mdc, 2 ch, skip st, 1 sc; rep from * to last 3 sts, 2 ch, skip st, 1 Mdc, 1 sc, turn.

Row 21: Using B, 1 ch, 1 sc, 2 ch, skip st, * 1 Mdc, 1 sc, 1 Mdc, 3 ch, skip 2 sts, 1 sc, 3 ch, skip 2 sts, 1 Mdc, 1 sc; rep from * to last 3 sts, 1 Mdc, 2 ch, skip st, 1 sc, turn.

Row 23: Using A, 1 ch, 1 sc, 1 Mdc, * 1 sc, 2 ch, skip st, 1 sc, 2 Mdc, 2 ch, skip st, 2 Mdc, 1 sc, 2 ch, skip st; rep from * to last 3 sts, 1 sc, 1 Mdc, 1 sc, turn.

Row 25: Using B, 1 ch, 1 sc, 2 ch, skip st, * 1 sc, 1 Mdc, 2 ch, skip st, 2 sc, 1 Mdc, 2 sc, 2 ch, skip st, 1 Mdc; rep from * to last 3 sts, 1 sc, 2 ch, skip st, 1 sc, turn.

Row 27: Using A, 1 ch, 1 sc, 1 Mdc, * 2 sc, 1 Mdc, [2 ch, skip st, 1 sc] twice, 2 ch, skip st, 1 Mdc, 1 sc; rep from * to last 3 sts, 1 sc, 1 Mdc, 1 sc, turn.

Row 29: Using B, 1 ch, 1 sc, 2 ch, skip st, * 1 sc, 2 ch, skip st, 1 sc, [1 Mdc, 2 ch, skip st] twice, 1 Mdc, 1 sc, 2 ch, skip st; rep from * to last 3 sts, 1 sc, 2 ch, skip st, 1 sc, turn.

Row 31: Using A, 1 ch, 1 sc, 1 Mdc, * 1 sc, 1 Mdc, 2 ch, skip st, 1 sc, 1 Mdc, 2 ch, skip st, 1 Mdc, 1 sc, 2 ch, skip st, 1 Mdc; rep from * to last 3 sts, 1 sc, 1 Mdc, 1 sc, turn.

Row 33: Using B, 1 ch, 1 sc, 2 ch, skip st, * 1 sc, 2 ch, skip st, 1 Mdc, 2 ch, skip st, 1 sc 1 Mdc, 1 sc, 2 ch, skip st, 1 Mdc, 2 ch, skip st; rep from * to last 3 sts, 1 sc, 2 ch, skip st, 1 sc, turn.

Row 35: Using A, 1 ch, 1 sc, 1 Mdc, * [1 sc, 1 Mdc] twice, 2 ch, skip st, 1 sc, 2 ch, skip st, 1 Mdc, 1 sc, 1 Mdc; rep from * to last 3 sts, 1 sc, 1 Mdc, 1 sc, turn.

Row 37: Using B, 1 ch, 1 sc, 2 ch, skip st, * 1 sc, 3 ch, skip 2 sts, [1 sc, 1 Mdc] twice, 1 sc, 3 ch, skip 2 sts; rep from * to last 3 sts, 1 sc, 2 ch, skip st, 1 sc, turn.

Row 39: Using A, 1 ch, 1 sc, 1 Mdc, * 1 sc, 2 Mdc, [2 ch, skip st, 1 sc] twice, 2 ch, skip st, 2 Mdc; rep from * to last 3 sts, 1 sc, 1 Mdc, 1 sc, turn.

Rep Rows 1 to 40, placing 1 Mdc in sps as required on Row 1. To finish, work Rows 41 to 43.

Row 41: Using B, 1 ch, 1 sc, 2 ch, skip st, * 1 sc, 3 ch, skip 2 sts, [1 Mdc, 1 sc] twice, 1 Mdc, 3 ch, skip 2 sts; rep from * to last 3 sts, 1 sc, 2 ch, skip st, 1 sc, turn.

Row 43: Using A, 1 ch, 1 sc in every st and Mdc in every sp.

Happy Little Trees

This design is inspired by fall and winter. It would look perfect on a cozy sweater or wrap, or even on decorative home accessories.

Knit Instructions

Multiple of 16 sts + 5

On RS rows, slip the sts purlwise with yarn in the back.

Cast on using B, k one row and p one row.

Row 1 (RS): Using A, k1, sl2, * [sl1, k1] 3 times, sl2, k1, sl1, k3, sl1, k1, sl1; rep from * to last 2 sts, sl1, k1.

Row 2 and all WS rows: P the knitted sts and sl the slipped sts purlwise with yarn in the front.

Row 3: Using B, k3, * k3, sl1, k6, sl3, k3; rep from * to last 2 sts, k2.

Row 5: Using A, k1, sl1, k1, * sl2, k3, sl2, k9; rep from * to last 2 sts, sl1, k1.

Row 7: Using B, k2, sl1, * k2, sl1, k1, sl1, k2, [sl1, k1] 4 times, sl1; rep from * to last 2 sts, k2.

Row 9: Using A, k1, sl1, k1, * sl1, k5, sl1, k9; rep from * to last 2 sts, sl1, k1.

Row 11: Using B, k3, * k1, [sl1, k1] twice, sl1, k2, [sl1, k1] 4 times; rep from * to last 2 sts, k2.

Row 13: Using A, k1, sl2, * [k7, sl1] twice; rep from * to last 2 sts, sl1, k1.

Row 15: Using B, k3, * [sl1, k1] 4 times, [k1, sl1] 3 times, k2; rep from * to last 2 sts, k2.

Row 17: Using A, k1, sl1, k1, * k8, sl1, k5, sl1, k1; rep from * to last 2 sts, sl1, k1.

Row 19: Using B, k2, sl1, * [k1, sl1] 4 times, k1, [k1, sl1] twice, k2, sl1; rep from * to last 2 sts, k2.

Row 21: Using A, k1, sl1, k1, * k8, sl2, k3, sl2, k1; rep from * to last 2 sts, sl1, k1.

Row 23: Using B, k3, * k2, sl3, k6, sl1, k4; rep from * to last 2 sts, k2.

Row 25: Using A, k1, sl2, * k1, sl1, k3, sl1, k1, sl2, [k1, sl1] 3 times, sl1; rep from * to last 2 sts, sl1, k1.

Row 27: Using B, k all sts.

Row 28: As Row 2.

Rep Rows 1 to 28. To finish, using B, work Row 27 by k all sts and Row 28 by p all sts.

Crochet Instructions

Multiple of 16 sts + 5

Pattern note: The repeat in written instructions differs from chart on Rows 1, 13, and 25.

Using B, make desired number of chainless sc.

Row 1 (RS): Using A, 1 ch, 1 sc, 4 ch, skip 3 sts, * [1 sc, 2 ch, skip st,] twice, 1 sc, 3 ch, skip 2 sts, 1 sc, 2 ch, skip st, 3 sc, 2 ch, skip st, 1 sc, 3 ch, skip 2 st; rep from * to last st, 1 sc, turn.

Row 2 and all WS rows: 1 ch, 1 sc in sts, ch and skip ch-sps, turn.

Row 3: Using B, 1 ch, 1 sc, 2 Mdc, * 1 Mdc, 1 sc, 1 Mdc, 2 ch, skip st, [1 Mdc, 1 sc, 1 Mdc] twice, 4 ch, skip 3 sts, 1 Mdc, 1 sc, 1 Mdc; rep from * to last 2 sts, 1 Mdc, 1 sc, turn.

Row 5: Using A, 1 ch, 1 sc, 2 ch, skip st, 1 sc, * 3 ch, skip 2 sts, 1 sc, 1 Mdc, 1 sc, 3 ch, skip 2 sts, 3 sc, 3 Mdc, 3 sc; rep from * to last 2 sts, 2 ch, skip st, 1 sc, turn.

Row 7: Using B, 1 ch, 1 sc, 1 Mdc, 2 ch, skip st, * 2 Mdc, 2 ch, skip st, 1 sc, 2 ch, skip st, 2 Mdc, [2 ch, skip st, 1 sc] 4 times, 2 ch, skip st; rep from * to last 2 sts, 1 Mdc, 1 sc, turn.

Row 9: Using A, 1 ch, 1 sc, 2 ch, skip st, 1 Mdc, * 2 ch, skip st, [1 sc, 1 Mdc] twice, 1 sc, 2 ch, skip st, [1 Mdc, 1 sc] 4 times, 1 Mdc; rep from * to last 2 sts, 2 ch, skip st, 1 sc, turn.

Row 11: Using B, 1 ch, 1 sc, 1 Mdc, 1 sc, * 1 Mdc, [2 ch, skip st, 1 sc] twice,

Yarn A = Cream

Yarn B = Green

2 ch, skip st, 1 Mdc, [1 sc, 2 ch, skip st,] 4 times, 1 sc; rep from * to last 2 sts, 1 Mdc, 1 sc, turn.

Row 13: Using A, 1 ch, 1 sc, 3 ch, skip 2 sts, * [1 sc, 1 Mdc] 3 times, 1 sc, 2 ch, skip st, [1 Mdc, 1 sc] 3 times, 1 Mdc, ** 2 ch, skip st; rep from * to last 3 sts, ending last rep at **, 3 ch, skip 2 sts, 1 sc, turn.

Row 15: Using B, 1 ch, 1 sc, 2 Mdc, * [2 ch, skip st, 1 sc] 3 times, 2 ch, skip st, 1 Mdc, [1 sc, 2 ch, skip st,] 3 times, 1 sc, 1 Mdc; rep from * to last 2 sts, 1 Mdc, 1 sc, turn.

Row 17: Using A, 1 ch, 1 sc, 2 ch, skip st, 1 sc, * [1 Mdc, 1 sc] 4 times, 2 ch, skip st, [1 Mdc, 1 sc] twice, 1 Mdc, 2 ch, skip st, 1 sc; rep from * to last 2 sts, 2 ch, skip st, 1 sc, turn.

Row 19: Using B, 1 ch, 1 sc, 1 Mdc, 2 ch, skip st, * [1 sc, 2 ch, skip st] 4 times, 1 Mdc, [1 sc, 2 ch, skip st] twice, 1 sc, 1 Mdc, 2 ch, skip st; rep from * to last 2 sts, 1 Mdc, 1 sc, turn.

Row 21: Using A, 1 ch, 1 sc, 2 ch, skip st, 1 Mdc, * [1 sc, 1 Mdc] 4 times, 3 ch, skip 2 sts, 1 Mdc, 1 sc, 1 Mdc, 3 ch, skip 2 sts, 1 Mdc; rep from * to last 2 sts, 2 ch, skip st, 1 sc, turn.

Row 23: Using B, 1 ch, 1 sc, 1 Mdc, 1 sc, * 2 sc, 4 ch, skip 3 sts, 3 sc, 2 Mdc, 1 sc, 2 ch, skip st, 1 sc, 2 Mdc, 1 sc; rep from * to last 2 sts, 1 Mdc, 1 sc, turn.

Row 25: Using A, 1 ch, 1 sc, 3 ch, skip 2 sts, * 1 sc, 2 ch, skip st, 3 Mdc, 2 ch, skip st, 1 sc, 3 ch, skip 2 sts, 1 sc, 2 ch, skip st, 1 Mdc, 2 ch, skip st, 1 sc, ** 3 ch, skip 2 sts; rep from * to last 4 sts, ending last rep at **, 4 ch, skip 3 sts, 1 sc, turn.

Row 27: Using B, 1 ch, 1 sc in every st and Mdc in every sp.

Row 28: As Row 2.

Rep Rows 1 to 28, ending last rep with Row 27.

CROCHET

Pine Forest

This design is ideal for a bigger project with many repeats. Incorporate it into an Afghan or throw to give the repeat enough space.

Knit Instructions

Multiple of 10 sts + 3

On RS rows, slip the sts purlwise with yarn in the back.

Cast on using A, k one row and p one row.

Row 1 (RS): Using B, k1, * k2, [sl1, k1] 4 times; rep from * to last 2 sts, k2.

Row 2 and all WS rows: P the knitted sts and sl the slipped sts purlwise with yarn in the front.

Row 3: Using A, k1, * [sl1, k4] twice; rep from * to last 2 sts, sl1, k1.

Row 5: Using B, k1, * k1, sl1, k7, sl1; rep from * to last 2 sts, k2.

Row 7: Using A, k1, * k5, sl1, k4; rep from * to last 2 sts, k2.

Row 9: Using B, k1, * k1, sl2, k5, sl2; rep from * to last 2 sts, k2.

Row 11: Using A, k1, * k5, sl1, k4; rep from * to last 2 sts, k2.

Row 13: Using B, k1, * [k1, sl1] twice, k3, sl1, k1, sl1; rep from * to last 2 sts, k2.

Row 15: Using A, k1, * sl1, k4, sl1, k4; rep from * to last 2 sts, sl1, k1.

Row 17: Using B, k1, * k4, sl1, k1, sl1, k3; rep from * to last 2 sts, k2.

Row 19: Using A, k1, * sl1, k9; rep from * to last 2 sts, sl1, k1.

Row 21: Using B, k1, * k3, sl2, k1, sl2, k2; rep from * to last 2 sts, k2.

Row 23: Using A, k1, * sl1, k9; rep from * to last 2 sts, sl1, k1.

Row 24: Using A, as Row 2.

Rep Rows 1 to 24.

Crochet Instructions

Multiple of 10 sts + 3

Using A, make desired number of chainless sc.

Row 1 (RS): Using B, 1 ch, 1 sc, * 2 sc, [2 ch, skip st, 1 sc] 4 times; rep from * to last 2 sts, 2 sc, turn.

Row 2 and all WS rows: 1 ch, 1 sc in sts, ch and skip ch-sps, turn.

Row 3: Using A, 1 ch, 1 sc, * 2 ch, skip st, [1 sc, 1 Mdc] twice, 2 ch, skip st, [1 Mdc, 1 sc] twice; rep from * to last 2 sts, 2 ch skip st, 1 sc, turn.

Row 5: Using B, 1 ch, 1 sc, * 1 Mdc, 2 ch, skip st, 3 sc, 1 Mdc, 3 sc, 2 ch, skip st; rep from * to last 2 sts, 1 Mdc, 1 sc, turn.

Row 7: Using A, 1 ch, 1 sc, * 1 sc, 1 Mdc, 3 sc, 2 ch, skip st, 3 sc, 1 Mdc; rep from * to last 2 sts, 2 sc, turn.

Row 9: Using B, 1 ch, 1 sc, * 1 sc, 3 ch, skip 2 sts, 2 sc, 1 Mdc, 2 sc, 3 ch, skip 2 sts; rep from * to last 2 sts, 2 sc, turn.

Row 11: Using A, 1 ch, 1 sc, * 1 sc, 2 Mdc, 2 sc, 2 ch, skip st, 2 sc, 2 Mdc; rep from * to last 2 sts, 2 sc, turn.

Row 13: Using B, 1 ch, 1 sc, * [1 sc, 2 ch, skip st] twice, 1 sc, 1 Mdc, [1 sc, 2 ch, skip st] twice; rep from * to last 2 sts, 2 sc, turn.

Row 15: Using A, 1 ch, 1 sc, * 2 ch, skip st, [1 Mdc, 1 sc] twice, 2 ch, skip st, [1 sc, 1 Mdc] twice; rep from * to last 2 sts, 2 ch, skip st, 1 sc, turn.

Row 17: Using B, 1 ch, 1 sc, * 1 Mdc, 3 sc, 2 ch, skip st, 1 Mdc, 2 ch, skip st, 3 sc; rep from * to last 2 sts, 1 Mdc, 1 sc, turn.

Row 19: Using A, 1 ch, 1 sc, * 2 ch, skip st, 3 sc, 1 Mdc, 1 sc, 1 Mdc, 3 sc; rep from * to last 2 sts, 2 ch, skip st, 1 sc, turn.

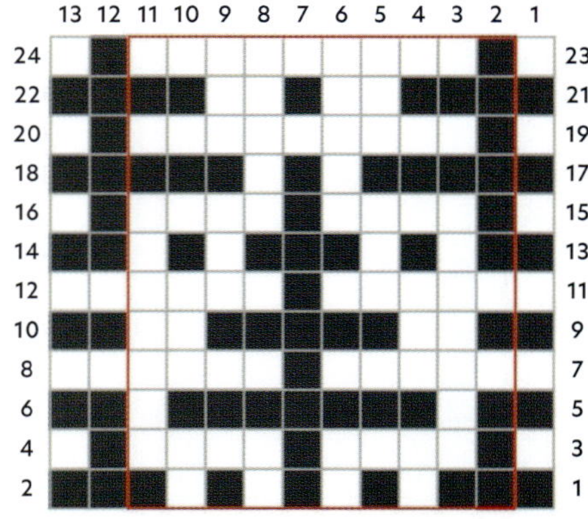

Row 21: Using B, 1 ch, 1 sc, * 1 Mdc, 2 sc, 3 ch, skip 2 sts, 1 sc, 3 ch, skip 2 sts, 2 sc; rep from * to last 2 sts, 1 Mdc, 1 sc, turn.

Row 23: Using A, 1 ch, 1 sc, * 2 ch, skip st, 2 sc, 2 Mdc, 1 sc, 2 Mdc, 2 sc; rep from * to last 2 sts, 2 ch, skip st, 1 sc, turn.

Row 24: As Row 2.

Rep Rows 1 to 24, placing 1 Mdc in sps as required on Row 1. To finish, using B, work Row 23 as follows: 1 ch, 1 sc in every st and Mdc in every sp.

CROCHET

TIP: For the crochet version: If you would like the trees to be shorter with a similar look to the sizing in the knitted swatch, convert the chart to overlay mosaic crochet (see page 24).

Forget-me-nots

Use this floral design in a large repeat section on a summer cardigan, dress, or shawl. Use cotton yarn to keep the fabric light.

Knit Instructions

Multiple of 10 sts + 2

On RS rows, slip the sts purlwise with yarn in the back.

Cast on using A, k one row and p one row.

Row 1 (RS): Using B, k1, * sl2, k3, sl2, k1, sl1, k1; rep from * to last st, k1.

Row 2 and all WS rows: P the knitted sts and sl the slipped sts purlwise with yarn in the front.

Row 3: Using A, k1, * k2, sl3, k5; rep from * to last st, k1.

Row 5: Using B, k1, * k7, sl1, k1, sl1; rep from * to last st, k1.

Row 7: Using A, k1, * sl3, k1, sl3, k3; rep from * to last st, k1.

Row 9: Using B, k1, * k7, sl1, k1, sl1; rep from * to last st, k1.

Row 11: Using A, k1, * k2, sl3, k5; rep from * to last st, k1.

Row 13: Using B, k1, * [sl2, k3] twice; rep from * to last st, k1.

Row 15: Using A, k1, * k7, sl3; rep from * to last st, k1.

Row 17: Using B, k1, * k2, sl1, k1, sl1, k5; rep from * to last st, k1.

Row 19: Using A, k1, * sl2, k3, sl3, k1, sl1; rep from * to last st, k1.

Row 21: Using B, k1, * k2, sl1, k1, sl1, k5; rep from * to last st, k1.

Row 23: Using A, k1, * k7, sl3; rep from * to last st, k1.

Row 25: Using B, k1, * sl2, k1, sl1, k1, sl2, k3; rep from * to last st, k1.

Row 27: Using A, k all sts.

Row 28: As Row 2.

Rep Rows 1 to 28.

Crochet Instructions

Multiple of 10 sts + 2

Pattern note: The repeat in written instructions differs from chart on Row 19.

Using A, make desired number of chainless sc.

Row 1 (RS): Using B, 1 ch, 1 sc, * 3 ch, skip 2 sts, 3 sc, 3 ch, skip 2 sts, 1 sc, 2 ch, skip st, 1 sc; rep from * to last st, 1 sc, turn.

Row 2 and all WS rows: 1 ch, 1 sc in sts, ch and skip ch-sps, turn.

Row 3: Using A, 1 ch, 1 sc, * 2 Mdc, 4 ch, skip 3 sts, 2 Mdc, 1 sc, 1 Mdc, 1 sc; rep from * to last st, 1 sc, turn.

Row 5: Using B, 1 ch, 1 sc, * 2 sc, 3 Mdc, 2 sc, 2 ch, skip st, 1 sc, 2 ch, skip st; rep from * to last st, 1 sc, turn.

Row 7: Using A, 1 ch, 1 sc, * 4 ch, skip 3 sts, 1 sc, 4 ch, skip 3 sts, 1 Mdc, 1 sc, 1 Mdc; rep from * to last st, 1 sc, turn.

Row 9: Using B, 1 ch, 1 sc, * 3 Mdc, 1 sc, 3 Mdc, 2 ch, skip st, 1 sc, 2 ch, skip st; rep from * to last st, 1 sc, turn.

Row 11: Using A, 1 ch, 1 sc, * 2 sc, 4 ch, skip 3 sts, 2 sc, 1 Mdc, 1 sc, 1 Mdc; rep from * to last st, 1 sc, turn.

Row 13: Using B, 1 ch, 1 sc, * 3 ch, skip 2 sts, 3 Mdc, 3 ch, skip 2 sts, 3 sc; rep

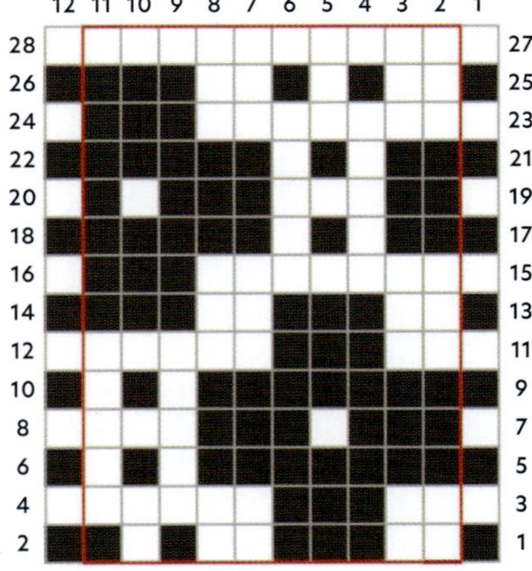

from * to last st, 1 sc, turn.
Row 15: Using A, 1 ch, 1 sc, * 2 Mdc, 3 sc, 2 Mdc, 4 ch, skip 3 sts; rep from * to last st, 1 sc, turn.
Row 17: Using B, 1 ch, 1 sc, * 2 sc, 2 ch, skip st, 1 sc, 2 ch, skip st, 2 sc, 3 Mdc; rep from * to last st, 1 sc, turn.
Row 19: Using A, 1 ch, 1 sc, 3 ch, skip 2 sts, * 1 Mdc, 1 sc, 1 Mdc, 4 ch, skip 3 sts, 1 sc, ** 4 ch, skip 3 sts; rep from * to last 2 sts, ending last rep at **, 2 ch, skip st, 1 sc, turn.
Row 21: Using B, 1 ch, 1 sc, * 2 Mdc, 2 ch, skip st, 1 sc, 2 ch, skip st, 3 Mdc, 1 sc, 1 Mdc; rep from * to last st, 1 sc, turn.
Row 23: Using A, 1 ch, 1 sc, * 2 sc, 1 Mdc, 1 sc, 1 Mdc, 2 sc, 4 ch, skip 3 sts; rep from * to last st, 1 sc, turn.
Row 25: Using B, 1 ch, 1 sc, * 3 ch, skip 2 sts, 1 sc, 2 ch, skip st, 1 sc, 3 ch, skip 2 sts, 3 Mdc; rep from * to last st, 1 sc, turn.
Row 27: Using A, 1 ch, 1 sc in every st and Mdc in every sp.
Row 28: As Row 2.
Rep Rows 1 to 28, ending last rep with Row 27.

KNIT

CROCHET

TIP: For the knit version: This pattern will look equally stunning if the background is worked in garter stitch and the flowers in stockinette stitch.

Leaves

This sweet leaf design would look amazing if it was worked with multicolored yarn as Yarn B and solid yarn as Yarn A.

Knit Instructions

Multiple of 20 sts + 3

On RS rows, slip the sts purlwise with yarn in the back.

Cast on using A, k one row and p one row.

Row 1 (RS): Using B, k1, * [sl1, k1] 10 times; rep from * to last 2 sts, sl1, k1.

Row 2 and all WS rows: P the knitted sts and sl the slipped sts purlwise with yarn in the front.

Row 3: Using A, k1, * k5, sl1, k9, sl1, k4; rep from * to last 2 sts, k2.

Row 5: Using B, k1, * sl2, k7, sl2, k1, sl2, k3, sl2, k1; rep from * to last 2 sts, sl1, k1.

Row 7: Using A, k1, * k2, sl1, k5, sl1, k5, sl1, k1, sl1, k3; rep from * to last 2 sts, k2.

Row 9: Using B, k1, * sl1, k2, [sl1, k1] 3 times, k1, sl1, k1, sl1, k2, sl1, k2, sl1, k1; rep from * to last 2 sts, sl1, k1.

Row 11: Using A, k1, * k1, sl1, k7, [sl1, k3] twice, sl1, k2; rep from * to last 2 sts, k2.

Row 13: Using B, k1, * sl1, k1, [sl1, k1] 4 times, sl2, k2, sl1, k1, sl1, k2, sl1; rep from * to last 2 sts, sl1, k1.

Row 15: Using A, k1, * k1, sl1, k7, sl1, k2, sl1, k5, sl1, k1; rep from * to last 2 sts, k2.

Row 17: Using B, k1, * sl1, k2, [sl1, k1] 3 times, k1, sl1, k2, [sl1, k1] 3 times, k1; rep from * to last 2 sts, sl1, k1.

Row 19: Using A, k1, * k2, sl1, k5, sl1, k2, sl1, k7, sl1; rep from * to last 2 sts, k2.

Row 21: Using B, k1, * sl2, k2, [sl1, k1] twice, k1, sl2, k1, [sl1, k1] 4 times; rep from * to last 2 sts, sl1, k1.

Row 23: Using A, k1, * [k3, sl1] 3 times, k7, sl1; rep from * to last 2 sts, k2.

Row 25: Using B, k1, * sl1, k1, [sl1, k2] twice, sl1, k1, sl1, k2, [sl1, k1] 3 times, k1; rep from * to last 2 sts, sl1, k1.

Row 27: Using A, *k1, k4, sl1, k1, sl1, [k5, sl1] twice, k1; rep from * to last 2 sts, k2.

Row 29: Using B, k1, * sl1, k1, sl2, k3, sl2, k1, sl2, k7, sl1; rep from * to last 2 sts, sl1, k1.

Row 31: Using A, k1, * k5, sl1, k9, sl1, k4; rep from * to last 2 sts, k2.

Row 33: Using B, k1, * [sl1, k1] 10 times; rep from * to last 2 sts, sl1, k1.

Row 35: Using A, k all sts.

Row 36: As Row 2.

Rep Rows 1 to 36. To finish, using B, work Row 35 by k all sts and Row 36 by p all sts.

Yarn A = Cream

Yarn B = Green

MOSAIC CHART

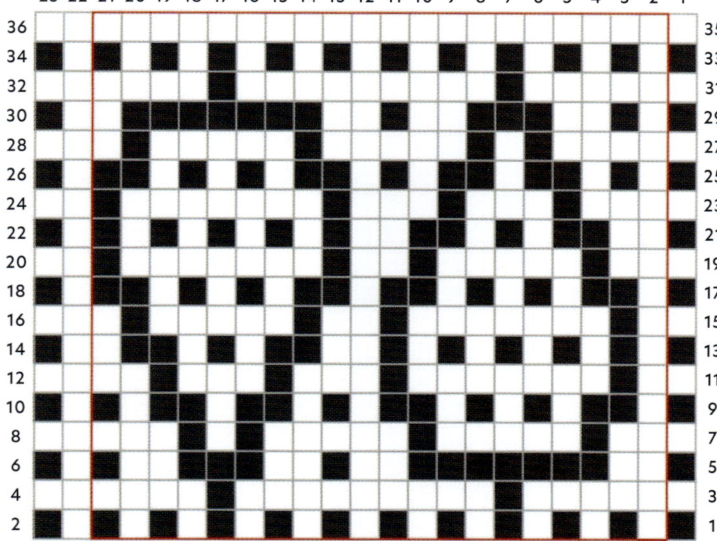

20 sts

Crochet Instructions

Multiple of 20 sts + 3

Pattern note: The repeat in written instructions differs from chart on Rows 13 and 29.

Using A, make desired number of chainless sc.

Row 1 (RS): Using B, 1 ch, 1 sc, * [2 ch, skip st, 1 sc] 10 times; rep from * to last 2 sts, 2 ch, skip st, 1 sc, turn.

Row 2 and all WS rows: 1 ch, 1 sc in sts, ch and skip ch-sps, turn.

Row 3: Using A, 1 ch, 1 sc, * [1 Mdc, 1 sc] twice, 1 Mdc, 2 ch, skip st, [1 Mdc, 1 sc] 4 times, 1 Mdc, 2 ch, skip st, [1 Mdc, 1 sc] twice; rep from * to last 2 sts, 1 Mdc, 1 sc, turn.

Row 5: Using B, 1 ch, 1 sc, * 3 ch, skip 2 sts, 3 sc, 1 Mdc, 3 sc, 3 ch, skip 2 sts, 1 sc, 3 ch, skip 2 sts, 1 sc, 1 Mdc, 1 sc, 3 ch, skip 2 sts, 1 sc; rep from * to last 2 sts, 2 ch, skip st, 1 sc, turn.

Row 7: Using A, 1 ch, 1 sc, * 2 Mdc, 2 ch, skip st, 5 sc, 2 ch, skip st, 2 Mdc, 1 sc, 2 Mdc, 2 ch, skip st, 1 sc, 2 ch, skip st, 2 Mdc, 1 sc; rep from * to last 2 sts, 1 Mdc, 1 sc, turn.

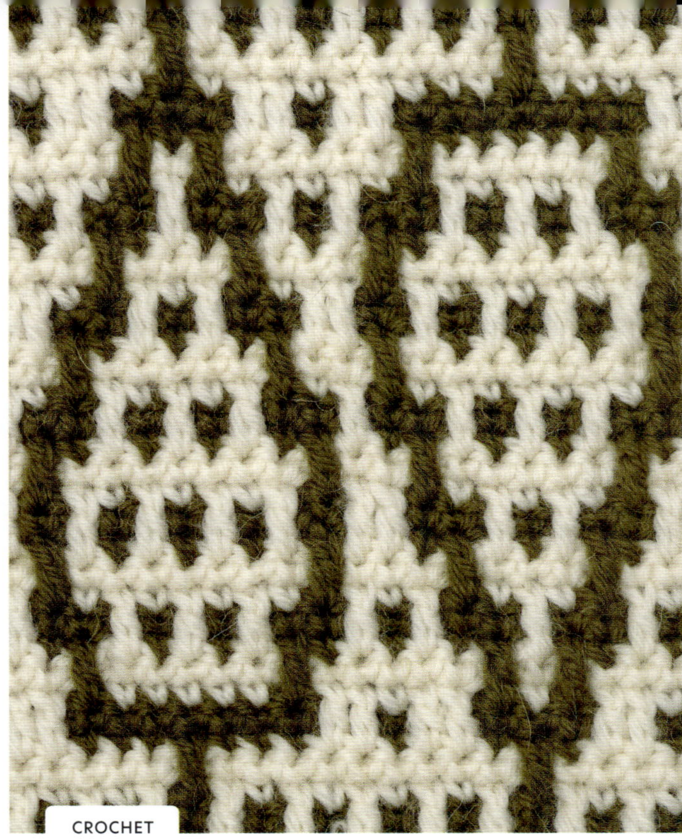

st, 1 sc, 1 Mdc, [2 ch, skip st, 1 sc] twice, 2 ch, skip st, 1 Mdc, 1 sc, [2 ch, skip st, 1 sc] twice, 1 Mdc, 2 ch, skip st, 1 Mdc, 1 sc, 2 ch, skip st, 1 sc; rep from * to last 2 sts, 2 ch, skip st, 1 sc, turn.

Row 11: Using A, 1 ch, 1 sc, * 1 Mdc, 2 ch, skip st, [1 sc, 1 Mdc] 3 times, 1 sc, 2 ch, skip st, 1 Mdc, 1 sc, 1 Mdc, 2 ch, skip st, 1 sc, 1 Mdc, 1 sc, 2 ch, skip st, 1 Mdc, 1 sc; rep from * to last 2 sts, 1 Mdc, 1 sc, turn.

Row 13: Using B, 1 ch, 1 sc, 2 ch, skip st, * 1 Mdc, [2 ch, skip st, 1 sc] 3 times, 2 ch, skip st, 1 Mdc, 3 ch, skip 2 sts, 1 sc, 1 Mdc, 2 ch, skip st, 1 sc, 2 ch, skip st, 1 Mdc, 1 sc, ** 3 ch, skip 2 sts; rep from * to last 3 sts, ending last rep at **, 3 ch, skip 2 sts, 1 sc, turn.

Row 15: Using A, 1 ch, 1 sc, * 1 Mdc, 2 ch, skip st, [1 Mdc, 1 sc] 3 times, 1 Mdc, 2 ch, skip st, 2 Mdc, 2 ch, skip st, 1 sc, 1 Mdc, 1 sc, 1 Mdc, 1 sc, 2 ch, skip st, 1 Mdc; rep from * to last 2 sts, 1 Mdc, 1 sc, turn.

Row 17: Using B, 1 ch, 1 sc, * 2 ch, skip st, 1 Mdc, 1 sc, [2 ch, skip st, 1 sc] 3 times, 1 Mdc, 2 ch, skip st, 1 sc, 1 Mdc, [2 ch, skip st, 1 sc] twice, 2 ch, skip st, 1 Mdc, 1 sc; rep from * to last 2 sts, 2 ch, skip st, 1 sc, turn.

Row 19: Using A, 1 ch, 1 sc, * 1 Mdc, 1 sc, 2 ch, skip st, [1 Mdc, 1 sc] twice, 1 Mdc, 2 ch, skip st, 1 sc, 1 Mdc, 2 ch, skip st, 1 sc, [1 Mdc, 1 sc] 3 times, 2 ch, skip st; rep from * to last 2 sts, 1 Mdc, 1 sc, turn.

Row 21: Using B, 1 ch, 1 sc, * 3 ch, skip 2 sts, 1 Mdc, 1 sc, [2 ch, skip st, 1 sc] twice, 1 Mdc, 3 ch, skip 2 sts, 1 Mdc, [2 ch, skip st, 1 sc] 3 times, 2 ch, skip st, 1 Mdc; rep from * to last 2 sts, 2 ch, skip st, 1 sc, turn.

Row 23: Using A, 1 ch, 1 sc, * 2 Mdc, 1 sc, 2 ch, skip st, 1 Mdc, 1 sc, 1 Mdc, 2 ch, skip st, 1 sc, 2 Mdc, 2 ch, skip st, [1 Mdc, 1 sc] 3 times, 1 Mdc, 2 ch, skip st; rep from * to last 2 sts, 1 Mdc, 1 sc, turn.

Row 25: Using B, 1 ch, 1 sc, * 2 ch, skip st, 1 sc, 2 ch, skip st, 1 Mdc, 1 sc, 2 ch, skip st, 1 sc, 1 Mdc, 2 ch, skip st, 1 sc, 2 ch, skip st, 1 Mdc, 1 sc , [2 ch, skip st, 1 sc] 3 times, 1 Mdc; rep from * to last 2 sts, 2 ch, skip st, 1 sc, turn.

Row 27: Using A, 1 ch, 1 sc, * [1 Mdc, 1 sc] twice, 2 ch, skip st, 1 Mdc, 2 ch, skip st, [1 sc, 1 Mdc] twice, 1 sc, 2 ch, skip st, [1 Mdc, 1 sc] twice, 1 Mdc, 2 ch, skip st, 1 sc; rep from * to last 2 sts, 1 Mdc, 1 sc, turn.

Row 29: Using B, 1 ch, 1 sc, 2 ch, skip st, * 1 sc, 3 ch, skip 2 sts, 1 Mdc, 1 sc, 1 Mdc, 3 ch, skip 2 sts, 1 sc, 3 ch, skip 2 sts, 1 Mdc, 5 sc, 1 Mdc, ** 3 ch, skip 2 sts; rep from * to last 3 sts, ending last rep at **, 3 ch, skip 2 sts, 1 sc, turn.

Row 31: Using A, 1 ch, 1 sc, * 1 Mdc, 1 sc, 2 Mdc, 1 sc, 2 ch, skip st, [1 sc, 2 Mdc] twice, 3 sc, 2 ch, skip st, 3 sc, 1 Mdc; rep from * to last 2 sts, 1 Mdc, 1 sc, turn.

Row 33: Using B, 1 ch, 1 sc, * [2 ch, skip st, 1 sc] twice, 2 ch, skip st, 1 Mdc, [2 ch, skip st, 1 sc] 4 times, 2 ch, skip st, 1 Mdc, [2 ch, skip st, 1 sc] twice; rep from * to last 2 sts, 2 ch, skip st, 1 sc, turn.

Row 35: Using A, 1 ch, 1 sc in every st and Mdc in every sp.

Row 36: As Row 2.

Rep Rows 1 to 36, ending last rep with Row 35.

Ivy

This pattern was inspired by the climbing ivy that you find on trees. Perfect to use as a panel along a wrap or to add a touch of interest to a sweater.

Knit Instructions

Multiple of 9 sts + 2

On RS rows, slip the sts purlwise with yarn in the back.

Cast on using B, k one row and p one row.

Row 1 (RS): Using A, k1, * sl1, k3, sl2, k1, sl2; rep from * to last st, k1.

Row 2 and all WS rows: P the knitted sts and sl the slipped sts purlwise with yarn in the front.

Row 3: Using B, k1, * k1, [sl1, k1] twice, k4; rep from * to last st, k1.

Row 5: Using A, k1, * sl1, k5, sl1, k1, sl1; rep from * to last st, k1.

Row 7: Using B, k1, * k3, sl1, k1, sl1, k3; rep from * to last st, k1.

Row 9: Using A, k1, * sl1, k1, sl1, k5, sl1; rep from * to last st, k1.

Row 11: Using B, k1, * k5, sl1, k1, sl1, k1; rep from * to last st, k1.

Row 13: Using A, k1, * sl2, k1, sl2, k3, sl1; rep from * to last st, k1.

Row 15: Using B, k1, * k7, sl1, k1; rep from * to last st, k1.

Row 17: Using A, k1 all sts.

Row 19: As Row 15.

Row 21: As Row 13.

Row 23: As Row 11.

Row 25: As Row 9.

Row 27: As Row 7.

Row 29: As Row 5.

Row 31: As Row 3.

Row 33: As Row 1.

Row 35: Using B, k all sts.

Row 36: As Row 2.

MOSAIC CHART

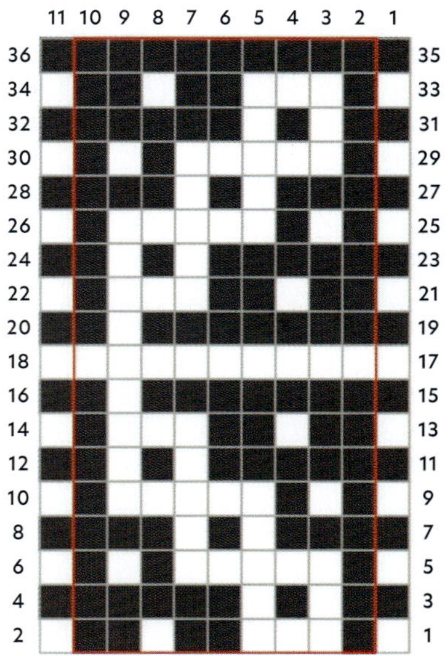

9 sts

Yarn A = Cream

Yarn B = Green

Crochet Instructions

Multiple of 9 sts + 2

Pattern note: The repeat in written instructions differs from chart on Rows 1, 5, 7, 9, 13, 21, 25, 29, and 33.

Using B, make desired number of chainless sc.

Row 1 (RS): Using A, 1 ch, 1 sc, 2 ch, skip st, * 3 sc, 3 ch, skip 2 sts, 1 sc, ** 4 ch, skip 3 sts; rep from * to last 3 sts, ending last rep at **, 3 ch, skip 2 sts, 1 sc, turn.

Row 2 and all WS rows: 1 ch, 1 sc in sts, ch and skip ch-sps, turn.

Row 3: Using B, 1 ch, 1 sc, * 1 Mdc, 2 ch, skip st, 1 sc, 2 ch, skip st, 2 Mdc, 1 sc, 2 Mdc; rep from * to last st, 1 sc, turn.

Row 5: Using A, 1 ch, 1 sc, 2 ch, skip st, * 1 Mdc, 1 sc, 1 Mdc, 2 sc, 2 ch, skip st, 1 sc, ** 3 ch, skip 2 sts; rep from * to last 2 sts, ending last rep at **, 2 ch, skip st, 1 sc, turn.

Row 7: Using B, 1 ch, 1 sc, * 1 Mdc, 2 sc, 2 ch, skip st, 1 sc, 2 ch, skip st, 1 Mdc, 1 sc, 1 Mdc; rep from * to last st, 1 sc, turn.

Row 9: Using A, 1 ch, 1 sc, 2 ch, skip st, * 1 sc, 2 ch, skip st, 1 Mdc, 1 sc, 1 Mdc, 2 sc, ** 3 ch, skip 2 sts; rep from * to last 2 sts, ending last rep at **, 2 ch, skip st, 1 sc, turn.

Row 11: Using B, 1 ch, 1 sc, * 1 Mdc, 1 sc, 1 Mdc, 2 sc, 2 ch, skip st, 1 sc, 2 ch, skip st, 1 Mdc; rep from * to last st, 1 sc, turn.

Row 13: Using A, 1 ch, 1 sc, 3 ch, skip 2 sts, * 1 sc, 3 ch, skip 2 sts, 1 Mdc, 1 sc, 1 Mdc, ** 4 ch, skip 3 sts; rep from * to last 2 sts, ending last rep at **, 2 ch, skip st, 1 sc, turn.

Row 15: Using B, 1 ch, 1 sc, * 2 Mdc, 1 sc, 2 Mdc, 2 sc, 2 ch, skip st, 1 Mdc; rep from * to last st, 1 sc, turn.

Row 17: Using A, 1 ch, 1 sc, * 7 sc, 1 Mdc, 1 sc; rep from * to last st, 1 sc, turn.

Row 19: Using B, 1 ch, 1 sc, * 7 sc, 2 ch, skip st, 1 sc; rep from * to last st, 1 sc, turn.

Row 21: Using A, 1 ch, 1 sc, 3 ch, skip 2 sts, * 1 sc, 3 ch, skip 2 sts, 3 sc, ** 4 ch, skip 3 sts; rep from * to last 2 sts, ending last rep at **, 2 ch, skip st, 1 sc, turn.

Row 23: Using B, 1 ch, 1 sc, * 2 Mdc, 1 sc, 2 Mdc, 2 ch, skip st, 1 sc, 2 ch, skip st, 1 Mdc; rep from * to last st, 1 sc, turn.

Row 25: Using A, 1 ch, 1 sc, 2 ch, skip st, * 1 sc, 2 ch, skip st, 2 sc, 1 Mdc, 1 sc, 1 Mdc, ** 3 ch, skip 2 sts; rep from * to last 2 sts, ending last rep at **, 2 ch, skip st, 1 sc, turn.

Row 27: Using B, 1 ch, 1 sc, * 1 Mdc, 1 sc, 1 Mdc, 2 ch, skip st, 1 sc, 2 ch, skip st, 2 sc, 1 Mdc; rep from * to last st, 1 sc, turn.

Row 29: Using A, 1 ch, 1 sc, 2 ch, skip st, * 2 sc, 1 Mdc, 1 sc, 1 Mdc, 2 ch, skip st, 1 sc, ** 3 ch, skip 2 sts; rep from * to last 2 sts, ending last rep at **, 2 ch, skip st, 1 sc, turn.

Row 31: Using B, 1 ch, 1 sc, * 1 Mdc, 2 ch, skip st, 1 sc, 2 ch, skip st, 2 sc, 1 Mdc, 1 sc, 1 Mdc; rep from * to last st, 1 sc, turn.

Row 33: Using A, 1 ch, 1 sc, 2 ch, skip st, * 1 Mdc, 1 sc, 1 Mdc, 3 ch, skip 2 sts, 1 sc, ** 4 ch, skip 3 sts; rep from * to last 3 sts, ending last rep at **, 3 ch, skip 2 sts, 1 sc, turn.

To finish, work Row 35.

Row 35: Using B, 1 ch, 1 sc in every st and Mdc in every sp.

KNIT

CROCHET

Queen Bee

This design is perfect for a panel on a cardigan or just by itself in the corner of a pillow. If you are working on a panel in the knit version, place the repeats close together for the best results or switch to garter stitch for the background.

Knit Instructions

Multiple of 23 sts + 2
On RS rows, slip the sts purlwise with yarn in the back.
Cast on using A, k one row and p one row.
Row 1 (RS): Using B, k all sts.
Row 2 and all WS rows: P the knitted sts and sl the slipped sts purlwise with yarn in the front.
Row 3: Using A, k all sts.
Row 5: Using B, k1, * k9, sl1, k3, sl1, k9; rep from * to last st, k1.
Row 7: Using A, k1, * k10, sl3, k10; rep from * to last st, k1.
Row 9: Using B, k1, * k7, sl1, k7, sl1, k7; rep from * to last st, k1.
Row 11: Using A, k1, * k8, sl1, k5, sl1, k8; rep from * to last st, k1.
Row 13: Using B, k1, * k7, sl1, k7, sl1, k7; rep from * to last st, k1.
Row 15: Using A, k1, * k8, sl1, k5, sl1, k8; rep from * to last st, k1.
Row 17: Using B, k1, * k3, sl1, k15, sl1, k3; rep from * to last st, k1.
Row 19: Using A, k1, * k4, sl1, k4, sl2, k1, sl2, k4, sl1, k4; rep from * to last st, k1.
Row 21: Using B, k1, * k1, sl1, k19, sl1, k1; rep from * to last st, k1.
Row 23: Using A, k1, * k2, sl1, k6, sl2, k1, sl2, k6, sl1, k2; rep from * to last st, k1.
Row 25: Using B, k1, * k1, sl1, k19, sl1, k1; rep from * to last st, k1.
Row 27: Using A, k1, * k9, [sl1, k1] 3 times, k8; rep from * to last st, k1.
Row 29: Using B, k1, * k8, sl1, k5, sl1, k8; rep from * to last st, k1.
Row 31: Using A, k1, * k10, [sl1, k1] twice, k9; rep from * to last st, k1.
Row 33: Using B, k1, * k7, sl1, [k3, sl1] twice, k7; rep from * to last st, k1.
Row 35: Using A, k all sts.
Row 37: Using B, k all sts.
Row 39: Using A, k all sts.
Row 40: As Row 2.

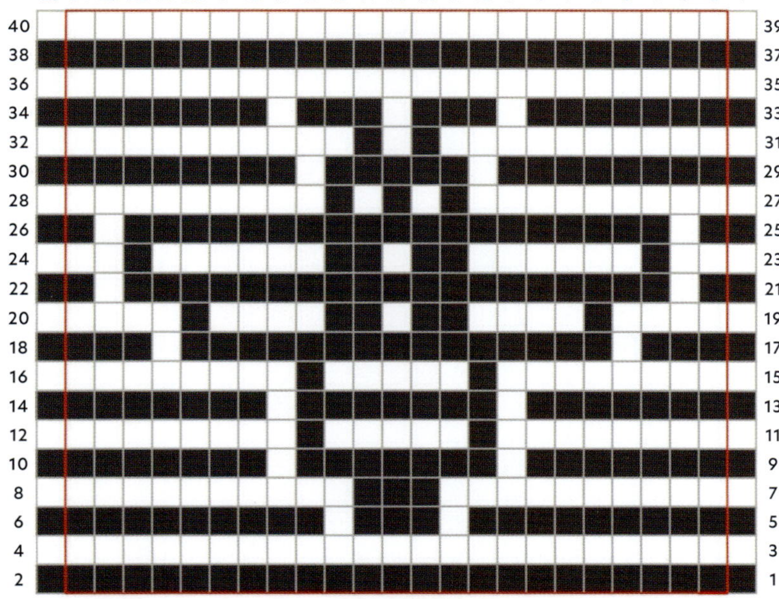

Yarn A = Cream
Yarn B = Yellow

Crochet Instructions

Multiple of 23 sts + 2
Using A, make desired number of chainless sc.
Row 1 (RS): Using B, 1 ch, 1 sc in every st to end.
Row 2 and all WS rows: 1 ch, 1 sc in sts, ch and skip ch-sps, turn.
Row 3: Using A, 1 ch, 1 sc in every st to end.
Row 5: Using B, 1 ch, 1 sc, * 9 sc, 2 ch, skip st, 3 sc, 2 ch, skip st, 9 sc; rep from * to last st, 1 sc, turn.
Row 7: Using A, 1 ch, 1 sc, * 9 sc, 1 Mdc, 4 ch, skip 3 sts, 1 Mdc, 9 sc; rep from * to last st, 1 sc, turn.
Row 9: Using B, 1 ch, 1 sc, * 7 sc, 2 ch, skip st, 2 sc, 3 Mdc, 2 sc, 2 ch, skip st, 7 sc; rep from * to last st, 1 sc, turn.
Row 11: Using A, 1 ch, 1 sc, * 7 sc, 1 Mdc, 2 ch, skip st, 5 sc, 2 ch, skip st, 1 Mdc, 7 sc; rep from * to last st, 1 sc, turn.
Row 13: Using B, 1 ch, 1 sc, * 7 sc, 2 ch, skip st, 1 Mdc, 5 sc, 1 Mdc, 2 ch, skip st, 7 sc; rep from * to last st, 1 sc, turn.
Row 15: Using A, 1 ch, 1 sc, * 7 sc, 1 Mdc, 2 ch, skip st, 5 sc, 2 ch, skip st, 1 Mdc, 7 sc; rep from * to last st, 1 sc, turn.
Row 17: Using B, 1 ch, 1 sc, * 3 sc, 2 ch, skip st, 4 sc, 1 Mdc, 5 sc, 1 Mdc, 4 sc, 2 ch, skip st, 3 sc; rep from * to last st, 1 sc, turn.

Row 19: Using A, 1 ch, 1 sc, * 3 sc, 1 Mdc, 2 ch, skip st, 4 sc, 3 ch, skip 2 sts, 1 sc, 3 ch, skip 2 sts, 4 sc, 2 ch, skip st, 1 Mdc, 3 sc; rep from * to last st, 1 sc, turn.

Row 21: Using B, 1 ch, 1 sc, * 1 sc, 2 ch, skip st, 2 sc, 1 Mdc, 4 sc, 2 Mdc, 1 sc, 2 Mdc, 4 sc, 1 Mdc, 2 sc, 2 ch, skip st, 1 sc; rep from * to last st, 1 sc, turn.

Row 23: Using A, 1 ch, 1 sc, * 1 sc, 1 Mdc, 2 ch, skip st, 6 sc, 3 ch, skip 2 sts, 1 sc, 3 ch, skip 2 sts, 6 sc, 2 ch, skip st, 1 Mdc, 1 sc; rep from * to last st, 1 sc, turn.

Row 25: Using B, 1 ch, 1 sc, * 1 sc, 2 ch, skip st, 1 Mdc, 6 sc, 2 Mdc, 1 sc, 2 Mdc, 6 sc, 1 Mdc, 2 ch, skip st, 1 sc; rep from * to last st, 1 sc, turn.

Row 27: Using A, 1 ch, 1 sc, * 1 sc, 1 Mdc, 7 sc, [2 ch, skip st, 1 sc] 3 times, 6 sc, 1 Mdc, 1 sc; rep from * to last st, 1 sc, turn.

Row 29: Using B, 1 ch, 1 sc, * 8 sc, 2 ch, skip st, [1 Mdc, 1 sc] twice, 1 Mdc, 2 ch, skip st, 8 sc; rep from * to last st, 1 sc, turn.

Row 31: Using A, 1 ch, 1 sc, * 8 sc, 1 Mdc, 1 sc, [2 ch, skip st, 1 sc] twice, 1 Mdc, 8 sc; rep from * to last st, 1 sc, turn.

Row 33: Using B, 1 ch, 1 sc, * 7 sc, 2 ch, skip st, 2 sc, 1 Mdc, 2 ch, skip st, 1 Mdc, 2 sc, 2 ch, skip st, 7 sc; rep from * to last st, 1 sc, turn.

Row 35: Using A, 1 ch, 1 sc, 7 sc, 1 Mdc, [3 sc, 1 Mdc] twice, 7 sc; rep from * to last st, 1 sc, turn.

Row 37: Using B, 1 ch, 1 sc in every st to end.

Row 39: Using A, 1 ch, 1 sc in every st to end.

Row 40: As Row 2.

Rep Rows 1 to 40, ending last rep with Row 39.

KNIT

CROCHET

Topiary

A cute pattern, perfect for a garden-themed present. Think about changing your Yarn A to a red or a yellow if you want it to look like an apple or lemon tree.

Knit Instructions

Multiple of 12 sts + 3

On RS rows, slip the sts purlwise with yarn in the back.

Cast on using A, k one row and p one row.

Row 1 (RS): Using B, k1, * [sl1, k1]; rep from * to last 2 sts, sl1, k1.

Row 2 and all WS rows: P the knitted sts and sl the slipped sts purlwise with yarn in the front.

Row 3: Using A, k all sts.

Row 5: Using B, k1, * [sl1, k1] twice, sl1, k3, [sl1, k1] twice; rep from * to last 2 sts, sl1, k1.

Row 7: Using A, k1, * k5, sl1, k1, sl1, k4; rep from * to last 2 sts, k2.

Row 9: Using B, k1, * sl1, k1, sl2, k5, sl2, k1; rep from * to last 2 sts, sl1, k1.

Row 11: Using A, k1, * k4, sl2, k1, sl2, k3; rep from * to last 2 sts, k2.

Row 13: Using B, k1, * sl2, k9, sl1; rep from * to last 2 sts, sl1, k1.

Row 15: Using A, k1, * k6, sl1, k5; rep from * to last 2 sts, k2.

Row 17: Using B, k1, * [sl1, k1] twice, sl2, k1, sl2, k1, sl1, k1; rep from * to last 2 sts, sl1, k1.

Row 19: Using A, k1, * k6, sl1, k5; rep from * to last 2 sts, k2.

Row 21: Using B, k1, * [sl1, k1] twice, sl2, k1, sl2, k1, sl1, k1; rep from * to last 2 sts, sl1, k1.

Row 23: Using A, k1, * k6, sl1, k5; rep from * to last 2 sts, k2.

Row 25: Using B, k1, * sl1, k1, sl1, k7, sl1, k1; rep from * to last 2 sts, sl1, k1.

Row 27: Using A, k1, * k3, [sl1, k1] 4 times, k1; rep from * to last 2 sts, k2.

Row 29: Using B, k1, * sl2, k9, sl1; rep from * to last 2 sts, sl1, k1.

Row 31: Using A, k1, * k2, [sl1, k1] 5 times; rep from * to last 2 sts, k2.

Row 33: Using B, k1, * sl2, k9, sl1; rep from * to last 2 sts, sl1, k1.

Row 35: Using A, k1, * k3, sl2, k1, sl1, k1, sl2, k2; rep from * to last 2 sts, k2.

Row 37: Using B, k1, * sl1, k1, sl1, k7, sl1, k1; rep from * to last 2 sts, sl1, k1.

Row 39: Using A, k1, * k5, sl1, k1, sl1, k4; rep from * to last 2 sts, k2.

Row 41: Using B, k1, * [sl1, k1] twice, sl1, k3, [sl1, k1] twice; rep from * to last 2 sts, sl1, k1.

Row 43: Using A, k all sts.

Row 45: Using B, k1, * [sl1, k1]; rep from * to last 2 sts, sl1, k1.

Row 47: Using A, k all sts.

Row 48: As Row 2.

Rep Rows 1 to 48.

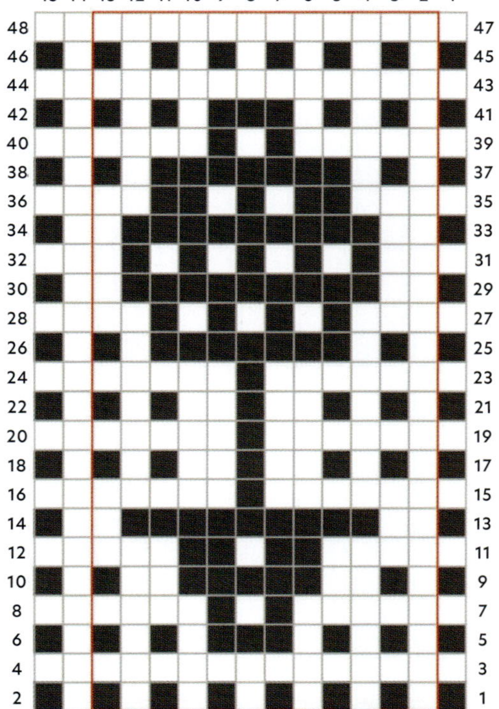

Yarn A = Cream

Yarn B = Green

Crochet Instructions

Multiple of 12 sts + 3

Pattern note: The repeat in written instructions differs from chart on Rows 13, 29, and 33.

Using A, make desired number of chainless sc.

Row 1 (RS): Using B, 1 ch, 1 sc, * [2 ch, skip st, 1 sc] 6 times; rep from * to last 2 sts, 2 ch, skip st, 1 sc, turn.

Row 2 and all WS rows: 1 ch, 1 sc in sts, ch and skip ch-sps, turn.

Row 3: Using A, 1 ch, 1 sc, * [1 Mdc, 1 sc] 6 times; rep from * to last 2 sts, 1 Mdc, 1 sc, turn.

Row 5: Using B, 1 ch, 1 sc, * [2 ch, skip st, 1 sc] twice, 2 ch, skip st, 3 sc, [2 ch, skip st, 1 sc] twice; rep from * to last 2 sts, 2 ch, skip st, 1 sc, turn.

KNIT

CROCHET

1 sc] twice, 1 Mdc, 2 ch, skip st, 1 sc, 2 ch, skip st, [1 Mdc, 1 sc] twice; rep from * to last 2 sts, 1 Mdc, 1 sc, turn.

Row 9: Using B, 1 ch, 1 sc, * 2 ch, skip st, 1 sc, 3 ch, skip 2 sts, [1 sc, 1 Mdc] twice, 1 sc, 3 ch, skip 2 sts, 1 sc; rep from * to last 2 sts, 2 ch, skip st, 1 sc, turn.

Row 11: Using A, 1 ch, 1 sc, * 1 Mdc, 1 sc, 2 Mdc, 3 ch, skip 2 sts, 1 sc, 3 ch, skip 2 sts, 2 Mdc, 1 sc; rep from * to last 2 sts, 1 Mdc, 1 sc, turn.

Row 13: Using B, 1 ch, 1 sc, 3 ch, skip 2 sts, * 2 sc, 2 Mdc, 1 sc, 2 Mdc, 2 sc, ** 4 ch, skip 3 sts; rep from * to last 3 sts, ending last rep at **, 3 ch, skip 2 sts, 1 sc, turn.

Row 15: Using A, 1 ch, 1 sc, * 2 Mdc, 4 sc, 2 ch, skip st, 4 sc, 1 Mdc; rep from * to last 2 sts, 1 Mdc, 1 sc, turn.

Row 17: Using B, 1 ch, 1 sc, * [2 ch, skip st, 1 sc] twice, 3 ch, skip 2 sts, 1 Mdc, 3 ch, skip 2 sts, 1 sc, 2 ch, skip st, 1 sc; rep from * to last 2 sts, 2 ch, skip st, 1 sc, turn.

Row 19: Using A, 1 ch, 1 sc, * [1 Mdc, 1 sc] twice, 2 Mdc, 2 ch, skip st, 2 Mdc, 1 sc, 1 Mdc, 1 sc; rep from * to last 2 sts, 1 Mdc, 1 sc, turn.

Row 21: Using B, 1 ch, 1 sc, * [2 ch, skip st, 1 sc] twice, 3 ch, skip 2 sts, 1 Mdc, 3 ch, skip 2 sts, 1 sc, 2 ch, skip st, 1 sc; rep from * to last 2 sts, 2 ch, skip st, 1 sc, turn.

Row 23: Using A, 1 ch, 1 sc, * [1 Mdc, 1 sc] twice, 2 Mdc, 2 ch, skip st, 2 Mdc, 1 sc, 1 Mdc, 1 sc; rep from * to last 2 sts, 1 Mdc, 1 sc, turn.

Row 25: Using B, 1 ch, 1 sc, * 2 ch, skip st, 1 sc, 2 ch, skip st, 3 sc, 1 Mdc, 3 sc, 2 ch, skip st, 1 sc; rep from * to last 2 sts, 2 ch, skip st, 1 sc, turn.

Row 27: Using A, 1 ch, 1 sc, * 1 Mdc, 1 sc, 1 Mdc, [2 ch, skip st, 1 sc] 3 times, 2 ch, skip st, 1 Mdc, 1 sc; rep from * to last 2 sts, 1 Mdc, 1 sc, turn.

Row 29: Using B, 1 ch, 1 sc, 3 ch, skip 2 sts, * 1 sc, [1 Mdc, 1 sc] 4 times, ** 4 ch, skip 3 sts; rep from * to last 3 sts, ending last rep at **, 3 ch, skip 2 sts, 1 sc, turn.

Row 31: Using A, 1 ch, 1 sc, * 2 Mdc, [2 ch, skip st, 1 sc] 4 times, 2 ch, skip st, 1 Mdc; rep from * to last 2 sts, 1 Mdc, 1 sc, turn.

Row 33: Using B, 1 ch, 1 sc, 3 ch, skip 2 sts, * [1 Mdc, 1 sc] 4 times, 1 Mdc, ** 4 ch, skip 3 sts; rep from * to last 3 sts, ending last rep at **, 3 ch, skip 2 sts, 1 sc, turn.

Row 35: Using A, 1 ch, 1 sc, * 2 Mdc, 1 sc, 3 ch, skip 2 sts, 1 sc, 2 ch, skip st, 1 sc, 3 ch, skip 2 sts, 1 sc, 1 Mdc; rep from * to last 2 sts, 1 Mdc, 1 sc, turn.

Row 37: Using B, 1 ch, 1 sc, * 2 ch, skip st, 1 sc, 2 ch, skip st, 2 Mdc, 1 sc, 1 Mdc, 1 sc, 2 Mdc, 2 ch, skip st, 1 sc; rep from * to last 2 sts, 2 ch, skip st, 1 sc, turn.

Row 39: Using A, 1 ch, 1 sc, * 1 Mdc, 1 sc, 1 Mdc, 2 sc, 2 ch, skip st, 1 sc, 2 ch, skip st, 2 sc, 1 Mdc, 1 sc; rep from * to last 2 sts, 1 Mdc, 1 sc, turn.

Row 41: Using B, 1 ch, 1 sc, * [2 ch, skip st, 1 sc] twice, 2 ch, skip st, 1 Mdc, 1 sc, 1 Mdc, [2 ch, skip st, 1 sc] twice; rep from * to last 2 sts, 2 ch, skip st, 1 sc, turn.

Row 43: Using A, 1 ch, 1 sc, * [1 Mdc, 1 sc] 3 times, 2 sc, [1 Mdc, 1 sc] twice; rep from * to last 2 sts, 1 Mdc, 1 sc, turn.

Row 45: Using B, 1 ch, 1 sc, * [2 ch, skip st, 1 sc] 6 times; rep from * to last 2 sts, 2 ch, skip st, 1 sc, turn.

To finish, work Row 47.

Row 47: Using A, 1 ch, 1 sc in every st and Mdc in every sp.

Trellis

This stunning design will look best on larger projects where a few repeats can be worked to let the pattern truly shine and reveal the surrounding design of leaves.

Knitting Instructions

Multiple of 10 sts + 5

On RS rows, slip the sts purlwise with yarn in the back.

Cast on using A, k one row and p one row.

Row 1 (RS): Using B, k1, sl1, * k2, sl1, k5, sl1, k1; rep from * to last 3 sts, k1, sl1, k1.

Row 2 and all WS rows: P the knitted sts and sl the slipped sts purlwise with yarn in the front.

Row 3: Using A, k2, * k1, sl1, k2, [sl1, k1] twice, k1, sl1; rep from * to last 3 sts, k3.

Row 5: Using B, k1, sl1, * sl1, k2, sl1, k3, sl1, k2; rep from * to last 3 sts, sl2, k1.

Row 7: Using A, k2, * [k2, sl1] 3 times, k1; rep from * to last 3 sts, k3.

Row 9: Using B, k1, sl1, * sl1, k2, sl1, k3, sl1, k2; rep from * to last 3 sts, sl2, k1.

Row 11: Using A, k2, * k1, sl1, k2, [sl1, k1] twice, k1, sl1; rep from * to last 3 sts, k3.

Row 13: Using B, k1, sl1, * k2, sl1, k5, sl1, k1; rep from * to last 3 sts, k1, sl1, k1.

Row 15: Using A, k2, *k3, [sl1, k1] 3 times, k1; rep from * to last 3 sts, k3.

Row 17: Using B, k1, sl1, * sl1, k9; rep from * to last 3 sts, sl2, k1.

Row 19: Using A, k2, * k1, sl1, k1, [sl2, k1] twice, sl1; rep from * to last 3 sts, k3.

Row 21: Using B, k1, sl1, * k10; rep from * to last 3 sts, k1, sl1, k1.

Row 23: Using A, k2, * k1, sl1, k1, [sl2, k1] twice, sl1; rep from * to last 3 sts, k3.

Row 25: Using B, k1, sl1, * sl1, k9; rep from * to last 3 sts, sl2, k1.

Row 27: Using A, k2, * k3, [sl1, k1] twice, sl1, k2; rep from * to last 3 sts, k3.

Row 29: Using B, k1, sl1, * k2, sl1, k5, sl1, k1; rep from * to last 3 sts, k1, sl1, k1.

Row 31: Using A, k2, * k1, sl1, k2, [sl1, k1] twice, k1, sl1; rep from * to last 3 sts, k3.

Rep Rows 5 to 32. To finish, work Rows 33 to 44.

Row 33: Using B, k1, sl1, * sl1, k2, sl1, k3, sl1, k2; rep from * to last 3 sts, sl2, k1.

Row 35: Using A, k2, * k2, sl1, k2, sl1, k2, sl1, k1; rep from * to last 3 sts, k3.

Row 37: Using B, k1, sl1, * sl1, k2, sl1, k3, sl1, k2; rep from * to last 3 sts, sl2, k1.

Row 39: Using A, k2, * k1, sl1, k2, sl1, k1, sl1, k2, sl1; rep from * to last 3 sts, k3.

Row 41: Using B, k1, sl1, * k2, sl1, k5, sl1, k1; rep from * to last 3 sts, k1, sl1, k1.

Row 43: Using A, k all sts.

Row 44: As Row 2.

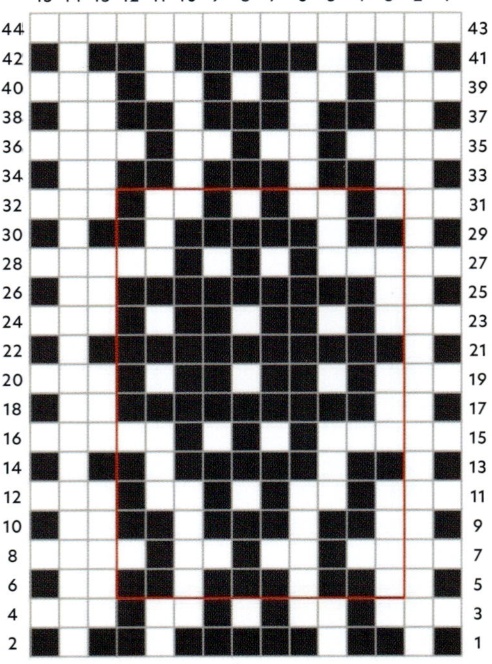

Crochet Instructions

Multiple of 10 sts + 5

Pattern note: The repeat in written instructions differs from chart on Rows 5, 9, 17, 25, 33, and 37.

Using A, make desired number of chainless sc.

Row 1 (RS): Using B, 1 ch, 1 sc, 2 ch, skip st, * 2 sc, 2 ch, skip st, 5 sc, 2 ch, skip st, 1 sc; rep from * to last 3 sts, 1 sc, 2 ch, skip st, 1 sc, turn.

Row 2 and all WS rows: 1 ch, 1 sc in sts, ch and skip ch-sps, turn.

Row 3: Using A, 1 ch, 1 sc, 1 Mdc, * 1 sc, 2 ch, skip st, 1 Mdc, [1 sc, 2 ch, skip st] twice, 1 sc, 1 Mdc, 2 ch, skip st; rep from * to last 3 sts, 1 sc, 1 Mdc, 1 sc, turn.

Row 5: Using B, 1 ch, 1 sc, 3 ch, skip 2 sts, * 1 Mdc, 1 sc, 2 ch, skip st, 1 Mdc, 1 sc, 1 Mdc, 2 ch, skip st, 1 sc, 1 Mdc, ** 2 ch, skip st; rep from * to last 3 sts, ending last rep at **, 3 ch, skip 2 sts, 1 sc, turn.

Row 7: Using A, 1 ch, 1 sc, 1 Mdc, * [1 Mdc, 1 sc, 2 ch, skip st] twice, 1 sc,

1 Mdc, 2 ch, skip st, 1 sc; rep from * to last 3 sts, 2 Mdc, 1 sc, turn.

Row 9: Using B, 1 ch, 1 sc, 3 ch, skip 2 sts, * 1 sc, 1 Mdc, 2 ch, skip st, 1 sc, 1 Mdc, 1 sc, 2 ch, skip st, 1 Mdc, 1 sc, ** 2 ch, skip st; rep from * to last 3 sts, ending last rep at **, 3 ch, skip 2 sts, 1 sc, turn.

Row 11: Using A, 1 ch, 1 sc, 1 Mdc, * 1 Mdc, 2 ch, skip st, 1 sc, 1 Mdc, 2 ch, skip st, 1 sc, 2 ch, skip st, 1 Mdc, 1 sc, 2 ch, skip st; rep from * to last 3 sts, 2 Mdc, 1 sc, turn.

Row 13: Using B, 1 ch, 1 sc, 2 ch, skip st, * 1 sc, 1 Mdc, 2 ch, skip st, [1 sc, 1 Mdc] twice, 1 sc, 2 ch, skip st, 1 Mdc; rep from * to last 3 sts, 1 sc, 2 ch, skip st, 1 sc, turn.

Row 15: Using A, 1 ch, 1 sc, 1 Mdc, * 2 sc, 1 Mdc, [2 ch, skip st, 1 sc] twice, 2 ch, skip st, 1 Mdc, 1 sc; rep from * to last 3 sts, 1 sc, 1 Mdc, 1 sc, turn.

Row 17: Using B, 1 ch, 1 sc, 3 ch, skip 2 sts, * 2 sc, [1 Mdc, 1 sc] twice, 1 Mdc, 2 sc, ** 2 ch, skip st; rep from * to last 3 sts, ending last rep at **, 3 ch, skip 2 sts, 1 sc, turn.

Row 19: Using A, 1 ch, 1 sc, 1 Mdc, * 1 Mdc, 2 ch, skip st, [1 sc, 3 ch, skip 2 sts] twice, 1 sc, 2 ch, skip st; rep from * to last 3 sts, 2 Mdc, 1 sc, turn.

Row 21: Using B, 1 ch, 1 sc, 2 ch, skip st, * 1 sc, 1 Mdc, [1 sc, 2 Mdc] twice, 1 sc, 1 Mdc; rep from * to last 3 sts, 1 sc, 2 ch, skip st, 1 sc, turn.

Row 23: Using A, 1 ch, 1 sc, 1 Mdc, * 1 sc, 2 ch, skip st, [1 sc, 3 ch, skip 2 sts] twice, 1 sc, 2 ch, skip st; rep from * to last 3 sts, 1 sc, 1 Mdc, 1 sc, turn.

Row 25: Using B, 1 ch, 1 sc, 3 ch, skip 2 sts, * 1 Mdc, [1 sc, 2 Mdc] twice, 1 sc, 1 Mdc, ** 2 ch, skip st; rep from * to last 3 sts, ending last rep at **, 3 ch, skip 2 sts, 1 sc, turn.

Row 27: Using A, 1 ch, 1 sc, 1 Mdc, * 1 Mdc, 2 sc, [2 ch, skip st, 1 sc] twice, 2 ch, skip st, 2 sc; rep from * to last 3 sts, 2 Mdc, 1 sc, turn.

Row 29: Using B, 1 ch, 1 sc, 2 ch, skip st, * 2 sc, 2 ch, skip st, 1 Mdc, [1 sc, 1 Mdc] twice, 2 ch, skip st, 1 sc; rep from * to last 3 sts, 1 sc, 2 ch, skip st, 1 sc, turn.

Row 31: Using A, 1 ch, 1 sc, 1 Mdc, * 1 sc, 2 ch, skip st, 1 Mdc, 1 sc, [2 ch, skip st, 1 sc] twice, 1 Mdc, 2 ch, skip st; rep from * to last 3 sts, 1 sc, 1 Mdc, 1 sc, turn.

Rep Rows 5 to 32. To finish, work Rows 33 to 43.

Rows 33 to 42: Rep Rows 5 to 14.

Row 43: Using A, 1 ch, 1 sc in every st and Mdc in every sp.

Tulip

Though this is classified as an easy design, it is advisable to pay close attention to the chart and text as it can get confusing when slipping stitches (knitting) or chaining (crochet) when repeating.

Knit Instructions

Multiple of 10 sts + 3

On RS rows, slip the sts purlwise with yarn in the back.

Cast on using B, k one row and p one row.

Row 1 (RS): Using A, k1, * sl1, k1, sl2, k1, sl1, k1, sl2, k1; rep from * to last 2 sts, sl1, k1.

Row 2 and all WS rows: P the knitted sts and sl the slipped sts purlwise with yarn in the front.

Row 3: Using B, k1, * k4, sl1, k1, sl1, k3; rep from * to last 2 sts, k2.

Row 5: Using A, k1, * [sl1, k1] twice, k1, sl1, k2, sl1, k1; rep from * to last 2 sts, sl1, k1.

Row 7: Using B, k1, * [k3, sl1] twice, k2; rep from * to last 2 sts, k2.

Row 9: Using A, k1, * sl2, k2, sl1, k1, sl1, k2, sl1; rep from * to last 2 sts, sl1, k1.

Row 11: Using B, k1, * [k2, sl1] 3 times, k1; rep from * to last 2 sts, k2.

Row 13: Using A, k1, * sl1, k2, sl1, k3, sl1, k2; rep from * to last 2 sts, sl1, k1.

Row 15: Using B, k1, * k1, sl1, k2, sl3, k2, sl1; rep from * to last 2 sts, k2.

Row 17: Using A, k1, * sl1, k1, sl1, k5, sl1, k1; rep from * to last 2 sts, sl1, k1.

Row 19: Using B, k1, * k3, [sl1, k1] 3 times, k1; rep from * to last 2 sts, k2.

Row 21: Using A, k1, * [sl1, k1] 5 times; rep from * to last 2 sts, sl1, k1.

Row 23: Using B, k1, * k5, sl1, k4; rep from * to last 2 sts, k2.

Row 25: Using A, k1, * [sl1, k1] 5 times; rep from * to last 2 sts, sl1, k1.

Row 27: Using B, k all sts.

Row 28: As Row 2.

Rep Rows 1 to 28.

Crochet Instructions

Multiple of 10 sts + 3

Pattern note: The repeat in written instructions differs from chart on Row 9.

Using B, make desired number of chainless sc.

Row 1 (RS): Using A, 1 ch, 1 sc, * [2 ch, skip st, 1 sc, 3 ch, skip 2 sts, 1 sc] twice; rep from * to last 2 sts, 2 ch, skip st, 1 sc, turn.

Row 2 and all WS rows: 1 ch, 1 sc in sts, ch and skip ch-sps, turn.

Row 3: Using B, 1 ch, 1 sc, * 1 Mdc, 1 sc, 2 Mdc, [2 ch, skip st, 1 Mdc] twice, 1 Mdc, 1 sc; rep from * to last 2 sts, 1 Mdc, 1 sc, turn.

Row 5: Using A, 1 ch, 1 sc, * [2 ch, skip st, 1 sc] twice, 1 Mdc, 2 ch, skip st, 1 Mdc, 1 sc, 2 ch, skip st, 1 sc; rep from * to last 2 sts, 2 ch, skip st, 1 sc, turn.

Row 7: Using B, 1 ch, 1 sc, * 1 Mdc, 1 sc, 1 Mdc, 2 ch, skip st, 1 sc, 1 Mdc, 1 sc, 2 ch, skip st, 1 Mdc, 1 sc; rep from * to last 2 sts, 1 Mdc, 1 sc, turn.

Row 9: Using A, 1 ch, 1 sc, 3 ch, skip 2 sts, * 1 sc, 1 Mdc, 2 ch, skip st, 1 sc, 2 ch, skip st, 1 Mdc, 1 sc, ** 4 ch, skip 3 sts; rep from * to last 3 sts, ending last rep at **, 3 ch, skip 2 sts, 1 sc, turn.

Row 11: Using B, 1 ch, 1 sc, * 2 Mdc,

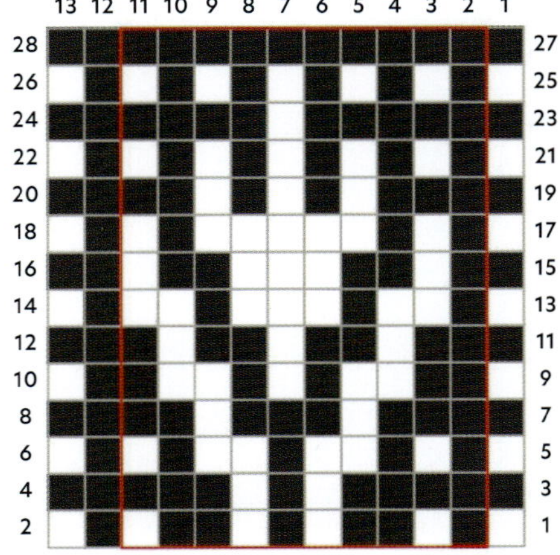

Yarn A = Cream

Yarn B = Red

2 ch, skip st, 1 sc, 1 Mdc, 2 ch, skip st, 1 Mdc, 1 sc, 2 ch, skip st, 1 Mdc; rep from * to last 2 sts, 1 Mdc, 1 sc, turn.

Row 13: Using A, 1 ch, 1 sc, * 2 ch, skip st, 1 sc, 1 Mdc, 2 ch, skip st, 1 sc, 1 Mdc, 1 sc, 2 ch, skip st, 1 Mdc, 1 sc; rep from * to last 2 sts, 2 ch, skip st, 1 sc, turn.

Row 15: Using B, 1 ch, 1 sc, * 1 Mdc, 2 ch, skip st, 1 sc, 1 Mdc, 4 ch, skip 3 sts, 1 Mdc, 1 sc, 2 ch, skip st; rep from * to last 2 sts, 1 Mdc, 1 sc, turn.

Row 17: Using A, 1 ch, 1 sc, * 2 ch, skip st, 1 Mdc, 2 ch, skip st, 1 sc, 3 Mdc, 1 sc, 2 ch, skip st, 1 Mdc; rep from * to last 2 sts, 2 ch, skip st, 1 sc, turn.

Row 19: Using B, 1 ch, 1 sc, * 1 Mdc, 1 sc, 1 Mdc, [2 ch, skip st, 1 sc] twice, 2 ch, skip st, 1 Mdc, 1 sc; rep from * to last 2 sts, 1 Mdc, 1 sc, turn.

Row 21: Using A, 1 ch, 1 sc, * 2 ch, skip st, 1 sc, [2 ch, skip st, 1 Mdc] 3 times, 2 ch, skip st, 1 sc; rep from * to last 2 sts, 2 ch, skip st, 1 sc, turn.

Row 23: Using B, 1 ch, 1 sc, * [1 Mdc, 1 sc] twice, 1 Mdc, 2 ch, skip st, [1 Mdc, 1 sc] twice; rep from * to last 2 sts, 1 Mdc, 1 sc, turn.

Row 25: Using A, 1 ch, 1 sc, * [2 ch, skip st, 1 sc] twice, 2 ch, skip st, 1 Mdc, [2 ch, skip st, 1 sc] twice; rep from * to last 2 sts, 2 ch, skip st, 1 sc, turn.

Row 27: Using B, 1 ch, 1 sc in every st and Mdc in every sp.

Row 28: As Row 2.

Rep Rows 1 to 28, ending last rep with Row 27.

CROCHET

Bloom

This pattern is perfect for blankets as a large repeat. Or use it as a horizontal panel in combination with other designs such as Topiary, Leaves, or Tulip for a unique result.

Knit Instructions

Multiple of 12 sts + 3

On RS rows, slip the sts purlwise with yarn in the back.

Cast on using A, k one row and p one row.

Row 1 (RS): Using B, k1, * sl1, k1, [sl1, k3] twice, sl1, k1; rep from * to last 2 sts, sl1, k1.

Row 2 and all WS rows: P the knitted sts and sl the slipped sts purlwise with yarn in the front.

Row 3: Using A, k1, * k3, [sl1, k1] 4 times, k1; rep from * to last 2 sts, k2.

Row 5: Using B, k1, * sl1, [k3, sl1] twice, k3; rep from * to last 2 sts, sl1, k1.

Row 7: Using A, k1, * k1, sl1, k3, sl1, k1, sl1, k3, sl1; rep from * to last 2 sts, k2.

Row 9: Using B, k1, * sl1, k11; rep from * to last 2 sts, sl1, k1.

Row 11: Using A, k1, * k3, [sl1, k1] 4 times, k1; rep from * to last 2 sts, k2.

Row 13: Using B, k1, * sl1, k11; rep from * to last 2 sts, sl1, k1.

Row 15: Using A, k1, * k1, sl1, k3, sl1, k1, sl1, k3, sl1; rep from * to last 2 sts, k2.

Row 17: Using B, k1, * sl1, [k3, sl1] twice, k3; rep from * to last 2 sts, sl1, k1.

Row 19: Using A, k1, * k3, [sl1, k1] 4 times, k1; rep from * to last 2 sts, k2.

Row 21: Using B, k1, * sl1, k1, [sl1, k3] twice, sl1, k1; rep from * to last 2 sts, sl1, k1.

Row 23: Using A, k all sts.

Row 24: As Row 2.

Repeat Rows 1 to 24.

Crochet Instructions

Multiple of 12 sts + 3

Using A, make desired number of chainless sc.

Row 1 (RS): Using B, 1 ch, 1 sc, * 2 ch, skip st, 1 sc, [2 ch, skip st, 3 sc] twice, 2 ch, skip st, 1 sc; rep from * to last 2 sts, 2 ch, skip st, 1 sc, turn.

Row 2 and all WS rows: 1 ch, 1 sc in sts, ch and skip ch-sps, turn.

Row 3: Using A, 1 ch, 1 sc, * 1 Mdc, 1 sc, 1 Mdc, [2 ch, skip st, 1 sc, 2 ch, skip st, 1 Mdc] twice, 1 sc; rep from * to last 2 sts, 1 Mdc, 1 sc, turn.

Row 5: Using B, 1 ch, 1 sc, * 2 ch, skip st, 2 sc, 1 Mdc, 2 ch, skip st, 1 Mdc, 1 sc, 1 Mdc, 2 ch, skip st, 1 Mdc, 2 sc; rep from * to last 2 sts, 2 ch, skip st, 1 sc, turn.

Row 7: Using A, 1 ch, 1 sc, * 1 Mdc, 2 ch, skip st, 2 sc, 1 Mdc, 2 ch, skip st, 1 sc, 2 ch, skip st, 1 Mdc, 2 sc, 2 ch, skip st; rep from * to last 2 sts, 1 Mdc, 1 sc, turn.

Row 9: Using B, 1 ch, 1 sc, * 2 ch, skip st, 1 Mdc, 3 sc, 1 Mdc, 1 sc, 1 Mdc, 3 sc, 1 Mdc; rep from * to last 2 sts, 2 ch, skip st, 1 sc, turn.

Row 11: Using A, 1 ch, 1 sc, * 1 Mdc, 2 sc, [2 ch, skip st, 1 sc] 4 times, 1 sc; rep from * to last 2 sts, 1 Mdc, 1 sc, turn.

Row 13: Using B, 1 ch, 1 sc, * 2 ch, skip st, 2 sc, [1 Mdc, 1 sc] 4 times, 1 sc; rep from * to last 2 sts, 2 ch, skip st, 1 sc, turn.

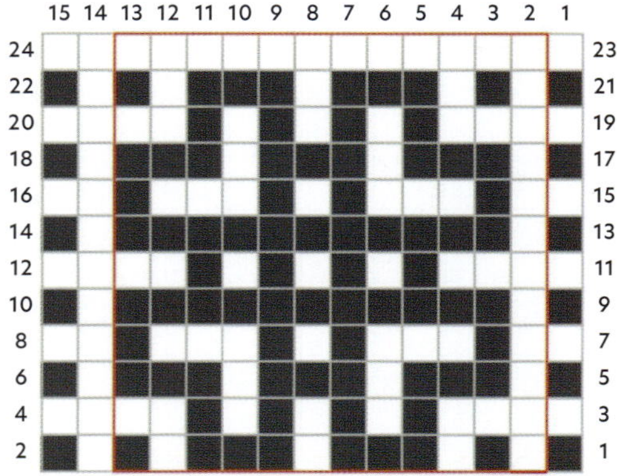

KNIT

CROCHET

Row 15: Using A, 1 ch, 1 sc, * 1 Mdc, 2 ch, skip st, 3 sc, 2 ch, skip st, 1 sc, 2 ch, skip st, 3 sc, 2 ch, skip st; rep from * to last 2 sts, 1 Mdc, 1 sc, turn.

Row 17: Using B, 1 ch, 1 sc, * 2 ch, skip st, 1 Mdc, 2 sc, 2 ch, skip st, 1 Mdc, 1 sc, 1 Mdc, 2 ch, skip st, 2 sc, 1 Mdc; rep from * to last 2 sts, 2 ch, skip st, 1 sc, turn.

Row 19: Using A, 1 ch, 1 sc, * 1 Mdc, 2 sc, 2 ch, skip st, 1 Mdc, 2 ch, skip st, 1 sc, 2 ch, skip st, 1 Mdc, 2 ch, skip st, 2 sc; rep from * to last 2 sts, 1 Mdc, 1 sc, turn.

Row 21: Using B, 1 ch, 1 sc, * 2 ch, skip st, 1 sc, 2 ch, skip st, [1 Mdc, 1 sc, 1 Mdc, 2 ch, skip st] twice, 1 sc; rep from * to last 2 sts, 2 ch, skip st, 1 sc, turn.

Row 23: Using A, 1 ch, 1 sc in every st and 1 Mdc in every sp.

Row 24: As Row 2.

Rep Rows 1 to 24, ending last rep with Row 23.

TIP: This design will work perfectly as a horizontal or vertical panel. When working a horizontal single panel, end work on Row 24 for knit and Row 23 for crochet.

Vine

This is another design inspired by climbing plants. This motif works best in a tall panel or as a large repeat to really show off the pattern.

Knit Instructions

Multiple of 12 sts + 5
On RS rows, slip the sts purlwise with yarn in the back.
Cast on using A, k one row and p one row.
Row 1 (RS): Using B, k1, sl1, * k1, sl1, k2, sl1, k3, sl1, k2, sl1; rep from * to last 3 sts, k1, sl1, k1.
Row 2 and all WS rows: P the knitted sts and sl the slipped sts purlwise with yarn in the front.
Row 3: Using A, k2, * k2, [sl1, k3] twice, sl1, k1; rep from * to last 3 sts, k3.
Row 5: Using B, k1, sl1, * sl1, k2, sl1, k5, sl1, k2; rep from * to last 3 sts, sl2, k1.
Row 7: Using A, k2, * k1, sl1, k2, [sl1, k1] 3 times, k1, sl1; rep from * to last 3 sts, k3.
Row 9: Using B, k1, sl1, * sl1, k1, sl1, k2, sl1, k1, sl1, k2, sl1, k1; rep from * to last 3 sts, sl2, k1.
Row 11: Using A, k2, * k3, [sl1, k2] 3 times; rep from * to last 3 sts, k3.
Rep Rows 1 to 12. To finish, work Rows 13 to 16.
Row 13: Using B, k1, sl1, * k1, sl1, k2, sl1, k3, sl1, k2, sl1; rep from * to last 3 sts, k1, sl1, k1.
Row 15: Using A, k all sts.
Row 16: As Row 2.

Crochet Instructions

Multiple of 12 sts + 5
Pattern note: The repeat in written instructions differs from chart on Rows 5 and 9.
Using A, make desired number of chainless sc.
Row 1 (RS): Using B, 1 ch, 1 sc, 2 ch, skip st, * 1 sc, 2 ch, skip st, 2 sc, 2 ch, skip st, 3 sc, 2 ch, skip st, 2 sc, 2 ch, skip st; rep from * to last 3 sts, 1 sc, 2 ch, skip st, 1 sc, turn.
Row 2 and all WS rows: 1 ch, 1 sc in sts, ch and skip ch-sps, turn.
Row 3: Using A, 1 ch, 1 sc, 1 Mdc, * 1 sc, 1 Mdc, [2 ch, skip st, 1 sc, 1 Mdc, 1 sc] twice, 2 ch, skip st, 1 Mdc; rep from * to last 3 sts, 1 sc, 1 Mdc, 1 sc, turn.
Row 5: Using B, 1 ch, 1 sc, 3 ch, skip 2 sts, * 1 sc, 1 Mdc, 2 ch, skip st, 2 sc, 1 Mdc, 2 sc, 2 ch, skip st, 1 Mdc, 1 sc, ** 2 ch, skip st; rep from * to last 3 sts, ending last rep at **, 3 ch, skip 2 sts, 1 sc, turn.
Row 7: Using A, 1 ch, 1 sc, 1 Mdc, * 1 Mdc, 2 ch, skip st, 1 sc, 1 Mdc, [2 ch, skip st, 1 sc] twice, 2 ch, skip st, 1 Mdc, 1 sc, 2 ch, skip st; rep from * to last

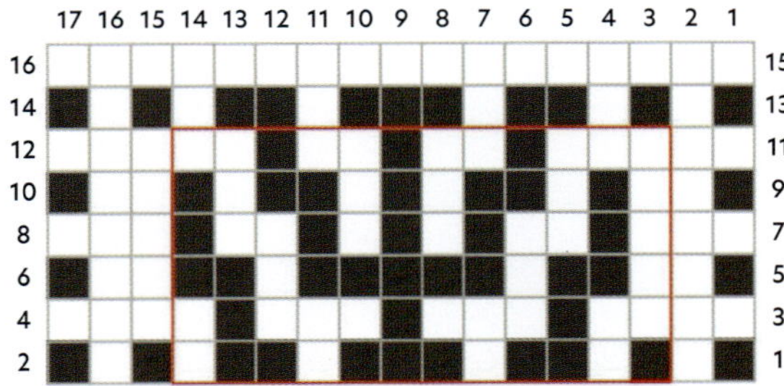

3 sts, 2 Mdc, 1 sc, turn.

Row 9: Using B, 1 ch, 1 sc, 3 ch, skip 2 sts, * 1 Mdc, 2 ch, skip st, 1 sc, [1 Mdc, 2 ch, skip st] twice, 1 Mdc, 1 sc, 2 ch, skip st, 1 Mdc, ** 2 ch, skip st; rep from * to last 3 sts, ending last rep at **, 3 ch, skip 2 sts, 1 sc, turn.

Row 11: Using A, 1 ch, 1 sc, 1 Mdc, * 1 Mdc, 1 sc, 1 Mdc, 2 ch, skip st, 1 sc, 1 Mdc, 2 ch, skip st, 1 Mdc, 1 sc, 2 ch, skip st, 1 Mdc, 1 sc; rep from * to last 3 sts, 2 Mdc, 1 sc, turn.

Rep Rows 1 to 12, placing 1 Mdc in sps as required on Row 1. To finish, work Rows 13 to 15.

Row 13: Using B, 1 ch, 1 sc, 2 ch, skip st, * 1 sc, 2 ch, skip st, 1 sc, 1 Mdc, 2 ch, skip st, 1 sc, 1 Mdc, 1 sc, 2 ch, skip st, 1 Mdc, 1 sc, 2 ch, skip st; rep from * to last 3 sts, 1 sc, 2 ch, skip st, 1 sc, turn.

Row 15: Using A, 1 ch, 1 sc in every st and Mdc in every sp.

KNIT

CROCHET

Seasonal

Easter Egg

The knitted version of this pattern looks rounder as the rows are smaller than crochet. Try the crochet version with overlay mosaic crochet (page 24) to achieve a similar look as the knit version.

Knit Instructions

Multiple of 20 sts + 5

On RS rows, slip the sts purlwise using yarn in the back.

Cast on using A, k one row and p one row.

Row 1 (RS): Using B, k all sts.

Row 2 and all WS rows: P the knitted sts and sl the slipped sts purlwise with yarn in the front.

Row 3: Using A, k1, sl1, k1, * sl1, k1; rep from * to last 2 sts, sl1, k1.

Row 5: Using B, k all sts.

Row 7: Using A, k all sts.

Row 9: Using B, k1, sl1, k1, * sl3, k1, sl1, k9, sl1, k1, sl3, k1; rep from * to last 2 sts, sl1, k1.

Row 11: Using A, k3, * k5, [sl1, k1] 5 times, k5; rep from * to last 2 sts, k2.

Row 13: Using B, k1, sl2, * sl1, k1, sl1, k13, sl1, k1, sl2; rep from * to last 2 sts, sl1, k1.

Row 15: Using A, k3, * k3, sl1, k11, sl1, k4; rep from * to last 2 sts, k2.

Row 17: Using B, k1, sl1, k1, * sl2, k15, sl2, k1; rep from * to last 2 sts, sl1, k1.

Row 19: Using A, k3, * k2, [sl1, k1] 8 times, k2; rep from * to last 2 sts, k2.

Row 21: Using B, k1, sl2, * sl1, k17, sl2; rep from * to last 2 sts, sl1, k1.

Row 23: Using A, k3, * k1, sl1, k15, sl1, k2; rep from * to last 2 sts, k2.

Row 25: Using B, k1, sl2, * k19, sl1; rep from * to last 2 sts, sl1, k1.

Row 27: Using A, k3, * sl1, k1; rep from * to last 2 sts, k2.

Row 29: As Row 25.

Row 31: Using A, k3, * sl2, [k1, sl1] 8 times, sl1, k1; rep from * to last 2 sts, k2.

Row 33: As Row 25.

Row 35: As Row 23.

Row 37: As Row 21.

Row 39: As Row 19.

Row 41: Using B, k1, sl2, * k1, sl1, k15, sl1, k1, sl1; rep from * to last 2 sts, sl1, k1.

Row 43: As Row 15.

Row 45: Using B, k1, sl1, k1, * sl3, k13, sl3, k1; rep from * to last 2 sts, sl1, k1.

Row 47: Using A, k3, * k4, sl1, k9, sl1, k5; rep from * to last 2 sts, k2.

Row 49: Using B, k1, sl2, * sl1, k1, sl2, k11, sl2, k1, sl2; rep from * to last 2 sts, sl1, k1.

Row 51: Using A, k3, * k6, sl1, k5, sl1, k7; rep from * to last 2 sts, k2.

Row 53: Using B, k1, sl1, k1, * sl3, k1, sl2, k7, sl2, k1, sl3, k1; rep from * to last 2 sts, sl1, k1.

Row 55: Using A, k all sts.

Row 57: Using B, k all sts.

Row 59: As Row 3.

Row 61: Using B, k all sts.

Rep Rows 7 to 62. To finish, work Rows 63 and 64.

Row 63: Using A, k all sts.

Row 64: As Row 2.

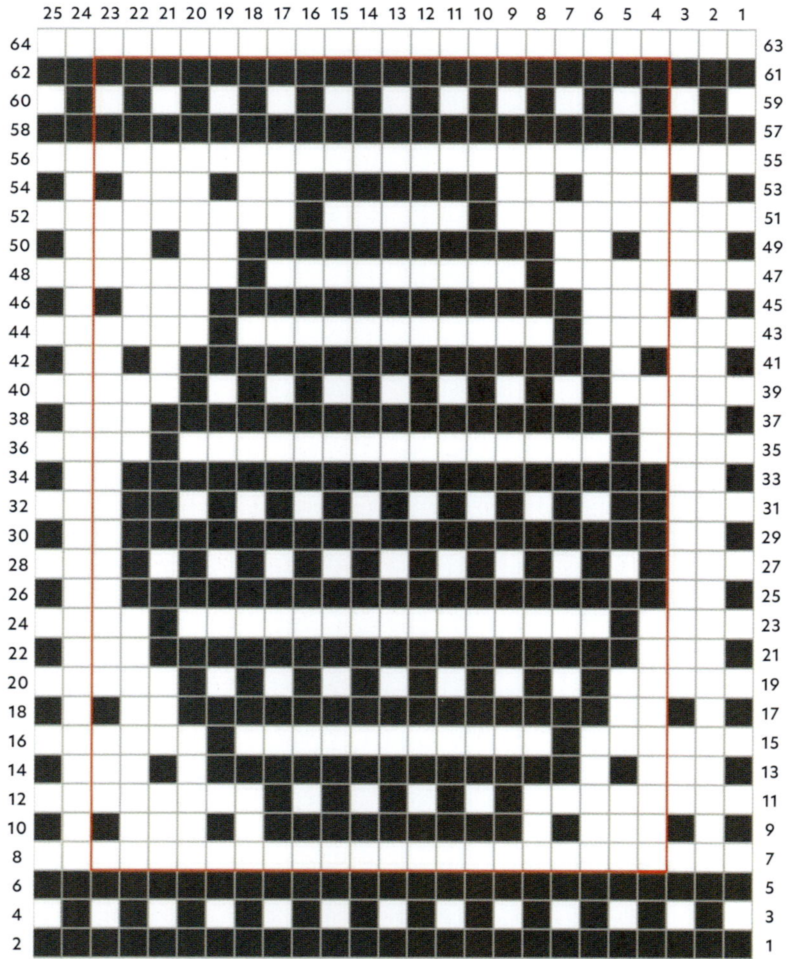

Crochet Instructions

Multiple of 20 sts + 5

Pattern note: The repeat in the written instructions differs from the chart on Rows 13, 21, 25, 29, 33, 37, 41, and 49.

Using A, make desired number of chainless sc.

Row 1 (RS): Using B, 1 ch, 1 sc in every st, turn.

Row 2 and all WS rows: 1 ch, 1 sc in sts, ch and skip ch-sps, turn.

Row 3: Using A, 1 ch, 1 sc, 2 ch, skip st, 1 sc, * [2 ch, skip st, 1 sc] 10 times; rep from * to last 2 sts, 2 ch, skip st, 1 sc, turn.

Row 5: Using B, 1 ch, 1 sc, 1 Mdc, 1 sc, * [1 Mdc, 1 sc] 10 times; rep from * to last 2 sts, 1 Mdc, 1 sc, turn.

Row 7: Using A, 1 ch, 1 sc in every st, turn.

Row 9: Using B, 1 ch, 1 sc, 2 ch, skip st, 1 sc, * 4 ch, skip 3 sts, 1 sc, 2 ch, skip st, 9 sc, 2 ch, skip st, 1 sc, 4 ch, skip 3 sts, 1 sc; rep from * to last 2 sts, 2 ch, skip st, 1 sc, turn.

Row 11: Using A, 1 ch, 1 sc, 1 Mdc, 1 sc, * 3 Mdc, 1 sc, 1 Mdc, [2 ch, skip st, 1 sc] 4 times, 2 ch, skip st, 1 Mdc, 1 sc, 3 Mdc, 1 sc; rep from * to last 2 sts, 1 Mdc, 1 sc, turn.

Row 13: Using B, 1 ch, 1 sc, 4 ch, skip 3 sts, * 1 sc, 2 ch, skip st, 2 sc, [1 Mdc, 1 sc] 5 times, 1 sc, 2 ch, skip st, 1 sc, 4 ch, skip 3 sts; rep from * to last st, 1 sc, turn.

Row 15: Using A, 1 ch, 1 sc, 2 Mdc, * 1 Mdc, 1 sc, 1 Mdc, 2 ch, skip st, 11 sc, 2 ch, skip st, 1 Mdc, 1 sc, 2 Mdc; rep from * to last 2 sts, 1 Mdc, 1 sc, turn.

Row 17: Using B, 1 ch, 1 sc, 2 ch, skip st, 1 sc, * 3 ch, skip 2 sts, 1 sc, 1 Mdc, 11 sc, 1 Mdc, 1 sc, 3 ch, skip 2 sts, 1 sc; rep from * to last 2 sts, 2 ch, skip st, 1 sc, turn.

Row 19: Using A, 1 ch, 1 sc, 1 Mdc, 1 sc, * 2 Mdc, [2 ch, skip st, 1 sc] 7 times, 2 ch, skip st, 2 Mdc, 1 sc; rep from * to last 2 sts, 1 Mdc, 1 sc, turn.

Row 21: Using B, 1 ch, 1 sc, 4 ch, skip 3 sts, * 1 sc, [1 Mdc, 1 sc] 8 times, 4 ch, skip 3 sts; rep from * to last st, 1 sc, turn.

Row 23: Using A, 1 ch, 1 sc, 2 Mdc, * 1 Mdc, 2 ch, skip st, 15 sc, 2 ch, skip st, 2 Mdc; rep from * to last 2 sts, 1 Mdc, 1 sc, turn.

Row 25: Using B, 1 ch, 1 sc, 3 ch, skip 2 sts, * 1 sc, 1 Mdc, 15 sc, 1 Mdc, 1 sc, 2 ch, skip st; rep from * to last 3 sts, ending last rep with 3 ch, skip 2 sts, 1 sc, turn.

Row 27: Using A, 1 ch, 1 sc, 2 Mdc, * [2 ch, skip st, 1 sc] 9 times, 2 ch, skip st, 1 Mdc; rep from * to last 2 sts, 1 Mdc, 1 sc, turn.

Row 29: Using B, 1 ch, 1 sc, 3 ch, skip 2 sts, * [1 Mdc, 1 sc] 9 times, 1 Mdc, ** 2 ch, skip st; rep from * to last 3 sts, ending last rep at **, 3 ch, skip 2 sts, 1 sc, turn.

Row 31: Using A, 1 ch, 1 sc, 2 Mdc, * 3 ch, skip 2 sts, [1 sc, 2 ch, skip st] 7 times, 1 sc, 3 ch, skip 2 sts, 1 Mdc; rep from * to last 2 sts, 1 Mdc, 1 sc, turn.

Row 33: Using B, 1 ch, 1 sc, 3 ch, skip 2 sts, * 2 Mdc, [1 sc, 1 Mdc] 7 times, 1 sc, 2 Mdc, ** 2 ch, skip st; rep from * to last 3 sts, ending last rep at **, 3 ch, skip 2 sts, 1 sc, turn.

Row 35: Using A, 1 ch, 1 sc, 2 Mdc, * 1 sc, 2 ch, skip st, 15 sc, 2 ch, skip st, 1 sc, 1 Mdc; rep from * to last 2 sts, 1 Mdc, 1 sc, turn.

Row 37: Using B, 1 ch, 1 sc, 4 ch, skip 3 sts, * 1 Mdc, 15 sc, 1 Mdc, 4 ch, skip 3 sts; rep from * to last st, 1 sc, turn.

Row 39: Using A, 1 ch, 1 sc, 2 Mdc, * 1 Mdc, 1 sc, [2 ch, skip st, 1 sc] 8 times, 2 Mdc; rep from * to last 2 sts, 1 Mdc, 1 sc, turn.

Row 41: Using B, 1 ch, 1 sc, 3 ch, skip 2 sts, * 1 sc, 2 ch, skip st, [1 Mdc, 1 sc] 7 times, 1 Mdc, 2 ch, skip st, 1 sc, ** 2 ch, skip st; rep from * to last 3 sts, ending last rep at **, 3 ch, skip 2 sts, 1 sc, turn.

Row 43: Using A, 1 ch, 1 sc, 2 Mdc, * 1 sc, 1 Mdc, 1 sc, 2 ch, skip st, 11 sc, 2 ch, skip st, [1 sc, 1 Mdc] twice; rep from * to last 2 sts, 1 Mdc, 1 sc, turn.

Row 45: Using B, 1 ch, 1 sc, 2 ch, skip st, 1 sc, * 4 ch, skip 3 sts, 1 Mdc, 11 sc, 1 Mdc, 4 ch, skip 3 sts, 1 sc; rep from * to last 2 sts, 2 ch, skip st, 1 sc, turn.

Row 47: Using A, 1 ch, 1 sc, 1 Mdc, 1 sc, * 3 Mdc, 1 sc, 2 ch, skip st, 9 sc, 2 ch, skip st, 1 sc, 3 Mdc, 1 sc; rep from * to last 2 sts, 1 Mdc, 1 sc, turn.

Row 49: Using B, 1 ch, 1 sc, 4 ch, skip 3 sts, * 1 sc, 3 ch, skip 2 sts, 1 Mdc, 9 sc, 1 Mdc, 3 ch, skip 2 sts, 1 sc, 4 ch, skip 3 sts; rep from * to last st, 1 sc, turn.

Row 51: Using A, 1 ch, 1 sc, 2 Mdc, * 1 Mdc, 1 sc, 2 Mdc, 2 sc, 2 ch, skip st, 5 sc, 2 ch, skip st, 2 sc, 2 Mdc, 1 sc, 2 Mdc; rep from * to last 2 sts, 1 Mdc, 1 sc, turn.

Row 53: Using B, 1 ch, 1 sc, 2 ch, skip st, 1 sc, * 4 ch, skip 3 sts, 1 sc, 3 ch, skip 2 sts, 1 Mdc, 5 sc, 1 Mdc, 3 ch, skip 2 sts, 1 sc, 4 ch, skip 3 sts, 1 sc; rep from * to last 2 sts, 2 ch, skip st, 1 sc, turn.

Row 55: Using A, 1 ch, 1 sc, 1 Mdc, 1 sc, * 3 Mdc, 1 sc, 2 Mdc, 7 sc, 2 Mdc, 1 sc, 3 Mdc, 1 sc; rep from * to last 2 sts, 1 Mdc, 1 sc, turn.

Row 57: Using B, 1 ch, 1 sc in every st, turn.

Row 59: As Row 3.

Row 61: As Row 5.

Rep Rows 7 to 62. To finish, work Row 63.

Row 63: Using A, 1 ch, 1 sc in every st.

Chicken

This is a great design to place around a yoke or just above the bottom rib of a garment. You could make a whole flock and place them on a blanket, or you could place a single chicken on a scarf or pocket.

Knit Instructions

Multiple of 14 sts + 5

On RS rows slip the sts purlwise with yarn in the back.

Cast on using B, k one row and p one row.

Row 1 (RS): Using A, k1, sl2, *sl1, k1, sl3, k3, sl3, k1, sl2; rep from * to last 2 sts, sl1, k1.

Row 2 and all WS rows: P the knitted sts and sl the slipped sts purlwise with yarn in the front.

Row 3: Using B, k3, * k6, sl1, k7; rep from * to last 2 sts, k2.

Row 5: Using A, k1, sl1, k1, * sl3, k7, sl3, k1; rep from * to last 2 sts, sl1, k1.

Row 7: Using B, k3, * k3, sl2, k1, sl1, k1, sl2, k4; rep from * to last 2 sts, k2.

Row 9: Using A, k1, sl2, * k1, sl1, k10, sl2; rep from * to last 2 sts, sl1, k1.

Row 11: Using B, k3, * k2, sl2, [k1, sl1] 3 times, sl2, k2; rep from * to last 2 sts, k2.

Row 13: Using A, k1, sl1, k1, * sl1, k12, sl1; rep from * to last 2 sts, sl1, k1.

Row 15: Using B, k3, * k1, sl2, [k1, sl1, k1, sl2] twice, k1; rep from * to last 2 sts, k2.

Row 17: Using A, k1, sl2, * sl1, k12, sl1; rep from * to last 2 sts, sl1, k1.

Row 19: Using B, k3, * k1, sl1, [k1, sl1] twice, k3, sl2, k1, sl1, k1; rep from * to last 2 sts, k2.

Row 21: Using A, k1, sl1, k1, * sl1, k5, sl3, k4, sl1; rep from * to last 2 sts, sl1, k1.

Row 23: Using B, k3, * k1, sl2, k1, sl1, k6, sl2, k1; rep from * to last 2 sts, k2.

Row 25: Using A, k1, sl2, * k5, sl2, k1, sl3, k2, sl1; rep from * to last 2 sts, sl1, k1.

Row 27: Using B, k3, * sl2, k1, sl1, k10; rep from * to last 2 sts, k2.

Row 29: Using A, k1, sl1, k1, * k4, sl1, k1, [sl3, k1] twice; rep from * to last 2 sts, sl1, k1.

Row 31: Using B, k all sts.

Row 33: Using A, k1, sl2, * k1, sl2, k1, [sl3, k1] twice, sl2; rep from * to last 2 sts, sl1, k1.

Row 35: Using B, k all sts.

Row 36: As Row 2.

Rep Rows 1 to 36.

Crochet Instructions

Multiple of 14 sts + 5

Pattern note: The repeat in the written instructions differs from the chart on Rows 1, 9, 13, 17, 21, 25, and 33.

Using B, make desired number of chainless sc.

Row 1 (RS): Using A, 1 ch, 1 sc, 4 ch, skip 3 sts, * 1 sc, 4 ch, skip 3 sts, 3 sc, 4 ch, skip 3 sts, 1 sc, 4 ch, skip 3 sts; rep from * to last st, 1 sc, turn.

Row 2 and all WS rows: 1 ch, 1 sc in sts, ch and skip ch-sps, turn.

Row 3: Using B, 1 ch, 1 sc, 2 Mdc, * 1 Mdc, 1 sc, 3 Mdc, 1 sc, 2 ch, skip st, 1 sc, 3 Mdc, 1 sc, 2 Mdc; rep from * to last 2 sts, 1 Mdc, 1 sc, turn.

Row 5: Using A, 1 ch, 1 sc, 2 ch, skip st, 1 sc, * 4 ch, skip 3 sts, 3 sc, 1 Mdc, 3 sc, 4 ch, skip 3 sts, 1 sc; rep from * to last 2 sts, 2 ch, skip st, 1 sc, turn.

Row 7: Using B, 1 ch, 1 sc, 1 Mdc, 1 sc, * 3 Mdc, 3 ch, skip 2 sts, 1 sc, 2 ch, skip st, 1 sc, 3 ch, skip 2 sts, 3 Mdc, 1 sc; rep from * to last 2 sts, 1 Mdc, 1 sc, turn.

Row 9: Using A, 1 ch, 1 sc, 3 ch, skip 2 sts, * 1 sc, 2 ch, skip st, 1 sc, 2 Mdc, 1 sc, 1 Mdc, 1 sc, 2 Mdc, 2 sc, ** 3 ch, skip 2 sts; rep from * to last st, ending last rep at **, 4 ch, skip 3 sts, 1 sc, turn.

Row 11: Using B, 1 ch, 1 sc, 2 Mdc, * 1 sc, 1 Mdc, 3 ch, skip 2 sts, 1 sc, [2 ch, skip st, 1 sc] twice, 4 ch, skip 3 sts, 2 Mdc; rep from * to last 2 sts, 1 Mdc, 1 sc, turn.

Row 13: Using A, 1 ch, 1 sc, 2 ch, skip st, 1 sc, 2 ch, skip st, * 1 sc, 2 Mdc, [1 sc, 1 Mdc] 3 times, 2 Mdc, 1 sc, 3 ch, skip 2 sts; rep from * to last st, 1 sc, turn.

Row 15: Using B, 1 ch, 1 sc, 1 Mdc, 1 sc,

MOSAIC CHART

* 1 Mdc, 3 ch, skip 2 sts, [1 sc, 2 ch, skip st, 1 sc, 3 ch, skip 2 sts] twice, 1 Mdc; rep from * to last 2 sts, 1 Mdc, 1 sc, turn.

Row 17: Using A, 1 ch, 1 sc, 4 ch, skip 3 sts, * 2 Mdc, [1 sc, 1 Mdc, 1 sc, 2 Mdc] twice, 3 ch, skip 2 sts; rep from * to last st, 1 sc, turn.

Row 19: Using B, 1 ch, 1 sc, 2 Mdc, * 1 Mdc, [2 ch, skip st, 1 sc] twice, 2 ch, skip st, 3 sc, 3 ch, skip 2 sts, 1 sc, 2 ch, skip st, 1 Mdc; rep from * to last 2 sts, 1 Mdc, 1 sc, turn.

Row 21: Using A, 1 ch, 1 sc, 2 ch, skip st, 1 sc, 2 ch, skip st, * [1 Mdc, 1 sc] twice, 1 Mdc, 4 ch, skip 3 sts, 2 Mdc, 1 sc, 1 Mdc, 3 ch, skip 2 sts; rep from * to last st, 1 sc, turn.

Row 23: Using B, 1 ch, 1 sc, 1 Mdc, 1 sc, * 1 Mdc, 3 ch, skip 2 sts, 1 sc, 2 ch, skip st, 1 sc, 3 Mdc, 2 sc, 3 ch, skip 2 sts, 1 Mdc; rep from * to last 2 sts, 1 Mdc, 1 sc, turn.

Row 25: Using A, 1 ch, 1 sc, 3 ch, skip 2 sts, 1 sc, * 2 Mdc, 1 sc, 1 Mdc, 3 ch, skip 2 sts, 1 sc, 4 ch, skip 3 sts, 2 Mdc, ** 2 ch, skip st; rep from * to last 3 sts, ending last rep at **, 3 ch, skip 2 sts, 1 sc, turn.

Row 27: Using B, 1 ch, 1 sc, 2 Mdc, * 3 ch, skip 2 sts, 1 sc, 2 ch, skip st, 1 sc, 2 Mdc, 1 sc, 3 Mdc, 2 sc, 1 Mdc; rep from * to last 2 sts, 1 Mdc, 1 sc, turn.

Row 29: Using A, 1 ch, 1 sc, 2 ch, skip st, 1 sc, * 2 Mdc, 1 sc, 1 Mdc, 2 ch, skip st, 1 sc, [4 ch, skip 3 sts, 1 sc] twice; rep from * to last 2 sts, 2 ch, skip st, 1 sc, turn.

Row 31: Using B, 1 ch, 1 sc, 1 Mdc, 1 sc, * 4 sc, 1 Mdc, 1 sc, [3 Mdc, 1 sc] twice; rep from * to last 2 sts, 1 Mdc, 1 sc, turn.

Row 33: Using A, 1 ch, 1 sc, 3 ch, skip 2 sts, * 1 sc, 3 ch, skip 2 sts, [1 sc, 4 ch, skip 3 sts] twice, 1 sc, ** 3 ch, skip 2 sts; rep from * to last st, ending last rep at **, 4 ch, skip 3 sts, 1 sc, turn.

Row 35: Using B, 1 ch, 1 sc, 2 Mdc, * 1 sc, 2 Mdc, 1 sc, [3 Mdc, 1 sc] twice, 2 Mdc; rep from * to last 2 sts, 1 Mdc, 1 sc, turn.

Row 36: As Row 2.

Rep Rows 1 to 36, ending last rep with Row 35.

KNIT

CROCHET

Reindeer

This festive reindeer is perfect for blankets or pillows. For the knit version, the stockinette stitch produces a loose fabric on the background stripes. Switch to garter stitch or place the repeats closer to even out the fabric a little.

Knit Instructions

Multiple of 21 sts + 3

On RS rows, slip the sts purlwise with yarn in the back.

Cast on using B, k one row and p one row.

Row 1 (RS): Using A, k1, * k1, sl1, k1, sl1, k17; rep from * to last 2 sts, k2.

Row 2 and all WS rows: P the knitted sts and sl the slipped sts purlwise with yarn in the front.

Row 3: Using B, k1, * k2, sl1, k18; rep from * to last 2 sts, k2.

Row 5: Using A, k1, * k1, sl1, k2, sl1, k8, sl1, k2, sl1, k4; rep from * to last 2 sts, k2.

Row 7: Using B, k1, * k3, sl1, k11, sl1, k5; rep from * to last 2 sts, k2.

Row 9: Using A, k1, * k2, sl1, k4, sl1, k6, sl1, k2, sl1, k3; rep from * to last 2 sts, k2.

Row 11: Using B, k1, * k5, sl2, k9, sl1, k4; rep from * to last 2 sts, k2.

Row 13: Using A, k1, * k4, sl1, k12, sl1, k3; rep from * to last 2 sts, k2.

Row 15: Using B, k1, * k5, sl3, [k1, sl1] 3 times, sl1, k6; rep from * to last 2 sts, k2.

Row 17: Using A, k1, * k4, sl1, k10, sl1, k5; rep from * to last 2 sts, k2.

Row 19: Using B, k1, * k5, sl2, [k1, sl1] 4 times, k6; rep from * to last 2 sts, k2.

Row 21: Using A, k1, * k3, sl1, k11, sl1, k5; rep from * to last 2 sts, k2.

Row 23: Using B, k1, * k4, sl1, k8, sl2, k6; rep from * to last 2 sts, k2.

Row 25: Using A, k1, * k1, sl1, k3, sl1, k6, sl1, k2, sl1, k5; rep from * to last 2 sts, k2.

Row 27: Using B, k1, * k13, sl2, k6; rep from * to last 2 sts, k2.

Row 29: Using A, k1, * k12, sl1, k6, sl1, k1; rep from * to last 2 sts, k2.

Row 31: Using B, k1, * k13, sl2, k1, sl3, k2; rep from * to last 2 sts, k2.

Row 33: Using A, k1, * k9, sl1, k10, sl1; rep from * to last 2 sts, k2.

Row 35: Using B, k1, * k10, sl1, k2, sl1, k7; rep from * to last 2 sts, k2.

Row 37: Using A, k1, * k7, sl1, k3, sl2, k1, sl1, k6; rep from * to last 2 sts, k2.

Row 39: Using B, k1, * k8, sl1, k4, sl1, k7; rep from * to last 2 sts, k2.

Row 41: Using A, k1, * k7, sl1, k1, sl1, k4, sl1, k6; rep from * to last 2 sts, k2.

Row 43: Using B, k1, * k13, sl1, k7; rep from * to last 2 sts, k2.

Row 45: Using A, k1, * k12, sl1, k1, sl1, k6; rep from * to last 2 sts, k2.

Row 47: Using B, k all sts.

Row 48: As Row 2.

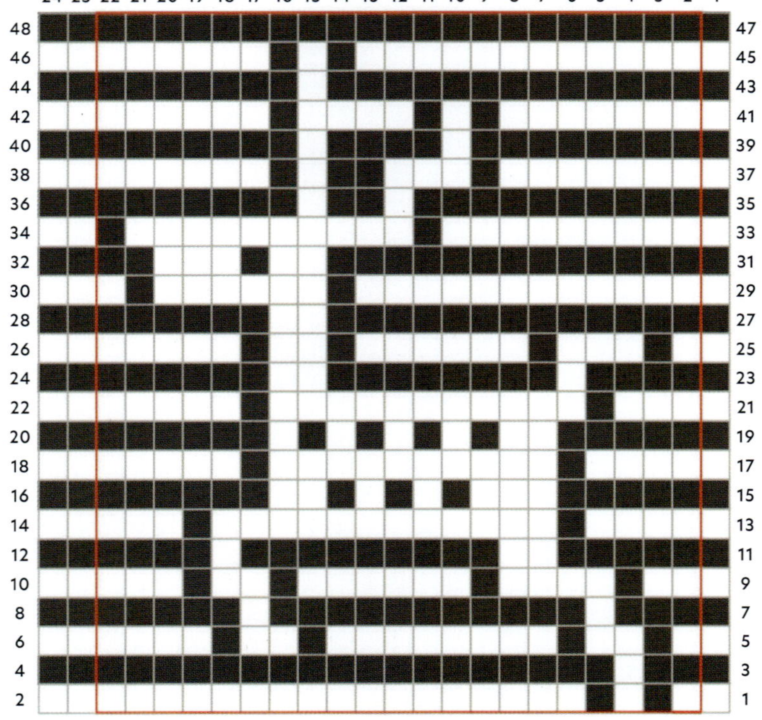

Yarn A = Cream

Yarn B = Burgundy

Crochet Instructions

Multiple of 21 sts + 3

Using B, make desired number of chainless sc.

Row 1 (RS): Using A, 1 ch, 1 sc, * 1 sc, 2 ch, skip st, 1 sc, 2 ch, skip st, 17 sc; rep from * to last 2 sts, 2 sc, turn.

Row 2 and all WS rows: 1 ch, 1 sc in sts, ch and skip ch-sps, turn.

Row 3: Using B, 1 ch, 1 sc, * 1 sc, 1 Mdc, 2 ch, skip st, 1 Mdc, 17 sc; rep from * to last 2 sts, 2 sc, turn.

Row 5: Using A, 1 ch, 1 sc, * 1 sc, 2 ch, skip st, 1 Mdc, 1 sc, 2 ch, skip st, 8 sc,

2 ch, skip st, 2 sc, 2 ch, skip st, 4 sc; rep from * to last 2 sts, 2 sc, turn.

Row 7: Using B, 1 ch, 1 sc, * 1 sc, 1 Mdc, 1 sc, 2 ch, skip st, 1 Mdc, 8 sc, 1 Mdc, 1 sc, 2 ch, skip st, 1 Mdc, 4 sc; rep from * to last 2 sts, 2 sc, turn.

Row 9: Using A, 1 ch, 1 sc, * 2 sc, 2 ch, skip st, 1 Mdc, 3 sc, 2 ch, skip st, 6 sc, 2 ch, skip st, 1 Mdc, 1 sc, 2 ch, skip st, 3 sc; rep from * to last 2 sts, 2 sc, turn.

Row 11: Using B, 1 ch, 1 sc, * 2 sc, 1 Mdc, 2 sc, 3 ch, skip 2 sts, 1 Mdc, 6 sc, 1 Mdc, 1 sc, 2 ch, skip st, 1 Mdc, 3 sc; rep from * to last 2 sts, 2 sc, turn.

Row 13: Using A, 1 ch, 1 sc, * 4 sc, 2 ch, skip st, 2 Mdc, 9 sc, 1 Mdc, 2 ch, skip st, 3 sc; rep from * to last 2 sts, 2 sc, turn.

Row 15: Using B, 1 ch, 1 sc, * 4 sc, 1 Mdc, 4 ch, skip 3 sts, [1 sc, 2 ch, skip st] twice, 1 sc, 3 ch, skip 2 sts, 2 sc, 1 Mdc, 3 sc; rep from * to last 2 sts, 2 sc, turn.

Row 17: Using A, 1 ch, 1 sc, * 4 sc, 2 ch, skip st, 3 Mdc, [1 sc, 1 Mdc] 3 times, 1 Mdc, 2 ch, skip st, 5 sc; rep from * to last 2 sts, 2 sc, turn.

Row 19: Using B, 1 ch, 1 sc, * 4 sc, 1 Mdc, 3 ch, skip 2 sts, [1 sc, 2 ch, skip st] 4 times, 1 Mdc, 5 sc; rep from * to last 2 sts, 2 sc, turn.

Row 21: Using A, 1 ch, 1 sc, * 3 sc, 2 ch, skip st, 1 sc, 2 Mdc, [1 sc, 1 Mdc] 4 times, 2 ch, skip st, 5 sc; rep from * to last 2 sts, 2 sc, turn.

Row 23: Using B, 1 ch, 1 sc, * 3 sc, 1 Mdc, 2 ch, skip st, 8 sc, 3 ch, skip 2 sts, 1 Mdc, 5 sc; rep from * to last 2 sts, 2 sc, turn.

Row 25: Using A, 1 ch, 1 sc, * 1 sc, 2 ch, skip st, 2 sc, 1 Mdc, 2 ch, skip st, 6 sc, 2 ch, skip st, 2 Mdc, 2 ch, skip st, 5 sc; rep from * to last 2 sts, 2 sc, turn.

Row 27: Using B, 1 ch, 1 sc, * 1 sc, 1 Mdc, 3 sc, 1 Mdc, 6 sc, 1 Mdc, 3 ch, skip 2 sts, 1 Mdc, 5 sc; rep from * to last 2 sts, 2 sc, turn.

Row 29: Using A, 1 ch, 1 sc, * 12 sc, 2 ch, skip st, 2 Mdc, 4 sc, 2 ch, skip st, 1 sc; rep from * to last 2 sts, 2 sc, turn.

Row 31: Using B, 1 ch, 1 sc, * 12 sc, 1 Mdc, 3 ch, skip 2 sts, 1 sc, 4 ch, skip 3 sts, 1 Mdc, 1 sc; rep from * to last 2 sts, 2 sc, turn.

Row 33: Using A, 1 ch, 1 sc, * 9 sc, 2 ch, skip st, 3 sc, 2 Mdc, 1 sc, 3 Mdc, 1 sc, 2 ch, skip st; rep from * to last 2 sts, 2 sc, turn.

Row 35: Using B, 1 ch, 1 sc, * 9 sc, 1 Mdc, 2 ch, skip st, 2 sc, 2 ch, skip st, 6 sc, 1 Mdc; rep from * to last 2 sts, 2 sc, turn.

Row 37: Using A, 1 ch, 1 sc, * 7 sc, 2 ch, skip st, 2 sc, 1 Mdc, 3 ch, skip 2 sts, 1 Mdc, 2 ch, skip st, 6 sc; rep from * to last 2 sts, 2 sc, turn.

Row 39: Using B, 1 ch, 1 sc, * 7 sc, 1 Mdc, 2 ch, skip st, 2 sc, 2 Mdc, 2 ch, skip st, 1 Mdc, 6 sc; rep from * to last 2 sts, 2 sc, turn.

Row 41: Using A, 1 ch, 1 sc, * 7 sc, 2 ch, skip st, 1 Mdc, 2 ch, skip st, 3 sc, 1 Mdc, 2 ch, skip st, 6 sc; rep from * to last 2 sts, 2 sc, turn.

Row 43: Using B, 1 ch, 1 sc, * 7 sc, 1 Mdc, 1 sc, 1 Mdc, 3 sc, 2 ch, skip st, 1 Mdc, 6 sc; rep from * to last 2 sts, 2 sc, turn.

Row 45: Using A, 1 ch, 1 sc, * 12 sc, 2 ch, skip st, 1 Mdc, 2 ch, skip st, 6 sc; rep from * to last 2 sts, 2 sc, turn.

To finish, work Row 47.

Row 47: Using B, 1 ch, 1 sc in every st and Mdc in every sp.

Snow Crystal

A classic symbol of Christmas, this snowflake or snow crystal is accompanied by falling snow in the background, creating a beautiful scene when repeated.

Knit Instructions

Multiple of 22 sts + 3

On RS rows, slip the sts purlwise with yarn in the back.

Cast on using B, k one row and p one row.

Row 1 (RS): Using A, k1, * sl2, k1, sl3, k3, sl2, k1, sl2, k3, sl3, k1, sl1; rep from * to last 2 sts, sl1, k1.

Row 2 and all WS rows: P the knitted sts and sl the slipped sts purlwise with yarn in the front.

Row 3: Using B, k1, * k6, sl1, k1, sl1, k5, sl1, k1, sl1, k5; rep from * to last 2 sts, k2.

Row 5: Using A, k1, * sl1, k1, sl2, k1, sl1, k5, sl1, k5, sl1, k1, sl2, k1; rep from * to last 2 sts, sl1, k1.

Row 7: Using B, k1, * k8, sl1, [k1, sl1] 3 times, k7; rep from * to last 2 sts, k2.

Row 9: Using A, k1, * sl2, k3, sl1, k1, [sl1, k3] twice, sl1, k1, sl1, k3, sl1; rep from * to last 2 sts, sl1, k1.

Row 11: Using B, k1, * k2, sl1, k1, sl1, k5, sl1, k1, sl1, k5, sl1, k1, sl1, k1; rep from * to last 2 sts, k2.

Row 13: Using A, k1, * sl2, k5, [sl1, k1] 4 times, sl1, k5, sl1; rep from * to last 2 sts, sl1, k1.

Row 15: Using B, k1, * k4, sl1, k1, sl1, k9, sl1, k1, sl1, k3; rep from * to last 2 sts, k2.

Row 17: Using A, k1, * sl1, k1, sl2, k5, [sl1, k1] twice, sl1, k5, sl2, k1; rep from * to last 2 sts, sl1, k1.

Row 19: Using B, k all sts.

Row 21: Using A, as Row 17.

Row 23: Using B, as Row 15.

Row 25: Using A, as Row 13.

Row 27: Using B, as Row 11.

Row 29: Using A, k1, as Row 9.

Row 31: Using B, k1, as Row 7.

Row 33: Using A, k1, as Row 5.

Row 35: Using B, k1, as Row 3.

Row 37: Using A, k1, as Row 1.

Row 39: Using B, k all sts.

Row 40: As Row 2.

Yarn A = Cream

Yarn B = Burgundy

MOSAIC CHART

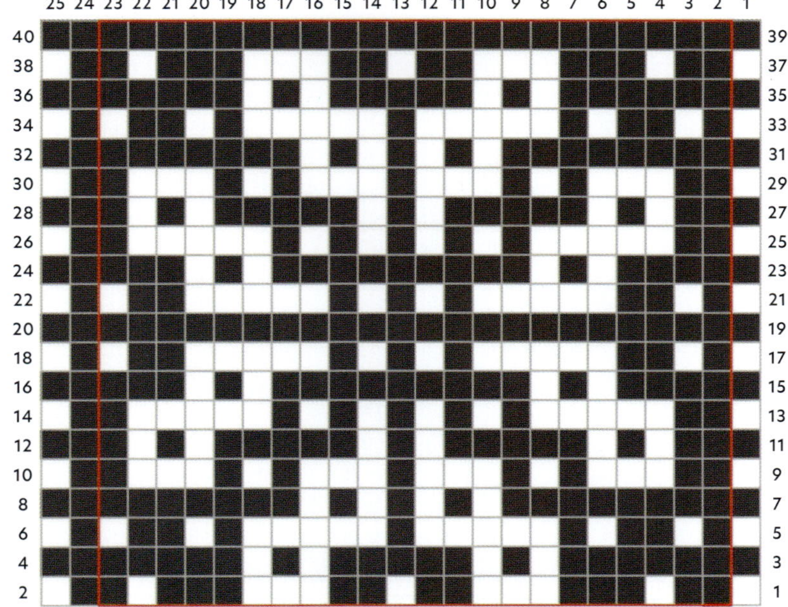

22 sts

Crochet Instructions

Multiple of 22 sts + 3

Pattern note: The repeat in written instructions differs from chart on Rows 9, 13, 25, 29, and 37.

Using B, make desired number of chainless sc.

Row 1: Using A, 1 ch, 1 sc, 3 ch, skip 2 sts, * 1 sc, 4 ch, skip 3 sts, 3 sc, 3 ch, skip 2 sts, 1 sc, 3 ch, skip 2 sts, 3 sc, 4 ch, skip 3 sts, 1 sc **, 4 ch, skip 3 sts; rep from * to last 3 sts, ending last rep at **, 3 ch, skip 2 sts, 1 sc.

Row 2 and all WS rows: 1 ch, 1 sc in sts, ch and skip ch-sps, turn.

Row 3: Using B, 1 ch, 1 sc, * 2 Mdc, 1 sc, 3 Mdc, 2 ch, skip st, 1 sc, 2 ch, skip st, 2 Mdc, 1 sc, 2 Mdc, 2 ch, skip st, 1 sc, 2 ch, skip st, 3 Mdc, 1 sc, 1 Mdc; rep from * to last 2 sts, 1 Mdc, 1 sc, turn.

Row 5: Using A, 1 ch, 1 sc, * 2 ch, skip st, 1 sc, 3 ch, skip 2 sts, 1 sc, 2 ch, skip st, 1 Mdc, 1 sc, 1 Mdc, 2 sc, 2 ch, skip st, 2 sc, 1 Mdc, 1 sc, 1 Mdc, 2 ch, skip st, 1 sc, 3 ch, skip 2 sts, 1 sc; rep from * to last 2 sts, 2 ch, skip st, 1 sc, turn.

Row 7: Using B, 1 ch, 1 sc, * 1 Mdc, 1 sc, 2 Mdc, 1 sc, 1 Mdc, 2 sc, 2 ch, skip st, 1 sc, 2 ch, skip st, 1 Mdc, 2 ch, skip st, 1 sc, 2 ch, skip st, 2 sc, 1 Mdc, 1 sc, 2 Mdc, 1 sc; rep from * to last 2 sts, 1 Mdc, 1 sc, turn.

Row 9: Using A, 1 ch, 1 sc, 3 ch, skip 2 sts, * 3 sc, 2 ch, skip st, 1 sc, 2 ch, skip st, 1 Mdc, 1 sc, 1 Mdc, 2 ch, skip st, 1 Mdc, 1 sc, 1 Mdc, 2 ch, skip st, 1 sc,

KNIT

CROCHET

2 ch, skip st, 3 sc, ** 4 ch, skip 3 sts; rep from * to last 3 sts, ending last rep at **, 3 ch, skip 2 sts, 1 sc, turn.

Row 11: Using B, 1 ch, 1 sc, * 2 Mdc, 2 ch, skip st, 1 sc, 2 ch, skip st, 1 Mdc, 1 sc, 1 Mdc, 2 sc, 2 ch, skip st, 1 Mdc, 2 ch, skip st, 2 sc, 1 Mdc, 1 sc, 1 Mdc, 2 ch, skip st, 1 sc, 2 ch, skip st, 1 Mdc; rep from * to last 2 sts, 1 Mdc, 1 sc, turn.

Row 13: Using A, 1 ch, 1 sc, 3 ch, skip 2 sts, * 1 Mdc, 1 sc, 1 Mdc, 2 sc, 2 ch, skip st, 1 sc, 2 ch, skip st, 1 Mdc, 2 ch, skip st, 1 Mdc, 2 ch, skip st, 1 sc, 2 ch, skip st, 2 sc, 1 Mdc, 1 sc, 1 Mdc, ** 4 ch, skip 3 sts; rep from * to last 3 sts, ending last rep at **, 3 ch, skip 2 sts, 1 sc, turn.

Row 15: Using B, 1 ch, 1 sc, * 2 Mdc, 2 sc, 2 ch, skip st, 1 sc, 2 ch, skip st, [1 Mdc, 1 sc] 4 times, 1 Mdc, 2 ch, skip st, 1 sc, 2 ch, skip st, 2 sc, 1 Mdc; rep from * to last 2 sts, 1 Mdc, 1 sc, turn.

Row 17: Using A, 1 ch, 1 sc, * 2 ch, skip st, 1 sc, 3 ch, skip 2 sts, 1 Mdc, 1 sc, 1 Mdc, 2 sc, [2 ch, skip st, 1 sc] twice, 2 ch, skip st, 2 sc, 1 Mdc, 1 sc, 1 Mdc, 3 ch, skip 2 sts, 1 sc; rep from * to last 2 sts, 2 ch, skip st, 1 sc, turn.

Row 19: Using B, 1 ch, 1 sc, * 1 Mdc, 1 sc, 2 Mdc, 5 sc, [1 Mdc, 1 sc] twice, 1 Mdc, 5 sc, 2 Mdc, 1 sc; rep from * to last 2 sts, 1 Mdc, 1 sc, turn.

Row 21: Using A, 1 ch, 1 sc, * 2 ch, skip st, 1 sc, 3 ch, skip 2 sts, 5 sc, 2 ch, skip st, [1 sc, 2 ch, skip st] twice, 5 sc, 3 ch, skip 2 sts, 1 sc; rep from * to last 2 sts, 2 ch, skip st, 1 sc, turn.

Row 23: Using B, 1 ch, 1 sc, * 1 Mdc, 1 sc, 2 Mdc, 2 ch, skip st, 1 sc, 2 ch, skip st, 2 sc, 1 Mdc, [1 sc, 1 Mdc] twice, 2 sc, 2 ch, skip st, 1 sc, 2 ch, skip st, 2 Mdc, 1 sc; rep from * to last 2 sts, 1 Mdc, 1 sc, turn.

Row 25: Using A, 1 ch, 1 sc, 3 ch, skip 2 sts, * 2 sc, 1 Mdc, 1 sc, 1 Mdc, 2 ch, skip st, [1 sc, 2 ch, skip st] 4 times, 1 Mdc, 1 sc, 1 Mdc, 2 sc, ** 4 ch, skip 3 sts; rep from * to last 3 sts, ending last rep at **, 3 ch, skip 2 sts, 1 sc, turn.

Row 27: Using B, 1 ch, 1 sc, * 2 Mdc, 2 ch, skip st, 1 sc, 2 ch, skip st, 2 sc, 1 Mdc, 1 sc, 1 Mdc, 2 ch, skip st, 1 Mdc, 2 ch, skip st, 1 Mdc, 1 sc, 1 Mdc, 2 sc, 2 ch, skip st, 1 sc, 2 ch, skip st, 1 Mdc; rep from * to last 2 sts, 1 Mdc, 1 sc, turn.

Row 29: Using A, 1 ch, 1 sc, 3 ch, skip 2 sts, * 1 Mdc, 1 sc, 1 Mdc, 2 ch, skip st, 1 sc, 2 ch, skip st, 2 sc, 1 Mdc, 2 ch, skip st, 1 Mdc, 2 sc, 2 ch, skip st, 1 sc, 2 ch, skip st, 1 Mdc, 1 sc, 1 Mdc, ** 4 ch, skip 3 sts; rep from * to last 3 sts, ending last rep at **, 3 ch, skip 2 sts, 1 sc, turn.

Row 31: Using B, 1 ch, 1 sc, * 2 Mdc, 3 sc, 1 Mdc, 1 sc, 1 Mdc, 2 ch, skip st, 1 sc, 2 ch, skip st, 1 Mdc, 2 ch, skip st, 1 sc, 2 ch, skip st, 1 Mdc, 1 sc, 1 Mdc, 3 sc, 1 Mdc; rep from * to last 2 sts, 1 Mdc, 1 sc, turn.

Row 33: Using A, 1 ch, 1 sc, * 2 ch, skip st, 1 sc, 3 ch, skip 2 sts, 1 sc, 2 ch, skip st, 2 sc, 1 Mdc, 1 sc, 1 Mdc, 2 ch, skip st, 1 Mdc, 1 sc, 1 Mdc, 2 sc, 2 ch, skip st, 1 sc, 3 ch, skip 2 sts, 1 sc; rep from * to last 2 sts, 2 ch, skip st, 1 sc, turn.

Row 35: Using B, 1 ch, 1 sc, * 1 Mdc, 1 sc, 2 Mdc, 1 sc, 1 Mdc, 2 ch, skip st, 1 sc, 2 ch, skip st, 2 sc, 1 Mdc, 2 sc, 2 ch, skip st, 1 sc, 2 ch, skip st, 1 Mdc, 1 sc, 2 Mdc, 1 sc; rep from * to last 2 sts, 1 Mdc, 1 sc, turn.

Row 37: Using A, 1 ch, 1 sc, 3 ch, skip 2 sts, * 1 sc, 4 ch, skip 3 sts, 1 Mdc, 1 sc, 1 Mdc, 3 ch, skip 2 sts, 1 sc, 3 ch, skip 2 sts, 1 Mdc, 1 sc, 1 Mdc, 4 ch, skip 3 sts, 1 sc, ** 4 ch, skip 3 sts; rep from * to last 3 sts, ending last rep at **, 3 ch, skip 2 sts, 1 sc, turn.

To finish, work Row 39.

Row 39: Using B, 1 ch, 1 sc in every st and Mdc in every sp.

Snowflake

Similar to the snow crystal on page 158, this motif is more robust in its formation, with eight distinct points. In both the knitted and crochet versions, a cross is visible at the center.

Knit Instructions

Multiple of 20 sts + 5

On RS rows, slip the sts purlwise with yarn in the back.

Cast on using A, k one row and p one row.

Row 1 (RS): Using B, k1, sl1, k1, * sl2, k3, [sl3, k3] twice, sl2, k1; rep from * to last 2 sts, sl1, k1.

Row 2 and all WS rows: P the knitted sts and sl the slipped sts purlwise with yarn in the front.

Row 3: Using A, k3, * k2, [sl1, k1, sl1, k3] 3 times; rep from * to last 2 sts, k2.

Row 5: Using B, k1, sl1, k1, * sl2, k5, sl1, k3, sl1, k5, sl2, k1; rep from * to last 2 sts, sl1, k1.

Row 7: Using A, k3, * k4, [sl1, k1] 6 times, k4; rep from * to last 2 sts, k2.

Row 9: Using B, k1, sl1, k1, * sl1, k1, sl2, k11, sl2, k1, sl1, k1; rep from * to last 2 sts, sl1, k1.

Row 11: Using A, k3, * k6, [sl1, k1] 4 times, k6; rep from * to last 2 sts, k2.

Row 13: Using B, k1, sl1, k1, * sl2, [k7, sl1] twice, sl1, k1; rep from * to last 2 sts, sl1, k1.

Row 15: Using A, k3, * k2, [sl1, k1] 3 times, k4, [sl1, k1] 3 times, k2; rep from * to last 2 sts, k2.

Row 17: As Row 13.

Row 19: As Row 11.

Row 21: As Row 9.

Row 23: As Row 7.

Row 25: As Row 5.

Row 27: As Row 3.

Row 29: As Row 1.

Row 31: Using A, k all sts.

Row 32: As Row 2.

Crochet Instructions

Multiple of 20 sts + 5

Using A, make desired number of chainless sc.

Row 1: Using B, 1 ch, 1 sc, 2 ch, skip st, 1 sc, * 3 ch, skip 2 sts, [3 sc, 4 ch, skip 3 sts] twice, 3 sc, 3 ch, skip 2 sts, 1 sc; rep from * to last 2 sts, 2 ch, skip st, 1 sc, turn.

Row 2 and all WS rows: 1 ch, 1 sc in sts, ch and skip ch-sps, turn.

Row 3: Using A, 1 ch, 1 sc, 1 Mdc, 1 sc, * [2 Mdc, 2 ch, skip st, 1 sc, 2 ch, skip st, 1 Mdc] 3 times, 1 Mdc, 1 sc; rep from * to last 2 sts, 1 Mdc, 1 sc, turn.

Row 5: Using B, 1 ch, 1 sc, 2 ch, skip st, 1 sc, * 3 ch, skip 2 sts, 1 Mdc, 1 sc, 1 Mdc, 2 sc, 2 ch, skip st, 1 Mdc, 1 sc, 1 Mdc, 2 ch, skip st, 2 sc, 1 Mdc, 1 sc, 1 Mdc, ch 3, skip 2 sts, 1 sc; rep from * to last 2 sts, 2 ch, skip st, 1 sc, turn.

Row 7: Using A, 1 ch, 1 sc, 1 Mdc, 1 sc, * 2 Mdc, 2 sc, [2 ch, skip st, 1 sc, 2 ch, skip st, 1 Mdc] twice, 2 ch, skip st, 1 sc, 2 ch, skip st, 2 sc, 2 Mdc, 1 sc; rep from * to last 2 sts, 1 Mdc, 1 sc, turn.

Row 9: Using B, 1 ch, 1 sc, 2 ch, skip st, 1 sc, * 2 ch, skip st, 1 sc, 3 ch, skip 2 sts, 1 Mdc, [1 sc, 1 Mdc] 5 times, 3 ch, skip 2 sts, 1 sc, 2 ch, skip st, 1 sc; rep from * to last 2 sts, 2 ch, skip st, 1 sc, turn.

Row 11: Using A, 1 ch, 1 sc, 1 Mdc, 1 sc, * 1 Mdc, 1 sc, 2 Mdc, 2 sc, [2 ch, skip st, 1 sc] 4 times, 1 sc, 2 Mdc, 1 sc, 1 Mdc, 1 sc; rep from * to last 2 sts, 1 Mdc, 1 sc, turn.

Row 13: Using B, 1 ch, 1 sc, 2 ch, skip st, 1 sc, * 3 ch, skip 2 sts, 4 sc, 1 Mdc, 1 sc, 1 Mdc, 2 ch, skip st, 1 Mdc, 1 sc, 1 Mdc, 4 sc, 3 ch, skip 2 sts, 1 sc; rep from * to last 2 sts, 2 ch, skip st, 1 sc, turn.

Row 15: Using A, 1 ch, 1 sc, 1 Mdc, 1 sc, * 2 Mdc, [2 ch, skip st, 1 sc] 3 times, 1 sc, 1 Mdc, 1 sc, [1 sc, 2 ch, skip st] 3 times,

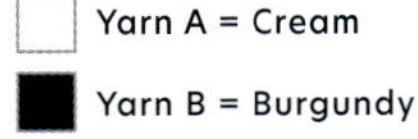

2 Mdc, 1 sc; rep from * to last 2 sts, 1 Mdc, 1 sc, turn.

Row 17: Using B, 1 ch, 1 sc, 2 ch, skip st, 1 sc,* 3 ch, skip 2 sts, [1 Mdc, 1 sc] 3 times, 1 sc, 2 ch, skip st, 1 sc, [1 sc, 1 Mdc] 3 times, 3 ch, skip 2 sts, 1 sc; rep from * to last 2 sts, 2 ch, skip st, 1 sc, turn.

Row 19: Using A, 1 ch, 1 sc, 1 Mdc, 1 sc, * 2 Mdc, 4 sc, 2 ch, skip st, 1 sc, 2 ch, skip st, 1 Mdc, 2 ch, skip st, 1 sc, 2 ch, skip st, 4 sc, 2 Mdc, 1 sc; rep from * to last 2 sts, 1 Mdc, 1 sc, turn.

Row 21: Using B, 1 ch, 1 sc, 2 ch, skip st, 1 sc, * 2 ch, skip st, 1 sc, 3 ch, skip 2 sts, 2 sc, [1 Mdc, 1 sc] 4 times, 1 sc, 3 ch, skip 2 sts, 1 sc, 2 ch, skip st, 1 sc; rep from * to last 2 sts, 2 ch, skip st, 1 sc, turn.

Row 23: Using A, 1 ch, 1 sc, 1 Mdc, 1 sc, * 1 Mdc, 1 sc, 2 Mdc, 2 ch, skip st, [1 sc, 2 ch, skip st] 5 times, 2 Mdc, 1 sc, 1 Mdc, 1 sc; rep from * to last 2 sts, 1 Mdc, 1 sc, turn.

Row 25: Using B, 1 ch, 1 sc, 2 ch, skip st, 1 sc, * 3 ch, skip 2 sts, 2 sc, [1 Mdc, 1 sc, 1 Mdc, 2 ch, skip st] twice, 1 Mdc, 1 sc, 1 Mdc, 2 sc, 3 ch, skip 2 sts, 1 sc; rep from * to last 2 sts, 2 ch, skip st, 1 sc, turn.

Row 27: Using A, 1 ch, 1 sc, 1 Mdc, 1 sc, * 2 Mdc, 2 ch, skip st, 1 sc, 2 ch, skip st, 2 sc, 1 Mdc, 2 ch, skip st, 1 sc, 2 ch, skip st, 1 Mdc, 2 sc, 2 ch, skip st, 1 sc, 2 ch, skip st, 2 Mdc, 1 sc; rep from * to last 2 sts, 1 Mdc, 1 sc, turn.

Row 29: Using B, 1 ch, 1 sc, 2 ch, skip st, 1 sc, * 3 ch, skip 2 sts, [1 Mdc, 1 sc, 1 Mdc, 4 ch, skip 3 sts] twice, 1 Mdc, 1 sc, 1 Mdc, 3 ch, skip st, 1 sc; rep from * to last 2 sts, 2 ch, skip st, 1 sc, turn.

To finish, work Row 31.

Row 31: Using A, 1 ch, 1 sc in every st and Mdc in every sp.

KNIT

CROCHET

Baubles

If you're able to knit and crochet, you may choose to do one or the other, depending on how rounded (knitted) or elongated (crochet) you would like your bauble to appear.

Knit Instructions

Multiple of 18 sts + 3

On RS rows, slip the sts purlwise with yarn in the back.

Cast on using B, k one row and p one row.

Row 1 (RS): Using A, k all sts.

Row 2 and all WS rows: P the knitted sts and sl the slipped sts purlwise with yarn in the front.

Row 3: Using B, k1, * k12, sl1, k1, sl1, k3; rep from * to last 2 sts, k2.

Row 5: Using A, k1, * k13, sl1, k4; rep from * to last 2 sts, k2.

Row 7: Using B, k1, * k2, sl1, k3, sl1, k4, sl1, k3, sl1, k2; rep from * to last 2 sts, k2.

Row 9: Using A, k1, * k3, sl3, k6, sl3, k3; rep from * to last 2 sts, k2.

Row 11: Using B, k1, * k1, sl1, k5, sl1, k2, sl1, k5, sl1, k1; rep from * to last 2 sts, k2.

Row 13: Using A, k1, *k2, sl1, k3, sl1, k4, sl1, k3, sl1, k2; rep from * to last 2 sts, k2.

Row 15: Using B, k1, * sl1, k2, sl1, k1, sl1, k2, sl2, k2, sl1, k1, sl1, k2, sl1; rep from * to last 2 sts, k2.

Row 17: Using A, k1, * k1, sl1, k5, sl1, k2, sl1, k5, sl1, k1; rep from * to last 2 sts, k2.

Row 19: Using B, k1, * sl1, k1, sl2, k1, sl2, k1, sl1, k2, sl1, [k1, sl1] twice, k2; rep from * to last 2 sts, sl1, k1.

Row 21: Using A, k1, * k1, sl1, k5, sl1, k1, sl1, k7, sl1; rep from * to last 2 sts, k2.

Row 23: Using B, k1, * sl1, k2, sl1, k1, sl1, k2, sl1, k1, sl2, k1, sl1, k1, sl2, k1; rep from * to last 2 sts, sl1, k1.

Row 25: Using A, k1, * k2, sl1, k3, sl1, k2, sl1, k7, sl1; rep from * to last 2 sts, k2.

Row 27: Using B, k1, * sl2, k5, sl2, k2, [sl1, k1] 3 times, k1; rep from * to last 2 sts, sl1, k1.

Row 29: Using A, k1, * k3, sl3, k4, sl1, k5, sl1, k1; rep from * to last 2 sts, k2.

Row 31: Using B, k1, * k2, sl1, k3, sl1, k2, sl1, k2, sl1, k1, sl1, k2, sl1; rep from * to last 2 sts, k2.

Row 33: Using A, k1, * k4, sl1, k6, sl1, k3, sl1, k2; rep from * to last 2 sts, k2.

Row 35: Using B, k1, * k3, sl1, k1, sl1, k4, sl1, k5, sl1, k1; rep from * to last 2 sts, k2.

Row 37: Using A, k1, * k4, sl1, k7, sl3, k3; rep from * to last 2 sts, k2.

Row 39: Using B, k1, * k3, sl1, k1, sl1, k5, sl1, k3, sl1, k2; rep from * to last 2 sts, k2.

Row 41: Using A, k1, * k4, sl1, k8, sl1, k4; rep from * to last 2 sts, k2.

Row 43: Using B, k1, * k3, sl1, k1, sl1, k6, sl1, k1, sl1, k3; rep from * to last 2 sts, k2.

Row 45: Using A, k1, * k4, sl1, k8, sl1, k4; rep from * to last 2 sts, k2.

Row 47: Using B, k all sts.

Row 48: As Row 2.

MOSAIC CHART

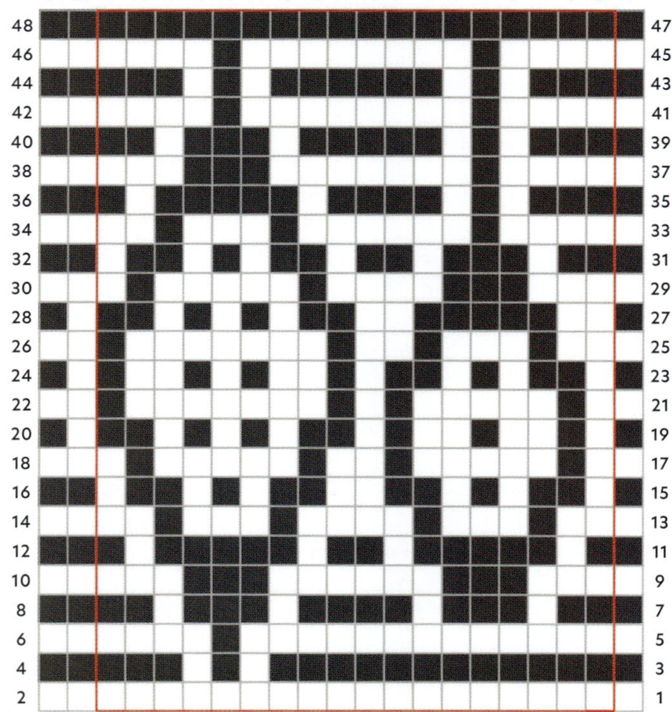

18 sts

Yarn A = Cream

Yarn B = Burgundy

Crochet Instructions

Multiple of 18 sts + 3

Pattern note: The repeat in written instructions differs from chart on Row 15.

Using B, make desired number of chainless sc.

Row 1: Using A, ch 1, 1 sc in every st to end, turn.

Row 2 and all WS rows: 1 ch, 1 sc in sts, ch and skip ch-sps, turn.

Row 3: Using B, 1 ch, 1 sc, * 12 sc, 2 ch, skip st, 1 sc, 2 ch, skip st, 3 sc; rep from * to last 2 sts, 2 sc, turn.

Row 5: Using A, 1 ch, 1 sc, * 12 sc, 1 Mdc, 2 ch, skip st, 1 Mdc, 3 sc; rep from * to last 2 sts, 2 sc, turn.
Row 7: Using B, 1 ch, 1 sc, * 2 sc, 2 ch, skip st, 3 sc, 2 ch, skip st, 4 sc, 2 ch, skip st, 1 sc, 1 Mdc, 1 sc, 2 ch, skip st, 2 sc; rep from * to last 2 sts, 2 sc, turn.
Row 9: Using A, 1 ch, 1 sc, * 2 sc, 1 Mdc, 4 ch, skip 3 sts, 1 Mdc, 4 sc, 1 Mdc, 4 ch, skip 3 sts, 1 Mdc, 2 sc; rep from * to last 2 sts, 2 sc, turn.
Row 11: Using B, 1 ch, 1 sc, * 1 sc, 2 ch, skip st, 1 sc, 3 Mdc, 1 sc, 2 ch, skip st, 2 sc, 2 ch, skip st, 1 sc, 3 Mdc, 1 sc, 2 ch, skip st, 1 sc; rep from * to last 2 sts, 2 sc, turn.
Row 13: Using A, 1 ch, 1 sc, * 1 sc, 1 Mdc, 2 ch, skip st, 3 sc, 2 ch, skip st, 1 Mdc, 2 sc, 1 Mdc, 2 ch, skip st, 3 sc, 2 ch, skip st, 1 Mdc, 1 sc; rep from * to last 2 sts, 2 sc, turn.
Row 15: Using B, 1 ch, 1 sc, 2 ch, skip st, * 1 sc, 1 Mdc, 2 ch, skip st, 1 sc, 2 ch, skip st, 1 Mdc, 1 sc, 3 ch, skip 2 sts, 1 sc, 1 Mdc, 2 ch, skip st, 1 sc, 2 ch, skip st, 1 Mdc, 1 sc **, 3 ch, skip 2 sts; rep from * ending last rep at **, 2 ch, skip st, 2 sc, turn.
Row 17: Using A, 1 ch, 1 sc, * 1 Mdc, 2 ch, skip st, [1 sc, 1 Mdc] twice, 1 sc, 2 ch, skip st, 2 Mdc, 2 ch, skip st, [1 sc, 1 Mdc] twice, 1 sc, 2 ch, skip st, 1 Mdc; rep from * to last 2 sts, 2 sc, turn.
Row 19: Using B, 1 ch, 1 sc, * 2 ch, skip st, 1 Mdc, 3 ch, skip 2 sts, 1 sc, 3 ch, skip 2 sts, 1 Mdc, 2 ch, skip st, 1 sc, 1 Mdc, [2 ch, skip st, 1 sc] twice, 2 ch, skip st, 1 Mdc, 1 sc; rep from * to last 2 sts, 2 ch, skip st, 1 sc, turn.
Row 21: Using A, 1 ch, 1 sc, * 1 Mdc, 2 ch, skip st, 2 Mdc, 1 sc, 2 Mdc, 2 ch, skip st, 1 Mdc, 2 ch, skip st, [1 sc, 1 Mdc] 3 times, 1 sc, 2 ch, skip st; rep from * to last 2 sts, 1 Mdc, 1 sc, turn.
Row 23: Using B, 1 ch, 1 sc, * 2 ch, skip st, 1 Mdc, 1 sc, [2 ch, skip st, 1 sc] twice, 1 Mdc, 2 ch, skip st, 1 Mdc, 3 ch, skip 2 sts, 1 sc, 2 ch, skip st, 1 sc, ch 3, skip 2 sts, 1 Mdc; rep from * to last 2 sts, 2 ch, skip st, 1 sc, turn.
Row 25: Using A, 1 ch, 1 sc, * 1 Mdc, 1 sc, 2 ch, skip st, 1 Mdc, 1 sc, 1 Mdc, 2 ch, skip st, 1 sc, 1 Mdc, 2 ch, skip st, 2 Mdc, 1 sc, 1 Mdc, 1 sc, 2 Mdc, 2 ch, skip st; rep from * to last 2 sts, 1 Mdc, 1 sc, turn.
Row 27: Using B, 1 ch, 1 sc, * 3 ch, skip 2 sts, 1 Mdc, 3 sc, 1 Mdc, 3 ch, skip 2 sts, 1 Mdc, 1 sc, [2 ch, skip st, 1 sc] 3 times, 1 Mdc, rep from * to last 2 sts, 2 ch, skip st, 1 sc, turn.
Row 29: Using A, 1 ch, 1 sc, * 2 Mdc, 1 sc, ch4, skip 3 sts, 1 sc, 2 Mdc, 1 sc, 2 ch, skip st, 1 Mdc, [1 sc, 1 Mdc] twice, 2 ch, skip st, 1 sc, rep from * to last 2 sts, 1 Mdc, 1 sc, turn.
Row 31: Using B, 1 ch, 1 sc, * 2 sc, 2 ch, skip st, 3 Mdc, 2 ch, skip st, 2 sc, 2 ch, skip st, 1 Mdc, [1 sc, 2 ch, skip st] twice, 1 sc, 1 Mdc, ch 2, skip st; rep from * to last 2 sts, 2 sc, turn.
Row 33: Using A, 1 ch, 1 sc, * 2 sc, 1 Mdc, 1 sc, 2 ch, skip st, 1 sc, 1 Mdc, 2 sc, 1 Mdc, 1 sc, 2 ch, skip st, 1 Mdc, 1 sc, 1 Mdc, 2 ch, skip st, 1 sc, 1 Mdc, rep from * to last 2 sts, 2 sc, turn.
Row 35: Using B, 1 ch, 1 sc, * 3 sc, 2 ch, skip st, 1 Mdc, 2 ch, skip st, 4 sc, 2 ch, skip st, 1 Mdc, 3 sc, 1 Mdc, ch 2, skip st, 1 sc; rep from * to last 2 sts, 2 sc, turn.
Row 37: Using A, 1 ch, 1 sc, * 3 sc, 1 Mdc, 2 ch, skip st, 1 Mdc, 4 sc, 1 Mdc, 1 sc, 4 ch, skip 3 sts, 1 sc, 1 Mdc, 1 sc, rep from * to last 2 sts, 2 sc, turn.
Row 39: Using B, 1 ch, 1 sc, * 3 sc, 2 ch, skip st, 1 Mdc, 2 ch, skip st, 5 sc, 2 ch, skip st, 3 Mdc, ch 2, skip st, 2 sc; rep from * to last 2 sts, 2 sc, turn.
Row 41: Using A, 1 ch, 1 sc, * 3 sc, 1 Mdc, 2 ch, skip st, 1 Mdc, 5 sc, 1 Mdc, 1 sc, 2 ch, skip st, 1 sc, 1 Mdc, 2 sc; rep from * to last 2 sts, 2 sc, turn.
Row 43: Using B, 1 ch, 1 sc, * 3 sc, 2 ch, skip st, 1 Mdc, 2 ch, skip st, 6 sc, 2 ch, skip st, 1 Mdc, ch 2, skip st, 3 sc; rep from * to last 2 sts, 2 sc, turn.
Row 45: Using A, 1 ch, 1 sc, * 3 sc, 1 Mdc, 2 ch, skip st, 1 Mdc, 6 sc, 1 Mdc, 2 ch, skip st, 1 Mdc, 3 sc; rep from * to last 2 sts, 2 sc, turn.
To finish, work Row 47.
Row 47: Using B, 1 ch, 1 sc in every st and Mdc in every sp.

Christmas Tree

Like the other traditional Christmas designs, this Christmas tree motif would work well on a blanket or a table runner. All the Christmas designs can be used together for a unique festive pattern.

Knit Instructions

Multiple of 21 sts + 5

On RS rows, slip the sts purlwise with yarn in the back.

Cast on using A, k one row and p one row.

Row 1 (RS): Using B, k1, sl1, * [k1, sl1] 5 times, k2, [sl1, k1] 4 times, sl1; rep from * to last 3 sts, k1, sl1, k1.

Row 2 and all WS rows: P the knitted sts and sl the slipped sts purlwise with yarn in the front.

Row 3: Using A, k2, * k10, sl2, k9; rep from * to last 3 sts, k3.

Row 5: Using B, k1, sl1, * k1, sl1, k18, sl1; rep from * to last 3 sts, k1, sl1, k1.

Row 7: Using A, k2, * k4, [sl1, k1] 3 times, sl2, [k1, sl1] 3 times, k3; rep from * to last 3 sts, k3.

Row 9: Using B, k1, sl1, * k1, sl2, k16, sl2; rep from * to last 3 sts, k1, sl1, k1.

Row 11: Using A, k2, * k5, [sl1, k1] twice, sl4, [k1, sl1] twice, k4; rep from * to last 3 sts, k3.

Row 13: Using B, k1, sl1, * k1, sl3, k14, sl3; rep from * to last 3 sts, k1, sl1, k1.

Row 15: Using A, k2, * k6, [sl1, k1] twice, sl2, [k1, sl1] twice, k5; rep from * to last 3 sts, k3.

Row 17: Using B, k1, sl1, * k1, sl1, k1, sl2, k12, sl2, k1, sl1; rep from * to last 3 sts, k1, sl1, k1.

Row 19: Using A, k2, * k7, sl1, k1, sl4, k1, sl1, k6; rep from * to last 3 sts, k3.

Row 21: Using B, k1, sl1, * k1, sl2, k1, sl2, k10, sl2, k1, sl2; rep from * to last 3 sts, k1, sl1, k1.

Row 23: Using A, k2, * k8, sl1, k1, sl2, k1, sl1, k7; rep from * to last 3 sts, k3.

Row 25: Using B, k1, sl1, * k1, sl3, k1, sl2, k8, sl2, k1, sl3; rep from * to last 3 sts, k1, sl1, k1.

Row 27: Using A, k2, * k9, sl4, k8; rep from * to last 3 sts, k3.

Row 29: Using B, k1, sl1, * k1, sl1, k1, sl2, k1, sl2, k6, [sl2, k1] twice, sl1; rep from * to last 3 sts, k1, sl1, k1.

Row 31: Using A, k2, * k10, sl2, k9; rep from * to last 3 sts, k3.

Row 33: Using B, k1, sl1, * [k1, sl2] 3 times, k4, [sl2, k1] twice, sl2; rep from * to last 3 sts, k1, sl1, k1.

Row 35: Using A, k2, * k10, sl2, k9; rep from * to last 3 sts, k3.

Row 37: Using B, k1, sl1, * k1, sl3, [k1, sl2] twice, k2, [sl2, k1] twice, sl3; rep from * to last 3 sts, k1, sl1, k1.

Row 39: Using A, k all sts.

Row 40: As Row 2.

Crochet Instructions

Multiple of 21 sts + 5

Using A, make desired number of chainless sc.

Row 1: Using B, 1 ch, 1 sc, 2 ch, skip st, * [1 sc, 2 ch, skip st] 5 times, 2 sc, [2 ch, skip st, 1 sc] 4 times, 2 ch, skip st; rep from * to last 3 sts, 1 sc, 2 ch, skip st, 1 sc, turn.

Row 2 and all WS rows: 1 ch, 1 sc in sts, ch and skip ch-sps, turn.

Row 3: Using A, 1 ch, 1 sc, 1 Mdc, * [1 sc, 1 Mdc] 5 times, 3 ch, skip 2 sts, [1 Mdc, 1 sc] 4 times, 1 Mdc; rep from * to last 3 sts, 1 sc, 1 Mdc, 1 sc, turn.

Row 5: Using B, 1 ch, 1 sc, 2 ch, skip st, * 1 sc, 2 ch, skip st, 8 sc, 2 Mdc, 8 sc, 2 ch, skip st; rep from * to last 3 sts, 1 sc, 2 ch, skip st, 1 sc, turn.

Row 7: Using A, 1 ch, 1 sc, 1 Mdc, * 1 sc, 1 Mdc, 2 sc, [2 ch, skip st, 1 sc] 3 times, 3 ch, skip 2 sts, [1 sc, 2 ch, skip st] 3 times, 2 sc, 1 Mdc; rep from * to last 3 sts, 1 sc, 1 Mdc, 1 sc, turn.

MOSAIC CHART

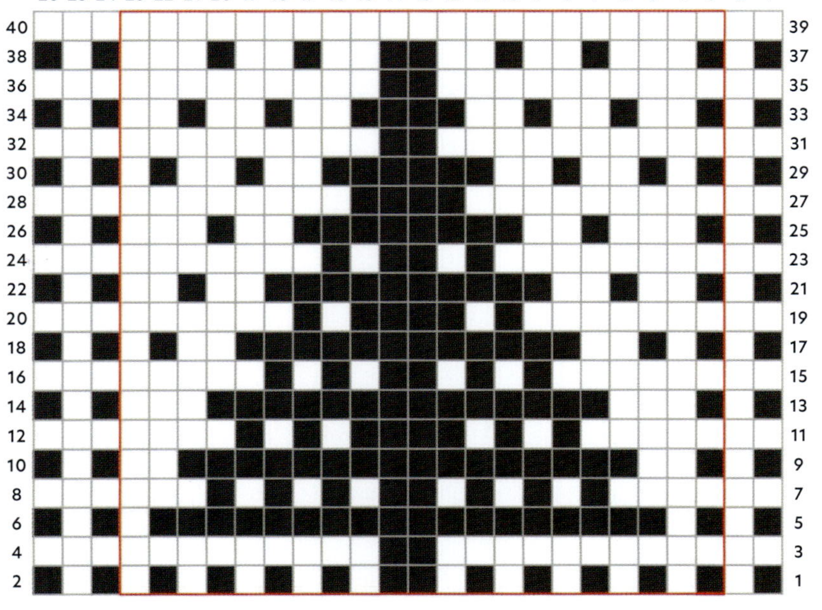

Yarn A = Cream

Yarn B = Burgundy

Row 9: Using B, 1 ch, 1 sc, 2 ch, skip st, * 1 sc, 3 ch, skip 2 sts, 1 sc, [1 Mdc, 1 sc] 3 times, 2 Mdc, [1 sc, 1 Mdc] 3 times, 1sc, 3 ch, skip 2 sts; rep from * to last 3 sts, 1 sc, 2 ch, skip st, 1 sc, turn.
Row 11: Using A, 1 ch, 1 sc, 1 Mdc, * 1 sc, 2 Mdc, 2 sc, [2 ch, skip st, 1 sc] twice, 5 ch, skip 4 sts, [1 sc, 2 ch, skip st] twice, 2 sc, 2 Mdc; rep from * to last 3 sts, 1 sc, 1 Mdc, 1 sc, turn.
Row 13: Using B, 1 ch, 1 sc, 2 ch, skip st, * 1 sc, 4 ch, skip 3 sts, 1 sc, [1 Mdc, 1 sc] twice, 4 Mdc, [1 sc, 1 Mdc] twice, 1 sc, 4 ch, skip 3 sts; rep from * to last 3 sts, 1 sc, 2 ch, skip st, 1 sc, turn.
Row 15: Using A, 1 ch, 1 sc, 1 Mdc, * 1 sc, 3 Mdc, 2 sc, [2 ch, skip st, 1 sc] twice, 3 ch, skip 2 sts, [1 sc, 2 ch, skip st] twice, 2 sc, 3 Mdc; rep from * to last 3 sts, 1 sc, 1 Mdc, 1 sc, turn.
Row 17: Using B, 1 ch, 1 sc, 2 ch, skip st, * 1 sc, 2 ch, skip st, 1 sc, 3 ch, skip 2 sts, 1 sc, [1 Mdc, 1 sc] twice, 2 Mdc, [1 sc, 1 Mdc] twice, 1 sc, 3 ch, skip 2 sts, 1 sc, 2 ch, skip st; rep from * to last 3 sts, 1 sc, 2 ch, skip st, 1 sc, turn.
Row 19: Using A, 1 ch, 1 sc, 1 Mdc, * 1 sc, 1 Mdc, 1 sc, 2 Mdc, 2 sc, 2 ch, skip st, 1 sc, 5 ch, skip 4 sts, 1 sc, 2 ch, skip st, 2 sc, 2 Mdc, 1 sc, 1 Mdc; rep from * to last 3 sts, 1 sc, 1 Mdc, 1 sc, turn.
Row 21: Using B, 1 ch, 1 sc, 2 ch, skip st, * 1 sc, [3 ch, skip 2 sts, 1 sc] twice, 1 Mdc, 1 sc, 4 Mdc, 1 sc, 1 Mdc, 1 sc, 3 ch, skip 2 sts, 1 sc, 3 ch, skip 2 sts; rep from * to last 3 sts, 1 sc, 2 ch, skip st, 1 sc, turn.
Row 23: Using A, 1 ch, 1 sc, 1 Mdc, * [1 sc, 2 Mdc] twice, 2 sc, 2 ch, skip st, 1 sc, 3 ch, skip 2 sts, 1 sc, 2 ch, skip st, 2 sc, 2 Mdc, 1 sc, 2 Mdc; rep from * to last 3 sts, 1 sc, 1 Mdc, 1 sc, turn.
Row 25: Using B, 1 ch, 1 sc, 2 ch, skip st, * 1 sc, 4 ch, skip 3 sts, 1 sc, 3 ch, skip 2 sts, 1 sc, 1 Mdc, 1 sc, 2 Mdc, 1 sc, 1 Mdc, 1 sc, 3 ch, skip 2 sts, 1 sc, 4 ch, skip 3 sts; rep from * to last 3 sts, 1 sc, 2 ch, skip st, 1 sc, turn.
Row 27: Using A, 1 ch, 1 sc, 1 Mdc, * 1 sc, 3 Mdc, 1 sc, 2 Mdc, 2 sc, 5 ch, skip 4 sts, 2 sc, 2 Mdc, 1 sc, 3 Mdc; rep from * to last 3 sts, 1 sc, 1 Mdc, 1 sc, turn.
Row 29: Using B, 1 ch, 1 sc, 2 ch, skip st, * 1 sc, 2 ch, skip st, 1 sc, [3 ch, skip 2 sts, 1 sc] twice, 4 Mdc, 1 sc, [3 ch, skip 2 sts, 1 sc] twice, 2 ch, skip st; rep from * to last 3 sts, 1 sc, 2 ch, skip st, 1 sc, turn.
Row 31: Using A, 1 ch, 1 sc, 1 Mdc, * 1 sc, 1 Mdc, [1 sc, 2 Mdc] twice, 2 sc, 3 ch, skip 2 sts, 2 sc, [2 Mdc, 1 sc] twice, 1 Mdc; rep from * to last 3 sts, 1 sc, 1 Mdc, 1 sc, turn.
Row 33: Using B, 1 ch, 1 sc, 2 ch, skip st, * [1 sc, 3 ch, skip 2 sts] 3 times, 1 sc, 2 Mdc, 1 sc, [3 ch, skip 2 sts, 1 sc] twice, 3 ch, skip 2 sts; rep from * to last 3 sts, 1 sc, 2 ch, skip st, 1 sc, turn.
Row 35: Using A, 1 ch, 1 sc, 1 Mdc, * [1 sc, 2 Mdc] 3 times, 1 sc, 3 ch, skip 2 sts, [1 sc, 2 Mdc] 3 times; rep from * to last 3 sts, 1 sc, 1 Mdc, 1 sc, turn.
Row 37: Using B, 1 ch, 1 sc, 2 ch, skip st, * 1 sc, 4 ch, skip 3 sts, 1 sc, 3 ch, skip 2 sts, 1 sc, 3 ch, skip 2 sts, 2 Mdc, [3 ch, skip 2 sts, 1 sc] twice, 4 ch, skip 3 sts; rep from * to last 3 sts, 1 sc, 2 ch, skip st, 1 sc, turn.
To finish, work Row 39.
Row 39: Using A, 1 ch, 1 sc in every st and Mdc in every sp.

Basic Crochet Skills

Understanding how to make simple stitches is key to mosaic crochet. If you're new to crochet, or need a refresher, all the basics are covered below.

Starting and Finishing

Crochet can be worked in rows, beginning with a foundation chain (see opposite page), or a chainless foundation row (see page 20).

HOLDING THE HOOK AND YARN

The two common ways of holding the hook, referred to as the pencil and knife hold, are shown here.

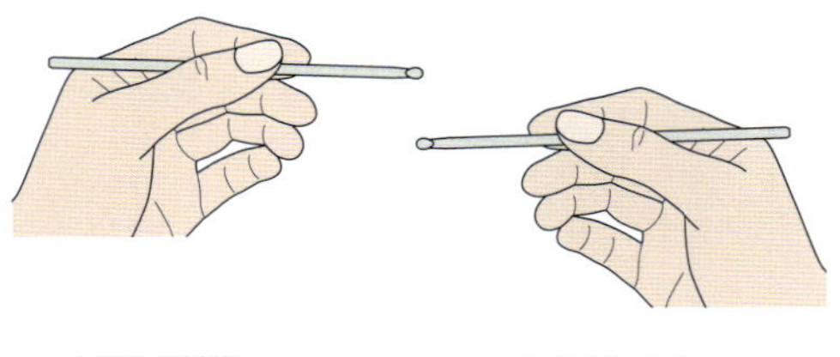

LEFT HAND RIGHT HAND

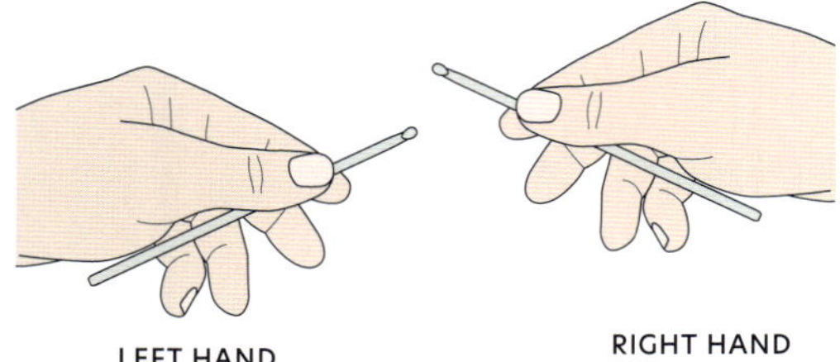

LEFT HAND RIGHT HAND

Pencil hold Center the tips of your dominant thumb and forefinger over the flat section of the hook, as shown, as if you were holding a pen or pencil.

Knife hold Grasp the flat section of the hook between your thumb and forefinger as if you were holding a knife.

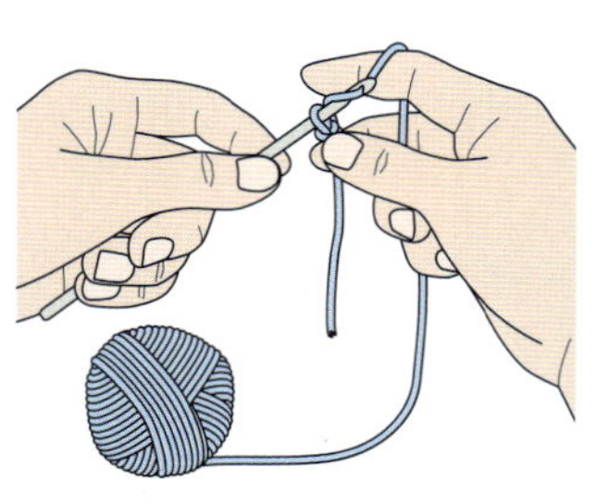

LEFT HAND

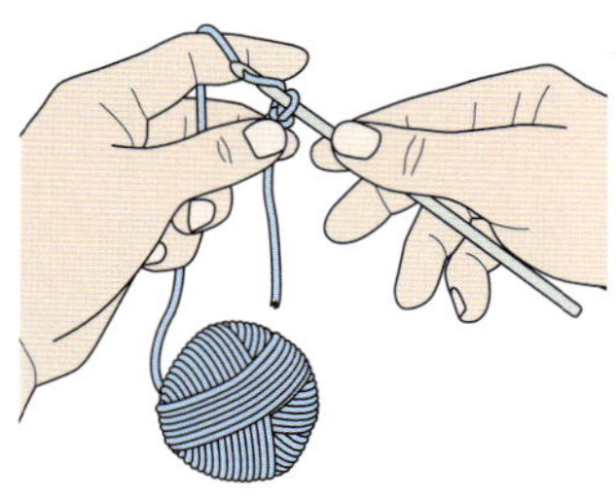

RIGHT HAND

Holding the yarn To control the supply and keep an even tension on the yarn, loop the short end of the yarn around your non-dominant forefinger, and take the yarn coming from the ball loosely around the little finger on the same hand. Use the middle finger on the same hand to help hold the work.

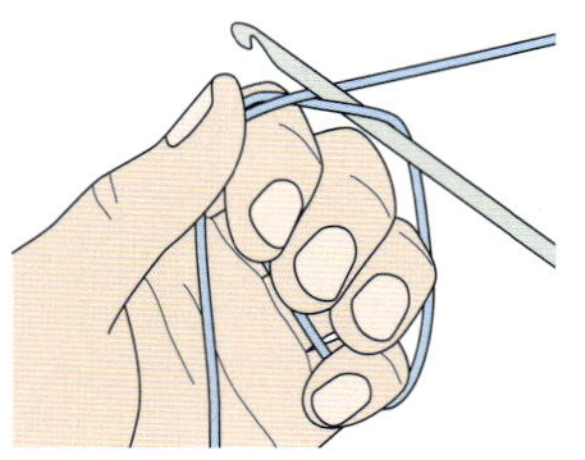

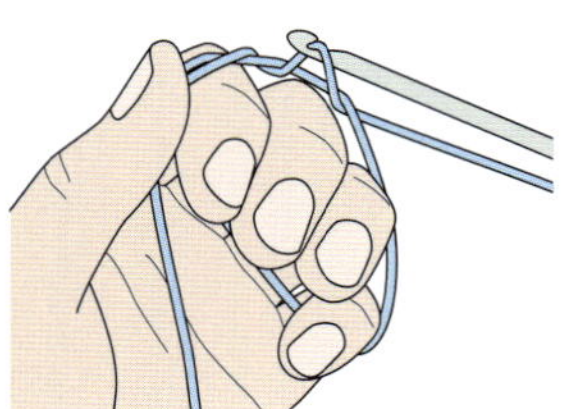

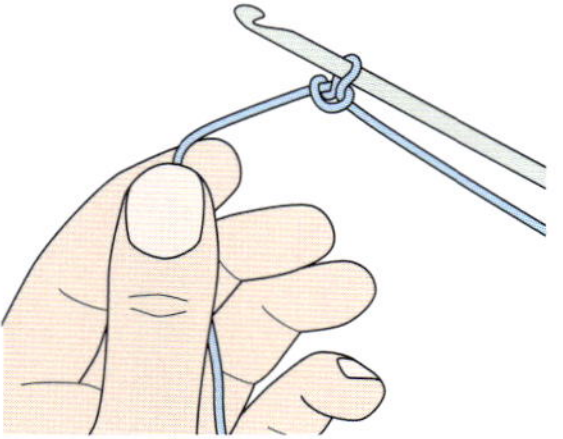

MAKING A SLIP KNOT

1. Loop the yarn as shown, insert the hook into the loop, catch the yarn with the hook, and pull it through to make a loop over the hook.

2. Gently pull the yarn to tighten the loop around the hook and complete the slip knot.

Basic Stitches

All crochet stitches are based on a loop pulled through another loop by a hook. There are only a few stitches to master, each of a different length. Here is a concise guide to the basic stitches used to make mosaic crochet.

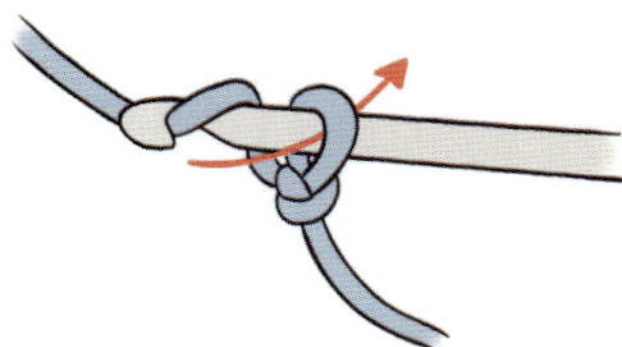

Chain (ch) Wrap the yarn over the hook and pull it through the loop on the hook to form a new loop on the hook.

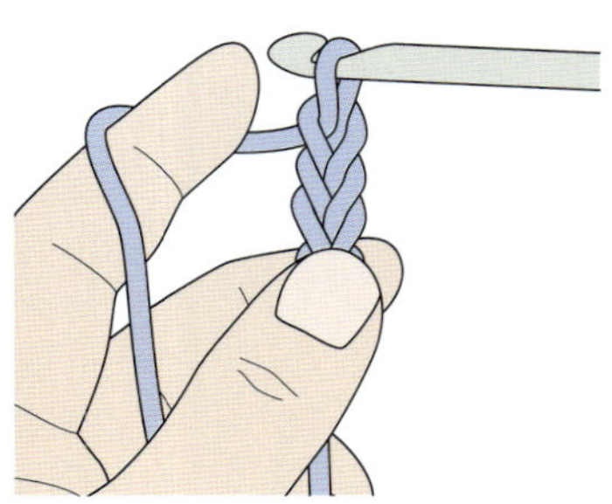

FOUNDATION CHAIN

The pattern will tell you how many chains to make. This may be a specific number or a multiple. If a pattern tells you to make a multiple of 3 + 2, this does not mean make a multiple of 5. It means that you should make a multiple of 3 and then add 2 chains—for example, 3 + 2, 6 + 2, 9 + 2, and so on. You may also be instructed to add a turning chain for the first row.

1. Follow the instruction to make a chain (see above) to complete the first chain stitch.
2. Repeat this process, drawing a new loop of yarn through the loop already on the hook until the chain is the required length. Count each V-shaped loop on the front of the chain as one chain stitch, except for the loop on the hook, which is not counted. After every few stitches, move up the thumb and finger that are grasping the chain to keep the chain stitches even.

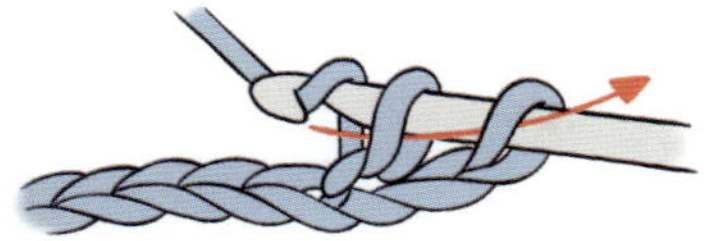

Single crochet (sc) Insert the hook into the specified stitch, wrap the yarn over the hook, and pull it through the stitch (2 loops on hook). Yarn over hook and pull it through both loops.

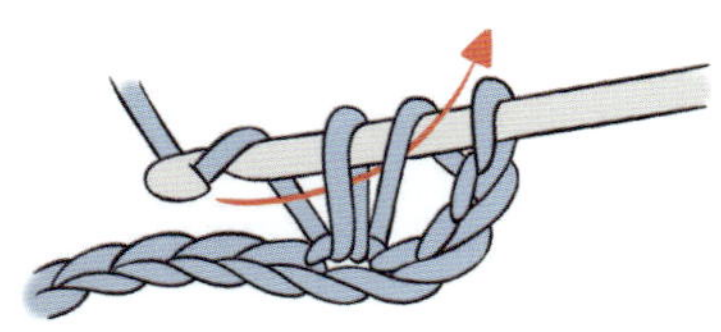

Double crochet (dc) Yarn over hook, insert the hook into the specified stitch, yarn over hook, and pull it through the stitch (3 loops on hook). * Yarn over hook and pull it through 2 loops; repeat from * once more.

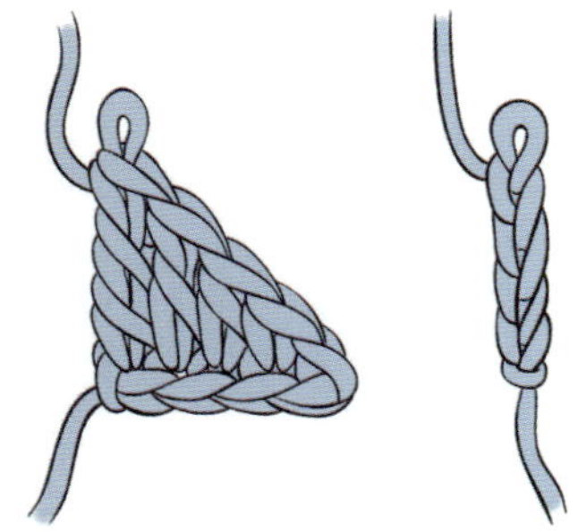

TURNING AND STARTING CHAINS

When working crochet, you will need to work a specific number of extra chains at the beginning of each row or round. When the work is turned at the end of a straight row, the extra chains are called a turning chain, and when they are worked at the beginning of a round, they are called a starting chain. The extra chains bring the hook up to the correct height for the stitch you will be working next.

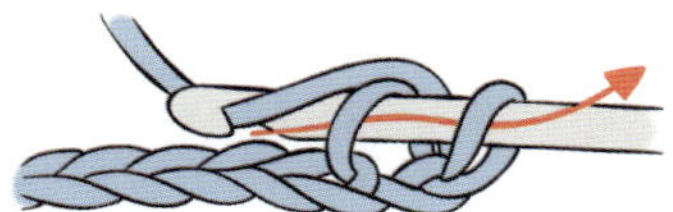

Slip stitch (sl st) Insert the hook into the specified stitch, wrap the yarn over the hook, and pull it through the stitch and the loop on the hook.

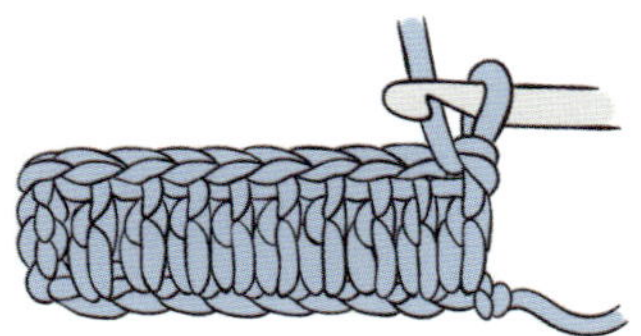

FASTENING OFF

When you have completed your crochet, cut the yarn about 6in (15cm) from the last stitch. Wrap the yarn over the hook and draw the yarn end through the loop on the hook. Gently pull the yarn to tighten the last stitch, then weave in the yarn end.

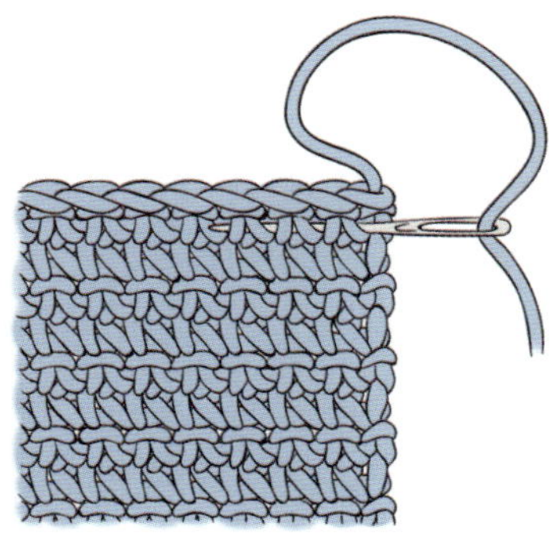

WEAVING IN ENDS

At the end of making your project, you will need to weave in any yarn ends. For crochet worked in rows, use a yarn needle to sew in ends diagonally on the wrong side. For crochet worked in rounds, sew in ends under stitches for an inch or two.

Basic Knitting Skills

If you're a new knitter, you will find all the information you need to get started below.

SLIP KNOT

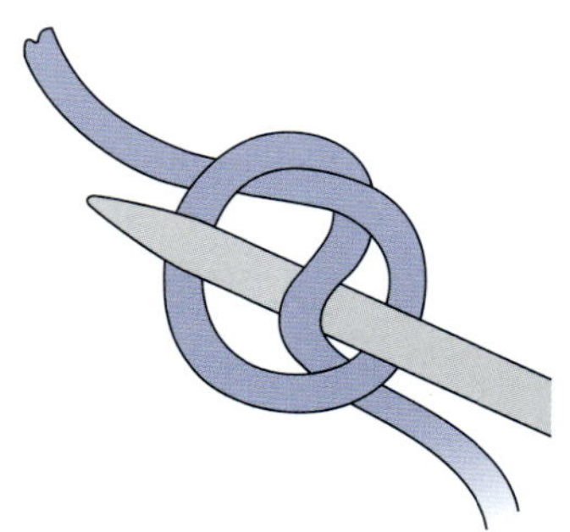

1. Putting a slip knot on the needle makes the first stitch of the cast-on. Loop the yarn around two fingers of the left hand, the ball end on top. Dip the needle into the loop, catch the ball end of the yarn, and pull it through the loop.

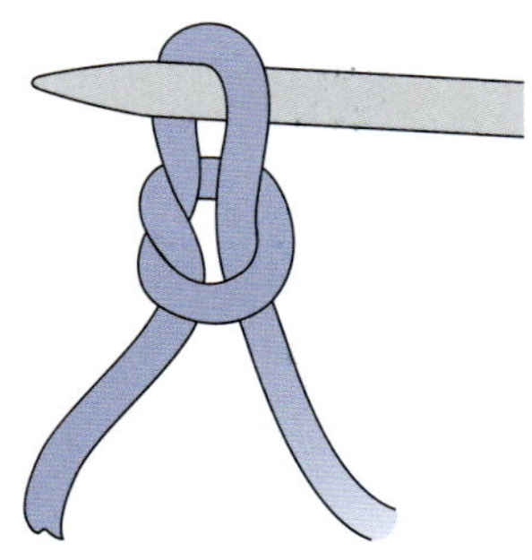

2. Pull the ends of the yarn to tighten the knot. Tighten the ball end to bring the knot up to the needle.

Ends

The end of yarn left after casting on should be a reasonable length so that it can be used for sewing up. The same applies to the end left after binding (casting) off. Darn in ends left when a new color is joined in along a seam or row end on the wrong side. These ends can also be very useful for covering up imperfections, such as awkward color changes.

Ends left while working a motif are better darned in behind the motif. Use a blunt-ended yarn needle for darning in.

CABLE CAST-ON

This two-needle method gives a firm result with the appearance of a rope edge.

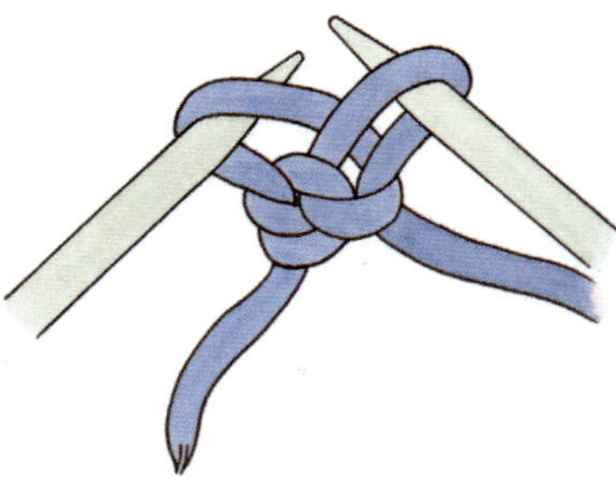

1. Put a slip knot on one needle. Use the other needle and the ball end of the yarn to knit into the loop on the left-hand needle without slipping it off. Transfer the new stitch to the left-hand needle.

2. Insert the right-hand needle between the new stitch and the next stitch and then make another stitch as before. Continue making stitches in this way.

CHAIN BIND-OFF

A simple knit-stitch bind-off can be used for these projects. Knit two stitches. * With the left needle, lift the first stitch over the second. Knit the next stitch. Repeat from * until one stitch remains. Break the yarn, take the end through this stitch, and tighten.

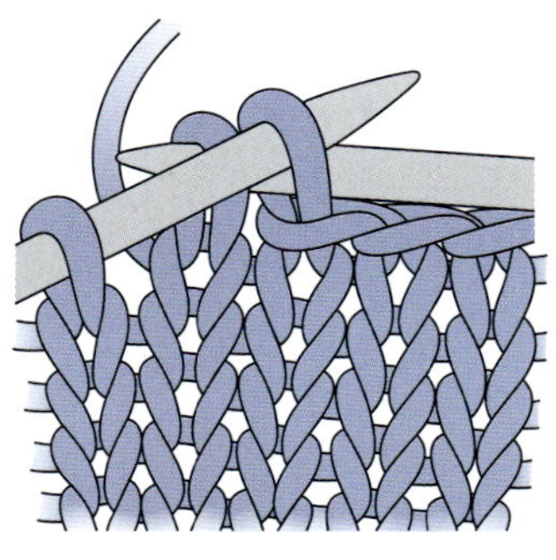

To bind off in pattern, simply work knit or purl stitches along the bind-off row as they would occur in the stitch pattern.

KNIT STITCH (K)

Choose to hold the yarn and needles in whichever way you feel most comfortable. To tension the yarn—that is, to keep it moving evenly—you will need to twist it through some fingers of the hand holding the yarn, and maybe even take it around your little finger. Continuous rows of knit stitch produce garter stitch.

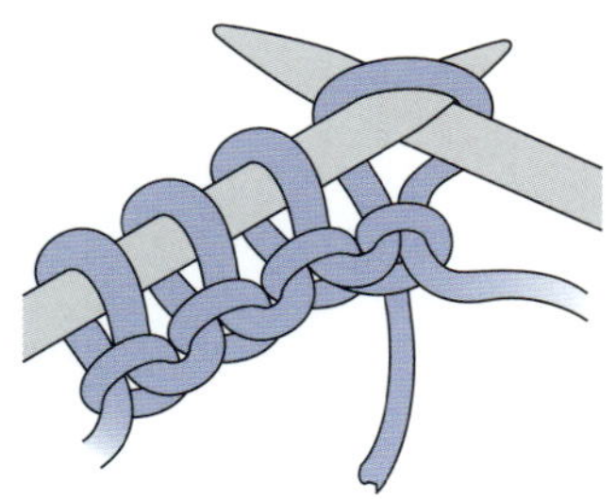

1. Insert the right needle into the first stitch on the left needle. Make sure it goes from left to right into the front of the stitch.

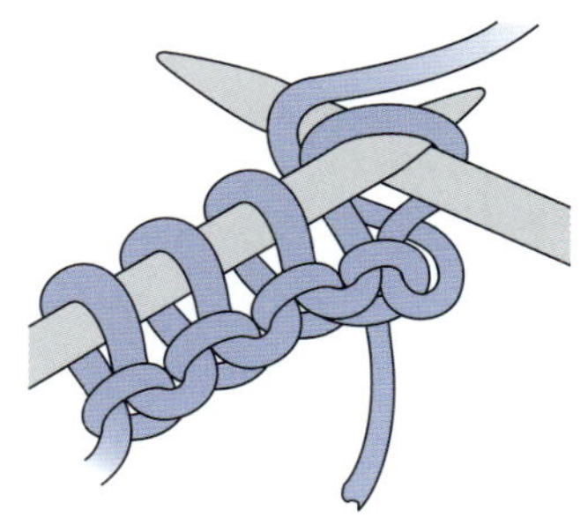

2. Taking the yarn behind, bring it up and around the right needle.

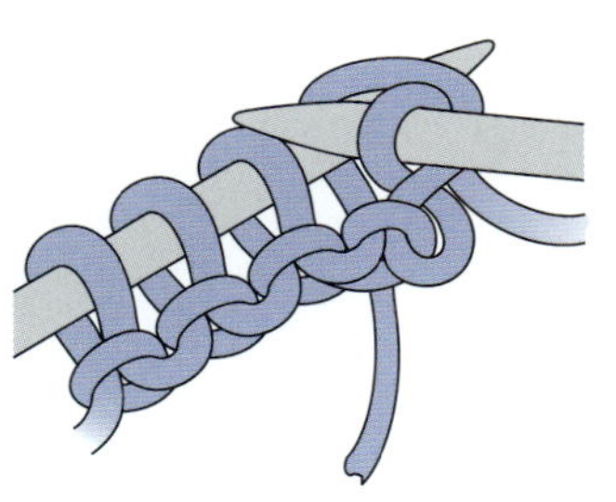

3. Using the tip of the right needle, draw a loop of yarn through the stitch.

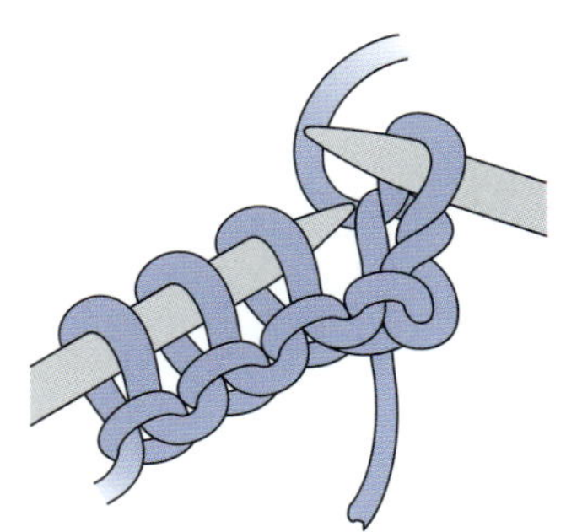

4. Slip the stitch off the left needle. There is now a new stitch on the right needle.

PURL STITCH (P)

Hold the yarn and needles in the same way as for making a knit stitch. A purl stitch is the exact opposite of a knit stitch, producing a nubbly stitch to the front and a smooth V-like knit stitch on the opposite side. Alternate rows of knit and purl produce a stockinette stitch.

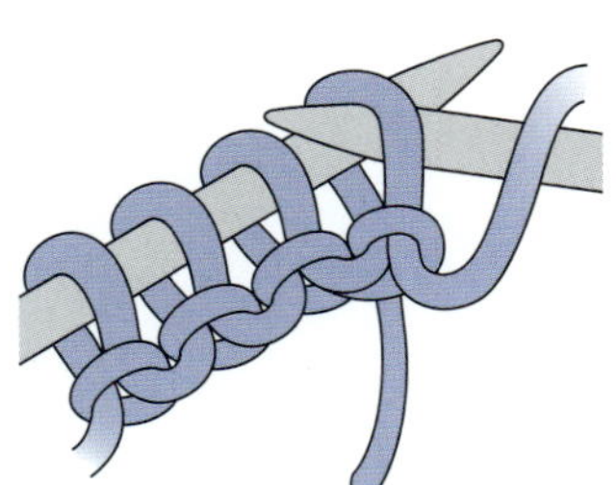

1. Insert the right needle into the first stitch on the left needle. Make sure it goes into the stitch from right to left.

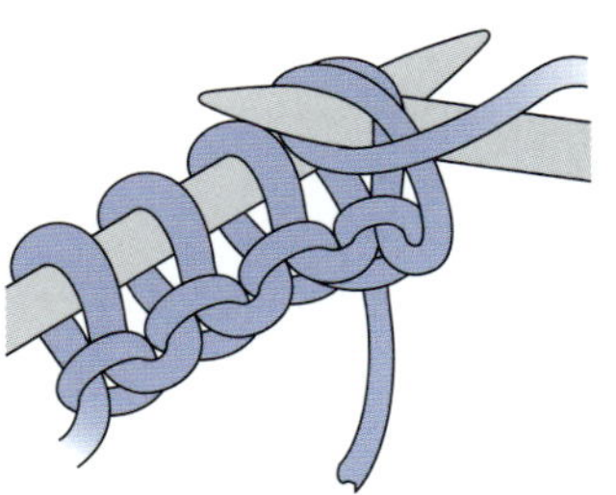

2. Taking the yarn to the front, loop it around the right needle.

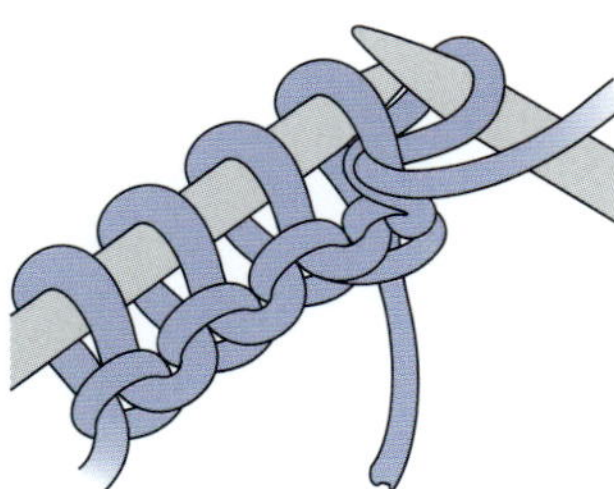

3. Lower the tip of the right needle, taking it away from you to draw a loop of yarn through the stitch.

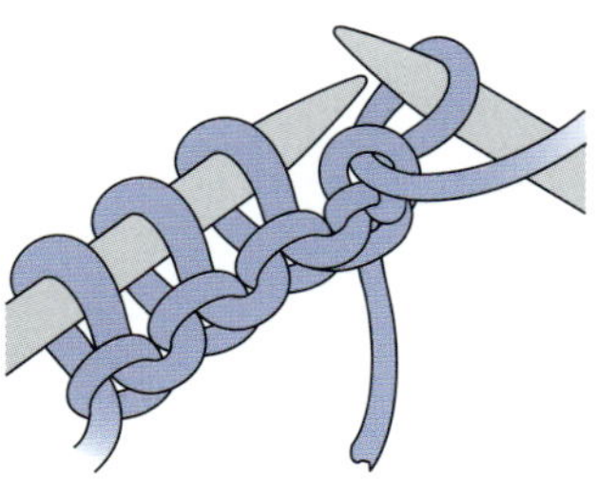

4. Slip the stitch off the left needle. There is now a new stitch on the right needle.

Joining

Panels can be joined by sewing or by crochet. Always block (see page 172) the pieces before joining. Pin seams together to help match up the panels and give a neat finish. Use the same yarn that you used for the panels, or a finer yarn, preferably with the same fiber content.

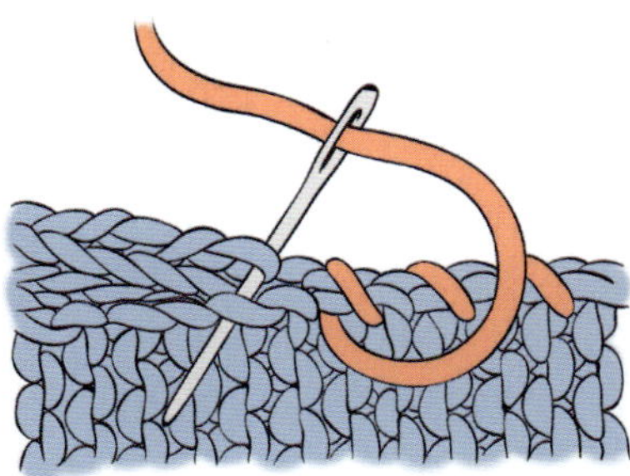

WHIP STITCH

Hold two panels together with the right sides facing, pinning if necessary. Work a line of diagonal stitches from back to front under the strands at the edges of the panels.

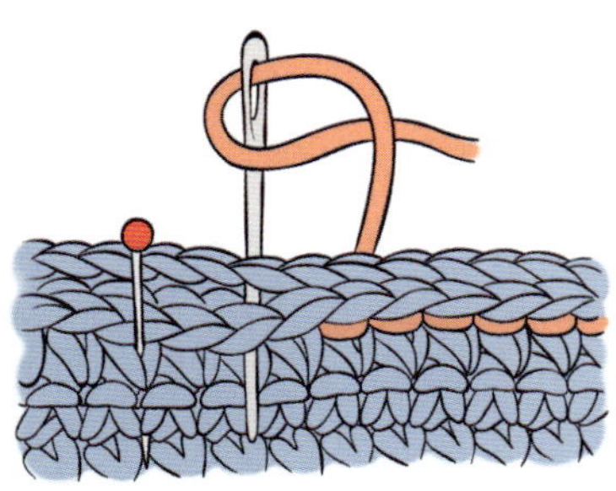

BACKSTITCH

Hold the panels with right sides together. Using a yarn needle, work a line of backstitches along the edge.

CROCHET SEAMS

Join the panels with wrong sides together for a visible seam, or with right sides together for an invisible one. Work a row of slip stitch or single crochet through both top loops of each panel. When using this method along the side edges of panels worked in rows, work enough evenly spaced stitches so that the seam is not too tight.

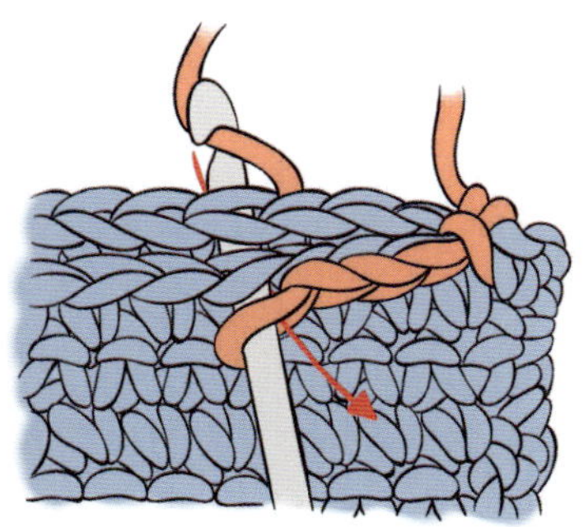

SLIP STITCH SEAM

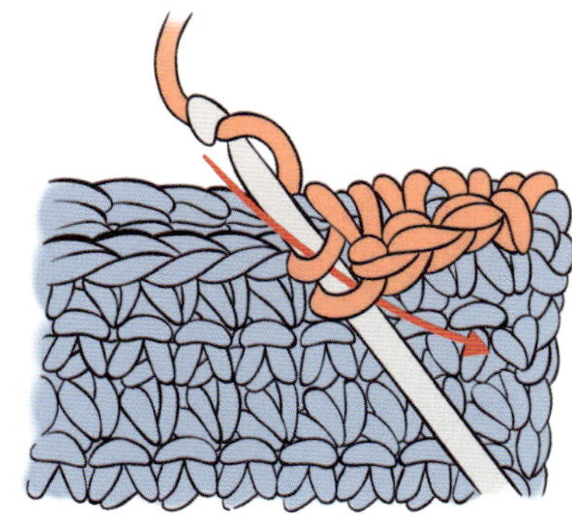

SINGLE CROCHET SEAM

Calculating yarn amounts

The best way to calculate how much yarn you will need to make a larger project is to work a few repeats of a pattern in the yarn and color combination you intend to use, then unravel them. Measure the amount of yarn used for each color, take the average length, and multiply by the number of pattern repeats you intend to make. Add extra yarn for joining panels and for working edgings.

Aftercare

It is a good idea to keep a ball band from each project you complete as a reference for washing instructions. Crochet and knit items are best washed gently by hand and dried flat on a towel, to keep their shape. Do not hang as the weight of the water will stretch the item.

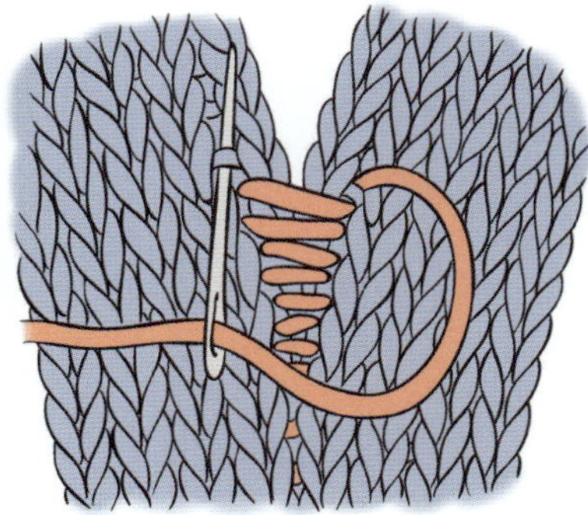

MATTRESS STITCH ON KNIT FABRIC
Lay the panels out with the edges touching and right sides facing upward. Using matching yarn threaded in a yarn needle, weave under the bar between the outer stitch and the next stitch on each edge as shown.

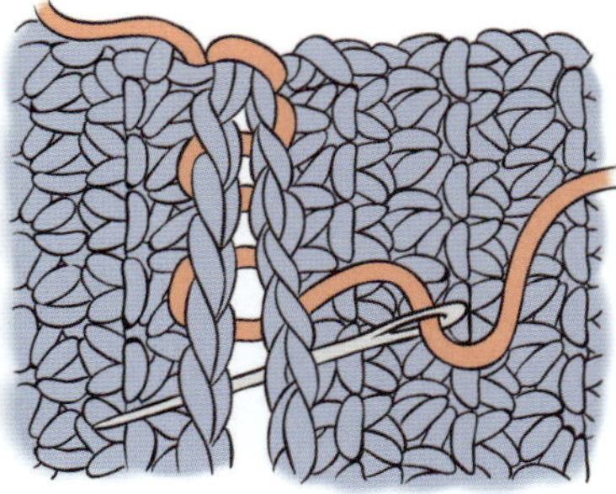

MATTRESS STITCH
ON CROCHET FABRIC
Lay the panels wrong side up and with edges touching. Using a yarn needle, weave back and forth around the centers of the stitches, without pulling the stitches too tight.

Blocking

Blocking is crucial to set the stitches and even out the piece. Blocking (also called dressing) is a means of finishing your knitting or crochet so that it is straightened out, the stitches are set and enhanced, and the knitting is restored to its intended shape and size. Most knit and crochet fabrics benefit from blocking, and this is normally done as part of the assembly stage.

Choose a method based on the care label of the yarn. When in doubt, use the wet method. Use an ironing board or a foam blocking mat to pin the pieces (you can buy special blocking boards or use children's foam play-mats).

Wet method—acrylic and wool/acrylic mix Using dressmaking pins or T-pins, pin the fabric to the correct measurements on a flat surface and dampen using a spray bottle of cold water. Pat the fabric to help the moisture penetrate. Ease stitches into position, keeping rows and stitches straight. Allow to dry before removing the pins.

Steam method—wools and cottons Pin out the fabric as above. For fabric with raised stitches, pin it right side up to avoid squashing the stitches; otherwise, pin it wrong side up. Steam lightly, holding the iron 1in (2.5cm) above the fabric. Allow the steam to penetrate for several seconds.

BLOCKING BOARDS
You can buy special foam jigsaw blocking mats (such as this one), or pick virtually the same things up at a toy store at a fraction of the cost. You can also use the top of an ironing board or a bath towel on the floor.

How to pin your swatches

Use good-quality, fine, rustproof dressmaking pins, and carefully pin the edges of the piece to its correct size and shape. Start by pinning the corners. Next, pin halfway along the edges. Continue, placing pins at regular intervals along each edge. Use plenty of pins to avoid distorting the fabric.

INCORRECTLY PINNED

See how the stitches are pulled and distorted.

CORRECTLY PINNED

Taut swatch retaining its natural shape. If the edge has points, pin out each point.

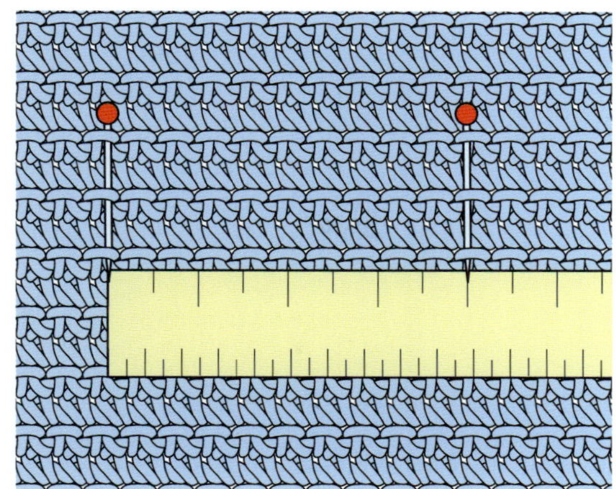

Gauge

It's important to crochet or knit a test swatch before you start any large project to establish gauge. You can also use the gauge swatch to test blocking and cleaning methods.

The term "gauge," or tension, refers to the number of stitches and rows contained in a given width and length of knitted or crocheted fabric. Patterns for garments include a recommended gauge and it's important that you match this gauge exactly so your work comes out the right size. Gauge can be affected by the size and brand of the crochet hook or knitting needle, the type of yarn used, the stitch pattern, and an individual worker's gauge.

Individual worker No two people will crochet to the exact same gauge, even when working with identical yarn and hooks.

Yarn variations Two yarns with the same description (e.g. sport or worsted) and fiber content made by different manufacturers will vary slightly in thickness. The color of yarn you choose may also affect gauge as a result of the different dyes used in manufacture.

Hook/Needle variations Hooks and needles can vary widely in shape and size even though they may all be branded with the same number or letter. Always use the same hook or needle for working both the gauge sample and the finished item.

Why should I make a gauge swatch? Always make a test swatch before starting a project so that you can compare your gauge with the pattern gauge and get an idea of how the finished project will feel and drape. It's also useful for testing out different color combinations.

How do I test the gauge? To test your gauge, make a sample swatch in the yarn you intend to use following the pattern directions. Block the sample and then measure again. If your sample is larger than the pattern requests, try making another using a smaller hook. If your sample is smaller, try making another using a bigger hook. Also do this if the fabric feels too loose and floppy or too dense and rigid. Keep trying until you find a hook size that will give you the required gauge, or until you are happy with the drape and feel of your work. Ultimately, it's more important that you use a hook or a needle that you are comfortable with than that you rigidly follow the pattern instructions.

Index

Credits

Thank you to all of the testers!

Crochet testers:
Jo Wright: @Sycamorecottagecraft
Karen Pimblett: @__kernowdesigns
Emma Griffiths-Brown: @mrsgbcrochet
Lucy Croft: @lucyacroft
Tayu Purnamasari: @TayuPurnamasari
Elena Trimarchi: @Elena.trimarchi
Claire Robinson
Sarah-Jane Hicks: @flo_and_dot
Chloe Jones
Amy Hancock: @Harmonytalc
Gee Wyles: @jadestar8
Christine Tait: @whatchristinemade
Pam Harrison: @Harrison_pam
Rachael Matthewman:@rachaellm

Knitting testers:
Alexandra Zeilinger: @arwenundomiel72
Marion Cook: @marionmakes_
Lauren Haighton: @knitasaurus
Faye Perriam-Reed: @fayeperriamreed
Nici Griffin: @beanieboat
Chloe Richardson @chesterfield_knitter
Elizabeth Ann Robinson: @millyknittens
Olivia Knoedt: @oliv_knits
Linda James
Vicky Wootten:@vixwootten
Sally Cowell: @levenknitandsew
Dooknits
Karen S. Henderson: @plot.twist.designs
Nicole Hawkesford: @certainstyle_makes
Becca Huben: @nutmegknitter

Acknowledgments

My biggest thank you is to my amazing husband, Dave, whose constant love, support, and belief in me spurs me on.

Thanks to Charlene and the fantastic team at Quarto for making this book a reality.

Thank you to Sharon and Linda, the best tech editors ever!

Huge thanks to Rhiannon and the West Yorkshire Spinners team for providing the beautiful yarn used in the book.

And thank you to all of you, for purchasing the book and loving to knit, or crochet, or both.

Anna x

About the Author

ANNA NIKIPIROWICZ is a crochet and knit designer, tutor, and author. Her designs are regularly featured in craft magazines such as *Inside Crochet* and she is the author of *Tunisian Crochet Stitch Dictionary*, *Crocheted Wreaths for the Home*, and more. Find her on her website www.moochka.co.uk and @annanikipirowicz on Instagram.

Yarn colors used in this book

COLOR A

LANGA 0010

GEOMETRIC

BRESSAY 1150

MAYWICK 0512

CLATE 1152

NISTA 0348

AZTEC

NORBY 0353

SKELBERRY 0580

WHALSAY 1151

NATURE

GRAVEN 1018

HARKLAND 0226

CHALLISTER 1019

GENERAL

SAMPFREY 1153

GREENBANK 0404

SEASONAL

SKELBERRY 0580

NISTA 0348

WEST YORKSHIRE SPINNERS

Please visit wyspinners/stockists to locate your local West Yorkshire Spinners yarn stockist.
Follow @westyorshirespinners on Facebook & Instagram